MznLnx

Missing Links Exam Preps

Exam Prep for

Economics: Principles and Policy

Baumol & Blinder, 11th Edition

The MznLnx Exam Prep is your link from the texbook and lecture to your exams.
The MznLnx Exam Preps are unauthorized and comprehensive reviews of your textbooks.

All material provided by MznLnx and Rico Publications (c) 2010
Textbook publishers and textbook authors do not particpate in or contribute to these reviews.

MznLnx

Rico Publications

Exam Prep for Economics: Principles and Policy
11th Edition
Baumol & Blinder

Publisher: Raymond Houge
Assistant Editor: Michael Rouger
Text and Cover Designer: Lisa Buckner
Marketing Manager: Sara Swagger
Project Manager, Editorial Production: Jerry Emerson
Art Director: Vernon Lowerui

Product Manager: Dave Mason
Editorial Assitant: Rachel Guzmanji
Pedagogy: Debra Long
Cover Image: Jim Reed/Getty Images
Text and Cover Printer: City Printing, Inc.
Compositor: Media Mix, Inc.

(c) 2010 Rico Publications
ALL RIGHTS RESERVED. No part of this work covered by the copyright may be reproduced or used in any form or by an means--graphic, electronic, or mechanical, including photocopying, recording, taping, Web distribution, information storage, and retrieval systems, or in any other manner--without the written permission of the publisher.

Printed in the United States
ISBN:

For more information about our products, contact us at:
Dave.Mason@RicoPublications.com

For permission to use material from this text or product, submit a request online to:
Dave.Mason@RicoPublications.com

Contents

CHAPTER 1
WHAT IS ECONOMICS?   1

CHAPTER 2
THE ECONOMY: MYTH AND REALITY   7

CHAPTER 3
THE FUNDAMENTAL ECONOMIC PROBLEM: SCARCITY AND CHOICE   22

CHAPTER 4
SUPPLY AND DEMAND: AN INITIAL LOOK   30

CHAPTER 5
CONSUMER CHOICE: INDIVIDUAL AND MARKET DEMAND   36

CHAPTER 6
DEMAND AND ELASTICITY   42

CHAPTER 7
PRODUCTION, INPUTS, AND COST: BUILDING BLOCKS FOR SUPPLY ANALYSIS   48

CHAPTER 8
OUTPUT, PRICE, AND PROFIT: THE IMPORTANCE OF MARGINAL ANALYSIS   57

CHAPTER 9
INVESTING IN BUSINESS: STOCKS AND BONDS   64

CHAPTER 10
THE FIRM AND THE INDUSTRY UNDER PERFECT COMPETITION   74

CHAPTER 11
MONOPOLY   83

CHAPTER 12
BETWEEN COMPETITION AND MONOPOLY   92

CHAPTER 13
LIMITING MARKET POWER: REGULATION AND ANTITRUST   101

CHAPTER 14
THE CASE FOR FREE MARKETS I: THE PRICE SYSTEM   111

CHAPTER 15
THE SHORTCOMINGS OF FREE MARKETS   118

CHAPTER 16
THE MARKET`S PRIME ACHIEVEMENT: INNOVATION AND GROWTH   128

CHAPTER 17
EXTERNALITIES, THE ENVIRONMENT, AND NATURAL RESOURCES   137

CHAPTER 18
TAXATION AND RESOURCE ALLOCATION   143

CHAPTER 19
PRICING THE FACTORS OF PRODUCTION   150

CHAPTER 20
LABOR AND ENTREPRENEURSHIP: THE HUMAN INPUTS   159

Contents (Cont.)

CHAPTER 21
POVERTY, INEQUALITY, AND DISCRIMINATION — 170

CHAPTER 22
AN INTRODUCTION TO MACROECONOMICS — 179

CHAPTER 23
THE GOALS OF MACROECONOMIC POLICY — 191

CHAPTER 24
ECONOMIC GROWTH: THEORY AND POLICY — 203

CHAPTER 25
AGGREGATE DEMAND AND THE POWERFUL CONSUMER — 214

CHAPTER 26
DEMAND-SIDE EQUILIBRIUM: UNEMPLOYMENT OR INFLATION? — 227

CHAPTER 27
BRINGING IN THE SUPPLY-SIDE: UNEMPLOYMENT AND INFLATION? — 234

CHAPTER 28
MANAGING AGGREGATE DEMAND: FISCAL POLICY — 242

CHAPTER 29
MONEY AND THE BANKING SYSTEM — 250

CHAPTER 30
MANAGING AGGREGATE DEMAND: MONETARY POLICY — 259

CHAPTER 31
THE DEBATE OVER MONETARY AND FISCAL POLICY — 267

CHAPTER 32
BUDGET DEFICITS IN THE SHORT AND LONG RUN — 279

CHAPTER 33
THE TRADE-OFF BETWEEN INFLATION AND UNEMPLOYMENT — 287

CHAPTER 34
INTERNATIONAL TRADE AND COMPARATIVE ADVANTAGE — 296

CHAPTER 35
THE INTERNATIONAL MONETARY SYSTEM: ORDER OR DISORDER? — 304

CHAPTER 36
EXCHANGE BATES AND THE MACROECONOMY — 313

ANSWER KEY — 320

TO THE STUDENT

COMPREHENSIVE

The *MznLnx* Exam Prep series is designed to help you pass your exams. Editors at MznLnx review your textbooks and then prepare these practice exams to help you master the textbook material. Unlike study guides, workbooks, and practice tests provided by the texbook publisher and textbook authors, *MznLnx* gives you **all** of the material in each chapter in exam form, not just samples, so you can be sure to nail your exam.

MECHANICAL

The MznLnx Exam Prep series creates exams that will help you learn the subject matter as well as test you on your understanding. Each question is designed to help you master the concept. Just working through the exams, you gain an understanding of the subject--its a simple mechanical process that produces success.

INTEGRATED STUDY GUIDE AND REVIEW

MznLnx is not just a set of exams designed to test you, its also a comprehensive review of the subject content. Each exam question is also a review of the concept, making sure that you will get the answer correct without having to go to other sources of material. You learn as you go! Its the easiest way to pass an exam.

HUMOR

Studying can be tedious and dry. MznLnx's instructional design includes moderate humor within the exam questions on occassion, to break the tedium and revitalize the brain

Chapter 1. WHAT IS ECONOMICS?

1. _____s is the social science that studies the production, distribution, and consumption of goods and services. The term _____s comes from the Ancient Greek oá¼°κονομῖα from oá¼¶κος (oikos, 'house') + vÏŒμος (nomos, 'custom' or 'law'), hence 'rules of the house(hold)'. Current _____ models developed out of the broader field of political economy in the late 19th century, owing to a desire to use an empirical approach more akin to the physical sciences.
   a. Economic
   b. Opportunity cost
   c. Inflation
   d. Energy economics

2. _____ or economic opportunity loss is the value of the next best alternative foregone as the result of making a decision. _____ analysis is an important part of a company's decision-making processes but is not treated as an actual cost in any financial statement. The next best thing that a person can engage in is referred to as the _____ of doing the best thing and ignoring the next best thing to be done.
   a. Industrial organization
   b. Economic
   c. Economic ideology
   d. Opportunity cost

3. The _____ is the expected return forgone by bypassing of other potential investment activities for a given capital. It is a rate of return that investors could earn in financial markets.
   a. ACEA agreement
   b. AD-IA Model
   c. Opportunity cost of capital
   d. ACCRA Cost of Living Index

4. The _____ is an expected return that the provider of capital plans to earn on their investment.

Capital (money) used for funding a business should earn returns for the capital providers who risk their capital. For an investment to be worthwhile, the expected return on capital must be greater than the _____.

   a. Cost of capital
   b. Capital intensive
   c. Modigliani-Miller theorem
   d. Capital expenditure

5. In economics, _____ refers to the ability of a person or a country to produce a particular good at a lower marginal cost and opportunity cost than another person or country. It is the ability to produce a product most efficiently given all the other products that could be produced. It can be contrasted with absolute advantage which refers to the ability of a person or a country to produce a particular good at a lower absolute cost than another.
   a. Gravity model of trade
   b. Triffin dilemma
   c. Hot money
   d. Comparative advantage

6. In economics, the _____ can be defined as the graph depicting the relationship between the price of a certain commodity, and the amount of it that consumers are willing and able to purchase at that given price. It is a graphic representation of a demand schedule. The _____ for all consumers together follows from the _____ of every individual consumer: the individual demands at each price are added together.
   a. Kuznets curve
   b. Wage curve
   c. Cost curve
   d. Demand curve

7. _____ is exchange of capital, goods, and services across international borders or territories. In most countries, it represents a significant share of gross domestic product (GDP.) While _____ has been present throughout much of history, its economic, social, and political importance has been on the rise in recent centuries.
   a. Intra-industry trade
   b. Incoterms
   c. Import license
   d. International trade

Chapter 1. WHAT IS ECONOMICS?

8. Economics:

   - _____, the desire to own something and the ability to pay for it
   - _____ curve, a graphic representation of a _____ schedule
   - _____ deposit, the money in checking accounts
   - _____ pull theory, the theory that inflation occurs when _____ for goods and services exceeds existing supplies
   - _____ schedule, a table that lists the quantity of a good a person will buy it each different price
   - _____ side economics, the school of economics at believes government spending and tax cuts open economy by raising _____

   a. Production
   b. Variability
   c. Demand
   d. McKesson ' Robbins scandal

9. In economics, a _____ is a table that lists the quantity of a good a person will buy it each different price See Demand curve.

   a. Federal Reserve districts
   b. Rational irrationality
   c. Free contract
   d. Demand schedule

10. In economics, the _____ is the term economists use to describe the self-regulating nature of the marketplace. The _____ is a metaphor coined by the economist Adam Smith in The Wealth of Nations.

    Adam Smith mentions the metaphor in Book IV of The Wealth of Nations, arguing that people in any society will certainly employ their capital in foreign trading only if the profits available by that method far exceed those available locally, and that in such a case it is better for society as a whole if they so did.

    a. Invisible hand
    b. AD-IA Model
    c. ACCRA Cost of Living Index
    d. ACEA agreement

11. In economics, _____ is equal to total cost divided by the number of goods produced (the output quantity, Q.) It is also equal to the sum of average variable costs (total variable costs divided by Q) plus average fixed costs (total fixed costs divided by Q.) _____ s may be dependent on the time period considered (increasing production may be expensive or impossible in the short term, for example.)

    a. Explicit cost
    b. Average cost
    c. Average variable cost
    d. Average fixed cost

12. In economics and finance, _____ is the change in total cost that arises when the quantity produced changes by one unit. It is the cost of producing one more unit of a good. Mathematically, the _____ function is expressed as the first derivative of the total cost (TC) function with respect to quantity (Q.)

    a. Khozraschyot
    b. Variable cost
    c. Quality costs
    d. Marginal cost

13. _____ is one of the ways government regulate a monopoly market. Monopolists tend to produce less than the optimal quantity pushing the prices up. Government may use _____ as a tool to regulate prices monopolists may charge.

Chapter 1. WHAT IS ECONOMICS?

a. Average cost pricing
c. ACCRA Cost of Living Index
b. AD-IA Model
d. ACEA agreement

14. In economics, an _____ is any good or commodity, transported from one country to another country in a legitimate fashion, typically for use in trade. _____ goods or services are provided to foreign consumers by domestic producers. _____ is an important part of international trade.
a. ACCRA Cost of Living Index
c. AD-IA Model
b. Export
d. ACEA agreement

15. _____ is one of the four Ps of the marketing mix. The other three aspects are product, promotion, and place. It is also a key variable in microeconomic price allocation theory.
a. Point of total assumption
c. Premium pricing
b. Guaranteed Maximum Price
d. Pricing

16. _____ is a broad label that refers to any individuals or households that use goods and services generated within the economy. The concept of a _____ is used in different contexts, so that the usage and significance of the term may vary.

Typically when business people and economists talk of _____s they are talking about person as _____, an aggregated commodity item with little individuality other than that expressed in the buy/not-buy decision.

a. 130-30 fund
c. Consumer
b. 1921 recession
d. 100-year flood

17. A _____ is a measure of the average price of consumer goods and services purchased by households. A _____ measures a price change for a constant market basket of goods and services from one period to the next within the same area (city, region, or nation.) It is a price index determined by measuring the price of a standard group of goods meant to represent the typical market basket of a typical urban consumer.
a. Lipstick index
c. Cost-of-living index
b. CPI
d. Consumer Price Index

18. _____ in economics and business is the result of an exchange and from that trade we assign a numerical monetary value to a good, service or asset. If Alice trades Bob 4 apples for an orange, the _____ of an orange is 4 apples. Inversely, the _____ of an apple is 1/4 oranges.
a. Price war
c. Premium pricing
b. Price book
d. Price

19. A _____ is a normalized average (typically a weighted average) of prices for a given class of goods or services in a given region, during a given interval of time. It is a statistic designed to help to compare how these prices, taken as a whole, differ between time periods or geographical locations.

Price indices have several potential uses.

Chapter 1. WHAT IS ECONOMICS?

a. Two-part tariff
b. Transactional Net Margin Method
c. Product sabotage
d. Price Index

20. In economics, _____ is a rise in the general level of prices of goods and services in an economy over a period of time. When the general price level rises, each unit of currency buys fewer goods and services; consequently, _____ is also a decline in the real value of money--a loss of purchasing power in the medium of exchange which is also the monetary unit of account in the economy. A chief measure of general price-level _____ is the general _____ rate, which is the percentage change in a general price index (normally the Consumer Price Index) over time.
a. Economic
b. Energy economics
c. Inflation
d. Opportunity cost

21. _____ is the shortage of common things such as food, clothing, shelter and safe drinking water, all of which determine the quality of life. It may also include the lack of access to opportunities such as education and employment which aid the escape from _____ and/or allow one to enjoy the respect of fellow citizens. According to Mollie Orshansky who developed the _____ measurements used by the U.S. government, 'to be poor is to be deprived of those goods and services and pleasures which others around us take for granted.' Ongoing debates over causes, effects and best ways to measure _____, directly influence the design and implementation of _____-reduction programs and are therefore relevant to the fields of public administration and international development.
a. Poverty map
b. Growth Elasticity of Poverty
c. Liberal welfare reforms
d. Poverty

22. _____ in economics refers to metrics and measures of output from production processes, per unit of input. Labor _____, for example, is typically measured as a ratio of output per labor-hour, an input. _____ may be conceived of as a metrics of the technical or engineering efficiency of production.
a. Piece work
b. Productivity
c. Fordism
d. Production-possibility frontier

23. In economics, _____ is the total supply of goods and services produced by a national economy during a specific time period. It is the total amount of goods and services in the economy available at all possible price levels.
a. Aggregate demand
b. Aggregation problem
c. Aggregate expenditure
d. Aggregate supply

24. In statistics, _____ indicates the strength and direction of a linear relationship between two random variables. That is in contrast with the usage of the term in colloquial speech, which denotes any relationship, not necessarily linear. In general statistical usage, _____ or co-relation refers to the departure of two random variables from independence.
a. 1921 recession
b. 130-30 fund
c. 100-year flood
d. Correlation

25. _____ is the increase in the amount of the goods and services produced by an economy over time. It is conventionally measured as the percent rate of increase in real gross domestic product, or real GDP. Growth is usually calculated in real terms, i.e. inflation-adjusted terms, in order to net out the effect of inflation on the price of the goods and services produced.
a. Economic growth
b. AD-IA Model
c. ACCRA Cost of Living Index
d. ACEA agreement

Chapter 1. WHAT IS ECONOMICS?

26. _____ and Keynesian Theory) is a macroeconomic theory based on the ideas of 20th-century British economist John Maynard Keynes. _____ argues that private sector decisions sometimes lead to inefficient macroeconomic outcomes and therefore advocates active policy responses by the public sector, including monetary policy actions by the central bank and fiscal policy actions by the government to stabilize output over the business cycle.

The theories forming the basis of _____ were first presented in The General Theory of Employment, Interest and Money, published in 1936.

a. Deflation
b. Rational choice theory
c. Market failure
d. Keynesian economics

27. In economics, the _____ is a historical inverse relation between the rate of unemployment and the rate of inflation in an economy. Stated simply, the lower the unemployment in an economy, the higher the rate of increase in nominal wages in the economy. Rate of Change of Wages against Unemployment, United Kingdom 1913-1948 from Phillips (1958)

William Phillips, a New Zealand born economist, wrote a paper in 1958 titled The Relationship between Unemployment and the Rate of Change of Money Wages in the United Kingdom 1861-1957, which was published in the quarterly journal Economica.

a. Phillips curve
b. Cost curve
c. Lorenz curve
d. Demand curve

28. In economics, _____ is the total demand for final goods and services in the economy (Y) at a given time and price level. It is the amount of goods and services in the economy that will be purchased at all possible price levels. This is the demand for the gross domestic product of a country when inventory levels are static.

a. Aggregation problem
b. Aggregate expenditure
c. Aggregate demand
d. Aggregate supply

29. _____ is the a method of technical and economic research of the systems for purpose to optimize a parity between system's consumer functions or properties and expenses to achieve those functions or properties.

This methodology for continuous perfection of production, industrial technologies, organizational structures was developed by Juryj Sobolev in 1948 at the 'Perm telephone factory'

- 1948 Juryj Sobolev - the first success in application of a method analysis at the 'Perm telephone factory'.
- 1949 - the first application for the invention as result of use of the new method.

Chapter 1. WHAT IS ECONOMICS?

Today in economically developed countries practically each enterprise or the company use methodology of the kind of functional-cost analysis as a practice of the quality management, most full satisfying to principles of standards of series ISO 9000.

- Interest of consumer not in products itself, but the advantage which it will receive from its usage.
- The consumer aspires to reduce his expenses
- Functions needed by consumer can be executed in the various ways, and, hence, with various efficiency and expenses. Among possible alternatives of realization of functions exist such in which the parity of quality and the price is the optimal for the consumer.

The goal of _____ is achievement of the highest consumer satisfaction of production at simultaneous decrease in all kinds of industrial expenses Classical _____ has three English synonyms - Value Engineering, Value Management, Value Analysis.

a. Monopoly wage
c. Function cost analysis
b. Staple financing
d. Willingness to pay

30. In coordinate geometry, the _____ is the y-value of the point where the graph of a function or relation intercepts the y-axis of the coordinate system.

In other words, the _____ of a function is the y-value of the point at which it intersects the line x = 0 (the y-axis.) Thus, if the function is specified in form y = f(x), the _____ is easy to find by calculating f.

a. 100-year flood
c. Ratio
b. 130-30 fund
d. Y-intercept

31. In microeconomics, _____ is quite simply the conversion of inputs into outputs. It is an economic process that uses resources to create a good or service that is suitable for exchange. This can include manufacturing, storing, shipping, and packaging.

a. MET
c. Solved
b. Production
d. Red Guards

32. In microeconomic theory a preference map or _____ is the collection of indifference curves possessed by an individual. Similar in nature to a topographical map, the contour lines of such a map demonstrating progressively more desirable options as they move upward or to the right. Because of the nature of indifference curves they cannot intersect and are effectively infinite in number, their sum defining all possible combinations of values.

a. Elasticity of substitution
c. Expenditure minimization problem
b. Engel curve
d. Indifference map

Chapter 2. THE ECONOMY: MYTH AND REALITY

1. The _____ is the largest national economy in the world. Its gross domestic product (GDP) was estimated as $14.2 trillion in 2008. The U.S. economy maintains a high level of output per person (GDP per capita, $46,800 in 2008, ranked at around number ten in the world.)
   - a. ACEA agreement
   - b. AD-IA Model
   - c. ACCRA Cost of Living Index
   - d. Economy of the United States

2. In economics, _____ are the resources employed to produce goods and services. They facilitate production but do not become part of the product (as with raw materials) or significantly transformed by the production process (as with fuel used to power machinery.) To 19th century economists, the _____ were land (natural resources, gifts from nature), labor (the ability to work), and capital goods (human-made tools and equipment.)
   - a. Long-run
   - b. Factors of production
   - c. Hicks-neutral technical change
   - d. Product Pipeline

3. The _____ or gross domestic income (GDI), a basic measure of an economy's economic performance, is the market value of all final goods and services produced within the borders of a nation in a year. _____ can be defined in three ways, all of which are conceptually identical. First, it is equal to the total expenditures for all final goods and services produced within the country in a stipulated period of time (usually a 365-day year.)
   - a. Countercyclical
   - b. Monopolistic competition
   - c. Market structure
   - d. Gross domestic product

4. An _____, in economics, is the amount by which the real Gross domestic product exceeds potential GDP. The real GDP is also known as GDP 'adjusted for inflation', 'constant prices' GDP or 'constant dollar' GDP, because it measures the aggregate output in a country's income accounts in a given year, expressed in base-year prices. On the other hand, the potential GDP is the quantity of real GDP when a country's economy is at full-employment.
   - a. ACEA agreement
   - b. ACCRA Cost of Living Index
   - c. AD-IA Model
   - d. Inflationary gap

5. _____ is the term denoting either an entrance or changes which are inserted into a system and which activate/modify a process. It is an abstract concept, used in the modeling, system(s) design and system(s) exploitation. It is usually connected with other terms, e.g., _____ field, _____ variable, _____ parameter, _____ value, _____ signal, _____ device and _____ file.
   - a. AD-IA Model
   - b. ACCRA Cost of Living Index
   - c. ACEA agreement
   - d. Input

6. _____ is a misspelled phrase from Latin 'pro capite' phrase meaning per head with pro meaning 'per' or 'for each' and capite meaning 'head.' Both words together equate to the phrase 'for each head.'

It is usually used in the field of statistics to indicate the average per person for any given concern, such as income, crime rate, etc.

It is also used in wills to indicate that each of the named beneficiaries should receive, by devise or bequest, equal shares of the estate. This is in contrast to a per stirpes division, in which each branch of the inheriting family inherits an equal share of the estate.

   - a. False positive rate
   - b. Sargan test
   - c. Population statistics
   - d. Per capita

7. In microeconomics, _____ is quite simply the conversion of inputs into outputs. It is an economic process that uses resources to create a good or service that is suitable for exchange. This can include manufacturing, storing, shipping, and packaging.
   a. Production
   b. Solved
   c. MET
   d. Red Guards

8. An autarky is an economy that is self-sufficient and does not take part in international trade, or severely limits trade with the outside world. Likewise the term refers to an ecosystem not affected by influences from the outside, which relies entirely on its own resources. In the economic meaning, it is also referred to as a _____.
   a. Transition economy
   b. Digital economy
   c. Network Economy
   d. Closed economy

9. In economics, an _____ is any good or commodity, transported from one country to another country in a legitimate fashion, typically for use in trade. _____ goods or services are provided to foreign consumers by domestic producers. _____ is an important part of international trade.
   a. ACEA agreement
   b. AD-IA Model
   c. ACCRA Cost of Living Index
   d. Export

10. In economics, an _____ is any good (e.g. a commodity) or service brought into one country from another country in a legitimate fashion, typically for use in trade. It is a good that is brought in from another country for sale. _____ goods or services are provided to domestic consumers by foreign producers. An _____ in the receiving country is an export to the sending country.
    a. Incoterms
    b. Import quota
    c. Economic integration
    d. Import

11. An _____ is an economy in which people, including businesses, can trade in goods and services with other people and businesses in the international community at large. This contrasts with a closed economy in which international trade cannot take place.

The act of selling goods or services to a foreign country is called exporting.

   a. Information economy
   b. Attention work
   c. Open economy
   d. Indicative planning

12. The _____ is a federally owned corporation in the United States created by congressional charter in May 1933 to provide navigation, flood control, electricity generation, fertilizer manufacturing, and economic development in the Tennessee Valley, a region particularly impacted by the Great Depression. The _____ was envisioned not only as an electricity provider, but also as a regional economic development agency that would use federal experts and electricity to rapidly modernize the region's economy and society.

The _____'s jurisdiction covers most of Tennessee, parts of Alabama, Mississippi, and Kentucky, and small slices of Georgia, North Carolina, and Virginia.

   a. 100-year flood
   b. Tennessee Valley Authority
   c. 1921 recession
   d. 130-30 fund

13. In economics, _____ is the total demand for final goods and services in the economy (Y) at a given time and price level. It is the amount of goods and services in the economy that will be purchased at all possible price levels. This is the demand for the gross domestic product of a country when inventory levels are static.
   a. Aggregation problem
   b. Aggregate supply
   c. Aggregate demand
   d. Aggregate expenditure

14. Economics:

   - _____ ,the desire to own something and the ability to pay for it
   - _____ curve, a graphic representation of a _____ schedule
   - _____ deposit, the money in checking accounts
   - _____ pull theory, the theory that inflation occurs when _____ for goods and services exceeds existing supplies
   - _____ schedule, a table that lists the quantity of a good a person will buy it each different price
   - _____ side economics, the school of economics at believes government spending and tax cuts open economy by raising _____

   a. Production
   b. Demand
   c. McKesson ' Robbins scandal
   d. Variability

15. In economics, the _____ can be defined as the graph depicting the relationship between the price of a certain commodity, and the amount of it that consumers are willing and able to purchase at that given price. It is a graphic representation of a demand schedule. The _____ for all consumers together follows from the _____ of every individual consumer: the individual demands at each price are added together.
   a. Wage curve
   b. Kuznets curve
   c. Cost curve
   d. Demand curve

16. The term _____ refers to economy-wide fluctuations in production or economic activity over several months or years. These fluctuations occur around a long-term growth trend, and typically involve shifts over time between periods of relatively rapid economic growth (expansion or boom), and periods of relative stagnation or decline (contraction or recession.)

   These fluctuations are often measured using the growth rate of real gross domestic product.
   a. Nominal value
   b. Tobit model
   c. Consumer theory
   d. Business cycle

17. In economics, a _____ is a general slowdown in economic activity over a sustained period of time, or a business cycle contraction. During _____ s, many macroeconomic indicators vary in a similar way. Production as measured by Gross Domestic Product (GDP), employment, investment spending, capacity utilization, household incomes and business profits all fall during _____ s.
   a. Treasury View
   b. Monetary economics
   c. Recession
   d. Leading indicators

18. A _____, reserve bank, or monetary authority is the entity responsible for the monetary policy of a country or of a group of member states. It is a bank that can lend money to other banks in times of need. Its primary responsibility is to maintain the stability of the national currency and money supply, but more active duties include controlling subsidized-loan interest rates, and acting as a lender of last resort to the banking sector during times of financial crisis (private banks often being integral to the national financial system.)

    a. 1921 recession
    b. 130-30 fund
    c. 100-year flood
    d. Central bank

19. _____ is money accepted for exchange of goods in an economy. The prevalence of one money over another arises, usually, when a government designates through decrees that the government shall accept only particular notes and coins in payment for taxes. Typically, money of _____ consists of stamped coins and minted paper bills.

    a. Totnes pound
    b. Security thread
    c. Currency
    d. Local currency

20. _____s is the social science that studies the production, distribution, and consumption of goods and services. The term _____s comes from the Ancient Greek οá¼°κονομῖα from οá¼¶κος (oikos, 'house') + vÏŒμος (nomos, 'custom' or 'law'), hence 'rules of the house(hold)'. Current _____ models developed out of the broader field of political economy in the late 19th century, owing to a desire to use an empirical approach more akin to the physical sciences.

    a. Inflation
    b. Energy economics
    c. Opportunity cost
    d. Economic

21. _____ refers to the economic policies of United States President Bill Clinton during the 1990s. Clinton assumed office at the tail end of a recession, and the economic theories he utilized and implemented are claimed by his supporters to have eventually led to a strong recovery, though Clinton's opponents deny this.

The strategy was outlined in the following three points:

- Establishing fiscal discipline, eliminating the budget deficit, keeping interest rates low, and spurring private-sector investment.
- Investing in people through education, training, science, and research.
- Opening foreign markets so American workers can compete abroad.

During the 1992 presidential campaign America had undergone twelve years of conservative policies implemented by Ronald Reagan and George Herbert Walker Bush. Clinton ran on the economic platform of balancing the budget, lowering inflation, lowering unemployment, and continuing the traditionally conservative policies of free trade.

    a. Jawboning
    b. Purchasing Managers Index
    c. Structural equation modeling
    d. Clintonomics

22. The _____ was a worldwide economic downturn starting in most places in 1929 and ending at different times in the 1930s or early 1940s for different countries. It was the largest and most important economic depression in the 20th century, and is used in the 21st century as an example of how far the world's economy can fall. The _____ originated in the United States; historians most often use as a starting date the stock market crash on October 29, 1929, known as Black Tuesday.

a. British Empire Economic Conference
b. Jarrow March
c. Wall Street Crash of 1929
d. Great Depression

23. _____, 1st Baron Keynes was a renowned economist from Britain whose many ideas on economic and political theories as well as on many governments' monetary policies influenced America. He advocated a government that played an active role in the lives of people regarding business, economy, etc. In this role, the government would use fiscal measures to reduce the consequences of recessions, economic depressions and booms.
   a. Adolph Fischer
   b. Adam Smith
   c. Adolf Hitler
   d. John Maynard Keynes

24. Unemployment occurs when a person is available to work and seeking work but currently without work. The prevalence of unemployment is usually measured using the _____, which is defined as the percentage of those in the labor force who are unemployed. The _____ is also used in economic studies and economic indexes such as the United States' Conference Board's Index of Leading Indicators as a measure of the state of the macroeconomics.
   a. AD-IA Model
   b. Unemployment rate
   c. ACCRA Cost of Living Index
   d. ACEA agreement

25. _____ was a global military conflict which involved a majority of the world's nations, including all of the great powers, organized into two opposing military alliances: the Allies and the Axis. The war involved the mobilization of over 100 million military personnel, making it the most widespread war in history. In a state of 'total war', the major participants placed their entire economic, industrial, and scientific capabilities at the service of the war effort, erasing the distinction between civilian and military resources.
   a. 130-30 fund
   b. 100-year flood
   c. 1921 recession
   d. World War II

26. A _____ occurs when an entity spends more money than it takes in. The opposite of a _____ is a budget surplus. Debt is essentially an accumulated flow of deficits.
   a. Budget deficit
   b. Funding body
   c. Public Financial Management
   d. Lump-sum tax

27. _____ is the increase in the amount of the goods and services produced by an economy over time. It is conventionally measured as the percent rate of increase in real gross domestic product, or real GDP. Growth is usually calculated in real terms, i.e. inflation-adjusted terms, in order to net out the effect of inflation on the price of the goods and services produced.
   a. ACEA agreement
   b. ACCRA Cost of Living Index
   c. Economic growth
   d. AD-IA Model

28. In economics, the _____ is a historical inverse relation between the rate of unemployment and the rate of inflation in an economy. Stated simply, the lower the unemployment in an economy, the higher the rate of increase in nominal wages in the economy. Rate of Change of Wages against Unemployment, United Kingdom 1913-1948 from Phillips (1958)

William Phillips, a New Zealand born economist, wrote a paper in 1958 titled The Relationship between Unemployment and the Rate of Change of Money Wages in the United Kingdom 1861-1957, which was published in the quarterly journal Economica.

a. Lorenz curve	b. Cost curve
c. Demand curve	d. Phillips curve

29. In a _____ there is both a monopoly (a single seller) and monopsony (a single buyer) in the same market.

In such market price and output will be determined by the non economic forces like bargaining power of both buyer and seller. A _____ model is often used in situations where the switching costs of both sides are prohibitively high.

a. Bilateral monopoly	b. Market concentration
c. Revenue-cap regulation	d. Price takers

30. In economics, a _____ exists when a specific individual or enterprise has sufficient control over a particular product or service to determine significantly the terms on which other individuals shall have access to it. Monopolies are thus characterized by a lack of economic competition for the good or service that they provide and a lack of viable substitute goods. The verb 'monopolize' refers to the process by which a firm gains persistently greater market share than what is expected under perfect competition.

a. Monopoly	b. 130-30 fund
c. 100-year flood	d. 1921 recession

31. The _____ is the labour pool in employment. It is generally used to describe those working for a single company or industry, but can also apply to a geographic region like a city, country, state, etc. The term generally excludes the employers or management, and implies those involved in manual labour.

a. Collective bargaining	b. Grenelle agreements
c. Departmentalization	d. Workforce

32. A _____ is a legal document that is often passed by the legislature, and approved by the chief executive-or president. For example, only certain types of revenue may be imposed and collected. Property tax is frequently the basis for municipal and county revenues, while sales tax and/or income tax are the basis for state revenues, and income tax and corporate tax are the basis for national revenues.

a. Right-financing	b. Lump-sum tax
c. Structural deficit	d. Government budget

33. The _____ is one of the three economic sectors, the others being the secondary sector and the primary sector The general definition of the Tertiary sector is producing a service instead of just a end product, in the case of the secondary sector. Sometimes an additional sector, the 'quaternary sector', is defined for the sharing of information

a. Production line	b. Secondary sector of the economy
c. Tertiary sector of economy	d. Primary products

34. _____ is a specific term used in companies' financial reporting from the company-whole point of view. Because that use excludes the effects of changing ownership interest, an economic measure of _____ is necessary for financial analysis from the shareholders' point of view

_____ is defined by the Financial Accounting Standards Board, or FASB, as e;the change in equity [net assets] of a business enterprise during a period from transactions and other events and circumstances from nonowner sources. It includes all changes in equity during a period except those resulting from investments by owners and distributions to owners.e;

_____ is the sum of net income and other items that must bypass the income statement because they have not been realized, including items like an unrealized holding gain or loss from available for sale securities and foreign currency translation gains or losses.

a. Windfall gain
b. Real income
c. Net national income
d. Comprehensive income

35. The _____, also commonly known as the Computer Age or Information Era, is an idea that the current age will be characterised by the ability of individuals to transfer information freely, and to have instant access to knowledge that would have been difficult or impossible to find previously. The idea is heavily linked to the concept of a Digital Age or Digital Revolution, and carries the ramifications of a shift from traditional industry that the Industrial Revolution brought through industrialisation, to an economy based around the manipulation of information. The period is generally said to have begun in the latter half of the 20th century, though the particular date varies.

a. ACEA agreement
b. ACCRA Cost of Living Index
c. AD-IA Model
d. Information Age

36. _____ is where a person works for themselves rather than someone else or a company that they do not own. To be self-employed, an individual is normally highly skilled in a trade or has a niche product or service for their local community. With the creation of the Internet the ability for an individual to become self-employed has increased dramatically.

a. Just cause
b. Self-employment
c. Work-at-home scheme
d. Performance improvement plan

37. _____ is a broad label that refers to any individuals or households that use goods and services generated within the economy. The concept of a _____ is used in different contexts, so that the usage and significance of the term may vary.

Typically when business people and economists talk of _____s they are talking about person as _____, an aggregated commodity item with little individuality other than that expressed in the buy/not-buy decision.

a. 100-year flood
b. 130-30 fund
c. 1921 recession
d. Consumer

38. _____ or consumer demand or consumption is also known as personal consumption expenditure. It is the largest part of aggregate demand or effective demand at the macroeconomic level. There are two variants of consumption in the aggregate demand model, including induced consumption and autonomous consumption.

a. Potential output
b. Dishoarding
c. Complex multiplier
d. Consumer spending

Chapter 2. THE ECONOMY: MYTH AND REALITY

39. _____ is a common concept in economics, and gives rise to derived concepts such as consumer debt. Generally _____ is defined by opposition to production. But the precise definition can vary because different schools of economists define production quite differently.

   a. Consumption
   b. Foreclosure data providers
   c. Federal Reserve Bank Notes
   d. Cash or share options

40. In finance, a _____ is a debt security, in which the authorized issuer owes the holders a debt and, depending on the terms of the _____, is obliged to pay interest (the coupon) and/or to repay the principal at a later date, termed maturity. A _____ is a formal contract to repay borrowed money with interest at fixed intervals.

Thus a _____ is like a loan: the issuer is the borrower (debtor), the holder is the lender (creditor), and the coupon is the interest.

   a. Zero-coupon
   b. Bond
   c. Prize Bond
   d. Callable

41. The _____ consists of a number of economic theories which describe the nature of the firm, company including its existence, its behaviour, and its relationship with the market.

In simplified terms, the _____ aims to answer these questions:

   1. Existence - why do firms emerge, why are not all transactions in the economy mediated over the market?
   2. Boundaries - why the boundary between firms and the market is located exactly there? Which transactions are performed internally and which are negotiated on the market?
   3. Organization - why are firms structured in such specific way? What is the interplay of formal and informal relationships?

Despite looking simple, these questions are not answered by the established economic theory, which usually views firms as given, and treats them as black boxes without any internal structure.

The First World War period saw a change of emphasis in economic theory away from industry-level analysis which mainly included analysing markets to analysis at the level of the firm, as it became increasingly clear that perfect competition was no longer an adequate model of how firms behaved. Economic theory till then had focussed on trying to understand markets alone and there had been little study on understanding why firms or organisations exist.

   a. Policy Ineffectiveness Proposition
   b. Theory of the firm
   c. Technology gap
   d. Khazzoom-Brookes postulate

42. A _____ or transnational corporation is a corporation or enterprise that manages production or delivers services in more than one country. It can also be referred to as an international corporation.

The first modern MNC is generally thought to be the Dutch East India Company, established in 1602.

a. Rakon
b. Multinational corporation
c. Foreign direct investment
d. Luxembourg Income Study

43. In neoclassical economics and microeconomics, _____ describes the perfect being a market in which there are many small firms, all producing homogeneous goods. In the short term, such markets are productively inefficient as output will not occur where mc is equal to ac, but allocatively efficient, as output under _____ will always occur where mc is equal to mr, and therefore where mc equals ar. However, in the long term, such markets are both allocatively and productively efficient.
   a. Law of supply
   b. Perfect competition
   c. General equilibrium
   d. Co-operative economics

44. Competition law, known in the United States as _____ law, has three main elements:

   - prohibiting agreements or practices that restrict free trading and competition between business entities. This includes in particular the repression of cartels.
   - banning abusive behaviour by a firm dominating a market, or anti-competitive practices that tend to lead to such a dominant position. Practices controlled in this way may include predatory pricing, tying, price gouging, refusal to deal, and many others.
   - supervising the mergers and acquisitions of large corporations, including some joint ventures. Transactions that are considered to threaten the competitive process can be prohibited altogether, or approved subject to 'remedies' such as an obligation to divest part of the merged business or to offer licences or access to facilities to enable other businesses to continue competing.

The substance and practice of competition law varies from jurisdiction to jurisdiction. Protecting the interests of consumers (consumer welfare) and ensuring that entrepreneurs have an opportunity to compete in the market economy are often treated as important objectives. Competition law is closely connected with law on deregulation of access to markets, state aids and subsidies, the privatisation of state owned assets and the establishment of independent sector regulators. In recent decades, competition law has been viewed as a way to provide better public services.

   a. Antitrust
   b. Anti-Inflation Act
   c. Intellectual property law
   d. United Kingdom competition law

45. _____, known in the United States as antitrust law, has three main elements:

   - prohibiting agreements or practices that restrict free trading and competition between business entities. This includes in particular the repression of cartels.
   - banning abusive behaviour by a firm dominating a market, or anti-competitive practices that tend to lead to such a dominant position. Practices controlled in this way may include predatory pricing, tying, price gouging, refusal to deal, and many others.
   - supervising the mergers and acquisitions of large corporations, including some joint ventures. Transactions that are considered to threaten the competitive process can be prohibited altogether, or approved subject to 'remedies' such as an obligation to divest part of the merged business or to offer licences or access to facilities to enable other businesses to continue competing.

The substance and practice of _____ varies from jurisdiction to jurisdiction. Protecting the interests of consumers (consumer welfare) and ensuring that entrepreneurs have an opportunity to compete in the market economy are often treated as important objectives. _____ is closely connected with law on deregulation of access to markets, state aids and subsidies, the privatisation of state owned assets and the establishment of independent sector regulators. In recent decades, _____ has been viewed as a way to provide better public services.

a. Due diligence
b. Competition law
c. Hostile work environment
d. Fee simple

46. In economics, the term _____ of income or _____ refers to a simple economic model which describes the reciprocal circulation of income between producers and consumers. In the _____ model, the inter-dependent entities of producer and consumer are referred to as 'firms' and 'households' respectively and provide each other with factors in order to facilitate the flow of income. Firms provide consumers with goods and services in exchange for consumer expenditure and 'factors of production' from households.

a. 1921 recession
b. 100-year flood
c. 130-30 fund
d. Circular flow

47. _____ is a fee paid on borrowed assets. It is the price paid for the use of borrowed money, or, money earned by deposited funds. Assets that are sometimes lent with _____ include money, shares, consumer goods through hire purchase, major assets such as aircraft, and even entire factories in finance lease arrangements.

a. Interest
b. Asset protection
c. Insolvency
d. Internal debt

48. In general, a _____ is an arrangement to provide people with an income when they are no longer earning a regular income from employment.

The terms retirement plan or superannuation refer to a _____ granted upon retirement. Retirement plans may be set up by employers, insurance companies, the government or other institutions such as employer associations or trade unions.

a. Pension
b. Real wage
c. Superannuation
d. Profit-sharing agreement

49. _____ is the economic policy of restraining trade between states, through methods such as tariffs on imported goods, restrictive quotas, and a variety of other restrictive government regulations designed to discourage imports, and prevent foreign take-over of local markets and companies. This policy is closely aligned with anti-globalization, and contrasts with free trade, where government barriers to trade are kept to a minimum. The term is mostly used in the context of economics, where _____ refers to policies or doctrines which 'protect' businesses and workers within a country by restricting or regulating trade with foreign nations.

a. Google economy
b. Digital economy
c. Protectionism
d. Knowledge economy

50. _____ refers to the economic policies promoted by United States President Ronald Reagan during the 1980s. The four pillars of Reagan's economic policy were to:

1. reduce the growth of government spending,
2. reduce income and capital gains marginal tax rates,
3. reduce government regulation of the economy,
4. control the money supply to reduce inflation.

In attempting to cut back on domestic spending while lowering taxes, Reagan's approach was a departure from his immediate predecessors.

Reagan became president during a period of high inflation and unemployment (commonly referred to as stagflation), which had largely abated by the time he left office eight years later.

Prior to the Reagan Administration was a roughly ten year period of economic stagnation and inflation, known as stagflation.

- a. Social savings
- b. Business sector
- c. Happiness economics
- d. Reaganomics

51. _____ is that which is owed; usually referencing assets owed, but the term can also cover moral obligations and other interactions not requiring money. In the case of assets, _____ is a means of using future purchasing power in the present before a summation has been earned. Some companies and corporations use _____ as a part of their overall corporate finance strategy.
- a. Hard money loan
- b. Debenture
- c. Collateral Management
- d. Debt

52.

_____ was a German philosopher, political economist, historian, political theorist, sociologist, communist and revolutionary credited as the founder of communism.

Marx summarized his approach to history and politics in the opening line of the first chapter of The Communist Manifesto : e;The history of all hitherto existing society is the history of class struggles.e; Marx argued that capitalism, like previous socioeconomic systems, will produce internal tensions which will lead to its destruction. Just as capitalism replaced feudalism, socialism will in its turn replace capitalism and lead to a stateless, classless society which will emerge after a transitional period, the 'dictatorship of the proletariat'.

- a. Adam Smith
- b. Karl Heinrich Marx
- c. Neo-Gramscianism
- d. Marxism

53. A _____ is a tax imposed so that the tax rate is fixed as the amount subject to taxation increases. In simple terms, it imposes an equal burden (relative to resources) on the rich and poor. 'Proportional' describes a distribution effect on income or expenditure, referring to the way the rate remains consistent (does not progress from 'low to high' or 'high to low' as income or consumption changes), where the marginal tax rate is equal to the average tax rate.

a. 130-30 fund
b. Regressive tax
c. 100-year flood
d. Proportional tax

54. _____ in political thought refers to economic theories of social organization advocating collective ownership and administration of the means of production and distribution of goods, and a society characterized by equality for all individuals, with an egalitarian method of compensation. Modern _____ originated in the late 19th-century intellectual and working class political movement that criticized the effects of industrialization and private ownership on society. Karl Marx posited that _____ would be achieved via class struggle and a proletarian revolution after a transitional stage from capitalism called the dictatorship of the proletariat.

a. Adolph Fischer
b. Socialism
c. Adam Smith
d. Adolf Hitler

55. In economics, a _____ is a redistribution of income in the market system. These payments are considered to be nonexhaustive because they do not directly absorb resources or create output. Examples of certain _____s include welfare (financial aid), social security, and government subsidies for certain businesses (firms.)

a. 130-30 fund
b. 1921 recession
c. 100-year flood
d. Transfer payment

56. In economics, _____ is a measure of the relative satisfaction from consumption of various goods and services. Given this measure, one may speak meaningfully of increasing or decreasing _____, and thereby explain economic behavior in terms of attempts to increase one's _____. For illustrative purposes, changes in _____ are sometimes expressed in units called utils.

a. Utility
b. Utility function
c. Ordinal utility
d. Expected utility hypothesis

57. A _____ is the transfer of wealth from one party (such as a person or company) to another. A _____ is usually made in exchange for the provision of goods, services or both, or to fulfill a legal obligation.

The simplest and oldest form of _____ is barter, the exchange of one good or service for another.

a. Soft count
b. Going concern
c. Social gravity
d. Payment

58. _____ is the incidence or process of transferring ownership of a business, enterprise, agency or public service from the public sector (government) to the private sector (business.) In a broader sense, _____ refers to transfer of any government function to the private sector including governmental functions like revenue collection and law enforcement.

The term '_____' also has been used to describe two unrelated transactions.

a. Ricardian equivalence
b. Performance reports
c. Compound empowerment
d. Privatization

Chapter 2. THE ECONOMY: MYTH AND REALITY 19

59. A _____ is:

- Rewrite _____, in generative grammar and computer science
- Standardization, a formal and widely-accepted statement, fact, definition, or qualification
- Operation, a determinate _____ for performing a mathematical operation and obtaining a certain result (Mathematics, Logic)
    - Unary operation
    - Binary operation
- _____ of inference, a function from sets of formulae to formulae (Mathematics, Logic)
- _____ of thumb, principle with broad application that is not intended to be strictly accurate or reliable for every situation. Also often simply referred to as a _____
- Moral, an atomic element of a moral code for guiding choices in human behavior
- Heuristic, a quantized '_____' which shows a tendency or probability for successful function
- A regulation, as in sports
- A Production _____, as in computer science
- Procedural law, a _____ set governing the application of laws to cases
    - A law, which may informally be called a '_____'
    - A court ruling, a decision by a court
- In the U.S. Government, a regulation mandated by Congress, but written or expanded upon by the Executive Branch.
- Norm (sociology), an informal but widely accepted _____, concept, truth, definition, or qualification (social norms, legal norms, coding norms)
- Norm (philosophy), a kind of sentence or a reason to act, feel or believe
- 'Rulership' is the concept of governance by a government:
    - Military _____, governance by a military body
    - Monastic _____, a collection of precepts that guides the life of monks or nuns in a religious order where the superior holds the place of Christ
- Slide _____

- '_____,' a song by Ayumi Hamasaki
- '_____,' a song by rapper Nas
- '_____s,' an album by the band The Whitest Boy Alive
- _____s: Pyaar Ka Superhit Formula, a 2003 Bollywood film
- ruler, an instrument for measuring lengths
- _____, a component of an astrolabe, circumferator or similar instrument
- The _____s, a bestselling self-help book
- _____ Project (Run Up-to-date Linux Everywhere), a project that aims to use up-to-date Linux software on old PCs
- _____ engine, a software system that helps managing business _____s
- Ja _____, a hip hop artist
    - R.U.L.E., a 2005 greatest hits album by rapper Ja _____
- '_____s,' a KMFDM song

a. Technocracy
c. Rule
b. Procter ' Gamble
d. Demand

Chapter 2. THE ECONOMY: MYTH AND REALITY

60. To _____ is to impose a financial charge or other levy upon a taxpayer by a state or the functional equivalent of a state.

_____es are also imposed by many subnational entities. _____es consist of direct _____ or indirect _____, and may be paid in money or as its labour equivalent (often but not always unpaid.)

a. Tax
b. 130-30 fund
c. 1921 recession
d. 100-year flood

61. To tax is to impose a financial charge or other levy upon a taxpayer by a state or the functional equivalent of a state.

_____ are also imposed by many subnational entities. _____ consist of direct tax or indirect tax, and may be paid in money or as its labour equivalent (often but not always unpaid.)

a. 130-30 fund
b. 100-year flood
c. Taxes
d. 1921 recession

62. The _____ is the multiple by which Aggregate demand will increase, when there is an increase in transfer payments (e.g. welfare spending, unemployment payments.) Changes in spending usually lead to a larger than one for one increase in Aggregate demand, because any increase in household incomes caused by the increase in spending also increases in consumption spending, which further increases Aggregate demand.

a. Legal monopoly
b. Cost-effectiveness analysis
c. Market-based instruments
d. Transfer payments Multiplier

63. _____ is a socioeconomic structure and political ideology that promotes the establishment of an egalitarian, classless, stateless society based on common ownership and control of the means of production and property in general. In political science, the term '_____' is sometimes used to refer to communist states, a form of government in which the state operates under a one-party system and declares allegiance to Marxism-Leninism or a derivative thereof, even if the party does not actually claim that it has already reached _____.

Forerunners of communist ideas existed in antiquity and particularly in the 18th and early 19th century France, with thinkers such as Jean-Jacques Rousseau and the more radical Gracchus Babeuf.

a. Social fascism
b. New Communist Movement
c. Democratic centralism
d. Communism

64. A _____ is an economic system that incorporates a mixture of private and government ownership or control, or a mixture of capitalism and socialism.

There is not one single definition for a _____, but relevant aspects include: a degree of private economic freedom (including privately owned industry) intermingled with centralized economic planning and government regulation (which may include regulation of the market for environmental concerns and social welfare, or state ownership and management of some of the means of production for national or social objectives.)

For some states, there is not a consensus on whether they are capitalist, socialist, or mixed economies.

a. Hunter-gatherer
c. Planned liberalism
b. Dual economy
d. Mixed economy

65. _____ is used to assign the available resources in an economic way. It is part of resource management.

In strategic planning,is a plan for using available resources, for example human resources, especially in the near term, to achieve goals for the future.

a. 100-year flood
c. 130-30 fund
b. 1921 recession
d. Resource allocation

Chapter 3. THE FUNDAMENTAL ECONOMIC PROBLEM: SCARCITY AND CHOICE

1. A _____ occurs when an entity spends more money than it takes in. The opposite of a _____ is a budget surplus. Debt is essentially an accumulated flow of deficits.
   a. Funding body
   b. Budget deficit
   c. Public Financial Management
   d. Lump-sum tax

2. A _____ is a situation in which the government takes in more than it spends.
   a. Budget set
   b. 100-year flood
   c. 130-30 fund
   d. Budget surplus

3. _____ is any long-term change in the patterns of average weather of a specific region or the Earth as a whole. _____ reflects abnormal variations to the Earth's climate and subsequent effects on other parts of the Earth, such as in the ice caps over durations ranging from decades to millions of years.

   In recent usage, especially in the context of environmental policy, _____ usually refers to changes in modern climate

   a. 130-30 fund
   b. 1921 recession
   c. Climate change
   d. 100-year flood

4. _____ or economic opportunity loss is the value of the next best alternative foregone as the result of making a decision. _____ analysis is an important part of a company's decision-making processes but is not treated as an actual cost in any financial statement. The next best thing that a person can engage in is referred to as the _____ of doing the best thing and ignoring the next best thing to be done.
   a. Industrial organization
   b. Economic ideology
   c. Economic
   d. Opportunity cost

5. The _____ is the expected return forgone by bypassing of other potential investment activities for a given capital. It is a rate of return that investors could earn in financial markets.
   a. ACEA agreement
   b. ACCRA Cost of Living Index
   c. AD-IA Model
   d. Opportunity cost of capital

6. The _____ is the largest national economy in the world. Its gross domestic product (GDP) was estimated as $14.2 trillion in 2008. The U.S. economy maintains a high level of output per person (GDP per capita, $46,800 in 2008, ranked at around number ten in the world.)
   a. AD-IA Model
   b. Economy of the United States
   c. ACCRA Cost of Living Index
   d. ACEA agreement

7. The _____ is an expected return that the provider of capital plans to earn on their investment.

   Capital (money) used for funding a business should earn returns for the capital providers who risk their capital. For an investment to be worthwhile, the expected return on capital must be greater than the _____.

   a. Modigliani-Miller theorem
   b. Capital expenditure
   c. Capital intensive
   d. Cost of capital

Chapter 3. THE FUNDAMENTAL ECONOMIC PROBLEM: SCARCITY AND CHOICE

8. Competition law, known in the United States as _____ law, has three main elements:

   - prohibiting agreements or practices that restrict free trading and competition between business entities. This includes in particular the repression of cartels.
   - banning abusive behaviour by a firm dominating a market, or anti-competitive practices that tend to lead to such a dominant position. Practices controlled in this way may include predatory pricing, tying, price gouging, refusal to deal, and many others.
   - supervising the mergers and acquisitions of large corporations, including some joint ventures. Transactions that are considered to threaten the competitive process can be prohibited altogether, or approved subject to 'remedies' such as an obligation to divest part of the merged business or to offer licences or access to facilities to enable other businesses to continue competing.

   The substance and practice of competition law varies from jurisdiction to jurisdiction. Protecting the interests of consumers (consumer welfare) and ensuring that entrepreneurs have an opportunity to compete in the market economy are often treated as important objectives. Competition law is closely connected with law on deregulation of access to markets, state aids and subsidies, the privatisation of state owned assets and the establishment of independent sector regulators. In recent decades, competition law has been viewed as a way to provide better public services.

   a. United Kingdom competition law
   b. Anti-Inflation Act
   c. Intellectual property law
   d. Antitrust

9. _____, known in the United States as antitrust law, has three main elements:

   - prohibiting agreements or practices that restrict free trading and competition between business entities. This includes in particular the repression of cartels.
   - banning abusive behaviour by a firm dominating a market, or anti-competitive practices that tend to lead to such a dominant position. Practices controlled in this way may include predatory pricing, tying, price gouging, refusal to deal, and many others.
   - supervising the mergers and acquisitions of large corporations, including some joint ventures. Transactions that are considered to threaten the competitive process can be prohibited altogether, or approved subject to 'remedies' such as an obligation to divest part of the merged business or to offer licences or access to facilities to enable other businesses to continue competing.

   The substance and practice of _____ varies from jurisdiction to jurisdiction. Protecting the interests of consumers (consumer welfare) and ensuring that entrepreneurs have an opportunity to compete in the market economy are often treated as important objectives. _____ is closely connected with law on deregulation of access to markets, state aids and subsidies, the privatisation of state owned assets and the establishment of independent sector regulators. In recent decades, _____ has been viewed as a way to provide better public services.

   a. Hostile work environment
   b. Competition law
   c. Due diligence
   d. Fee simple

10. _____ is an economic concept with commonplace familiarity. It is the price that a good or service is offered at, or will fetch, in the marketplace. It is of interest mainly in the study of microeconomics.

Chapter 3. THE FUNDAMENTAL ECONOMIC PROBLEM: SCARCITY AND CHOICE

a. Market anomaly
b. Noisy market hypothesis
c. Paper trading
d. Market price

11. In economics, a _____ is a general slowdown in economic activity over a sustained period of time, or a business cycle contraction. During _____s, many macroeconomic indicators vary in a similar way. Production as measured by Gross Domestic Product (GDP), employment, investment spending, capacity utilization, household incomes and business profits all fall during _____s.
   a. Treasury View
   b. Recession
   c. Monetary economics
   d. Leading indicators

12. _____ in economics and business is the result of an exchange and from that trade we assign a numerical monetary value to a good, service or asset. If Alice trades Bob 4 apples for an orange, the _____ of an orange is 4 apples. Inversely, the _____ of an apple is 1/4 oranges.
   a. Premium pricing
   b. Price book
   c. Price war
   d. Price

13. _____ is the term denoting either an entrance or changes which are inserted into a system and which activate/modify a process. It is an abstract concept, used in the modeling, system(s) design and system(s) exploitation. It is usually connected with other terms, e.g., _____ field, _____ variable, _____ parameter, _____ value, _____ signal, _____ device and _____ file.
   a. ACCRA Cost of Living Index
   b. ACEA agreement
   c. AD-IA Model
   d. Input

14. _____ is the price at which an asset would trade in a competitive Walrasian auction setting. _____ is often used interchangeably with open _____, fair value or fair _____, although these terms have distinct definitions in different standards, and may differ in some circumstances.

International Valuation Standards defines _____ as 'the estimated amount for which a property should exchange on the date of valuation between a willing buyer and a willing seller in an arm's-length transaction after proper marketing wherein the parties had each acted knowledgeably, prudently, and without compulsion.'

_____ is a concept distinct from market price, which is 'the price at which one can transact', while _____ is 'the true underlying value' according to theoretical standards.

   a. Personal financial management
   b. Secured loan
   c. Netting
   d. Market value

15. An _____ is a decision such that no other available decision options will lead to a better outcome. It is an important concept in decision theory. In order to compare the different decision outcomes, one commonly assigns a relative utility to each of them.
   a. Influence diagram
   b. Intertemporal choice
   c. Expected value of sample information
   d. Optimal decision

16. _____ is a categorical label used to describe states that are considered to be underdeveloped in terms of their economy or level of industrialization, globalization, standard of living, health, education or other criteria for 'advancements'.

Chapter 3. THE FUNDAMENTAL ECONOMIC PROBLEM: SCARCITY AND CHOICE

_____ was a reference to the 'the Third Estate, the commoners of France before and during the French Revolution, opposed to the priests and nobles who composed the First Estate and the Second Estate.

a. Bulgarian-American trade
c. Third World

b. 2008 budget crisis
d. Developed markets

17. _____ is the a method of technical and economic research of the systems for purpose to optimize a parity between system's consumer functions or properties and expenses to achieve those functions or properties.

This methodology for continuous perfection of production, industrial technologies, organizational structures was developed by Juryj Sobolev in 1948 at the 'Perm telephone factory'

- 1948 Juryj Sobolev - the first success in application of a method analysis at the 'Perm telephone factory' .
- 1949 - the first application for the invention as result of use of the new method.

Today in economically developed countries practically each enterprise or the company use methodology of the kind of functional-cost analysis as a practice of the quality management, most full satisfying to principles of standards of series ISO 9000.

- Interest of consumer not in products itself, but the advantage which it will receive from its usage.
- The consumer aspires to reduce his expenses
- Functions needed by consumer can be executed in the various ways, and, hence, with various efficiency and expenses. Among possible alternatives of realization of functions exist such in which the parity of quality and the price is the optimal for the consumer.

The goal of _____ is achievement of the highest consumer satisfaction of production at simultaneous decrease in all kinds of industrial expenses Classical _____ has three English synonyms - Value Engineering, Value Management, Value Analysis.

a. Staple financing
c. Willingness to pay

b. Function cost analysis
d. Monopoly wage

18. In microeconomics, _____ is quite simply the conversion of inputs into outputs. It is an economic process that uses resources to create a good or service that is suitable for exchange. This can include manufacturing, storing, shipping, and packaging.

a. Red Guards
c. MET

b. Solved
d. Production

19. In calculus, a function f defined on a subset of the real numbers with real values is called _____, if for all x and y such that x >≤ y one has f(x) >≤ f(y), so f preserves the order. In layman's terms, the sign of the slope is always positive (the curve tending upwards) or zero (i.e., non-decreasing, or asymptotic, or depicted as a horizontal, flat line) Likewise, a function is called monotonically decreasing (non-increasing) if, whenever x >≤ y, then f(x) >≥ f(y), so it reverses the order.

Chapter 3. THE FUNDAMENTAL ECONOMIC PROBLEM: SCARCITY AND CHOICE

a. 130-30 fund
c. 100-year flood
b. 1921 recession
d. Monotonic

20. _____ is a common concept in economics, and gives rise to derived concepts such as consumer debt. Generally _____ is defined by opposition to production. But the precise definition can vary because different schools of economists define production quite differently.

a. Federal Reserve Bank Notes
c. Foreclosure data providers
b. Consumption
d. Cash or share options

21. In law and economics, the _____, describes the economic efficiency of an economic allocation or outcome in the presence of externalities. The theorem states that when trade in an externality is possible and there are no transaction costs, bargaining will lead to an efficient outcome regardless of the initial allocation of property rights. In practice, obstacles to bargaining or poorly defined property rights can prevent Coasian bargaining.

a. Means test
c. General Mining Act of 1872
b. Coase theorem
d. Prior appropriation water rights

22. _____ is used to assign the available resources in an economic way. It is part of resource management.

In strategic planning, is a plan for using available resources, for example human resources, especially in the near term, to achieve goals for the future.

a. 130-30 fund
c. 100-year flood
b. 1921 recession
d. Resource allocation

23. _____s is the social science that studies the production, distribution, and consumption of goods and services. The term _____s comes from the Ancient Greek οἰκονομία from οἶκος (oikos, 'house') + νόμος (nomos, 'custom' or 'law'), hence 'rules of the house(hold)'. Current _____ models developed out of the broader field of political economy in the late 19th century, owing to a desire to use an empirical approach more akin to the physical sciences.

a. Inflation
c. Economic
b. Energy economics
d. Opportunity cost

24. _____ was a survey conducted by the U.S. Department of Justice to gauge the prevalence of alcohol and illegal drug use among prior arrestees. It was a reformulation of the prior Drug Use Forecasting (DUF) program, focused on five drugs in particular: cocaine, marijuana, methamphetamine, opiates, and PCP.

Participants were randomly selected from arrest records in major metropolitan areas; because no personally identifying information is taken from each record chosen, the resulting data can be correlated to arrest rates, but not to the total population of persons charged.

a. AD-IA Model
c. ACEA agreement
b. ACCRA Cost of Living Index
d. Arrestee Drug Abuse Monitoring

Chapter 3. THE FUNDAMENTAL ECONOMIC PROBLEM: SCARCITY AND CHOICE

25. A _____ is an economy based on the division of labor in which the prices of goods and services are determined in a free price system set by supply and demand. This is often contrasted with a planned economy, in which a central government determines the price of goods and services using a fixed price system. Market economies are contrasted with mixed economy where the price system is not entirely free but under some government control that is not extensive enough to constitute a planned economy.

- a. Nutritional Economics
- b. Commons-based peer production
- c. Network Economy
- d. Market economy

26. _____ was a Scottish moral philosopher and a pioneer of political economy. One of the key figures of the Scottish Enlightenment, Smith is the author of The Theory of Moral Sentiments and An Inquiry into the Nature and Causes of the Wealth of Nations. The latter, usually abbreviated as The Wealth of Nations, is considered his magnum opus and the first modern work of economics.

- a. Alan Greenspan
- b. Adam Smith
- c. Adolf Hitler
- d. Adolph Fischer

27. An Inquiry into the Nature and Causes of the _____ is the magnum opus of the Scottish economist Adam Smith. It is a clearly written account of economics at the dawn of the Industrial Revolution, as well as a rhetorical piece written for the generally educated individual of the 18th century - advocating a free market economy as more productive and more beneficial to society.

The work is credited as a watershed in history and economics due to its comprehensive, largely accurate characterization of economic mechanisms that survive in modern economics; and also for its effective use of rhetorical technique, including structuring the work to contrast real world examples of free and fettered markets.

- a. The Bell Curve
- b. The Rise and Fall of the Great Powers
- c. Wealth of Nations
- d. Black Book of Communism

28. In a _____ there is both a monopoly (a single seller) and monopsony (a single buyer) in the same market.

In such market price and output will be determined by the non economic forces like bargaining power of both buyer and seller. A _____ model is often used in situations where the switching costs of both sides are prohibitively high.

- a. Revenue-cap regulation
- b. Price takers
- c. Market concentration
- d. Bilateral monopoly

29. In economics, a _____ exists when a specific individual or enterprise has sufficient control over a particular product or service to determine significantly the terms on which other individuals shall have access to it. Monopolies are thus characterized by a lack of economic competition for the good or service that they provide and a lack of viable substitute goods. The verb 'monopolize' refers to the process by which a firm gains persistently greater market share than what is expected under perfect competition.

- a. 100-year flood
- b. 130-30 fund
- c. 1921 recession
- d. Monopoly

Chapter 3. THE FUNDAMENTAL ECONOMIC PROBLEM: SCARCITY AND CHOICE

30. In economics, _____ refers to the ability of a person or a country to produce a particular good at a lower marginal cost and opportunity cost than another person or country. It is the ability to produce a product most efficiently given all the other products that could be produced. It can be contrasted with absolute advantage which refers to the ability of a person or a country to produce a particular good at a lower absolute cost than another.
   a. Triffin dilemma
   b. Hot money
   c. Gravity model of trade
   d. Comparative advantage

31. _____ is exchange of capital, goods, and services across international borders or territories. In most countries, it represents a significant share of gross domestic product (GDP.) While _____ has been present throughout much of history, its economic, social, and political importance has been on the rise in recent centuries.
   a. Import license
   b. Incoterms
   c. Intra-industry trade
   d. International trade

32. A _____ is a theoretical term that economists use to describe a market which is free from government intervention (i.e. no regulation, no subsidization, no single monetary system and no governmental monopolies.) In a _____, property rights are voluntarily exchanged at a price arranged solely by the mutual consent of sellers and buyers. By definition, buyers and sellers do not coerce each other, in the sense that they obtain each other's property without the use of physical force, threat of physical force, or fraud, nor is the coerced by a third party (such as by government via transfer payments) and they engage in trade simply because they both consent and believe that it is a good enough choice.
   a. Delegation
   b. Leninism
   c. Free market
   d. Third camp

33. _____ is a type of trade policy that allows traders to act and transact without interference from government. Thus, the policy permits trading partners mutual gains from trade, with goods and services produced according to the theory of comparative advantage.

Under a _____ policy, prices are a reflection of true supply and demand, and are the sole determinant of resource allocation.

   a. Free trade
   b. 100-year flood
   c. 1921 recession
   d. 130-30 fund

34. A _____ is any systematic process enabling many market players to bid and ask: helping bidders and sellers interact and make deals. It is not just the price mechanism but the entire system of regulation, qualification, credentials, reputations and clearing that surrounds that mechanism and makes it operate in a social context.

Because a _____ relies on the assumption that players are constantly involved and unequally enabled, a _____ is distinguished specifically from a voting system where candidates seek the support of voters on a less regular basis.

   a. Price mechanism
   b. Competitive equilibrium
   c. Contestable market
   d. Market system

35. In economics, a _____ is any economic system that effects its distribution of goods and services with prices and employing any form of money or debt tokens. Except for possible remote and primitive communities, all modern societies use _____s to allocate resources. However, _____s are not used for all resource allocation decisions today.

a. Hanseatic League
c. Price system
b. Neomercantilism
d. Family economy

36.

_____ was a German philosopher, political economist, historian, political theorist, sociologist, communist and revolutionary credited as the founder of communism.

Marx summarized his approach to history and politics in the opening line of the first chapter of The Communist Manifesto : e;The history of all hitherto existing society is the history of class struggles.e; Marx argued that capitalism, like previous socioeconomic systems, will produce internal tensions which will lead to its destruction. Just as capitalism replaced feudalism, socialism will in its turn replace capitalism and lead to a stateless, classless society which will emerge after a transitional period, the 'dictatorship of the proletariat'.

a. Neo-Gramscianism
c. Marxism
b. Adam Smith
d. Karl Heinrich Marx

Chapter 4. SUPPLY AND DEMAND: AN INITIAL LOOK

1. _____ is an economic model based on price, utility and quantity in a market. It predicts that in a competitive market, price will function to equalize the quantity demanded by consumers, and the quantity supplied by producers, resulting in an economic equilibrium of price and quantity. The model incorporates other factors changing equilibrium as a shift of demand and/or supply.

   a. Rational addiction   b. Deferred gratification
   c. Joint demand   d. Supply and demand

2. Economics:

- _____,the desire to own something and the ability to pay for it
- _____ curve,a graphic representation of a _____ schedule
- _____ deposit, the money in checking accounts
- _____ pull theory,the theory that inflation occurs when _____ for goods and services exceeds existing supplies
- _____ schedule,a table that lists the quantity of a good a person will buy it each different price
- _____ side economics,the school of economics at believes government spending and tax cuts open economy by raising _____

   a. Variability   b. McKesson ' Robbins scandal
   c. Production   d. Demand

3. _____ was a survey conducted by the U.S. Department of Justice to gauge the prevalence of alcohol and illegal drug use among prior arrestees. It was a reformulation of the prior Drug Use Forecasting (DUF) program, focused on five drugs in particular: cocaine, marijuana, methamphetamine, opiates, and PCP.

Participants were randomly selected from arrest records in major metropolitan areas; because no personally identifying information is taken from each record chosen, the resulting data can be correlated to arrest rates, but not to the total population of persons charged.

   a. ACEA agreement   b. AD-IA Model
   c. Arrestee Drug Abuse Monitoring   d. ACCRA Cost of Living Index

4. The _____ is the central banking system of the United States. Created in 1913 by the enactment of the Federal Reserve Act (signed by Woodrow Wilson), it is a quasi-public and quasi-private (government entity with private components) banking system that comprises (1) the presidentially appointed Board of Governors of the _____ in Washington, D.C.; (2) the Federal Open Market Committee; (3) twelve regional Federal Reserve Banks located in major cities throughout the nation acting as fiscal agents for the U.S. Treasury, each with its own nine-member board of directors; (4) numerous other private U.S. member banks, which subscribe to required amounts of non-transferable stock in their regional Federal Reserve Banks; and (5) various advisory councils. Since February 2006, Ben Bernanke has served as the Chairman of the Board of Governors of the _____.

   a. Monetary Policy Report to the Congress   b. Federal Reserve System
   c. Federal Reserve System Open Market Account   d. Term auction facility

5. In economics, the _____ is the term economists use to describe the self-regulating nature of the marketplace. The _____ is a metaphor coined by the economist Adam Smith in The Wealth of Nations.

Chapter 4. SUPPLY AND DEMAND: AN INITIAL LOOK

Adam Smith mentions the metaphor in Book IV of The Wealth of Nations, arguing that people in any society will certainly employ their capital in foreign trading only if the profits available by that method far exceed those available locally, and that in such a case it is better for society as a whole if they so did.

a. Invisible hand
b. AD-IA Model
c. ACCRA Cost of Living Index
d. ACEA agreement

6. _____s (economically referred to as land or raw materials) occur naturally within environments that exist relatively undisturbed by mankind, in a natural form. A _____'s is often characterized by amounts of biodiversity existent in various ecosystems.

Mining, petroleum extraction, fishing, hunting, and forestry are generally considered natural-resource industries.

a. Natural resource
b. 1921 recession
c. 100-year flood
d. 130-30 fund

7. _____ in economics and business is the result of an exchange and from that trade we assign a numerical monetary value to a good, service or asset. If Alice trades Bob 4 apples for an orange, the _____ of an orange is 4 apples. Inversely, the _____ of an apple is 1/4 oranges.

a. Premium pricing
b. Price book
c. Price war
d. Price

8. _____ was a Scottish moral philosopher and a pioneer of political economy. One of the key figures of the Scottish Enlightenment, Smith is the author of The Theory of Moral Sentiments and An Inquiry into the Nature and Causes of the Wealth of Nations. The latter, usually abbreviated as The Wealth of Nations, is considered his magnum opus and the first modern work of economics.

a. Alan Greenspan
b. Adolph Fischer
c. Adolf Hitler
d. Adam Smith

9. In economics, a _____ is any economic system that effects its distribution of goods and services with prices and employing any form of money or debt tokens. Except for possible remote and primitive communities, all modern societies use _____s to allocate resources. However, _____s are not used for all resource allocation decisions today.

a. Hanseatic League
b. Price system
c. Neomercantilism
d. Family economy

10. In economics, the _____ can be defined as the graph depicting the relationship between the price of a certain commodity, and the amount of it that consumers are willing and able to purchase at that given price. It is a graphic representation of a demand schedule. The _____ for all consumers together follows from the _____ of every individual consumer: the individual demands at each price are added together.

a. Kuznets curve
b. Cost curve
c. Demand curve
d. Wage curve

11. In economics, a _____ is a table that lists the quantity of a good a person will buy it each different price See Demand curve.

Chapter 4. SUPPLY AND DEMAND: AN INITIAL LOOK

a. Demand schedule
b. Free contract
c. Federal Reserve districts
d. Rational irrationality

12. _____ is a broad label that refers to any individuals or households that use goods and services generated within the economy. The concept of a _____ is used in different contexts, so that the usage and significance of the term may vary.

Typically when business people and economists talk of _____s they are talking about person as _____, an aggregated commodity item with little individuality other than that expressed in the buy/not-buy decision.

a. 130-30 fund
b. 1921 recession
c. Consumer
d. 100-year flood

13. _____ or consumer demand or consumption is also known as personal consumption expenditure. It is the largest part of aggregate demand or effective demand at the macroeconomic level. There are two variants of consumption in the aggregate demand model, including induced consumption and autonomous consumption.

a. Potential output
b. Consumer spending
c. Dishoarding
d. Complex multiplier

14. _____ is a common concept in economics, and gives rise to derived concepts such as consumer debt. Generally _____ is defined by opposition to production. But the precise definition can vary because different schools of economists define production quite differently.

a. Foreclosure data providers
b. Cash or share options
c. Federal Reserve Bank Notes
d. Consumption

15. The _____ is the United States federal agency with jurisdiction over interstate electricity sales, wholesale electric rates, hydroelectric licensing, natural gas pricing, and oil pipeline rates. _____ also reviews and authorizes liquefied natural gas (LNG) terminals, interstate natural gas pipelines and non-federal hydropower projects.

A predecessor agency, the Federal Power Commission, was founded in 1920 to allow cabinet members to coordinate federal hydropower development.

a. Commodity trading advisors
b. Demographics of India
c. Constrained Pareto optimality
d. Federal Energy Regulatory Commission

16. A _____ is an object whose consumption increases the utility of the consumer, for which the quantity demanded exceeds the quantity supplied at zero price. _____s are usually modeled as having diminishing marginal utility. The first individual purchase has high utility; the second has less.

a. Composite good
b. Good
c. Merit good
d. Pie method

17. _____ is the term denoting either an entrance or changes which are inserted into a system and which activate/modify a process. It is an abstract concept, used in the modeling, system(s) design and system(s) exploitation. It is usually connected with other terms, e.g., _____ field, _____ variable, _____ parameter, _____ value, _____ signal, _____ device and _____ file.

Chapter 4. SUPPLY AND DEMAND: AN INITIAL LOOK
33

a. ACCRA Cost of Living Index
b. AD-IA Model
c. ACEA agreement
d. Input

18. The Demand side is a term used in economics to refer to a number of things:

   - The demand element of a supply and demand partial equilibrium diagram, in microeconomics
   - The aggregate demand in an economy, in macroeconomics
   - Economic policy actions which are designed to affect aggregate demand.
   - _____ learning referring to the incentive to learn how to use and modify free software as opposed to buying conventional software.

The term is also used broadly to distinguish supply-side economics from other schools, for instance Keynesian economics.

a. Delayed differentiation
b. Reverse auction
c. Demand-side
d. CPFR

19. In economics, _____ is the total supply of goods and services produced by a national economy during a specific time period. It is the total amount of goods and services in the economy available at all possible price levels.

a. Aggregation problem
b. Aggregate supply
c. Aggregate expenditure
d. Aggregate demand

20. To _____ is to impose a financial charge or other levy upon a taxpayer by a state or the functional equivalent of a state.

_____es are also imposed by many subnational entities. _____es consist of direct _____ or indirect _____, and may be paid in money or as its labour equivalent (often but not always unpaid.)

a. 130-30 fund
b. 1921 recession
c. 100-year flood
d. Tax

21. _____ is a socioeconomic structure and political ideology that promotes the establishment of an egalitarian, classless, stateless society based on common ownership and control of the means of production and property in general. In political science, the term '_____' is sometimes used to refer to communist states, a form of government in which the state operates under a one-party system and declares allegiance to Marxism-Leninism or a derivative thereof, even if the party does not actually claim that it has already reached _____.

Forerunners of communist ideas existed in antiquity and particularly in the 18th and early 19th century France, with thinkers such as Jean-Jacques Rousseau and the more radical Gracchus Babeuf.

a. Social fascism
b. Democratic centralism
c. New Communist Movement
d. Communism

22. A _____ is a government imposed limit on how high a price can be charged on a product. For a _____ to be effective, it must differ from the free market price. In the graph at right, the supply and demand curves intersect to determine the free-market quantity and price.

Chapter 4. SUPPLY AND DEMAND: AN INITIAL LOOK

a. Product sabotage
c. Fire sale
b. Price ceiling
d. Pricing

23. The underground economy or _____ is a market where all commerce is conducted without regard to taxation, law or regulations of trade. The term is also often known as the underdog, shadow economy, black economy, parallel economy or phantom trades.

In modern societies the underground economy covers a vast array of activities.

a. Protectionism
c. Social market economy
b. Market economy
d. Black market

24. In coordinate geometry, the _____ is the y-value of the point where the graph of a function or relation intercepts the y-axis of the coordinate system.

In other words, the _____ of a function is the y-value of the point at which it intersects the line x = 0 (the y-axis.) Thus, if the function is specified in form y = f(x), the _____ is easy to find by calculating f.

a. Y-intercept
c. 130-30 fund
b. Ratio
d. 100-year flood

25. Economic _____ is defined as an excess distribution to any factor in a production process above that which is required to induce the factor into the process or any excess above that which is necessary to keep the factor in its current use..

Classical Factor _____ is primarily concerned with the fee paid for the use of fixed (e.g. natural) resources. The classical definition is expressed as any excess payment above that required to induce or provide for production.

a. 1921 recession
c. 100-year flood
b. 130-30 fund
d. Rent

26. _____ refers to laws or ordinances that set price controls on the renting of residential housing. It functions as a price ceiling.

_____ exists in approximately 40 countries around the world.

a. National Housing Conference
c. Rent control
b. Tenant rights
d. 100-year flood

27. The _____ was a worldwide economic downturn starting in most places in 1929 and ending at different times in the 1930s or early 1940s for different countries. It was the largest and most important economic depression in the 20th century, and is used in the 21st century as an example of how far the world's economy can fall. The _____ originated in the United States; historians most often use as a starting date the stock market crash on October 29, 1929, known as Black Tuesday.

Chapter 4. SUPPLY AND DEMAND: AN INITIAL LOOK 35

   a. British Empire Economic Conference
   b. Wall Street Crash of 1929
   c. Jarrow March
   d. Great Depression

28. _____, 1st Baron Keynes was a renowned economist from Britain whose many ideas on economic and political theories as well as on many governments' monetary policies influenced America. He advocated a government that played an active role in the lives of people regarding business, economy, etc. In this role, the government would use fiscal measures to reduce the consequences of recessions, economic depressions and booms.
   a. Adam Smith
   b. Adolf Hitler
   c. Adolph Fischer
   d. John Maynard Keynes

29. A _____ is a government- or group-imposed limit on how low a price can be charged for a product. In order for a _____ to be effective, it must be greater than the equilibrium price. An ineffective _____, below equilibrium price.

A _____ can be set below the free-market equilibrium price.

   a. Price floor
   b. Price markdown
   c. Two-part tariff
   d. Flat rate

30. In economics, a _____ may be either a subsidy or a price control, both with the intended effect of keeping the market price of a good higher than the competitive equilibrium level.

In the case of a price control, a _____ is the minimum legal price a seller may charge, typically placed above equilibrium. It is the support of certain price levels at or above market values by the government.

   a. Price support
   b. Labor intensity
   c. Marginal profit
   d. Payment schedule

31. _____ is used to assign the available resources in an economic way. It is part of resource management.

In strategic planning, is a plan for using available resources, for example human resources, especially in the near term, to achieve goals for the future.

   a. Resource allocation
   b. 130-30 fund
   c. 1921 recession
   d. 100-year flood

Chapter 5. CONSUMER CHOICE: INDIVIDUAL AND MARKET DEMAND

1. _____ is a broad label that refers to any individuals or households that use goods and services generated within the economy. The concept of a _____ is used in different contexts, so that the usage and significance of the term may vary.

Typically when business people and economists talk of _____s they are talking about person as _____, an aggregated commodity item with little individuality other than that expressed in the buy/not-buy decision.

   a. 1921 recession
   b. 100-year flood
   c. 130-30 fund
   d. Consumer

2. In economics, the _____ can be defined as the graph depicting the relationship between the price of a certain commodity, and the amount of it that consumers are willing and able to purchase at that given price. It is a graphic representation of a demand schedule. The _____ for all consumers together follows from the _____ of every individual consumer: the individual demands at each price are added together.
   a. Wage curve
   b. Kuznets curve
   c. Demand curve
   d. Cost curve

3. _____ is an economic model based on price, utility and quantity in a market. It predicts that in a competitive market, price will function to equalize the quantity demanded by consumers, and the quantity supplied by producers, resulting in an economic equilibrium of price and quantity. The model incorporates other factors changing equilibrium as a shift of demand and/or supply.
   a. Joint demand
   b. Deferred gratification
   c. Supply and demand
   d. Rational addiction

4. In economics, _____ is a measure of the relative satisfaction from consumption of various goods and services. Given this measure, one may speak meaningfully of increasing or decreasing _____, and thereby explain economic behavior in terms of attempts to increase one's _____. For illustrative purposes, changes in _____ are sometimes expressed in units called utils.
   a. Ordinal utility
   b. Utility
   c. Utility function
   d. Expected utility hypothesis

5. Economics:

   - _____,the desire to own something and the ability to pay for it
   - _____ curve,a graphic representation of a _____ schedule
   - _____ deposit, the money in checking accounts
   - _____ pull theory,the theory that inflation occurs when _____ for goods and services exceeds existing supplies
   - _____ schedule,a table that lists the quantity of a good a person will buy it each different price
   - _____ side economics,the school of economics at believes government spending and tax cuts open economy by raising _____

   a. Demand
   b. Production
   c. Variability
   d. McKesson ' Robbins scandal

Chapter 5. CONSUMER CHOICE: INDIVIDUAL AND MARKET DEMAND

6. In economics, _____ is the ratio of the percent change in one variable to the percent change in another variable. It is a tool for measuring the responsiveness of a function to changes in parameters in a relative way. Commonly analyzed are _____ of substitution, price and wealth.
   a. ACCRA Cost of Living Index
   b. Elasticity of demand
   c. Elasticity
   d. ACEA agreement

7. In economics, the _____ of a good or of a service is the utility of the specific use to which an agent would put a given increase in that good or service, or of the specific use that would be abandoned in response to a given decrease. In other words, _____ is the utility of the marginal use -- which, on the assumption of economic rationality, would be the least urgent use of the good or service, from the best feasible combination of actions in which its use is included. Under the mainstream assumptions, the _____ of a good or service is the posited quantified change in utility obtained by increasing or by decreasing use of that good or service.
   a. 1921 recession
   b. 130-30 fund
   c. 100-year flood
   d. Marginal utility

38   *Chapter 5. CONSUMER CHOICE: INDIVIDUAL AND MARKET DEMAND*

8. A _____ is:

- Rewrite _____, in generative grammar and computer science
- Standardization, a formal and widely-accepted statement, fact, definition, or qualification
- Operation, a determinate _____ for performing a mathematical operation and obtaining a certain result (Mathematics, Logic)
    - Unary operation
    - Binary operation
- _____ of inference, a function from sets of formulae to formulae (Mathematics, Logic)
- _____ of thumb, principle with broad application that is not intended to be strictly accurate or reliable for every situation. Also often simply referred to as a _____
- Moral, an atomic element of a moral code for guiding choices in human behavior
- Heuristic, a quantized '_____' which shows a tendency or probability for successful function
- A regulation, as in sports
- A Production _____, as in computer science
- Procedural law, a _____ set governing the application of laws to cases
    - A law, which may informally be called a '_____'
    - A court ruling, a decision by a court
- In the U.S. Government, a regulation mandated by Congress, but written or expanded upon by the Executive Branch.
- Norm (sociology), an informal but widely accepted _____, concept, truth, definition, or qualification (social norms, legal norms, coding norms)
- Norm (philosophy), a kind of sentence or a reason to act, feel or believe
- 'Rulership' is the concept of governance by a government:
    - Military _____, governance by a military body
    - Monastic _____, a collection of precepts that guides the life of monks or nuns in a religious order where the superior holds the place of Christ
- Slide _____

- '_____,' a song by Ayumi Hamasaki
- '_____,' a song by rapper Nas
- '_____s,' an album by the band The Whitest Boy Alive
- _____s: Pyaar Ka Superhit Formula, a 2003 Bollywood film
- ruler, an instrument for measuring lengths
- _____, a component of an astrolabe, circumferator or similar instrument
- The _____s, a bestselling self-help book
- _____ Project (Run Up-to-date Linux Everywhere), a project that aims to use up-to-date Linux software on old PCs
- _____ engine, a software system that helps managing business _____s
- Ja _____, a hip hop artist
    - R.U.L.E., a 2005 greatest hits album by rapper Ja _____
- '_____s,' a KMFDM song

a. Procter ' Gamble   b. Demand
c. Rule   d. Technocracy

Chapter 5. CONSUMER CHOICE: INDIVIDUAL AND MARKET DEMAND

9. In economics, a _____ is a table that lists the quantity of a good a person will buy it each different price See Demand curve.
   a. Federal Reserve districts
   b. Rational irrationality
   c. Free contract
   d. Demand schedule

10. _____ and behavioral finance are closely related fields that have evolved to be a separate branch of economic and financial analysis which applies scientific research on human and social, cognitive and emotional factors to better understand economic decisions by consumers, borrowers, investors, and how they affect market prices, returns and the allocation of resources.

The field is primarily concerned with the bounds of rationality (selfishness, self-control) of economic agents. Behavioral models typically integrate insights from psychology with neo-classical economic theory.

   a. Mainstream economics
   b. Georgism
   c. Behavioral economics
   d. Neoclassical economics

11. _____ or economic opportunity loss is the value of the next best alternative foregone as the result of making a decision. _____ analysis is an important part of a company's decision-making processes but is not treated as an actual cost in any financial statement. The next best thing that a person can engage in is referred to as the _____ of doing the best thing and ignoring the next best thing to be done.
   a. Economic ideology
   b. Industrial organization
   c. Economic
   d. Opportunity cost

12. The _____ is the expected return forgone by bypassing of other potential investment activities for a given capital. It is a rate of return that investors could earn in financial markets.
   a. AD-IA Model
   b. ACCRA Cost of Living Index
   c. ACEA agreement
   d. Opportunity cost of capital

13. The _____ is an expected return that the provider of capital plans to earn on their investment.

Capital (money) used for funding a business should earn returns for the capital providers who risk their capital. For an investment to be worthwhile, the expected return on capital must be greater than the _____.

   a. Capital expenditure
   b. Modigliani-Miller theorem
   c. Capital intensive
   d. Cost of capital

14. _____s is the social science that studies the production, distribution, and consumption of goods and services. The term _____s comes from the Ancient Greek oá¼°κονομῖα from oá¼¶κος (oikos, 'house') + νÏŒμος (nomos, 'custom' or 'law'), hence 'rules of the house(hold)'. Current _____ models developed out of the broader field of political economy in the late 19th century, owing to a desire to use an empirical approach more akin to the physical sciences.
   a. Energy economics
   b. Economic
   c. Inflation
   d. Opportunity cost

15. A _____ is a situation that involves losing one quality or aspect of something in return for gaining another quality or aspect. It implies a decision to be made with full comprehension of both the upside and downside of a particular choice.

In economics the term is expressed as opportunity cost, referring the most preferred alternative given up.

a. Trade-off
b. Nonmarket
c. Whitemail
d. Friedman-Savage utility function

16. _____ was a survey conducted by the U.S. Department of Justice to gauge the prevalence of alcohol and illegal drug use among prior arrestees. It was a reformulation of the prior Drug Use Forecasting (DUF) program, focused on five drugs in particular: cocaine, marijuana, methamphetamine, opiates, and PCP.

Participants were randomly selected from arrest records in major metropolitan areas; because no personally identifying information is taken from each record chosen, the resulting data can be correlated to arrest rates, but not to the total population of persons charged.

a. ACCRA Cost of Living Index
b. ACEA agreement
c. Arrestee Drug Abuse Monitoring
d. AD-IA Model

17. _____ was a Scottish moral philosopher and a pioneer of political economy. One of the key figures of the Scottish Enlightenment, Smith is the author of The Theory of Moral Sentiments and An Inquiry into the Nature and Causes of the Wealth of Nations. The latter, usually abbreviated as The Wealth of Nations, is considered his magnum opus and the first modern work of economics.

a. Adam Smith
b. Adolf Hitler
c. Alan Greenspan
d. Adolph Fischer

18. In economics, the term _____ of income or _____ refers to a simple economic model which describes the reciprocal circulation of income between producers and consumers. In the _____ model, the inter-dependent entities of producer and consumer are referred to as 'firms' and 'households' respectively and provide each other with factors in order to facilitate the flow of income. Firms provide consumers with goods and services in exchange for consumer expenditure and 'factors of production' from households.

a. 100-year flood
b. Circular flow
c. 1921 recession
d. 130-30 fund

19. A _____ is an object whose consumption increases the utility of the consumer, for which the quantity demanded exceeds the quantity supplied at zero price. _____s are usually modeled as having diminishing marginal utility. The first individual purchase has high utility; the second has less.

a. Pie method
b. Good
c. Merit good
d. Composite good

20. In consumer theory, an _____ is a good that decreases in demand when consumer income rises, unlike normal goods, for which the opposite is observed. It is a good that consumers demand increases when their income increases. Inferiority, in this sense, is an observable fact relating to affordability rather than a statement about the quality of the good.

a. Inferior good
b. Independent goods
c. Export-oriented
d. Information good

Chapter 5. CONSUMER CHOICE: INDIVIDUAL AND MARKET DEMAND

21. In economics, _____s are any goods for which demand increases when income increases and falls when income decreases but price remains constant, i.e. with a positive income elasticity of demand. The term does not necessarily refer to the quality of the good.

Depending on the indifference curves, the amount of a good bought can either increase, decrease, or stay the same when income increases.

   a. Normative economics
   b. Bord halfpenny
   c. Financial contagion
   d. Normal good

22. In microeconomic theory, an _____ is a graph showing different bundles of goods, each measured as to quantity, between which a consumer is indifferent. That is, at each point on the curve, the consumer has no preference for one bundle over another. In other words, they are all equally preferred.
   a. Expenditure minimization problem
   b. Indifference curve
   c. Indifference map
   d. Engel curve

23. _____ in economics and business is the result of an exchange and from that trade we assign a numerical monetary value to a good, service or asset. If Alice trades Bob 4 apples for an orange, the _____ of an orange is 4 apples. Inversely, the _____ of an apple is 1/4 oranges.
   a. Premium pricing
   b. Price war
   c. Price book
   d. Price

24. _____, or a _____ is the concept of a resulting effect (cf. cause and effect, arising from another action. In general terms, it is used to indicate that all human actions, particularly crime and sin, have profound effects.
   a. Solved
   b. Variability
   c. Rule
   d. Consequence

Chapter 6. DEMAND AND ELASTICITY

1. Economics:

   - _____, the desire to own something and the ability to pay for it
   - _____ curve, a graphic representation of a _____ schedule
   - _____ deposit, the money in checking accounts
   - _____ pull theory, the theory that inflation occurs when _____ for goods and services exceeds existing supplies
   - _____ schedule, a table that lists the quantity of a good a person will buy it each different price
   - _____ side economics, the school of economics at believes government spending and tax cuts open economy by raising _____

   a. Demand
   b. Production
   c. McKesson ' Robbins scandal
   d. Variability

2. In economics, _____ is the ratio of the percent change in one variable to the percent change in another variable. It is a tool for measuring the responsiveness of a function to changes in parameters in a relative way. Commonly analyzed are _____ of substitution, price and wealth.
   a. ACCRA Cost of Living Index
   b. Elasticity
   c. Elasticity of demand
   d. ACEA agreement

3. In algebra, a _____ is a function depending on n that associates a scalar, det(A), to an n×n square matrix A. The fundamental geometric meaning of a _____ is a scale factor for measure when A is regarded as a linear transformation. _____s are important both in calculus, where they enter the substitution rule for several variables, and in multilinear algebra.

   For a fixed nonnegative integer n, there is a unique _____ function for the n×n matrices over any commutative ring R. In particular, this function exists when R is the field of real or complex numbers.

   a. 130-30 fund
   b. 1921 recession
   c. Determinant
   d. 100-year flood

4. Price _____ is defined as the measure of responsiveness in the quantity demanded for a commodity as a result of change in price of the same commodity. It is a measure of how consumers react to a change in price. In other words, it is percentage change in quantity demanded by the percentage change in price of the same commodity.
   a. ACCRA Cost of Living Index
   b. Elasticity
   c. ACEA agreement
   d. Elasticity of demand

5. _____ in economics and business is the result of an exchange and from that trade we assign a numerical monetary value to a good, service or asset. If Alice trades Bob 4 apples for an orange, the _____ of an orange is 4 apples. Inversely, the _____ of an apple is 1/4 oranges.
   a. Price
   b. Price war
   c. Premium pricing
   d. Price book

6. _____ is defined as the measure of responsiveness in the quantity demanded for a commodity as a result of change in price of the same commodity. It is a measure of how consumers react to a change in price. In other words, it is percentage change in quantity demanded as per the percentage change in price of the same commodity.

Chapter 6. DEMAND AND ELASTICITY

a. 130-30 fund
b. 1921 recession
c. 100-year flood
d. Price elasticity of demand

7. In economics, the _____ can be defined as the graph depicting the relationship between the price of a certain commodity, and the amount of it that consumers are willing and able to purchase at that given price. It is a graphic representation of a demand schedule. The _____ for all consumers together follows from the _____ of every individual consumer: the individual demands at each price are added together.
   a. Cost curve
   b. Wage curve
   c. Kuznets curve
   d. Demand curve

8. _____ is a broad label that refers to any individuals or households that use goods and services generated within the economy. The concept of a _____ is used in different contexts, so that the usage and significance of the term may vary.

Typically when business people and economists talk of _____s they are talking about person as _____, an aggregated commodity item with little individuality other than that expressed in the buy/not-buy decision.

   a. 100-year flood
   b. 130-30 fund
   c. 1921 recession
   d. Consumer

9. In economics, _____ describes demand that is not very sensitive to a change in price.
   a. Export-led growth
   b. Effective unemployment rate
   c. Inflation hedge
   d. Inelastic

10. A _____ or labor union is an organization of workers who have banded together to achieve common goals in key areas and working conditions. The _____, through its leadership, bargains with the employer on behalf of union members (rank and file members) and negotiates labor contracts (Collective bargaining) with employers. This may include the negotiation of wages, work rules, complaint procedures, rules governing hiring, firing and promotion of workers, benefits, workplace safety and policies.
   a. Guaranteed investment contracts
   b. Case-Shiller Home Price Indices
   c. Consumer goods
   d. Trade union

11. _____ is the total money received from the sale of any given quantity of output.

The _____ is calculated by taking the price of the sale times the quantity sold, i.e.

_____ = price X quantity.

   a. Small numbers game
   b. Ceteris paribus
   c. Total revenue
   d. Market development funds

12. A _____ is an object whose consumption increases the utility of the consumer, for which the quantity demanded exceeds the quantity supplied at zero price. _____s are usually modeled as having diminishing marginal utility. The first individual purchase has high utility; the second has less.

Chapter 6. DEMAND AND ELASTICITY

a. Good
b. Pie method
c. Merit good
d. Composite good

13. In economics, a _____ is a good for which demand increases more than proportionally as income rises, in contrast to a 'necessity good', for which demand increases less than proportionally as income rises.

_____s are said to have high income elasticity of demand: as people become wealthier, they will buy more and more of the _____. This also means, however, that should there be a decline in income its demand will drop.

a. Free good
b. Pie method
c. Luxury good
d. Search good

14. In economics, the _____ of demand measures the responsiveness of the demand of a good to the change in the income of the people demanding the good. It is calculated as the ratio of the percent change in demand to the percent change in income. For example, if, in response to a 10% increase in income, the demand of a good increased by 20%, the _____ of demand would be 20%/10% = 2.

a. AD-IA Model
b. ACCRA Cost of Living Index
c. ACEA agreement
d. Income elasticity

15. In economics, the _____ measures the responsiveness of the demand of a good to the change in the income of the people demanding the good. It is calculated as the ratio of the percent change in demand to the percent change in income. For example, if, in response to a 10% increase in income, the demand of a good increased by 20%, the _____ would be 20%/10% = 2.

a. Indifference map
b. Expenditure minimization problem
c. Elasticity of substitution
d. Income elasticity of demand

16. In economics, the _____ and cross price elasticity of demand measures the responsiveness of the demand of a good to a change in the price of another good.

It is measured as the percentage change in demand for the first good that occurs in response to a percentage change in price of the second good. For example, if, in response to a 10% increase in the price of fuel, the demand of new cars that are fuel inefficient decreased by 20%, the _____ would be −20%/10% = −2.

a. Snob effect
b. Convex preferences
c. Quality bias
d. Cross elasticity of demand

17. In economics, the _____ is defined as a numerical measure of the responsiveness of the quantity supplied of product (A) to a change in price of product (A) alone. It is the measure of the way quantity supplied reacts to a change in price.

For example, if, in response to a 10% rise in the price of a good, the quantity supplied increases by 20%, the _____ would be 20%/10% = 2.

| a. Price elasticity of supply | b. Hedonimetry |
| c. Demand shaping | d. Passive income |

18. _____ is an economic model based on price, utility and quantity in a market. It predicts that in a competitive market, price will function to equalize the quantity demanded by consumers, and the quantity supplied by producers, resulting in an economic equilibrium of price and quantity. The model incorporates other factors changing equilibrium as a shift of demand and/or supply.

| a. Rational addiction | b. Deferred gratification |
| c. Supply and demand | d. Joint demand |

19. In economics, a _____ is a table that lists the quantity of a good a person will buy it each different price See Demand curve.

| a. Free contract | b. Demand schedule |
| c. Federal Reserve districts | d. Rational irrationality |

20. _____s is the social science that studies the production, distribution, and consumption of goods and services. The term _____s comes from the Ancient Greek οá¼°κονομῖα from οá¼¶κος (oikos, 'house') + vÏŒμος (nomos, 'custom' or 'law'), hence 'rules of the house(hold)'. Current _____ models developed out of the broader field of political economy in the late 19th century, owing to a desire to use an empirical approach more akin to the physical sciences.

| a. Energy economics | b. Inflation |
| c. Opportunity cost | d. Economic |

21. _____ is that which is owed; usually referencing assets owed, but the term can also cover moral obligations and other interactions not requiring money. In the case of assets, _____ is a means of using future purchasing power in the present before a summation has been earned. Some companies and corporations use _____ as a part of their overall corporate finance strategy.

| a. Hard money loan | b. Debt |
| c. Debenture | d. Collateral Management |

22. Competition law, known in the United States as _____ law, has three main elements:

- prohibiting agreements or practices that restrict free trading and competition between business entities. This includes in particular the repression of cartels.
- banning abusive behaviour by a firm dominating a market, or anti-competitive practices that tend to lead to such a dominant position. Practices controlled in this way may include predatory pricing, tying, price gouging, refusal to deal, and many others.
- supervising the mergers and acquisitions of large corporations, including some joint ventures. Transactions that are considered to threaten the competitive process can be prohibited altogether, or approved subject to 'remedies' such as an obligation to divest part of the merged business or to offer licences or access to facilities to enable other businesses to continue competing.

Chapter 6. DEMAND AND ELASTICITY

The substance and practice of competition law varies from jurisdiction to jurisdiction. Protecting the interests of consumers (consumer welfare) and ensuring that entrepreneurs have an opportunity to compete in the market economy are often treated as important objectives. Competition law is closely connected with law on deregulation of access to markets, state aids and subsidies, the privatisation of state owned assets and the establishment of independent sector regulators. In recent decades, competition law has been viewed as a way to provide better public services.

- a. United Kingdom competition law
- b. Intellectual property law
- c. Anti-Inflation Act
- d. Antitrust

23. _____, known in the United States as antitrust law, has three main elements:

- prohibiting agreements or practices that restrict free trading and competition between business entities. This includes in particular the repression of cartels.
- banning abusive behaviour by a firm dominating a market, or anti-competitive practices that tend to lead to such a dominant position. Practices controlled in this way may include predatory pricing, tying, price gouging, refusal to deal, and many others.
- supervising the mergers and acquisitions of large corporations, including some joint ventures. Transactions that are considered to threaten the competitive process can be prohibited altogether, or approved subject to 'remedies' such as an obligation to divest part of the merged business or to offer licences or access to facilities to enable other businesses to continue competing.

The substance and practice of _____ varies from jurisdiction to jurisdiction. Protecting the interests of consumers (consumer welfare) and ensuring that entrepreneurs have an opportunity to compete in the market economy are often treated as important objectives. _____ is closely connected with law on deregulation of access to markets, state aids and subsidies, the privatisation of state owned assets and the establishment of independent sector regulators. In recent decades, _____ has been viewed as a way to provide better public services.

- a. Hostile work environment
- b. Due diligence
- c. Fee simple
- d. Competition law

24. _____, in strategic management and marketing is, according to Carlton O'Neal, the percentage or proportion of the total available market or market segment that is being serviced by a company. It can be expressed as a company's sales revenue (from that market) divided by the total sales revenue available in that market. It can also be expressed as a company's unit sales volume (in a market) divided by the total volume of units sold in that market.

- a. Product differentiation
- b. Customer to customer
- c. Pricing science
- d. Market share

25. In economics, a _____ exists when a specific individual or enterprise has sufficient control over a particular product or service to determine significantly the terms on which other individuals shall have access to it. Monopolies are thus characterized by a lack of economic competition for the good or service that they provide and a lack of viable substitute goods. The verb 'monopolize' refers to the process by which a firm gains persistently greater market share than what is expected under perfect competition.

a. 1921 recession
c. 130-30 fund
b. 100-year flood
d. Monopoly

26. An _____ is a decision such that no other available decision options will lead to a better outcome. It is an important concept in decision theory. In order to compare the different decision outcomes, one commonly assigns a relative utility to each of them.
   a. Influence diagram
   b. Intertemporal choice
   c. Expected value of sample information
   d. Optimal decision

27. A _____ is a set of exclusive rights granted by a state to an inventor or his assignee for a limited period of time in exchange for a disclosure of an invention.

The procedure for granting _____s, the requirements placed on the _____ee and the extent of the exclusive rights vary widely between countries according to national laws and international agreements. Typically, however, a _____ application must include one or more claims defining the invention which must be new, inventive, and useful or industrially applicable.

   a. Bank regulation
   b. Patent
   c. Bona fide occupational qualification
   d. Long service leave

28. To _____ is to impose a financial charge or other levy upon a taxpayer by a state or the functional equivalent of a state.

_____es are also imposed by many subnational entities. _____es consist of direct _____ or indirect _____, and may be paid in money or as its labour equivalent (often but not always unpaid.)

   a. 100-year flood
   b. 130-30 fund
   c. Tax
   d. 1921 recession

Chapter 7. PRODUCTION, INPUTS, AND COST: BUILDING BLOCKS FOR SUPPLY ANALYSIS

1. _____, originally the American Telephone ' Telegraph Company, is an American telecommunications company that provided voice, video, data, and Internet telecommunications and professional services to businesses, consumers, and government agencies. During its long history, AT'T was at times the world's largest telephone company, the world's largest cable television operator, and a regulated monopoly. Today, the company is a subsidiary of AT'T Inc.
   - a. AT'T Corporation
   - b. AD-IA Model
   - c. ACEA agreement
   - d. ACCRA Cost of Living Index

2. In finance, a _____ is a debt security, in which the authorized issuer owes the holders a debt and, depending on the terms of the _____, is obliged to pay interest (the coupon) and/or to repay the principal at a later date, termed maturity. A _____ is a formal contract to repay borrowed money with interest at fixed intervals.

   Thus a _____ is like a loan: the issuer is the borrower (debtor), the holder is the lender (creditor), and the coupon is the interest.
   - a. Zero-coupon
   - b. Bond
   - c. Prize Bond
   - d. Callable

3. _____, in microeconomics, are the cost advantages that a business obtains due to expansion. They are factors that cause a producere;s average cost per unit to fall as scale is increased. _____ is a long run concept and refers to reductions in unit cost as the size of a facility, or scale, increases.
   - a. Economies of scale
   - b. Underinvestment employment relationship
   - c. Isoquant
   - d. Economic production quantity

4. _____ is the term denoting either an entrance or changes which are inserted into a system and which activate/modify a process. It is an abstract concept, used in the modeling, system(s) design and system(s) exploitation. It is usually connected with other terms, e.g., _____ field, _____ variable, _____ parameter, _____ value, _____ signal, _____ device and _____ file.
   - a. ACCRA Cost of Living Index
   - b. ACEA agreement
   - c. Input
   - d. AD-IA Model

5. In economics, a _____ is a general slowdown in economic activity over a sustained period of time, or a business cycle contraction. During _____s, many macroeconomic indicators vary in a similar way. Production as measured by Gross Domestic Product (GDP), employment, investment spending, capacity utilization, household incomes and business profits all fall during _____s.
   - a. Monetary economics
   - b. Leading indicators
   - c. Treasury View
   - d. Recession

Chapter 7. PRODUCTION, INPUTS, AND COST: BUILDING BLOCKS FOR SUPPLY ANALYSIS   49

6. Economics:

   - _____ , the desire to own something and the ability to pay for it
   - _____ curve, a graphic representation of a _____ schedule
   - _____ deposit, the money in checking accounts
   - _____ pull theory, the theory that inflation occurs when _____ for goods and services exceeds existing supplies
   - _____ schedule, a table that lists the quantity of a good a person will buy it each different price
   - _____ side economics, the school of economics at believes government spending and tax cuts open economy by raising _____

   a. McKesson ' Robbins scandal
   c. Variability
   b. Production
   d. Demand

7. In economics, the _____ can be defined as the graph depicting the relationship between the price of a certain commodity, and the amount of it that consumers are willing and able to purchase at that given price. It is a graphic representation of a demand schedule. The _____ for all consumers together follows from the _____ of every individual consumer: the individual demands at each price are added together.
   a. Kuznets curve
   b. Demand curve
   c. Wage curve
   d. Cost curve

8. In economic models, the _____ time frame assumes no fixed factors of production. Firms can enter or leave the marketplace, and the cost (and availability) of land, labor, raw materials, and capital goods can be assumed to vary. In contrast, in the short-run time frame, certain factors are assumed to be fixed, because there is not sufficient time for them to change.
   a. Diseconomies of scale
   b. Productivity world
   c. Price/performance ratio
   d. Long-run

9. In neoclassical economics and microeconomics, _____ describes the perfect being a market in which there are many small firms, all producing homogeneous goods. In the short term, such markets are productively inefficient as output will not occur where mc is equal to ac, but allocatively efficient, as output under _____ will always occur where mc is equal to mr, and therefore where mc equals ar. However, in the long term, such markets are both allocatively and productively efficient.
   a. Co-operative economics
   b. General equilibrium
   c. Law of supply
   d. Perfect competition

10. In economics, the concept of the _____ refers to the decision-making time frame of a firm in which at least one factor of production is fixed. Costs which are fixed in the _____ have no impact on a firms decisions. For example a firm can raise output by increasing the amount of labour through overtime.
    a. Hicks-neutral technical change
    b. Product Pipeline
    c. Productivity model
    d. Short-run

11. The term _____, 'the state or characteristic of being variable', _____ describes how spread out or closely clustered a set of data is. may be applied to many different subjects:

- Climate _____
- Genetic _____
- Heart rate _____
- Human _____
- Solar van
- Spatial _____
- Statistical _____
- _____

a. Demand
b. Characteristic
c. Total product
d. Variability

12. In economics, _____ is equal to total cost divided by the number of goods produced (the output quantity, Q.) It is also equal to the sum of average variable costs (total variable costs divided by Q) plus average fixed costs (total fixed costs divided by Q.) _____s may be dependent on the time period considered (increasing production may be expensive or impossible in the short term, for example.)

a. Average cost
b. Explicit cost
c. Average fixed cost
d. Average variable cost

13. In economics, _____ are business expenses that are not dependent on the activities of the business They tend to be time-related, such as salaries or rents being paid per month. This is in contrast to variable costs, which are volume-related (and are paid per quantity.)

In management accounting, _____ are defined as expenses that do not change in proportion to the activity of a business, within the relevant period or scale of production.

a. Cost of poor quality
b. Quality costs
c. Cost-Volume-Profit Analysis
d. Fixed costs

14. In economics and finance, _____ is the change in total cost that arises when the quantity produced changes by one unit. It is the cost of producing one more unit of a good. Mathematically, the _____ function is expressed as the first derivative of the total cost (TC) function with respect to quantity (Q.)

a. Marginal cost
b. Khozraschyot
c. Variable cost
d. Quality costs

15. _____s are expenses that change in proportion to the activity of a business. In other words, _____ is the sum of marginal costs. It can also be considered normal costs.

a. Cost allocation
b. Variable cost
c. Quality costs
d. Cost-Volume-Profit Analysis

Chapter 7. PRODUCTION, INPUTS, AND COST: BUILDING BLOCKS FOR SUPPLY ANALYSIS

16. An _____ is a person who has possession of an enterprise and assumes significant accountability for the inherent risks and the outcome. It is an ambitious leader who combines land, labor, and capital to create and market new goods or services. The term is a loanword from French and was first defined by the Irish economist Richard Cantillon.
    a. Expansionary policies
    b. ACCRA Cost of Living Index
    c. Entrepreneur
    d. ACEA agreement

17. In economics, the marginal product or _____ is the extra output produced by one more unit of an input (for instance, the difference in output when a firm's labour is increased from five to six units.) Assuming that no other inputs to production change, the marginal product of a given input (X) can be expressed as:

    MP = ΔY/ΔX = (the change of Y)/(the change of X.)

    In neoclassical economics, this is the mathematical derivative of the production function....

    a. Multifactor productivity
    b. Diseconomies of scale
    c. Productive capacity
    d. Marginal physical product

18. In microeconomics, _____ is quite simply the conversion of inputs into outputs. It is an economic process that uses resources to create a good or service that is suitable for exchange. This can include manufacturing, storing, shipping, and packaging.
    a. Red Guards
    b. MET
    c. Solved
    d. Production

19. The _____ of a variable factor of Production identifies what outputs are possible using various levels of the variable input. This can be displayed in either a chart that lists the output level corresponding to various levels of input, or a graph that summarizes the data into a '_____ curve'. The diagram shows a typical _____ curve. In this example, output increases as more inputs are employed up until point A. The maximum output possible with this Production process is Qm. (If there are other inputs used in the process, they are assumed to be fixed).
    a. Tightness
    b. Consequence
    c. Convexity
    d. Total product

20. In economics, _____ refers to how the marginal contribution of a factor of production usually decreases as more of the factor is used. According to this relationship, in a production system with fixed and variable inputs, beyond some point, each additional unit of the variable input yields smaller and smaller increases in output. Conversely, producing one more unit of output costs more and more in variable inputs.
    a. Community property
    b. Diminishing returns
    c. Patent troll
    d. Derivatives law

21. In microeconomics, _____ is the extra revenue that an additional unit of product will bring. It is the additional income from selling one more unit of a good; sometimes equal to price. It can also be described as the change in total revenue/change in number of units sold.
    a. Marginal revenue
    b. Reservation price
    c. Long term
    d. Market demand schedule

Chapter 7. PRODUCTION, INPUTS, AND COST: BUILDING BLOCKS FOR SUPPLY ANALYSIS

22. The marginal revenue productivity theory of wages, also referred to as the _____ of labor, is the change in total revenue earned by a firm that results from employing one more unit of labor. It is a neoclassical model that determines, under some conditions, the optimal number of workers to employ at an exogenously determined market wage rate.

The _____ of a worker is equal to the product of the marginal product of labor (MP) and the marginal revenue (MR), given by MR×MP = _____.

   a. Real prices and ideal prices
   b. Marginal revenue product
   c. Marginal revenue productivity theory of wages
   d. Coal depletion

Chapter 7. PRODUCTION, INPUTS, AND COST: BUILDING BLOCKS FOR SUPPLY ANALYSIS   53

23. A _____ is:

- Rewrite _____, in generative grammar and computer science
- Standardization, a formal and widely-accepted statement, fact, definition, or qualification
- Operation, a determinate _____ for performing a mathematical operation and obtaining a certain result (Mathematics, Logic)
    - Unary operation
    - Binary operation
- _____ of inference, a function from sets of formulae to formulae (Mathematics, Logic)
- _____ of thumb, principle with broad application that is not intended to be strictly accurate or reliable for every situation. Also often simply referred to as a _____
- Moral, an atomic element of a moral code for guiding choices in human behavior
- Heuristic, a quantized '_____' which shows a tendency or probability for successful function
- A regulation, as in sports
- A Production _____, as in computer science
- Procedural law, a _____ set governing the application of laws to cases
    - A law, which may informally be called a '_____'
    - A court ruling, a decision by a court
- In the U.S. Government, a regulation mandated by Congress, but written or expanded upon by the Executive Branch.
- Norm (sociology), an informal but widely accepted _____, concept, truth, definition, or qualification (social norms, legal norms, coding norms)
- Norm (philosophy), a kind of sentence or a reason to act, feel or believe
- 'Rulership' is the concept of governance by a government:
    - Military _____, governance by a military body
    - Monastic _____, a collection of precepts that guides the life of monks or nuns in a religious order where the superior holds the place of Christ
- Slide _____

- '_____,' a song by Ayumi Hamasaki
- '_____,' a song by rapper Nas
- '_____s,' an album by the band The Whitest Boy Alive
- _____s: Pyaar Ka Superhit Formula, a 2003 Bollywood film
- ruler, an instrument for measuring lengths
- _____, a component of an astrolabe, circumferator or similar instrument
- The _____s, a bestselling self-help book
- _____ Project (Run Up-to-date Linux Everywhere), a project that aims to use up-to-date Linux software on old PCs
- _____ engine, a software system that helps managing business _____s
- Ja _____, a hip hop artist
    - R.U.L.E., a 2005 greatest hits album by rapper Ja _____
- '_____s,' a KMFDM song

a. Technocracy   b. Demand
c. Rule   d. Procter ' Gamble

Chapter 7. PRODUCTION, INPUTS, AND COST: BUILDING BLOCKS FOR SUPPLY ANALYSIS

24. _____ in economics and business is the result of an exchange and from that trade we assign a numerical monetary value to a good, service or asset. If Alice trades Bob 4 apples for an orange, the _____ of an orange is 4 apples. Inversely, the _____ of an apple is 1/4 oranges.
   a. Price
   b. Premium pricing
   c. Price book
   d. Price war

25. In economics, a _____ is a graph of the costs of production as a function of total quantity produced. In a free market economy, productively efficient firms use these curves to find the optimal point of production, where they make the most profits. There are a few different types of _____s, each relevant to a different area of economics.
   a. Cost curve
   b. Demand curve
   c. Phillips curve
   d. Kuznets curve

26. _____ or economic opportunity loss is the value of the next best alternative foregone as the result of making a decision. _____ analysis is an important part of a company's decision-making processes but is not treated as an actual cost in any financial statement. The next best thing that a person can engage in is referred to as the _____ of doing the best thing and ignoring the next best thing to be done.
   a. Opportunity cost
   b. Economic
   c. Industrial organization
   d. Economic ideology

27. The _____ is the expected return forgone by bypassing of other potential investment activities for a given capital. It is a rate of return that investors could earn in financial markets.
   a. AD-IA Model
   b. ACCRA Cost of Living Index
   c. ACEA agreement
   d. Opportunity cost of capital

28. In economics, and cost accounting, _____ describes the total economic cost of production and is made up of variable costs, which vary according to the quantity of a good produced and include inputs such as labor and raw materials, plus fixed costs, which are independent of the quantity of a good produced and include inputs (capital) that cannot be varied in the short term, such as buildings and machinery. _____ in economics includes the total opportunity cost of each factor of production in addition to fixed and variable costs.

The rate at which _____ changes as the amount produced changes is called marginal cost.

   a. 1921 recession
   b. 100-year flood
   c. 130-30 fund
   d. Total cost

29. The _____ is an expected return that the provider of capital plans to earn on their investment.

Capital (money) used for funding a business should earn returns for the capital providers who risk their capital. For an investment to be worthwhile, the expected return on capital must be greater than the _____.

   a. Modigliani-Miller theorem
   b. Capital expenditure
   c. Capital intensive
   d. Cost of capital

Chapter 7. PRODUCTION, INPUTS, AND COST: BUILDING BLOCKS FOR SUPPLY ANALYSIS

30. In economics, _____ are the resources employed to produce goods and services. They facilitate production but do not become part of the product (as with raw materials) or significantly transformed by the production process (as with fuel used to power machinery.) To 19th century economists, the _____ were land (natural resources, gifts from nature), labor (the ability to work), and capital goods (human-made tools and equipment.)
   a. Long-run
   b. Product Pipeline
   c. Factors of production
   d. Hicks-neutral technical change

31. _____ in economics refers to metrics and measures of output from production processes, per unit of input. Labor _____, for example, is typically measured as a ratio of output per labor-hour, an input. _____ may be conceived of as a metrics of the technical or engineering efficiency of production.
   a. Production-possibility frontier
   b. Piece work
   c. Fordism
   d. Productivity

32. In economics, _____ is the total supply of goods and services produced by a national economy during a specific time period. It is the total amount of goods and services in the economy available at all possible price levels.
   a. Aggregate demand
   b. Aggregation problem
   c. Aggregate supply
   d. Aggregate expenditure

33. In calculus, a function f defined on a subset of the real numbers with real values is called _____, if for all x and y such that x >≤ y one has f(x) >≤ f(y), so f preserves the order. In layman's terms, the sign of the slope is always positive (the curve tending upwards) or zero (i.e., non-decreasing, or asymptotic, or depicted as a horizontal, flat line) Likewise, a function is called monotonically decreasing (non-increasing) if, whenever x >≤ y, then f(x) >≥ f(y), so it reverses the order.
   a. 100-year flood
   b. 130-30 fund
   c. Monotonic
   d. 1921 recession

34. In economics, _____ and economies of scale are related terms that describe what happens as the scale of production increases. They are different terms and should not be used interchangeably.

   _____ refers to a technical property of production that examines changes in output subsequent to a proportional change in all inputs (where all inputs increase by a constant factor.)

   a. Customer equity
   b. Necessity good
   c. Returns to scale
   d. Constant returns to scale

35. In accounting, _____ is the original monetary value of an economic item. In some circumstances, assets and liabilities may be shown at their _____, as if there had been no change in value since the date of acquisition. The balance sheet value of the item may therefore differ from the 'true' value.
   a. Deferred financing costs
   b. Salvage value
   c. Net income per employee
   d. Historical Cost

36. In microeconomic theory, an _____ is a graph showing different bundles of goods, each measured as to quantity, between which a consumer is indifferent. That is, at each point on the curve, the consumer has no preference for one bundle over another. In other words, they are all equally preferred.
   a. Engel curve
   b. Expenditure minimization problem
   c. Indifference curve
   d. Indifference map

Chapter 7. PRODUCTION, INPUTS, AND COST: BUILDING BLOCKS FOR SUPPLY ANALYSIS

37. In microeconomic theory a preference map or _____ is the collection of indifference curves possessed by an individual. Similar in nature to a topographical map, the contour lines of such a map demonstrating progressively more desirable options as they move upward or to the right. Because of the nature of indifference curves they cannot intersect and are effectively infinite in number, their sum defining all possible combinations of values.

   a. Engel curve
   b. Elasticity of substitution
   c. Expenditure minimization problem
   d. Indifference map

38. _____ is a broad label that refers to any individuals or households that use goods and services generated within the economy. The concept of a _____ is used in different contexts, so that the usage and significance of the term may vary.

Typically when business people and economists talk of _____s they are talking about person as _____, an aggregated commodity item with little individuality other than that expressed in the buy/not-buy decision.

   a. 100-year flood
   b. 130-30 fund
   c. 1921 recession
   d. Consumer

Chapter 8. OUTPUT, PRICE, AND PROFIT: THE IMPORTANCE OF MARGINAL ANALYSIS

1. An _____ is a decision such that no other available decision options will lead to a better outcome. It is an important concept in decision theory. In order to compare the different decision outcomes, one commonly assigns a relative utility to each of them.
   - a. Optimal decision
   - b. Influence diagram
   - c. Expected value of sample information
   - d. Intertemporal choice

2. _____ was a survey conducted by the U.S. Department of Justice to gauge the prevalence of alcohol and illegal drug use among prior arrestees. It was a reformulation of the prior Drug Use Forecasting (DUF) program, focused on five drugs in particular: cocaine, marijuana, methamphetamine, opiates, and PCP.

   Participants were randomly selected from arrest records in major metropolitan areas; because no personally identifying information is taken from each record chosen, the resulting data can be correlated to arrest rates, but not to the total population of persons charged.

   - a. ACEA agreement
   - b. ACCRA Cost of Living Index
   - c. AD-IA Model
   - d. Arrestee Drug Abuse Monitoring

3. _____ was a Scottish moral philosopher and a pioneer of political economy. One of the key figures of the Scottish Enlightenment, Smith is the author of The Theory of Moral Sentiments and An Inquiry into the Nature and Causes of the Wealth of Nations. The latter, usually abbreviated as The Wealth of Nations, is considered his magnum opus and the first modern work of economics.
   - a. Adolf Hitler
   - b. Alan Greenspan
   - c. Adolph Fischer
   - d. Adam Smith

4. Competition law, known in the United States as _____ law, has three main elements:

   - prohibiting agreements or practices that restrict free trading and competition between business entities. This includes in particular the repression of cartels.
   - banning abusive behaviour by a firm dominating a market, or anti-competitive practices that tend to lead to such a dominant position. Practices controlled in this way may include predatory pricing, tying, price gouging, refusal to deal, and many others.
   - supervising the mergers and acquisitions of large corporations, including some joint ventures. Transactions that are considered to threaten the competitive process can be prohibited altogether, or approved subject to 'remedies' such as an obligation to divest part of the merged business or to offer licences or access to facilities to enable other businesses to continue competing.

   The substance and practice of competition law varies from jurisdiction to jurisdiction. Protecting the interests of consumers (consumer welfare) and ensuring that entrepreneurs have an opportunity to compete in the market economy are often treated as important objectives. Competition law is closely connected with law on deregulation of access to markets, state aids and subsidies, the privatisation of state owned assets and the establishment of independent sector regulators. In recent decades, competition law has been viewed as a way to provide better public services.

   - a. United Kingdom competition law
   - b. Intellectual property law
   - c. Anti-Inflation Act
   - d. Antitrust

Chapter 8. OUTPUT, PRICE, AND PROFIT: THE IMPORTANCE OF MARGINAL ANALYSIS

5. _____, known in the United States as antitrust law, has three main elements:

   - prohibiting agreements or practices that restrict free trading and competition between business entities. This includes in particular the repression of cartels.
   - banning abusive behaviour by a firm dominating a market, or anti-competitive practices that tend to lead to such a dominant position. Practices controlled in this way may include predatory pricing, tying, price gouging, refusal to deal, and many others.
   - supervising the mergers and acquisitions of large corporations, including some joint ventures. Transactions that are considered to threaten the competitive process can be prohibited altogether, or approved subject to 'remedies' such as an obligation to divest part of the merged business or to offer licences or access to facilities to enable other businesses to continue competing.

   The substance and practice of _____ varies from jurisdiction to jurisdiction. Protecting the interests of consumers (consumer welfare) and ensuring that entrepreneurs have an opportunity to compete in the market economy are often treated as important objectives. _____ is closely connected with law on deregulation of access to markets, state aids and subsidies, the privatisation of state owned assets and the establishment of independent sector regulators. In recent decades, _____ has been viewed as a way to provide better public services.

   a. Competition law
   c. Due diligence
   b. Hostile work environment
   d. Fee simple

6. Economics:

   - _____,the desire to own something and the ability to pay for it
   - _____ curve,a graphic representation of a _____ schedule
   - _____ deposit, the money in checking accounts
   - _____ pull theory,the theory that inflation occurs when _____ for goods and services exceeds existing supplies
   - _____ schedule,a table that lists the quantity of a good a person will buy it each different price
   - _____ side economics,the school of economics at believes government spending and tax cuts open economy by raising _____

   a. McKesson ' Robbins scandal
   c. Demand
   b. Production
   d. Variability

7. In economics, the _____ can be defined as the graph depicting the relationship between the price of a certain commodity, and the amount of it that consumers are willing and able to purchase at that given price. It is a graphic representation of a demand schedule. The _____ for all consumers together follows from the _____ of every individual consumer: the individual demands at each price are added together.

   a. Wage curve
   c. Cost curve
   b. Demand curve
   d. Kuznets curve

Chapter 8. OUTPUT, PRICE, AND PROFIT: THE IMPORTANCE OF MARGINAL ANALYSIS

8. In economics, a _____ exists when a specific individual or enterprise has sufficient control over a particular product or service to determine significantly the terms on which other individuals shall have access to it. Monopolies are thus characterized by a lack of economic competition for the good or service that they provide and a lack of viable substitute goods. The verb 'monopolize' refers to the process by which a firm gains persistently greater market share than what is expected under perfect competition.

a. Monopoly
b. 1921 recession
c. 100-year flood
d. 130-30 fund

9. _____ in economics and business is the result of an exchange and from that trade we assign a numerical monetary value to a good, service or asset. If Alice trades Bob 4 apples for an orange, the _____ of an orange is 4 apples. Inversely, the _____ of an apple is 1/4 oranges.

a. Price war
b. Price book
c. Premium pricing
d. Price

10. _____ is a broad label that refers to any individuals or households that use goods and services generated within the economy. The concept of a _____ is used in different contexts, so that the usage and significance of the term may vary.

Typically when business people and economists talk of _____ s they are talking about person as _____, an aggregated commodity item with little individuality other than that expressed in the buy/not-buy decision.

a. 100-year flood
b. 130-30 fund
c. 1921 recession
d. Consumer

11. _____ s is the social science that studies the production, distribution, and consumption of goods and services. The term _____ s comes from the Ancient Greek οἰκονομία from οἶκος (oikos, 'house') + νόμος (nomos, 'custom' or 'law'), hence 'rules of the house(hold)'. Current _____ models developed out of the broader field of political economy in the late 19th century, owing to a desire to use an empirical approach more akin to the physical sciences.

a. Opportunity cost
b. Economic
c. Energy economics
d. Inflation

12. In economics, _____ is the difference between a company's total revenue and its opportunity costs. It is the increase in wealth that an investor has from making an investment, taking into consideration all costs associated with that investment including the opportunity cost of capital.

Profit is the factor income of the entrepreneur.

a. Operating profit
b. Accounting profit
c. ACCRA Cost of Living Index
d. Economic profit

13. In finance, the _____ s between two currencies specifies how much one currency is worth in terms of the other. It is the value of a foreign natione;s currency in terms of the home natione;s currency. For example an _____ of 102 Japanese yen to the United States dollar means that JPY 102 is worth the same as USD 1.

Chapter 8. OUTPUT, PRICE, AND PROFIT: THE IMPORTANCE OF MARGINAL ANALYSIS

a. ACCRA Cost of Living Index
b. Interbank market
c. ACEA agreement
d. Exchange rate

14. In microeconomics, _____ is the extra revenue that an additional unit of product will bring. It is the additional income from selling one more unit of a good; sometimes equal to price. It can also be described as the change in total revenue/change in number of units sold.
   a. Long term
   b. Reservation price
   c. Market demand schedule
   d. Marginal revenue

15. _____ is the total money received from the sale of any given quantity of output.

The _____ is calculated by taking the price of the sale times the quantity sold, i.e.

_____ = price X quantity.

   a. Small numbers game
   b. Ceteris paribus
   c. Market development funds
   d. Total revenue

16. In economics, _____ is equal to total cost divided by the number of goods produced (the output quantity, Q.) It is also equal to the sum of average variable costs (total variable costs divided by Q) plus average fixed costs (total fixed costs divided by Q.) _____s may be dependent on the time period considered (increasing production may be expensive or impossible in the short term, for example.)
   a. Explicit cost
   b. Average fixed cost
   c. Average variable cost
   d. Average cost

17. In economics and finance, _____ is the change in total cost that arises when the quantity produced changes by one unit. It is the cost of producing one more unit of a good. Mathematically, the _____ function is expressed as the first derivative of the total cost (TC) function with respect to quantity (Q.)
   a. Quality costs
   b. Khozraschyot
   c. Marginal cost
   d. Variable cost

18. In economics, and cost accounting, _____ describes the total economic cost of production and is made up of variable costs, which vary according to the quantity of a good produced and include inputs such as labor and raw materials, plus fixed costs, which are independent of the quantity of a good produced and include inputs (capital) that cannot be varied in the short term, such as buildings and machinery. _____ in economics includes the total opportunity cost of each factor of production in addition to fixed and variable costs.

The rate at which _____ changes as the amount produced changes is called marginal cost.

   a. 130-30 fund
   b. 1921 recession
   c. 100-year flood
   d. Total cost

19. _____ is one of the ways government regulate a monopoly market. Monopolists tend to produce less than the optimal quantity pushing the prices up. Government may use _____ as a tool to regulate prices monopolists may charge.

Chapter 8. OUTPUT, PRICE, AND PROFIT: THE IMPORTANCE OF MARGINAL ANALYSIS 61

    a. ACEA agreement
    b. AD-IA Model
    c. ACCRA Cost of Living Index
    d. Average cost pricing

20. _____ is one of the four Ps of the marketing mix. The other three aspects are product, promotion, and place. It is also a key variable in microeconomic price allocation theory.
    a. Guaranteed Maximum Price
    b. Point of total assumption
    c. Premium pricing
    d. Pricing

21. In microeconomics, _____ is the term used to refer to total when marginal cost is subtracted from marginal revenue. Under the marginal approach to profit maximization, to maximize profits, a firm should continue to produce a good until _____ is zero. Profit Maximization - The Marginal Approach.
    a. Holding period return
    b. Corporate synergy
    c. Marginal profit
    d. Lehman scale

22. _____ is a socioeconomic structure and political ideology that promotes the establishment of an egalitarian, classless, stateless society based on common ownership and control of the means of production and property in general. In political science, the term '_____' is sometimes used to refer to communist states, a form of government in which the state operates under a one-party system and declares allegiance to Marxism-Leninism or a derivative thereof, even if the party does not actually claim that it has already reached _____.

Forerunners of communist ideas existed in antiquity and particularly in the 18th and early 19th century France, with thinkers such as Jean-Jacques Rousseau and the more radical Gracchus Babeuf.

    a. New Communist Movement
    b. Social fascism
    c. Democratic centralism
    d. Communism

23. The _____ or gross domestic income (GDI), a basic measure of an economy's economic performance, is the market value of all final goods and services produced within the borders of a nation in a year. _____ can be defined in three ways, all of which are conceptually identical. First, it is equal to the total expenditures for all final goods and services produced within the country in a stipulated period of time (usually a 365-day year.)
    a. Market structure
    b. Monopolistic competition
    c. Countercyclical
    d. Gross domestic product

24. A _____ is an economy based on the division of labor in which the prices of goods and services are determined in a free price system set by supply and demand. This is often contrasted with a planned economy, in which a central government determines the price of goods and services using a fixed price system. Market economies are contrasted with mixed economy where the price system is not entirely free but under some government control that is not extensive enough to constitute a planned economy.
    a. Nutritional Economics
    b. Market economy
    c. Network Economy
    d. Commons-based peer production

25. A _____ is any systematic process enabling many market players to bid and ask: helping bidders and sellers interact and make deals. It is not just the price mechanism but the entire system of regulation, qualification, credentials, reputations and clearing that surrounds that mechanism and makes it operate in a social context.

62 *Chapter 8. OUTPUT, PRICE, AND PROFIT: THE IMPORTANCE OF MARGINAL ANALYSIS*

Because a _____ relies on the assumption that players are constantly involved and unequally enabled, a _____ is distinguished specifically from a voting system where candidates seek the support of voters on a less regular basis.

- a. Competitive equilibrium
- b. Contestable market
- c. Price mechanism
- d. Market system

26. In neoclassical economics and microeconomics, _____ describes the perfect being a market in which there are many small firms, all producing homogeneous goods. In the short term, such markets are productively inefficient as output will not occur where mc is equal to ac, but allocatively efficient, as output under _____ will always occur where mc is equal to mr, and therefore where mc equals ar. However, in the long term, such markets are both allocatively and productively efficient.
- a. Law of supply
- b. General equilibrium
- c. Co-operative economics
- d. Perfect competition

27. In economics, a _____ is any economic system that effects its distribution of goods and services with prices and employing any form of money or debt tokens. Except for possible remote and primitive communities, all modern societies use _____s to allocate resources. However, _____s are not used for all resource allocation decisions today.
- a. Hanseatic League
- b. Neomercantilism
- c. Family economy
- d. Price system

28. _____ is money accepted for exchange of goods in an economy. The prevalence of one money over another arises, usually, when a government designates through decrees that the government shall accept only particular notes and coins in payment for taxes. Typically, money of _____ consists of stamped coins and minted paper bills.
- a. Totnes pound
- b. Security thread
- c. Local currency
- d. Currency

29. _____ is a term from economics referring to the use of money exchanged by buyers and sellers with an open and understood system of value and time trade offs to produce the best distribution of goods and services. The use of the _____ does not imply a free market: there can be captive or controlled markets which seek to use supply and demand, or some other form of charging for scarcity, both in social situations and in engineering.

The _____ assumes perfect competition and is regulated by demand and supply.

- a. Product-Market Growth Matrix
- b. Partial equilibrium
- c. Market mechanism
- d. Two-sided markets

30. In economics, _____ are business expenses that are not dependent on the activities of the business They tend to be time-related, such as salaries or rents being paid per month. This is in contrast to variable costs, which are volume-related (and are paid per quantity.)

In management accounting, _____ are defined as expenses that do not change in proportion to the activity of a business, within the relevant period or scale of production.

Chapter 8. OUTPUT, PRICE, AND PROFIT: THE IMPORTANCE OF MARGINAL ANALYSIS

a. Cost-Volume-Profit Analysis
b. Cost of poor quality
c. Quality costs
d. Fixed costs

31. An _____ is a person who has possession of an enterprise and assumes significant accountability for the inherent risks and the outcome. It is an ambitious leader who combines land, labor, and capital to create and market new goods or services. The term is a loanword from French and was first defined by the Irish economist Richard Cantillon.

a. Entrepreneur
b. ACEA agreement
c. Expansionary policies
d. ACCRA Cost of Living Index

Chapter 9. INVESTING IN BUSINESS: STOCKS AND BONDS

1. _____ is an American economist and was the Chairman of the Federal Reserve of the United States from 1987 to 2006. He currently works as a private advisor and providing consulting for firms through his company, Greenspan Associates LLC.

First appointed Federal Reserve chairman by President Ronald Reagan in August 1987, he was reappointed at successive four-year intervals until retiring on January 31, 2006 after the second-longest tenure in the position.

   a. Adolf Hitler
   b. Adam Smith
   c. Adolph Fischer
   d. Alan Greenspan

2. '_____' is a phrase used by former Federal Reserve Board Chairman Alan Greenspan in a speech given at the American Enterprise Institute during the stock market boom of the 1990s. The phrase was interpreted by financial pundits as a typical extraordinary economy.

Greenspan's comment was made on December 5, 1996 (emphasis added in excerpt):

The presence of the short comment--not repeated by Greenspan since--within a rather dry and complex speech would not normally have been so memorable; however, it was followed by immediate slumps in stock markets worldwide, provoking a strong reaction in financial circles and making its way into colloquial speech.

   a. AD-IA Model
   b. ACEA agreement
   c. ACCRA Cost of Living Index
   d. Irrational exuberance

3. The _____ is an American stock exchange. It is the largest electronic screen-based equity securities trading market in the United States. With approximately 3,800 companies, it has more trading volume per hour than any other stock exchange in the world.
   a. NASDAQ
   b. 130-30 fund
   c. 1921 recession
   d. 100-year flood

4. A _____ is a public market for the trading of company stock and derivatives at an agreed price; these are securities listed on a stock exchange as well as those only traded privately.

The size of the world _____ was estimated at about $36.6 trillion US at the beginning of October 2008 . The total world derivatives market has been estimated at about $791 trillion face or nominal value, 11 times the size of the entire world economy.

   a. Adolf Hitler
   b. Adolph Fischer
   c. Adam Smith
   d. Stock market

5. The _____ consists of a number of economic theories which describe the nature of the firm, company including its existence, its behaviour, and its relationship with the market.

Chapter 9. INVESTING IN BUSINESS: STOCKS AND BONDS

In simplified terms, the _____ aims to answer these questions:

1. Existence - why do firms emerge, why are not all transactions in the economy mediated over the market?
2. Boundaries - why the boundary between firms and the market is located exactly there? Which transactions are performed internally and which are negotiated on the market?
3. Organization - why are firms structured in such specific way? What is the interplay of formal and informal relationships?

Despite looking simple, these questions are not answered by the established economic theory, which usually views firms as given, and treats them as black boxes without any internal structure.

The First World War period saw a change of emphasis in economic theory away from industry-level analysis which mainly included analysing markets to analysis at the level of the firm, as it became increasingly clear that perfect competition was no longer an adequate model of how firms behaved. Economic theory till then had focussed on trying to understand markets alone and there had been little study on understanding why firms or organisations exist.

- a. Theory of the firm
- b. Khazzoom-Brookes postulate
- c. Technology gap
- d. Policy Ineffectiveness Proposition

6. In finance, a _____ is a debt security, in which the authorized issuer owes the holders a debt and, depending on the terms of the _____, is obliged to pay interest (the coupon) and/or to repay the principal at a later date, termed maturity. A _____ is a formal contract to repay borrowed money with interest at fixed intervals.

Thus a _____ is like a loan: the issuer is the borrower (debtor), the holder is the lender (creditor), and the coupon is the interest.

- a. Zero-coupon
- b. Callable
- c. Prize Bond
- d. Bond

7. _____ is a concept whereby a person's financial liability is limited to a fixed sum, most commonly the value of a person's investment in a company or partnership with _____. A shareholder in a limited company is not personally liable for any of the debts of the company, other than for the value of his investment in that company. The same is true for the members of a _____ partnership and the limited partners in a limited partnership.

- a. Nexus of contracts
- b. Personal Responsibility and Work Opportunity Reconciliation Act of 1996
- c. Deficiency judgment
- d. Limited liability

8. _____ is a broad label that refers to any individuals or households that use goods and services generated within the economy. The concept of a _____ is used in different contexts, so that the usage and significance of the term may vary.

Chapter 9. INVESTING IN BUSINESS: STOCKS AND BONDS

Typically when business people and economists talk of _____s they are talking about person as _____, an aggregated commodity item with little individuality other than that expressed in the buy/not-buy decision.

a. 130-30 fund
b. 100-year flood
c. 1921 recession
d. Consumer

9. A _____ is a measure of the average price of consumer goods and services purchased by households. A _____ measures a price change for a constant market basket of goods and services from one period to the next within the same area (city, region, or nation.) It is a price index determined by measuring the price of a standard group of goods meant to represent the typical market basket of a typical urban consumer.

a. Consumer Price Index
b. Lipstick index
c. Cost-of-living index
d. CPI

10. _____ is a fee paid on borrowed assets. It is the price paid for the use of borrowed money , or, money earned by deposited funds . Assets that are sometimes lent with _____ include money, shares, consumer goods through hire purchase, major assets such as aircraft, and even entire factories in finance lease arrangements.

a. Insolvency
b. Asset protection
c. Interest
d. Internal debt

11. An _____ is the price a borrower pays for the use of money they do not own, for instance a small company might borrow from a bank to kick start their business, and the return a lender receives for deferring the use of funds, by lending it to the borrower. _____s are normally expressed as a percentage rate over the period of one year.

_____s targets are also a vital tool of monetary policy and are used to control variables like investment, inflation, and unemployment.

a. ACCRA Cost of Living Index
b. Arrow-Debreu model
c. Enterprise value
d. Interest rate

12. _____ in economics and business is the result of an exchange and from that trade we assign a numerical monetary value to a good, service or asset. If Alice trades Bob 4 apples for an orange, the _____ of an orange is 4 apples. Inversely, the _____ of an apple is 1/4 oranges.

a. Price
b. Premium pricing
c. Price war
d. Price book

13. A _____ is a normalized average (typically a weighted average) of prices for a given class of goods or services in a given region, during a given interval of time. It is a statistic designed to help to compare how these prices, taken as a whole, differ between time periods or geographical locations.

Price indices have several potential uses.

a. Two-part tariff
b. Price Index
c. Product sabotage
d. Transactional Net Margin Method

Chapter 9. INVESTING IN BUSINESS: STOCKS AND BONDS

14. _____ is a specific term used in companies' financial reporting from the company-whole point of view. Because that use excludes the effects of changing ownership interest, an economic measure of _____ is necessary for financial analysis from the shareholders' point of view

_____ is defined by the Financial Accounting Standards Board, or FASB, as e;the change in equity [net assets] of a business enterprise during a period from transactions and other events and circumstances from nonowner sources. It includes all changes in equity during a period except those resulting from investments by owners and distributions to owners.e;

_____ is the sum of net income and other items that must bypass the income statement because they have not been realized, including items like an unrealized holding gain or loss from available for sale securities and foreign currency translation gains or losses.

   a. Net national income
   b. Real income
   c. Windfall gain
   d. Comprehensive income

15. A security is a fungible, negotiable instrument representing financial value. _____ are broadly categorized into debt _____; equity _____, e.g., common stocks; and derivative (finance) contracts such as forwards, futures, options and swaps. The company or other entity issuing the security is called the issuer.
   a. Pass-Through Certificates
   b. Securities
   c. Settlement risk
   d. Red herring prospectus

16. The U.S. _____ is an independent agency of the United States government which holds primary responsibility for enforcing the federal securities laws and regulating the securities industry, the nation's stock and options exchanges, and other electronic securities markets. The SEC was created by section 4 of the Securities Exchange Act of 1934 (now codified as 15 U.S.C. § 78d and commonly referred to as the 1934 Act.)
   a. 1921 recession
   b. 100-year flood
   c. Securities and Exchange Commission
   d. 130-30 fund

17. _____, 1st Baron Keynes was a renowned economist from Britain whose many ideas on economic and political theories as well as on many governments' monetary policies influenced America. He advocated a government that played an active role in the lives of people regarding business, economy, etc. In this role, the government would use fiscal measures to reduce the consequences of recessions, economic depressions and booms.
   a. Adam Smith
   b. John Maynard Keynes
   c. Adolph Fischer
   d. Adolf Hitler

18. A _____ is an order to buy a security at no more than a specific price. This gives the trader some control over the price at which the trade is executed; on the other hand, the order may never be executed ('filled'.)

A buy _____ can only be executed by the broker at the limit price or lower.

   a. Demat account
   b. Non-voting stock
   c. Nifty Fifty
   d. Limit order

Chapter 9. INVESTING IN BUSINESS: STOCKS AND BONDS

19. In economics, a _____ exists when the production or use of goods and services by the market is not efficient. That is, there exists another outcome where all involved can be made better off. _____s can be viewed as scenarios where individuals' pursuit of pure self-interest leads to results that are not efficient - that can be improved upon from the societal point-of-view.
    a. General equilibrium
    b. Fixed exchange rate
    c. Market failure
    d. Financial economics

20. An _____ or index tracker is a collective investment scheme (usually a mutual fund or exchange-traded fund) that aims to replicate the movements of an index of a specific financial market regardless of market conditions.

    Tracking can be achieved by trying to hold all of the securities in the index, in the same proportions as the index. Other methods include statistically sampling the market and holding 'representative' securities.

    a. Investment trust
    b. Unit trust
    c. Asset management company
    d. Index fund

21. A _____ is a professionally managed type of collective investment scheme that pools money from many investors and invests it in stocks, bonds, short-term money market instruments, and/or other securities. The _____ will have a fund manager that trades the pooled money on a regular basis. As of early 2008, the worldwide value of all _____s totals more than $26 trillion.
    a. Mutual fund
    b. Self-invested personal pension
    c. Dark pools of liquidity
    d. Participating policy

22. _____ is an equity (stock) exchange located at 11 Wall Street in lower Manhattan, New York, USA. It is the largest stock exchange in the world by dollar value of its listed companies' securities. As of October 2008, the combined capitalization of all domestic _____ listed companies was US$10.1 trillion.
    a. 1921 recession
    b. 130-30 fund
    c. 100-year flood
    d. New York Stock Exchange

23. A _____ is a corporation or mutual organization which provides trading facilities for stock brokers and traders, to trade stocks and other securities. It may be a physical trading room where the traders gather, or a formalised communications network. Creation of a _____ is a strategy of economic development.
    a. SEAQ
    b. Primary shares
    c. 100-year flood
    d. Stock Exchange

24. _____ is a voluntary transfer of resources from one country to another, given at least partly with the objective of benefiting the recipient country. It may have other functions as well: it may be given as a signal of diplomatic approval, or to strengthen a military ally, to reward a government for behaviour desired by the donor, to extend the donor's cultural influence, to provide infrastructure needed by the donor for resource extraction from the recipient country, or to gain other kinds of commercial access. Humanitarianism and altruism are, nevertheless, significant motivations for the giving of _____.
    a. ACEA agreement
    b. AD-IA Model
    c. ACCRA Cost of Living Index
    d. Aid

25. The _____ is one of several stock market indices, created by nineteenth-century Wall Street Journal editor and Dow Jones ' Company co-founder Charles Dow. It is an index that shows how certain stocks have traded. Dow compiled the index to gauge the performance of the industrial sector of the American stock market.

Chapter 9. INVESTING IN BUSINESS: STOCKS AND BONDS

a. Federal Reserve Bank Notes
b. Fama-French three factor model
c. Commodity fetishism
d. Dow Jones Industrial Average

26. An _____ is a financial institution that raises capital, trades in securities and manages corporate mergers and acquisitions. _____s profit from companies and governments by raising money through issuing and selling securities in the capital markets (both equity, bond) and insuring bonds (selling credit default swaps), as well as providing advice on transactions such as mergers and acquisitions. To perform these services in the United States, an adviser must be a licensed broker-dealer, and is subject to SEC (FINRA) regulation see SEC.

a. Anonymous internet banking
b. Investment bank
c. Annual percentage rate
d. Interbanca

27. A _____ is a kind of negotiable instrument, a promissory note made by a bank payable to the bearer on demand, used as money, and in many jurisdictions is legal tender. Along with coins, _____s make up the cash or bearer forms of all modern money. With the exception of non-circulating high-value or precious metal commemorative issues, coins are generally used for lower valued monetary units, while _____s are used for higher values.

a. Banknote
b. Microprinting
c. Local currency
d. Security thread

28. _____s are financial contracts whose values are derived from the value of something else (known as the underlying.) The underlying value on which a _____ is based can be an asset (e.g., commodities, equities (stocks), residential mortgages, commercial real estate, loans, bonds), an index (e.g., interest rates, exchange rates, stock market indices, consumer price index (CPI) -- see inflation _____s), weather conditions bonds or other forms of credit.

a. 100-year flood
b. Second derivative
c. 130-30 fund
d. Derivative

29. A _____ is an investment fund open to a limited range of investors that is permitted by regulators to undertake a wider range of investment and trading activities than other investment funds and pays a performance fee to its investment manager. Each fund has its own strategy which determines the type of investments and the methods of investment it undertakes. _____s, as a class, invest in a broad range of investments including shares, debt, commodities and so forth.

a. 1921 recession
b. 130-30 fund
c. 100-year flood
d. Hedge fund

30. In economics, the _____ is an economic law that states that consumers buy more of a good when its price decreases and less when its price increases.

There are certain goods which do not follow this law. These include Veblen and Giffen goods

a. Financial crisis
b. Georgism
c. Law of demand
d. Market failure

31. _____ was a U.S. hedge fund which used trading strategies such as fixed income arbitrage, statistical arbitrage, and pairs trading, combined with high leverage. It failed spectacularly in the late 1990s, leading to a massive bailout by other major banks and investment houses, which was supervised by the Federal Reserve.

Chapter 9. INVESTING IN BUSINESS: STOCKS AND BONDS

LTCM was founded in 1994 by John Meriwether, the former vice-chairman and head of bond trading at Salomon Brothers.

a. General purpose technologies
b. Collectivization of agriculture in Romania
c. Consumer protection
d. Long-Term Capital Management

32. Economics:

- _____,the desire to own something and the ability to pay for it
- _____ curve,a graphic representation of a _____ schedule
- _____ deposit, the money in checking accounts
- _____ pull theory,the theory that inflation occurs when _____ for goods and services exceeds existing supplies
- _____ schedule,a table that lists the quantity of a good a person will buy it each different price
- _____ side economics,the school of economics at believes government spending and tax cuts open economy by raising _____

a. Variability
b. Demand
c. Production
d. McKesson ' Robbins scandal

33. In finance, _____ is a financial action that does not promise safety of the initial investment along with the return on the principal sum. _____ typically involves the lending of money or the purchase of assets, equity or debt but in a manner that has not been given thorough analysis or is deemed to have low margin of safety or a significant risk of the loss of the principal investment. The term, '_____,' which is formally defined as above in Graham and Dodd's 1934 text, Security Analysis, contrasts with the term 'investment,' which is a financial operation that, upon thorough analysis, promises safety of principal and a satisfactory return.

a. Global Financial Centres Index
b. Hybrid market
c. Municipal Bond Arbitrage
d. Speculation

34. _____ is a concept with somewhat disparate meanings in several fields. It also has a common meaning which has a loose connection with some of those more definite meanings.

Casually, it is typically used to denote a lack of order, or purpose, or cause.

a. 130-30 fund
b. 100-year flood
c. Randomness
d. 1921 recession

35. A _____, sometimes denoted _____, is a mathematical formalization of a trajectory that consists of taking successive random steps. The results of _____ analysis have been applied to computer science, physics, ecology, economics, and a number of other fields as a fundamental model for random processes in time. For example, the path traced by a molecule as it travels in a liquid or a gas, the search path of a foraging animal, the price of a fluctuating stock and the financial status of a gambler can all be modeled as _____s.

Chapter 9. INVESTING IN BUSINESS: STOCKS AND BONDS

a. Random walk
b. 130-30 fund
c. 100-year flood
d. 1921 recession

36. _____ was written by the English economist John Maynard Keynes. The book, generally considered to be his magnum opus, is largely credited with creating the terminology and shape of modern macroeconomics. Published in February 1936 it sought to bring about a revolution, commonly referred to as the 'Keynesian Revolution', in the way economists thought - especially in relation to the proposition that a market economy tends naturally to restore itself to full employment after temporary shocks.

a. The General Theory of Employment, Interest and Money
b. Principles of Political Economy
c. Wealth of Nations
d. General Theory of Employment, Interest and Money

37. A _____ is a type of economic bubble taking place in stock markets when price of stocks rise and become overvalued by any measure of stock valuation.

The existence of _____s is at odds with the assumptions of efficient market theory which assumes rational investor behaviour. Behavioral finance theory attribute _____s to cognitive biases that lead to groupthink and herd behavior.

a. Scrip issue
b. Growth investing
c. Stock market bubble
d. Fill or kill

38. _____ was a survey conducted by the U.S. Department of Justice to gauge the prevalence of alcohol and illegal drug use among prior arrestees. It was a reformulation of the prior Drug Use Forecasting (DUF) program, focused on five drugs in particular: cocaine, marijuana, methamphetamine, opiates, and PCP.

Participants were randomly selected from arrest records in major metropolitan areas; because no personally identifying information is taken from each record chosen, the resulting data can be correlated to arrest rates, but not to the total population of persons charged.

a. ACCRA Cost of Living Index
b. ACEA agreement
c. AD-IA Model
d. Arrestee Drug Abuse Monitoring

39. _____ was a Scottish moral philosopher and a pioneer of political economy. One of the key figures of the Scottish Enlightenment, Smith is the author of The Theory of Moral Sentiments and An Inquiry into the Nature and Causes of the Wealth of Nations. The latter, usually abbreviated as The Wealth of Nations, is considered his magnum opus and the first modern work of economics.

a. Alan Greenspan
b. Adolph Fischer
c. Adolf Hitler
d. Adam Smith

40. Competition law, known in the United States as _____ law, has three main elements:

- prohibiting agreements or practices that restrict free trading and competition between business entities. This includes in particular the repression of cartels.
- banning abusive behaviour by a firm dominating a market, or anti-competitive practices that tend to lead to such a dominant position. Practices controlled in this way may include predatory pricing, tying, price gouging, refusal to deal, and many others.
- supervising the mergers and acquisitions of large corporations, including some joint ventures. Transactions that are considered to threaten the competitive process can be prohibited altogether, or approved subject to 'remedies' such as an obligation to divest part of the merged business or to offer licences or access to facilities to enable other businesses to continue competing.

The substance and practice of competition law varies from jurisdiction to jurisdiction. Protecting the interests of consumers (consumer welfare) and ensuring that entrepreneurs have an opportunity to compete in the market economy are often treated as important objectives. Competition law is closely connected with law on deregulation of access to markets, state aids and subsidies, the privatisation of state owned assets and the establishment of independent sector regulators. In recent decades, competition law has been viewed as a way to provide better public services.

a. United Kingdom competition law
b. Intellectual property law
c. Anti-Inflation Act
d. Antitrust

41. _____, known in the United States as antitrust law, has three main elements:

- prohibiting agreements or practices that restrict free trading and competition between business entities. This includes in particular the repression of cartels.
- banning abusive behaviour by a firm dominating a market, or anti-competitive practices that tend to lead to such a dominant position. Practices controlled in this way may include predatory pricing, tying, price gouging, refusal to deal, and many others.
- supervising the mergers and acquisitions of large corporations, including some joint ventures. Transactions that are considered to threaten the competitive process can be prohibited altogether, or approved subject to 'remedies' such as an obligation to divest part of the merged business or to offer licences or access to facilities to enable other businesses to continue competing.

The substance and practice of _____ varies from jurisdiction to jurisdiction. Protecting the interests of consumers (consumer welfare) and ensuring that entrepreneurs have an opportunity to compete in the market economy are often treated as important objectives. _____ is closely connected with law on deregulation of access to markets, state aids and subsidies, the privatisation of state owned assets and the establishment of independent sector regulators. In recent decades, _____ has been viewed as a way to provide better public services.

a. Hostile work environment
b. Fee simple
c. Due diligence
d. Competition law

Chapter 9. INVESTING IN BUSINESS: STOCKS AND BONDS

42. An _____ is a market form in which a market or industry is dominated by a small number of sellers (oligopolists.) Because there are few participants in this type of market, each oligopolist is aware of the actions of the others. The decisions of one firm influence, and are influenced by, the decisions of other firms.
    a. Oligopsony
    b. ACEA agreement
    c. ACCRA Cost of Living Index
    d. Oligopoly

43. In neoclassical economics and microeconomics, _____ describes the perfect being a market in which there are many small firms, all producing homogeneous goods. In the short term, such markets are productively inefficient as output will not occur where mc is equal to ac, but allocatively efficient, as output under _____ will always occur where mc is equal to mr, and therefore where mc equals ar. However, in the long term, such markets are both allocatively and productively efficient.
    a. Law of supply
    b. Co-operative economics
    c. General equilibrium
    d. Perfect competition

44. In economics, a _____ exists when a specific individual or enterprise has sufficient control over a particular product or service to determine significantly the terms on which other individuals shall have access to it. Monopolies are thus characterized by a lack of economic competition for the good or service that they provide and a lack of viable substitute goods. The verb 'monopolize' refers to the process by which a firm gains persistently greater market share than what is expected under perfect competition.
    a. 100-year flood
    b. Monopoly
    c. 1921 recession
    d. 130-30 fund

Chapter 10. THE FIRM AND THE INDUSTRY UNDER PERFECT COMPETITION

1. In neoclassical economics and microeconomics, _____ describes the perfect being a market in which there are many small firms, all producing homogeneous goods. In the short term, such markets are productively inefficient as output will not occur where mc is equal to ac, but allocatively efficient, as output under _____ will always occur where mc is equal to mr, and therefore where mc equals ar. However, in the long term, such markets are both allocatively and productively efficient.

   a. Co-operative economics
   b. General equilibrium
   c. Law of supply
   d. Perfect competition

2. _____ is any (course of) action deliberately taken (or not taken) to manage human activities with a view to prevent, reduce or mitigate harmful effects on nature and natural resources, and ensuring that man-made changes to the environment do not have harmful effects on humans.

   It is useful to consider that _____ comprises two major terms: environment and policy. Environment primarily refers to the ecological (ecosystems) dimension, but can also take account of social (quality of life) dimension and an economic (resource management) dimension.

   a. ACCRA Cost of Living Index
   b. ACEA agreement
   c. AD-IA Model
   d. Environmental policy

3. _____ was a survey conducted by the U.S. Department of Justice to gauge the prevalence of alcohol and illegal drug use among prior arrestees. It was a reformulation of the prior Drug Use Forecasting (DUF) program, focused on five drugs in particular: cocaine, marijuana, methamphetamine, opiates, and PCP.

   Participants were randomly selected from arrest records in major metropolitan areas; because no personally identifying information is taken from each record chosen, the resulting data can be correlated to arrest rates, but not to the total population of persons charged.

   a. ACEA agreement
   b. AD-IA Model
   c. ACCRA Cost of Living Index
   d. Arrestee Drug Abuse Monitoring

4. In finance, a _____ is a debt security, in which the authorized issuer owes the holders a debt and, depending on the terms of the _____, is obliged to pay interest (the coupon) and/or to repay the principal at a later date, termed maturity. A _____ is a formal contract to repay borrowed money with interest at fixed intervals.

   Thus a _____ is like a loan: the issuer is the borrower (debtor), the holder is the lender (creditor), and the coupon is the interest.

   a. Prize Bond
   b. Bond
   c. Callable
   d. Zero-coupon

Chapter 10. THE FIRM AND THE INDUSTRY UNDER PERFECT COMPETITION

5. Economics:

   - _____, the desire to own something and the ability to pay for it
   - _____ curve, a graphic representation of a _____ schedule
   - _____ deposit, the money in checking accounts
   - _____ pull theory, the theory that inflation occurs when _____ for goods and services exceeds existing supplies
   - _____ schedule, a table that lists the quantity of a good a person will buy it each different price
   - _____ side economics, the school of economics at believes government spending and tax cuts open economy by raising _____

   a. Demand
   b. Production
   c. McKesson ' Robbins scandal
   d. Variability

6. In economics, the _____ can be defined as the graph depicting the relationship between the price of a certain commodity, and the amount of it that consumers are willing and able to purchase at that given price. It is a graphic representation of a demand schedule. The _____ for all consumers together follows from the _____ of every individual consumer: the individual demands at each price are added together.

   a. Kuznets curve
   b. Demand curve
   c. Wage curve
   d. Cost curve

7. _____ in economics and business is the result of an exchange and from that trade we assign a numerical monetary value to a good, service or asset. If Alice trades Bob 4 apples for an orange, the _____ of an orange is 4 apples. Inversely, the _____ of an apple is 1/4 oranges.

   a. Premium pricing
   b. Price war
   c. Price book
   d. Price

8. Monopoly power is an example of market failure which occurs when one or more of the participants has the ability to influence the price or other outcomes in some general or specialized market. The most commonly discussed form of market power is that of a monopoly, but other forms such as monopsony, and more moderate versions of these two extremes, exist. Market participants that have market power are sometimes referred to as 'price makers', while those without are sometimes called '_____'.

   a. Market power
   b. Market concentration
   c. Monopolization
   d. Price takers

9. In economics, a _____ is a general slowdown in economic activity over a sustained period of time, or a business cycle contraction. During _____s, many macroeconomic indicators vary in a similar way. Production as measured by Gross Domestic Product (GDP), employment, investment spending, capacity utilization, household incomes and business profits all fall during _____s.

   a. Recession
   b. Treasury View
   c. Monetary economics
   d. Leading indicators

Chapter 10. THE FIRM AND THE INDUSTRY UNDER PERFECT COMPETITION

10. _____ was a Scottish moral philosopher and a pioneer of political economy. One of the key figures of the Scottish Enlightenment, Smith is the author of The Theory of Moral Sentiments and An Inquiry into the Nature and Causes of the Wealth of Nations. The latter, usually abbreviated as The Wealth of Nations, is considered his magnum opus and the first modern work of economics.

   a. Adolf Hitler
   b. Alan Greenspan
   c. Adolph Fischer
   d. Adam Smith

11. _____ is a broad label that refers to any individuals or households that use goods and services generated within the economy. The concept of a _____ is used in different contexts, so that the usage and significance of the term may vary.

   Typically when business people and economists talk of _____s they are talking about person as _____, an aggregated commodity item with little individuality other than that expressed in the buy/not-buy decision.

   a. 1921 recession
   b. 130-30 fund
   c. 100-year flood
   d. Consumer

12. The Demand side is a term used in economics to refer to a number of things:

   - The demand element of a supply and demand partial equilibrium diagram, in microeconomics
   - The aggregate demand in an economy, in macroeconomics
   - Economic policy actions which are designed to affect aggregate demand.
   - _____ learning referring to the incentive to learn how to use and modify free software as opposed to buying conventional software.

   The term is also used broadly to distinguish supply-side economics from other schools, for instance Keynesian economics.

   a. CPFR
   b. Demand-side
   c. Delayed differentiation
   d. Reverse auction

13. In economics and finance, _____ is the change in total cost that arises when the quantity produced changes by one unit. It is the cost of producing one more unit of a good. Mathematically, the _____ function is expressed as the first derivative of the total cost (TC) function with respect to quantity (Q.)

   a. Quality costs
   b. Marginal cost
   c. Variable cost
   d. Khozraschyot

14. In microeconomics, _____ is the extra revenue that an additional unit of product will bring. It is the additional income from selling one more unit of a good; sometimes equal to price. It can also be described as the change in total revenue/change in number of units sold.

   a. Long term
   b. Reservation price
   c. Marginal revenue
   d. Market demand schedule

15. In economics, _____ is the total supply of goods and services produced by a national economy during a specific time period. It is the total amount of goods and services in the economy available at all possible price levels.

Chapter 10. THE FIRM AND THE INDUSTRY UNDER PERFECT COMPETITION

a. Aggregation problem
b. Aggregate expenditure
c. Aggregate demand
d. Aggregate supply

16. In economics, _____ is equal to total cost divided by the number of goods produced (the output quantity, Q.) It is also equal to the sum of average variable costs (total variable costs divided by Q) plus average fixed costs (total fixed costs divided by Q.) _____s may be dependent on the time period considered (increasing production may be expensive or impossible in the short term, for example.)
   a. Average fixed cost
   b. Average variable cost
   c. Explicit cost
   d. Average cost

17. _____ is one of the ways government regulate a monopoly market. Monopolists tend to produce less than the optimal quantity pushing the prices up. Government may use _____ as a tool to regulate prices monopolists may charge.
   a. AD-IA Model
   b. Average cost pricing
   c. ACEA agreement
   d. ACCRA Cost of Living Index

18. _____ is one of the four Ps of the marketing mix. The other three aspects are product, promotion, and place. It is also a key variable in microeconomic price allocation theory.
   a. Pricing
   b. Premium pricing
   c. Guaranteed Maximum Price
   d. Point of total assumption

19. In economics, the concept of the _____ refers to the decision-making time frame of a firm in which at least one factor of production is fixed. Costs which are fixed in the _____ have no impact on a firms decisions. For example a firm can raise output by increasing the amount of labour through overtime.
   a. Productivity model
   b. Short-run
   c. Hicks-neutral technical change
   d. Product Pipeline

20. _____ is an economic model based on price, utility and quantity in a market. It predicts that in a competitive market, price will function to equalize the quantity demanded by consumers, and the quantity supplied by producers, resulting in an economic equilibrium of price and quantity. The model incorporates other factors changing equilibrium as a shift of demand and/or supply.
   a. Deferred gratification
   b. Joint demand
   c. Rational addiction
   d. Supply and demand

21. In economics and business, specifically cost accounting, the _____ point (BEP) is the point at which cost or expenses and revenue are equal: there is no net loss or gain, and one has 'broken even'. A profit or a loss has not been made, although opportunity costs have been paid, and capital has received the risk-adjusted, expected return.

For example, if the business sells less than 200 tables each month, it will make a loss, if it sells more, it will be a profit.

   a. Buffer stock scheme
   b. Small numbers game
   c. Nonmarket
   d. Break-even

Chapter 10. THE FIRM AND THE INDUSTRY UNDER PERFECT COMPETITION

22. The break-even point for a product is the point where total revenue received equals the total costs associated with the sale of the product (TR=TC.) A break-even point is typically calculated in order for businesses to determine if it would be profitable to sell a proposed product, as opposed to attempting to modify an existing product instead so it can be made lucrative. _____ can also be used to analyse the potential profitability of an expenditure in a sales-based business.

a. Break even analysis
b. Flat rate
c. Competitor indexing
d. Price

23. In economics, and cost accounting, _____ describes the total economic cost of production and is made up of variable costs, which vary according to the quantity of a good produced and include inputs such as labor and raw materials, plus fixed costs, which are independent of the quantity of a good produced and include inputs (capital) that cannot be varied in the short term, such as buildings and machinery. _____ in economics includes the total opportunity cost of each factor of production in addition to fixed and variable costs.

The rate at which _____ changes as the amount produced changes is called marginal cost.

a. 130-30 fund
b. 1921 recession
c. 100-year flood
d. Total cost

24. _____ is the total money received from the sale of any given quantity of output.

The _____ is calculated by taking the price of the sale times the quantity sold, i.e.

_____ = price X quantity.

a. Ceteris paribus
b. Total revenue
c. Market development funds
d. Small numbers game

25. _____s are expenses that change in proportion to the activity of a business. In other words, _____ is the sum of marginal costs. It can also be considered normal costs.

a. Cost allocation
b. Variable cost
c. Quality costs
d. Cost-Volume-Profit Analysis

26. _____ is an economics term to describe a firms variable costs (labor, electricity, etc.) divided by the quantity (Q) of total units of output.

$$AVC = \frac{TVC}{Q}$$

Where:

- TVC = Total Variable Cost
- _____ = Average variable cost
- Q = Quantity of Units Produced

Chapter 10. THE FIRM AND THE INDUSTRY UNDER PERFECT COMPETITION

_____ plus average fixed cost equals average total cost:

_____ + AFC = ATC.

- a. Inventory valuation
- c. Explicit cost
- b. Average fixed cost
- d. Average variable cost

27. In economics, the term _____ of income or _____ refers to a simple economic model which describes the reciprocal circulation of income between producers and consumers. In the _____ model, the inter-dependent entities of producer and consumer are referred to as 'firms' and 'households' respectively and provide each other with factors in order to facilitate the flow of income. Firms provide consumers with goods and services in exchange for consumer expenditure and 'factors of production' from households.
- a. 1921 recession
- c. 100-year flood
- b. 130-30 fund
- d. Circular flow

28. In economic models, the _____ time frame assumes no fixed factors of production. Firms can enter or leave the marketplace, and the cost (and availability) of land, labor, raw materials, and capital goods can be assumed to vary. In contrast, in the short-run time frame, certain factors are assumed to be fixed, because there is not sufficient time for them to change.
- a. Price/performance ratio
- c. Productivity world
- b. Diseconomies of scale
- d. Long-run

29. _____s is the social science that studies the production, distribution, and consumption of goods and services. The term _____s comes from the Ancient Greek oá¼°κονομῖα from oá¼¶κος (oikos, 'house') + vĺŒμος (nomos, 'custom' or 'law'), hence 'rules of the house(hold)'. Current _____ models developed out of the broader field of political economy in the late 19th century, owing to a desire to use an empirical approach more akin to the physical sciences.
- a. Opportunity cost
- c. Inflation
- b. Economic
- d. Energy economics

30. In economics, _____ is the difference between a company's total revenue and its opportunity costs. It is the increase in wealth that an investor has from making an investment, taking into consideration all costs associated with that investment including the opportunity cost of capital.

Profit is the factor income of the entrepreneur.

- a. Accounting profit
- c. Economic profit
- b. ACCRA Cost of Living Index
- d. Operating profit

31. _____ or economic opportunity loss is the value of the next best alternative foregone as the result of making a decision. _____ analysis is an important part of a company's decision-making processes but is not treated as an actual cost in any financial statement. The next best thing that a person can engage in is referred to as the _____ of doing the best thing and ignoring the next best thing to be done.

Chapter 10. THE FIRM AND THE INDUSTRY UNDER PERFECT COMPETITION

a. Economic ideology
b. Economic
c. Industrial organization
d. Opportunity cost

32. The _____ is the expected return forgone by bypassing of other potential investment activities for a given capital. It is a rate of return that investors could earn in financial markets.

a. ACCRA Cost of Living Index
b. ACEA agreement
c. Opportunity cost of capital
d. AD-IA Model

33. The _____ is an expected return that the provider of capital plans to earn on their investment.

Capital (money) used for funding a business should earn returns for the capital providers who risk their capital. For an investment to be worthwhile, the expected return on capital must be greater than the _____.

a. Modigliani-Miller theorem
b. Capital expenditure
c. Capital intensive
d. Cost of Capital

34. Competition law, known in the United States as _____ law, has three main elements:

- prohibiting agreements or practices that restrict free trading and competition between business entities. This includes in particular the repression of cartels.
- banning abusive behaviour by a firm dominating a market, or anti-competitive practices that tend to lead to such a dominant position. Practices controlled in this way may include predatory pricing, tying, price gouging, refusal to deal, and many others.
- supervising the mergers and acquisitions of large corporations, including some joint ventures. Transactions that are considered to threaten the competitive process can be prohibited altogether, or approved subject to 'remedies' such as an obligation to divest part of the merged business or to offer licences or access to facilities to enable other businesses to continue competing.

The substance and practice of competition law varies from jurisdiction to jurisdiction. Protecting the interests of consumers (consumer welfare) and ensuring that entrepreneurs have an opportunity to compete in the market economy are often treated as important objectives. Competition law is closely connected with law on deregulation of access to markets, state aids and subsidies, the privatisation of state owned assets and the establishment of independent sector regulators. In recent decades, competition law has been viewed as a way to provide better public services.

a. Antitrust
b. United Kingdom competition law
c. Intellectual property law
d. Anti-Inflation Act

Chapter 10. THE FIRM AND THE INDUSTRY UNDER PERFECT COMPETITION

35. _____, known in the United States as antitrust law, has three main elements:

- prohibiting agreements or practices that restrict free trading and competition between business entities. This includes in particular the repression of cartels.
- banning abusive behaviour by a firm dominating a market, or anti-competitive practices that tend to lead to such a dominant position. Practices controlled in this way may include predatory pricing, tying, price gouging, refusal to deal, and many others.
- supervising the mergers and acquisitions of large corporations, including some joint ventures. Transactions that are considered to threaten the competitive process can be prohibited altogether, or approved subject to 'remedies' such as an obligation to divest part of the merged business or to offer licences or access to facilities to enable other businesses to continue competing.

The substance and practice of _____ varies from jurisdiction to jurisdiction. Protecting the interests of consumers (consumer welfare) and ensuring that entrepreneurs have an opportunity to compete in the market economy are often treated as important objectives. _____ is closely connected with law on deregulation of access to markets, state aids and subsidies, the privatisation of state owned assets and the establishment of independent sector regulators. In recent decades, _____ has been viewed as a way to provide better public services.

- a. Hostile work environment
- b. Due diligence
- c. Competition law
- d. Fee simple

36. In economics, a _____ is a graph of the costs of production as a function of total quantity produced. In a free market economy, productively efficient firms use these curves to find the optimal point of production, where they make the most profits. There are a few different types of _____s, each relevant to a different area of economics.
- a. Kuznets curve
- b. Demand curve
- c. Phillips curve
- d. Cost curve

37. _____, in microeconomics, are the cost advantages that a business obtains due to expansion. They are factors that cause a producere;s average cost per unit to fall as scale is increased. _____ is a long run concept and refers to reductions in unit cost as the size of a facility, or scale, increases.
- a. Economic production quantity
- b. Economies of scale
- c. Underinvestment employment relationship
- d. Isoquant

38. A _____ is a legal document that is often passed by the legislature, and approved by the chief executive-or president. For example, only certain types of revenue may be imposed and collected. Property tax is frequently the basis for municipal and county revenues, while sales tax and/or income tax are the basis for state revenues, and income tax and corporate tax are the basis for national revenues.
- a. Structural deficit
- b. Lump-sum tax
- c. Right-financing
- d. Government budget

39. In economics, the _____ is the term economists use to describe the self-regulating nature of the marketplace. The _____ is a metaphor coined by the economist Adam Smith in The Wealth of Nations.

Chapter 10. THE FIRM AND THE INDUSTRY UNDER PERFECT COMPETITION

Adam Smith mentions the metaphor in Book IV of The Wealth of Nations, arguing that people in any society will certainly employ their capital in foreign trading only if the profits available by that method far exceed those available locally, and that in such a case it is better for society as a whole if they so did.

- a. Invisible hand
- c. AD-IA Model
- b. ACEA agreement
- d. ACCRA Cost of Living Index

40. An _____ is a market form in which a market or industry is dominated by a small number of sellers (oligopolists.) Because there are few participants in this type of market, each oligopolist is aware of the actions of the others. The decisions of one firm influence, and are influenced by, the decisions of other firms.
- a. Oligopoly
- c. ACCRA Cost of Living Index
- b. Oligopsony
- d. ACEA agreement

Chapter 11. MONOPOLY

1. _____ was a survey conducted by the U.S. Department of Justice to gauge the prevalence of alcohol and illegal drug use among prior arrestees. It was a reformulation of the prior Drug Use Forecasting (DUF) program, focused on five drugs in particular: cocaine, marijuana, methamphetamine, opiates, and PCP.

Participants were randomly selected from arrest records in major metropolitan areas; because no personally identifying information is taken from each record chosen, the resulting data can be correlated to arrest rates, but not to the total population of persons charged.

   a. ACCRA Cost of Living Index
   b. AD-IA Model
   c. Arrestee Drug Abuse Monitoring
   d. ACEA agreement

2. _____ was a Scottish moral philosopher and a pioneer of political economy. One of the key figures of the Scottish Enlightenment, Smith is the author of The Theory of Moral Sentiments and An Inquiry into the Nature and Causes of the Wealth of Nations. The latter, usually abbreviated as The Wealth of Nations, is considered his magnum opus and the first modern work of economics.
   a. Adolf Hitler
   b. Adam Smith
   c. Alan Greenspan
   d. Adolph Fischer

3. Competition law, known in the United States as _____ law, has three main elements:

   - prohibiting agreements or practices that restrict free trading and competition between business entities. This includes in particular the repression of cartels.
   - banning abusive behaviour by a firm dominating a market, or anti-competitive practices that tend to lead to such a dominant position. Practices controlled in this way may include predatory pricing, tying, price gouging, refusal to deal, and many others.
   - supervising the mergers and acquisitions of large corporations, including some joint ventures. Transactions that are considered to threaten the competitive process can be prohibited altogether, or approved subject to 'remedies' such as an obligation to divest part of the merged business or to offer licences or access to facilities to enable other businesses to continue competing.

The substance and practice of competition law varies from jurisdiction to jurisdiction. Protecting the interests of consumers (consumer welfare) and ensuring that entrepreneurs have an opportunity to compete in the market economy are often treated as important objectives. Competition law is closely connected with law on deregulation of access to markets, state aids and subsidies, the privatisation of state owned assets and the establishment of independent sector regulators. In recent decades, competition law has been viewed as a way to provide better public services.

   a. Anti-Inflation Act
   b. Antitrust
   c. Intellectual property law
   d. United Kingdom competition law

Chapter 11. MONOPOLY

4. _____, known in the United States as antitrust law, has three main elements:

- prohibiting agreements or practices that restrict free trading and competition between business entities. This includes in particular the repression of cartels.
- banning abusive behaviour by a firm dominating a market, or anti-competitive practices that tend to lead to such a dominant position. Practices controlled in this way may include predatory pricing, tying, price gouging, refusal to deal, and many others.
- supervising the mergers and acquisitions of large corporations, including some joint ventures. Transactions that are considered to threaten the competitive process can be prohibited altogether, or approved subject to 'remedies' such as an obligation to divest part of the merged business or to offer licences or access to facilities to enable other businesses to continue competing.

The substance and practice of _____ varies from jurisdiction to jurisdiction. Protecting the interests of consumers (consumer welfare) and ensuring that entrepreneurs have an opportunity to compete in the market economy are often treated as important objectives. _____ is closely connected with law on deregulation of access to markets, state aids and subsidies, the privatisation of state owned assets and the establishment of independent sector regulators. In recent decades, _____ has been viewed as a way to provide better public services.

a. Fee simple
b. Hostile work environment
c. Due diligence
d. Competition law

5. In economics, a _____ exists when a specific individual or enterprise has sufficient control over a particular product or service to determine significantly the terms on which other individuals shall have access to it. Monopolies are thus characterized by a lack of economic competition for the good or service that they provide and a lack of viable substitute goods. The verb 'monopolize' refers to the process by which a firm gains persistently greater market share than what is expected under perfect competition.

a. 100-year flood
b. 130-30 fund
c. 1921 recession
d. Monopoly

6. _____, originally the American Telephone ' Telegraph Company, is an American telecommunications company that provided voice, video, data, and Internet telecommunications and professional services to businesses, consumers, and government agencies. During its long history, AT'T was at times the world's largest telephone company, the world's largest cable television operator, and a regulated monopoly. Today, the company is a subsidiary of AT'T Inc.

a. ACEA agreement
b. AD-IA Model
c. ACCRA Cost of Living Index
d. AT'T Corporation

7. In economics, a _____ occurs when, due to the economies of scale of a particular industry, the maximum efficiency of production and distribution is realized through a single supplier.

Natural monopolies arise where the largest supplier in an industry, often the first supplier in a market, has an overwhelming cost advantage over other actual or potential competitors. This tends to be the case in industries where capital costs predominate, creating economies of scale which are large in relation to the size of the market, and hence high barriers to entry; examples include water services and electricity.

Chapter 11. MONOPOLY

a. Privatizing profits and socializing losses
b. Common-pool resource
c. Natural monopoly
d. Collective goods

8. In economics and especially in the theory of competition, _____ are obstacles in the path of a firm that make it difficult to enter a given market.

_____ are the source of a firm's pricing power - the ability of a firm to raise prices without losing all its customers.

The term refers to hindrances that an individual may face while trying to gain entrance into a profession or trade.

a. Group boycott
b. Social dumping
c. Limit price
d. Barriers to entry

9. The _____ consists of a number of economic theories which describe the nature of the firm, company including its existence, its behaviour, and its relationship with the market.

In simplified terms, the _____ aims to answer these questions:

1. Existence - why do firms emerge, why are not all transactions in the economy mediated over the market?
2. Boundaries - why the boundary between firms and the market is located exactly there? Which transactions are performed internally and which are negotiated on the market?
3. Organization - why are firms structured in such specific way? What is the interplay of formal and informal relationships?

Despite looking simple, these questions are not answered by the established economic theory, which usually views firms as given, and treats them as black boxes without any internal structure.

The First World War period saw a change of emphasis in economic theory away from industry-level analysis which mainly included analysing markets to analysis at the level of the firm, as it became increasingly clear that perfect competition was no longer an adequate model of how firms behaved. Economic theory till then had focussed on trying to understand markets alone and there had been little study on understanding why firms or organisations exist.

a. Khazzoom-Brookes postulate
b. Policy Ineffectiveness Proposition
c. Technology gap
d. Theory of the firm

10. _____ is the term denoting either an entrance or changes which are inserted into a system and which activate/modify a process. It is an abstract concept, used in the modeling, system(s) design and system(s) exploitation. It is usually connected with other terms, e.g., _____ field, _____ variable, _____ parameter, _____ value, _____ signal, _____ device and _____ file.

a. AD-IA Model
b. ACCRA Cost of Living Index
c. ACEA agreement
d. Input

Chapter 11. MONOPOLY

11. A _____ is a set of exclusive rights granted by a state to an inventor or his assignee for a limited period of time in exchange for a disclosure of an invention.

The procedure for granting _____s, the requirements placed on the _____ee and the extent of the exclusive rights vary widely between countries according to national laws and international agreements. Typically, however, a _____ application must include one or more claims defining the invention which must be new, inventive, and useful or industrially applicable.

    a. Bona fide occupational qualification
    b. Bank regulation
    c. Long service leave
    d. Patent

12. In economics and business decision-making, _____ are costs that cannot be recovered once they have been incurred. _____ are sometimes contrasted with variable costs, which are the costs that will change due to the proposed course of action, and prospective costs which are costs that will be incurred if an action is taken.

In traditional microeconomic theory, only variable costs are relevant to a decision.

    a. Sunk costs
    b. Halo effect
    c. Post-purchase rationalization
    d. Hyperbolic discounting

13. _____, in microeconomics, are the cost advantages that a business obtains due to expansion. They are factors that cause a producere;s average cost per unit to fall as scale is increased. _____ is a long run concept and refers to reductions in unit cost as the size of a facility, or scale, increases.

    a. Isoquant
    b. Economies of scale
    c. Economic production quantity
    d. Underinvestment employment relationship

14. _____ is a term used to collectively describe topics relating to the operations of firms with interests in multiple countries. Such firms are sometimes called multinational corporations . Well known MNCs include fast food companies McDonald's and Yum Brands, vehicle manufacturers such as General Motors and Toyota, consumer electronics companies like Samsung, LG and Sony, and energy companies such as ExxonMobil and BP.

    a. International Business
    b. ACCRA Cost of Living Index
    c. AD-IA Model
    d. ACEA agreement

15. _____ is a branch of economics that studies how individuals, households and firms and some states make decisions to allocate limited resources, typically in markets where goods or services are being bought and sold. _____ examines how these decisions and behaviours affect the supply and demand for goods and services, which determines prices; and how prices, in turn , determine the supply and demand of goods and services.

Whereas macroeconomics involves the 'sum total of economic activity, dealing with the issues of growth, inflation and unemployment, and with national economic policies relating to these issues' and the effects of government actions on them.

    a. New Keynesian economics
    b. Recession
    c. Countercyclical
    d. Microeconomics

Chapter 11. MONOPOLY

16. A public utility (usually just utility) is an organization that maintains the infrastructure for a public service (often also providing a service using that infrastructure.) _____ are subject to forms of public control and regulation ranging from local community-based groups to state-wide government monopolies. Common arguments in favor of regulation include the desire to control market power, facilitate competition, promote investment or system expansion, or stabilize markets.
   a. 100-year flood
   b. 1921 recession
   c. Public utilities
   d. 130-30 fund

17. _____ is a branch of economics that deals with the performance, structure, and behavior of a national or regional economy as a whole. Along with microeconomics, _____ is one of the two most general fields in economics. It is the study of the behavior and decision-making of entire economies.
   a. New Trade Theory
   b. Nominal value
   c. Tobit model
   d. Macroeconomics

18. Economics:

   - _____, the desire to own something and the ability to pay for it
   - _____ curve, a graphic representation of a _____ schedule
   - _____ deposit, the money in checking accounts
   - _____ pull theory, the theory that inflation occurs when _____ for goods and services exceeds existing supplies
   - _____ schedule, a table that lists the quantity of a good a person will buy it each different price
   - _____ side economics, the school of economics at believes government spending and tax cuts open economy by raising _____

   a. Production
   b. McKesson ' Robbins scandal
   c. Variability
   d. Demand

19. In economics, the _____ can be defined as the graph depicting the relationship between the price of a certain commodity, and the amount of it that consumers are willing and able to purchase at that given price. It is a graphic representation of a demand schedule. The _____ for all consumers together follows from the _____ of every individual consumer: the individual demands at each price are added together.
   a. Cost curve
   b. Demand curve
   c. Wage curve
   d. Kuznets curve

20. _____ in economics and business is the result of an exchange and from that trade we assign a numerical monetary value to a good, service or asset. If Alice trades Bob 4 apples for an orange, the _____ of an orange is 4 apples. Inversely, the _____ of an apple is 1/4 oranges.
   a. Price war
   b. Price book
   c. Premium pricing
   d. Price

21. Monopoly power is an example of market failure which occurs when one or more of the participants has the ability to influence the price or other outcomes in some general or specialized market. The most commonly discussed form of market power is that of a monopoly, but other forms such as monopsony, and more moderate versions of these two extremes, exist. Market participants that have market power are sometimes referred to as '_____', while those without are sometimes called 'price takers'.

a. Rate-of-return regulation
b. Revenue-cap regulation
c. Pacman conjecture
d. Price makers

22. _____ is a broad label that refers to any individuals or households that use goods and services generated within the economy. The concept of a _____ is used in different contexts, so that the usage and significance of the term may vary.

Typically when business people and economists talk of _____s they are talking about person as _____, an aggregated commodity item with little individuality other than that expressed in the buy/not-buy decision.

a. 130-30 fund
b. 100-year flood
c. 1921 recession
d. Consumer

23. In economics, a firm is said to reap _____s when a lack of viable market competition allows it to set its prices above the equilibrium price for a good or service without losing profits to competitors. _____ is a type of economic profit, that is, it is a profit greater than the normal profit that is typical in a perfectly competitive industry. The resulting price is known as the monopoly price.

a. Cleanup clause
b. First-price sealed-bid auction
c. Borrowing base
d. Monopoly profit

24. In neoclassical economics and microeconomics, _____ describes the perfect being a market in which there are many small firms, all producing homogeneous goods. In the short term, such markets are productively inefficient as output will not occur where mc is equal to ac, but allocatively efficient, as output under _____ will always occur where mc is equal to mr, and therefore where mc equals ar. However, in the long term, such markets are both allocatively and productively efficient.

a. General equilibrium
b. Co-operative economics
c. Perfect competition
d. Law of supply

25. _____s is the social science that studies the production, distribution, and consumption of goods and services. The term _____s comes from the Ancient Greek oá¼°κονομῖα from oá¼¶κος (oikos, 'house') + νÏŒμος (nomos, 'custom' or 'law'), hence 'rules of the house(hold)'. Current _____ models developed out of the broader field of political economy in the late 19th century, owing to a desire to use an empirical approach more akin to the physical sciences.

a. Economic
b. Inflation
c. Energy economics
d. Opportunity cost

26. In economics, _____ is the difference between a company's total revenue and its opportunity costs. It is the increase in wealth that an investor has from making an investment, taking into consideration all costs associated with that investment including the opportunity cost of capital.

Profit is the factor income of the entrepreneur.

a. Operating profit
b. ACCRA Cost of Living Index
c. Accounting profit
d. Economic profit

Chapter 11. MONOPOLY

27. In economics, the concept of the _____ refers to the decision-making time frame of a firm in which at least one factor of production is fixed. Costs which are fixed in the _____ have no impact on a firms decisions. For example a firm can raise output by increasing the amount of labour through overtime.
    a. Product Pipeline
    b. Productivity model
    c. Hicks-neutral technical change
    d. Short-run

28. _____ is used to assign the available resources in an economic way. It is part of resource management.

    In strategic planning,is a plan for using available resources, for example human resources, especially in the near term, to achieve goals for the future.

    a. Resource allocation
    b. 130-30 fund
    c. 100-year flood
    d. 1921 recession

29. _____ is an economic model based on price, utility and quantity in a market. It predicts that in a competitive market, price will function to equalize the quantity demanded by consumers, and the quantity supplied by producers, resulting in an economic equilibrium of price and quantity. The model incorporates other factors changing equilibrium as a shift of demand and/or supply.
    a. Deferred gratification
    b. Joint demand
    c. Supply and demand
    d. Rational addiction

30. In economics, _____ is the ratio of the percent change in one variable to the percent change in another variable. It is a tool for measuring the responsiveness of a function to changes in parameters in a relative way. Commonly analyzed are _____ of substitution, price and wealth.
    a. Elasticity of demand
    b. ACEA agreement
    c. ACCRA Cost of Living Index
    d. Elasticity

31. In economic models, the _____ time frame assumes no fixed factors of production. Firms can enter or leave the marketplace, and the cost (and availability) of land, labor, raw materials, and capital goods can be assumed to vary. In contrast, in the short-run time frame, certain factors are assumed to be fixed, because there is not sufficient time for them to change.
    a. Price/performance ratio
    b. Productivity world
    c. Diseconomies of scale
    d. Long-run

32. In economics, a _____ is a graph of the costs of production as a function of total quantity produced. In a free market economy, productively efficient firms use these curves to find the optimal point of production, where they make the most profits. There are a few different types of _____s, each relevant to a different area of economics.
    a. Cost curve
    b. Phillips curve
    c. Demand curve
    d. Kuznets curve

33. _____ is a pejorative term used to refer to the perceived business practice of a company providing a product or a service to only provide it to the high-value or low-cost customers of that product or service. It is considered a type of moral hazard. The term derives from the practice of extracting cream from fresh milk at a dairy, in which a device called a 'separator' draws off the cream (which is lighter, and floats) from fresh or raw milk.

a. 100-year flood
c. 1921 recession
b. 130-30 fund
d. Cream skimming

34. _____ exists when sales of identical goods or services are transacted at different prices from the same provider. In a theoretical market with perfect information, no transaction costs or prohibition on secondary exchange (or re-selling) to prevent arbitrage, _____ can only be a feature of monopoly and oligopoly markets, where market power can be exercised. Otherwise, the moment the seller tries to sell the same good at different prices, the buyer at the lower price can arbitrage by selling to the consumer buying at the higher price but with a tiny discount.
a. Transfer pricing
c. Price discrimination
b. Lerner Index
d. Loss leader

Chapter 11. MONOPOLY

35. A _____ is:

- Rewrite _____, in generative grammar and computer science
- Standardization, a formal and widely-accepted statement, fact, definition, or qualification
- Operation, a determinate _____ for performing a mathematical operation and obtaining a certain result (Mathematics, Logic)
    - Unary operation
    - Binary operation
- _____ of inference, a function from sets of formulae to formulae (Mathematics, Logic)
- _____ of thumb, principle with broad application that is not intended to be strictly accurate or reliable for every situation. Also often simply referred to as a _____
- Moral, an atomic element of a moral code for guiding choices in human behavior
- Heuristic, a quantized '_____' which shows a tendency or probability for successful function
- A regulation, as in sports
- A Production _____, as in computer science
- Procedural law, a _____ set governing the application of laws to cases
    - A law, which may informally be called a '_____'
    - A court ruling, a decision by a court
- In the U.S. Government, a regulation mandated by Congress, but written or expanded upon by the Executive Branch.
- Norm (sociology), an informal but widely accepted _____, concept, truth, definition, or qualification (social norms, legal norms, coding norms)
- Norm (philosophy), a kind of sentence or a reason to act, feel or believe
- 'Rulership' is the concept of governance by a government:
    - Military _____, governance by a military body
    - Monastic _____, a collection of precepts that guides the life of monks or nuns in a religious order where the superior holds the place of Christ
- Slide _____

- '_____,' a song by Ayumi Hamasaki
- '_____,' a song by rapper Nas
- '_____s,' an album by the band The Whitest Boy Alive
- _____s: Pyaar Ka Superhit Formula, a 2003 Bollywood film
- ruler, an instrument for measuring lengths
- _____, a component of an astrolabe, circumferator or similar instrument
- The _____s, a bestselling self-help book
- _____ Project (Run Up-to-date Linux Everywhere), a project that aims to use up-to-date Linux software on old PCs
- _____ engine, a software system that helps managing business _____s
- Ja _____, a hip hop artist
    - R.U.L.E., a 2005 greatest hits album by rapper Ja _____
- '_____s,' a KMFDM song

a. Demand
c. Procter ' Gamble
b. Rule
d. Technocracy

Chapter 12. BETWEEN COMPETITION AND MONOPOLY

1. _____ is a socioeconomic structure and political ideology that promotes the establishment of an egalitarian, classless, stateless society based on common ownership and control of the means of production and property in general. In political science, the term '_____' is sometimes used to refer to communist states, a form of government in which the state operates under a one-party system and declares allegiance to Marxism-Leninism or a derivative thereof, even if the party does not actually claim that it has already reached _____.

Forerunners of communist ideas existed in antiquity and particularly in the 18th and early 19th century France, with thinkers such as Jean-Jacques Rousseau and the more radical Gracchus Babeuf.

   a. Communism
   b. Social fascism
   c. Democratic centralism
   d. New Communist Movement

2. _____ is a common market structure where many competing producers sell products that are differentiated from one another (ie. the products are substitutes, but are not exactly alike.) Many markets are monopolistically competitive, common examples include the markets for restaurants, cereal, clothing, shoes and service industries in large cities.
   a. Monopolistic competition
   b. Perfect competition
   c. Financial crisis
   d. Mathematical economics

3. An _____ is a market form in which a market or industry is dominated by a small number of sellers (oligopolists.) Because there are few participants in this type of market, each oligopolist is aware of the actions of the others. The decisions of one firm influence, and are influenced by, the decisions of other firms.
   a. ACCRA Cost of Living Index
   b. Oligopsony
   c. Oligopoly
   d. ACEA agreement

4. _____ in economics and business is the result of an exchange and from that trade we assign a numerical monetary value to a good, service or asset. If Alice trades Bob 4 apples for an orange, the _____ of an orange is 4 apples. Inversely, the _____ of an apple is 1/4 oranges.
   a. Price book
   b. Premium pricing
   c. Price
   d. Price war

5. Procter is a surname, and may also refer to:

   - Bryan Waller Procter (pseud. Barry Cornwall), English poet
   - Goodwin Procter, American law firm
   - _____, consumer products multinational

   a. Bucket shop
   b. Tightness
   c. Drawdown
   d. Procter ' Gamble

Chapter 12. BETWEEN COMPETITION AND MONOPOLY

6. _____ has several particular meanings:

    - in mathematics
        - _____ function
        - Euler _____
        - _____
        - _____ subgroup
        - method of _____s (partial differential equations)
    - in physics and engineering
        - any _____ curve that shows the relationship between certain input- and output parameters, e.g.
        - an I-V or current-voltage _____ is the current in a circuit as a function of the applied voltage
        - Receiver-Operator _____
    - in fiction
        - in Dungeons ' Dragons, _____ is another name for ability score

    a. Demand
    b. Technocracy
    c. Russian financial crisis
    d. Characteristic

7. The Demand side is a term used in economics to refer to a number of things:

    - The demand element of a supply and demand partial equilibrium diagram, in microeconomics
    - The aggregate demand in an economy, in macroeconomics
    - Economic policy actions which are designed to affect aggregate demand.
    - _____ learning referring to the incentive to learn how to use and modify free software as opposed to buying conventional software.

    The term is also used broadly to distinguish supply-side economics from other schools, for instance Keynesian economics.

    a. Delayed differentiation
    b. CPFR
    c. Demand-side
    d. Reverse auction

8. _____ is used to assign the available resources in an economic way. It is part of resource management.

    In strategic planning,is a plan for using available resources, for example human resources, especially in the near term, to achieve goals for the future.

    a. 130-30 fund
    b. 100-year flood
    c. 1921 recession
    d. Resource allocation

9. In economics, _____ is the total supply of goods and services produced by a national economy during a specific time period. It is the total amount of goods and services in the economy available at all possible price levels.

    a. Aggregate supply
    b. Aggregate expenditure
    c. Aggregate demand
    d. Aggregation problem

Chapter 12. BETWEEN COMPETITION AND MONOPOLY

10. Economics:

- _____, the desire to own something and the ability to pay for it
- _____ curve, a graphic representation of a _____ schedule
- _____ deposit, the money in checking accounts
- _____ pull theory, the theory that inflation occurs when _____ for goods and services exceeds existing supplies
- _____ schedule, a table that lists the quantity of a good a person will buy it each different price
- _____ side economics, the school of economics at believes government spending and tax cuts open economy by raising _____

a. Variability
b. Demand
c. McKesson ' Robbins scandal
d. Production

11. In economic models, the _____ time frame assumes no fixed factors of production. Firms can enter or leave the marketplace, and the cost (and availability) of land, labor, raw materials, and capital goods can be assumed to vary. In contrast, in the short-run time frame, certain factors are assumed to be fixed, because there is not sufficient time for them to change.

a. Price/performance ratio
b. Productivity world
c. Diseconomies of scale
d. Long-run

12. _____ is an economic model based on price, utility and quantity in a market. It predicts that in a competitive market, price will function to equalize the quantity demanded by consumers, and the quantity supplied by producers, resulting in an economic equilibrium of price and quantity. The model incorporates other factors changing equilibrium as a shift of demand and/or supply.

a. Rational addiction
b. Deferred gratification
c. Joint demand
d. Supply and demand

13. As of 2007, modern day behaviorism, known as '_____,' is a thriving field. The Association for _____: International currently has 32 state and regional chapters within the United States. Approximately 30 additional chapters have also developed throughout Europe, Asia, South America, and Australia.

a. 100-year flood
b. Behavior analysis
c. 1921 recession
d. 130-30 fund

14. In marketing, _____ is the process of distinguishing the differences of a product or offering from others, to make it more attractive to a particular target market. This involves differentiating it from competitors' products as well as one's own product offerings.

Differentiation is a source of competitive advantage.

a. Technology acceptance model
b. Pricing science
c. Market segment
d. Product differentiation

Chapter 12. BETWEEN COMPETITION AND MONOPOLY

15. A _____ is a counterfeit agreement among industries. It is an informal organization of producers that agree to coordinate prices and production. _____s usually occur in an oligopolistic industry, where there is a small number of sellers and usually involve homogeneous products.
   a. Shill
   b. Shanzhai
   c. 100-year flood
   d. Cartel

16. The Organization of the Petroleum Exporting Countries is a cartel of twelve countries made up of Algeria, Angola, Ecuador, Iran, Iraq, Kuwait, Libya, Nigeria, Qatar, Saudi Arabia, the United Arab Emirates, and Venezuela. The cartel has maintained its headquarters in Vienna since 1965, and hosts regular meetings among the oil ministers of its Member Countries. Indonesia withdrew its membership in _____ in 2008 after it became a net importer of oil, but stated it would likely return if it became a net exporter in the world.
   a. ACCRA Cost of Living Index
   b. AD-IA Model
   c. OPEC
   d. ACEA agreement

17. _____ refers to the state of not requiring any outside aid, support for survival; it is therefore a type of personal or collective autonomy. On a large scale, a totally self-sufficient economy that does not trade with the outside world is called an autarky.

The term _____ is usually applied to varieties of sustainable living in which nothing is consumed outside of what is produced by the self-sufficient individuals.

   a. Sustainable forest management
   b. Sustainability science
   c. Global Reporting Initiative
   d. Self-sufficiency

18. _____ is an agreement, usually secretive, which occurs between two or more persons to deceive, mislead or to obtain an objective forbidden by law typically involving fraud or gaining an unfair advantage. It is an agreement among firms to divide the market, set prices kickbacks, or misrepresenting the independence of the relationship between the colluding parties.' All acts effected by _____ are considered void.
   a. Collusion
   b. Dividing territories
   c. Bid rigging
   d. Net Book Agreement

19. _____ occurs when cartels are illegal or overt collusion is absent. Put another way, two firms agree to play a certain strategy without explicitly saying so. This is also known as price leadership, as firms may stay within the law but still tacitly collude by monitoring each other's prices and keeping them the same.
   a. Poverty penalty
   b. Product innovation
   c. Staple port
   d. Tacit collusion

Chapter 12. BETWEEN COMPETITION AND MONOPOLY

20. Competition law, known in the United States as _____ law, has three main elements:

- prohibiting agreements or practices that restrict free trading and competition between business entities. This includes in particular the repression of cartels.
- banning abusive behaviour by a firm dominating a market, or anti-competitive practices that tend to lead to such a dominant position. Practices controlled in this way may include predatory pricing, tying, price gouging, refusal to deal, and many others.
- supervising the mergers and acquisitions of large corporations, including some joint ventures. Transactions that are considered to threaten the competitive process can be prohibited altogether, or approved subject to 'remedies' such as an obligation to divest part of the merged business or to offer licences or access to facilities to enable other businesses to continue competing.

The substance and practice of competition law varies from jurisdiction to jurisdiction. Protecting the interests of consumers (consumer welfare) and ensuring that entrepreneurs have an opportunity to compete in the market economy are often treated as important objectives. Competition law is closely connected with law on deregulation of access to markets, state aids and subsidies, the privatisation of state owned assets and the establishment of independent sector regulators. In recent decades, competition law has been viewed as a way to provide better public services.

a. Antitrust
b. Intellectual property law
c. Anti-Inflation Act
d. United Kingdom competition law

21. _____, known in the United States as antitrust law, has three main elements:

- prohibiting agreements or practices that restrict free trading and competition between business entities. This includes in particular the repression of cartels.
- banning abusive behaviour by a firm dominating a market, or anti-competitive practices that tend to lead to such a dominant position. Practices controlled in this way may include predatory pricing, tying, price gouging, refusal to deal, and many others.
- supervising the mergers and acquisitions of large corporations, including some joint ventures. Transactions that are considered to threaten the competitive process can be prohibited altogether, or approved subject to 'remedies' such as an obligation to divest part of the merged business or to offer licences or access to facilities to enable other businesses to continue competing.

The substance and practice of _____ varies from jurisdiction to jurisdiction. Protecting the interests of consumers (consumer welfare) and ensuring that entrepreneurs have an opportunity to compete in the market economy are often treated as important objectives. _____ is closely connected with law on deregulation of access to markets, state aids and subsidies, the privatisation of state owned assets and the establishment of independent sector regulators. In recent decades, _____ has been viewed as a way to provide better public services.

a. Hostile work environment
b. Due diligence
c. Fee simple
d. Competition law

Chapter 12. BETWEEN COMPETITION AND MONOPOLY

22. The _____ Corporation (1857-2003), based in Bethlehem, Pennsylvania, was once the second-largest steel producer in the United States, after Pittsburgh, Pennsylvania-based U.S. Steel. After a decline in the U.S. steel industry and management problems leading to the company's 2001 bankruptcy, the company was dissolved and the remaining assets sold to International Steel Group in 2003. In 2005, ISG merged with Mittal Steel, ending U.S. ownership of the assets of _____.
   - a. 130-30 fund
   - b. Bethlehem Steel
   - c. 1921 recession
   - d. 100-year flood

23. A _____ is a place of residence or refuge and comfort. It is usually a place in which an individual or a family can rest and be able to store personal property. Most modern-day households contain sanitary facilities and a means of preparing food.
   - a. 130-30 fund
   - b. 100-year flood
   - c. Home
   - d. 1921 recession

24. In economics, a _____ exists when a specific individual or enterprise has sufficient control over a particular product or service to determine significantly the terms on which other individuals shall have access to it. Monopolies are thus characterized by a lack of economic competition for the good or service that they provide and a lack of viable substitute goods. The verb 'monopolize' refers to the process by which a firm gains persistently greater market share than what is expected under perfect competition.
   - a. Monopoly
   - b. 1921 recession
   - c. 100-year flood
   - d. 130-30 fund

25. _____ is an agreement between business competitors to sell the same product or service at the same price. In general, it is an agreement intended to ultimately push the price of a product as high as possible, leading to profits for all the sellers. Price-fixing can also involve any agreement to fix, peg, discount or stabilize prices.
   - a. Moral victory
   - b. Price fixing
   - c. Non-price competition
   - d. Cut-throat competition

26. _____ is a term used in business to indicate a state of intense competitive rivalry accompanied by a multi-lateral series of price reduction. One competitor will lower its price, then others will lower their prices to match. If one of them reduces their price again, a new round of reductions starts.
   - a. Big ticket item
   - b. Discounts and allowances
   - c. Transactional Net Margin Method
   - d. Price war

27. In game theory, _____ is a solution concept of a game involving two or more players, in which each player is assumed to know the equilibrium strategies of the other players, and no player has anything to gain by changing only his or her own strategy unilaterally. If each player has chosen a strategy and no player can benefit by changing his or her strategy while the other players keep theirs unchanged, then the current set of strategy choices and the corresponding payoffs constitute a _____.

   Stated simply, Amy and Bill are in _____ if Amy is making the best decision she can, taking into account Bill's decision, and Bill is making the best decision he can, taking into account Amy's decision.

   - a. Lump of labour
   - b. Nash equilibrium
   - c. Linear production game
   - d. Proper equilibrium

Chapter 12. BETWEEN COMPETITION AND MONOPOLY

28. In economics, the _____ can be defined as the graph depicting the relationship between the price of a certain commodity, and the amount of it that consumers are willing and able to purchase at that given price. It is a graphic representation of a demand schedule. The _____ for all consumers together follows from the _____ of every individual consumer: the individual demands at each price are added together.
    a. Demand curve
    b. Wage curve
    c. Kuznets curve
    d. Cost curve

29. The _____ curve theory is an economic theory regarding oligopoly and monopolistic competition. When it was created, the idea fundamentally challenged classical economic tenets such as efficient markets and rapidly-changing prices, ideas that underly basic supply and demand models. _____ was an initial attempt to explain sticky prices.
    a. Marginal demand
    b. Precautionary demand
    c. Kinked demand curve
    d. Kinked demand

30. The _____ theory is an economic theory regarding oligopoly and monopolistic competition. When it was created, the idea fundamentally challenged classical economic tenets such as efficient markets and rapidly-changing prices, ideas that underly basic supply and demand models. Kinked demand was an initial attempt to explain sticky prices.
    a. Kinked demand curve
    b. Precautionary demand
    c. Kinked demand
    d. Hicksian demand function

31. _____ is a broad label that refers to any individuals or households that use goods and services generated within the economy. The concept of a _____ is used in different contexts, so that the usage and significance of the term may vary.

    Typically when business people and economists talk of _____s they are talking about person as _____, an aggregated commodity item with little individuality other than that expressed in the buy/not-buy decision.

    a. 100-year flood
    b. 130-30 fund
    c. 1921 recession
    d. Consumer

32. A true _____ is a specific type of oligopoly where only two producers exist in one market. In reality, this definition is generally used where only two firms have dominant control over a market. In the field of industrial organization, it is the most commonly studied form of oligopoly due to its simplicity.
    a. Megacorpstate
    b. 100-year flood
    c. 130-30 fund
    d. Duopoly

33. In finance, the _____s between two currencies specifies how much one currency is worth in terms of the other. It is the value of a foreign natione;s currency in terms of the home natione;s currency. For example an _____ of 102 Japanese yen to the United States dollar means that JPY 102 is worth the same as USD 1.
    a. ACCRA Cost of Living Index
    b. Exchange rate
    c. ACEA agreement
    d. Interbank market

34. _____ is a branch of applied mathematics that is used in the social sciences (most notably economics), biology, engineering, political science, international relations, computer science, and philosophy. _____ attempts to mathematically capture behavior in strategic situations, in which an individual's success in making choices depends on the choices of others. While initially developed to analyze competitions in which one individual does better at another's expense (zero sum games), it has been expanded to treat a wide class of interactions, which are classified according to several criteria.

   a. Game theory
   b. Proper equilibrium
   c. Dollar auction
   d. Discriminatory price auction

35. The concept was first developed in game theory and consequently zero-sum situations are often called _____s though this does not imply that the concept applies only to what are commonly referred to as games.

For 2-player finite _____s, the different game theoretic Solution concepts of Nash equilibrium, minimax, and maximin all give the same solution. In the solution, players play a mixed strategy.

   a. Zero-sum game
   b. Gordon growth model
   c. General purpose technologies
   d. Cash or share options

36. In game theory, a _____ is an extensive form game which consists in some number of repetitions of some base game (called a stage game.) The stage game is usually one of the well-studied 2-person games. It captures the idea that a player will have to take into account the impact of his current action on the future actions of other players; this is sometimes called his reputation.

   a. Quasi-perfect equilibrium
   b. Correlated equilibrium
   c. Pursuit-evasion
   d. Repeated game

37. A non-_____ is a term used in game theory economics to describe a threat by a player known to be rational in a sequential game that he would not carry out as it would not be in his best interest to do so. In game theoretical analysis the threat does not need to be a literally outspoken.

A simple example could be given by a person A walking up to another person B with a bomb.

   a. Debt to Assets
   b. Commodity fetishism
   c. Black-Scholes
   d. Credible threat

38.

The _____ is an independent agency of the United States government, created, directed, and empowered by Congressional statute , and with the majority of its commissioners appointed by the current President. The _____ works towards six strategic goals in the areas of broadband, competition, the spectrum, the media, public safety and homeland security, and modernizing the _____.

   a. 100-year flood
   b. 130-30 fund
   c. 1921 recession
   d. Federal Communications Commission

Chapter 12. BETWEEN COMPETITION AND MONOPOLY

39. _____ was a survey conducted by the U.S. Department of Justice to gauge the prevalence of alcohol and illegal drug use among prior arrestees. It was a reformulation of the prior Drug Use Forecasting (DUF) program, focused on five drugs in particular: cocaine, marijuana, methamphetamine, opiates, and PCP.

Participants were randomly selected from arrest records in major metropolitan areas; because no personally identifying information is taken from each record chosen, the resulting data can be correlated to arrest rates, but not to the total population of persons charged.

   a. ACEA agreement
   b. AD-IA Model
   c. ACCRA Cost of Living Index
   d. Arrestee Drug Abuse Monitoring

40. In economics, the _____ is the term economists use to describe the self-regulating nature of the marketplace. The _____ is a metaphor coined by the economist Adam Smith in The Wealth of Nations.

Adam Smith mentions the metaphor in Book IV of The Wealth of Nations, arguing that people in any society will certainly employ their capital in foreign trading only if the profits available by that method far exceed those available locally, and that in such a case it is better for society as a whole if they so did.

   a. ACCRA Cost of Living Index
   b. AD-IA Model
   c. Invisible hand
   d. ACEA agreement

41. A _____ refers to any program which seeks to provide a minimum level of income, service or other support for many marginalized groups such as the poor, elderly, and disabled people. Social welfare programs are undertaken by governments as well as non-governmental organizations (NGOs.) Social welfare payments and services are typically provided at the expense of taxpayers generally, funded by benefactors, or by compulsory enrollment of the poor themselves.
   a. 130-30 fund
   b. 1921 recession
   c. 100-year flood
   d. Social welfare provision

42. _____ was a Scottish moral philosopher and a pioneer of political economy. One of the key figures of the Scottish Enlightenment, Smith is the author of The Theory of Moral Sentiments and An Inquiry into the Nature and Causes of the Wealth of Nations. The latter, usually abbreviated as The Wealth of Nations, is considered his magnum opus and the first modern work of economics.
   a. Alan Greenspan
   b. Adolf Hitler
   c. Adolph Fischer
   d. Adam Smith

43. In neoclassical economics and microeconomics, _____ describes the perfect being a market in which there are many small firms, all producing homogeneous goods. In the short term, such markets are productively inefficient as output will not occur where mc is equal to ac, but allocatively efficient, as output under _____ will always occur where mc is equal to mr, and therefore where mc equals ar. However, in the long term, such markets are both allocatively and productively efficient.
   a. Law of supply
   b. General equilibrium
   c. Co-operative economics
   d. Perfect competition

Chapter 13. LIMITING MARKET POWER: REGULATION AND ANTITRUST

1. _____ was a survey conducted by the U.S. Department of Justice to gauge the prevalence of alcohol and illegal drug use among prior arrestees. It was a reformulation of the prior Drug Use Forecasting (DUF) program, focused on five drugs in particular: cocaine, marijuana, methamphetamine, opiates, and PCP.

Participants were randomly selected from arrest records in major metropolitan areas; because no personally identifying information is taken from each record chosen, the resulting data can be correlated to arrest rates, but not to the total population of persons charged.

   a. Arrestee Drug Abuse Monitoring
   b. AD-IA Model
   c. ACCRA Cost of Living Index
   d. ACEA agreement

2. _____ was a Scottish moral philosopher and a pioneer of political economy. One of the key figures of the Scottish Enlightenment, Smith is the author of The Theory of Moral Sentiments and An Inquiry into the Nature and Causes of the Wealth of Nations. The latter, usually abbreviated as The Wealth of Nations, is considered his magnum opus and the first modern work of economics.
   a. Adam Smith
   b. Adolph Fischer
   c. Adolf Hitler
   d. Alan Greenspan

3. Competition law, known in the United States as _____ law, has three main elements:

   - prohibiting agreements or practices that restrict free trading and competition between business entities. This includes in particular the repression of cartels.
   - banning abusive behaviour by a firm dominating a market, or anti-competitive practices that tend to lead to such a dominant position. Practices controlled in this way may include predatory pricing, tying, price gouging, refusal to deal, and many others.
   - supervising the mergers and acquisitions of large corporations, including some joint ventures. Transactions that are considered to threaten the competitive process can be prohibited altogether, or approved subject to 'remedies' such as an obligation to divest part of the merged business or to offer licences or access to facilities to enable other businesses to continue competing.

The substance and practice of competition law varies from jurisdiction to jurisdiction. Protecting the interests of consumers (consumer welfare) and ensuring that entrepreneurs have an opportunity to compete in the market economy are often treated as important objectives. Competition law is closely connected with law on deregulation of access to markets, state aids and subsidies, the privatisation of state owned assets and the establishment of independent sector regulators. In recent decades, competition law has been viewed as a way to provide better public services.

   a. Intellectual property law
   b. Anti-Inflation Act
   c. United Kingdom competition law
   d. Antitrust

Chapter 13. LIMITING MARKET POWER: REGULATION AND ANTITRUST

4. _____, known in the United States as antitrust law, has three main elements:

- prohibiting agreements or practices that restrict free trading and competition between business entities. This includes in particular the repression of cartels.
- banning abusive behaviour by a firm dominating a market, or anti-competitive practices that tend to lead to such a dominant position. Practices controlled in this way may include predatory pricing, tying, price gouging, refusal to deal, and many others.
- supervising the mergers and acquisitions of large corporations, including some joint ventures. Transactions that are considered to threaten the competitive process can be prohibited altogether, or approved subject to 'remedies' such as an obligation to divest part of the merged business or to offer licences or access to facilities to enable other businesses to continue competing.

The substance and practice of _____ varies from jurisdiction to jurisdiction. Protecting the interests of consumers (consumer welfare) and ensuring that entrepreneurs have an opportunity to compete in the market economy are often treated as important objectives. _____ is closely connected with law on deregulation of access to markets, state aids and subsidies, the privatisation of state owned assets and the establishment of independent sector regulators. In recent decades, _____ has been viewed as a way to provide better public services.

a. Hostile work environment
b. Competition law
c. Fee simple
d. Due diligence

5. _____, in microeconomics, are the cost advantages that a business obtains due to expansion. They are factors that cause a producere;s average cost per unit to fall as scale is increased. _____ is a long run concept and refers to reductions in unit cost as the size of a facility, or scale, increases.

a. Economic production quantity
b. Underinvestment employment relationship
c. Isoquant
d. Economies of scale

6. In economics, a _____ exists when a specific individual or enterprise has sufficient control over a particular product or service to determine significantly the terms on which other individuals shall have access to it. Monopolies are thus characterized by a lack of economic competition for the good or service that they provide and a lack of viable substitute goods. The verb 'monopolize' refers to the process by which a firm gains persistently greater market share than what is expected under perfect competition.

a. 100-year flood
b. 1921 recession
c. 130-30 fund
d. Monopoly

7. In economics, _____ refers to excess of supply over demand of products being offered to the market. This leads to lower prices and/or unsold goods.

_____ is the accumulation of unsalable inventories in the hands of businesses.

a. Intra Regional Trade
b. Incomplete markets
c. Inflation adjustment
d. Overproduction

Chapter 13. LIMITING MARKET POWER: REGULATION AND ANTITRUST

8. _____ in economics and business is the result of an exchange and from that trade we assign a numerical monetary value to a good, service or asset. If Alice trades Bob 4 apples for an orange, the _____ of an orange is 4 apples. Inversely, the _____ of an apple is 1/4 oranges.
   a. Premium pricing
   c. Price book
   b. Price
   d. Price war

9. In microeconomics, _____ is quite simply the conversion of inputs into outputs. It is an economic process that uses resources to create a good or service that is suitable for exchange. This can include manufacturing, storing, shipping, and packaging.
   a. Solved
   c. Production
   b. MET
   d. Red Guards

10. A _____ refers to any program which seeks to provide a minimum level of income, service or other support for many marginalized groups such as the poor, elderly, and disabled people. Social welfare programs are undertaken by governments as well as non-governmental organizations (NGOs.) Social welfare payments and services are typically provided at the expense of taxpayers generally, funded by benefactors, or by compulsory enrollment of the poor themselves.
    a. 1921 recession
    c. 100-year flood
    b. 130-30 fund
    d. Social welfare provision

11. _____ is used to assign the available resources in an economic way. It is part of resource management.

In strategic planning,is a plan for using available resources, for example human resources, especially in the near term, to achieve goals for the future.

   a. 100-year flood
   c. 1921 recession
   b. 130-30 fund
   d. Resource allocation

12. The _____ is an independent agency of the United States government, established in 1914 by the _____ Act. Its principal mission is the promotion of 'consumer protection' and the elimination and prevention of what regulators perceive to be harmfully 'anti-competitive' business practices, such as coercive monopoly.

The _____ Act was one of President Wilson's major acts against trusts.

   a. 130-30 fund
   c. 100-year flood
   b. Federal Trade Commission
   d. 1921 recession

13. The _____ of 1914 (15 U.S.C §§ 41-58, as amended) established the Federal Trade Commission (FTC), a bipartisan body of five members appointed by the President of the United States for seven year terms. This Commission was authorized to issue Cease and Desist orders to large corporations to curb unfair trade practices. This Act also gave more flexibility to the US congress for judicial matters.
    a. Federal Trade Commission Act
    c. Minimum wage law
    b. Competition law theory
    d. Buydown

14. The _____ of 1936 (or Anti-Price Discrimination Act, 15 U.S.C. § 13) is a United States federal law that prohibits what were considered, at the time of passage, to be anticompetitive practices by producers, specifically price discrimination. It grew out of practices in which chain stores were allowed to purchase goods at lower prices than other retailers.

Chapter 13. LIMITING MARKET POWER: REGULATION AND ANTITRUST

a. Contract theory
c. Flextime
b. Robinson-Patman Act
d. Feoffee

15. _____, originally the American Telephone ' Telegraph Company, is an American telecommunications company that provided voice, video, data, and Internet telecommunications and professional services to businesses, consumers, and government agencies. During its long history, AT'T was at times the world's largest telephone company, the world's largest cable television operator, and a regulated monopoly. Today, the company is a subsidiary of AT'T Inc.
a. ACEA agreement
c. ACCRA Cost of Living Index
b. AD-IA Model
d. AT'T Corporation

16. In economics, the _____ of an industry is used as an indicator of the relative size of firms in relation to the industry as a whole. It is calculated as the sum of the percent market share of the top n industries. This may also assist in determining the market structure of the industry.
a. Quasi-rent
c. Monopolization
b. Pacman conjecture
d. Concentration ratio

17. _____ is a fee paid on borrowed assets. It is the price paid for the use of borrowed money , or, money earned by deposited funds . Assets that are sometimes lent with _____ include money, shares, consumer goods through hire purchase, major assets such as aircraft, and even entire factories in finance lease arrangements.
a. Insolvency
c. Asset protection
b. Internal debt
d. Interest

18. An _____ is the price a borrower pays for the use of money they do not own, for instance a small company might borrow from a bank to kick start their business, and the return a lender receives for deferring the use of funds, by lending it to the borrower. _____s are normally expressed as a percentage rate over the period of one year.

_____s targets are also a vital tool of monetary policy and are used to control variables like investment, inflation, and unemployment.

a. Interest rate
c. Enterprise value
b. Arrow-Debreu model
d. ACCRA Cost of Living Index

19. _____ is a term used to collectively describe topics relating to the operations of firms with interests in multiple countries. Such firms are sometimes called multinational corporations . Well known MNCs include fast food companies McDonald's and Yum Brands, vehicle manufacturers such as General Motors and Toyota, consumer electronics companies like Samsung, LG and Sony, and energy companies such as ExxonMobil and BP.
a. ACEA agreement
c. AD-IA Model
b. ACCRA Cost of Living Index
d. International Business

20. In economics, _____ is the ability of a firm to alter the market price of a good or service. A firm with _____ can raise prices without losing all customers to competitors.

When a firm has _____ it faces a downward-sloping demand curve.

Chapter 13. LIMITING MARKET POWER: REGULATION AND ANTITRUST

a. Pacman conjecture
b. Revenue-cap regulation
c. Price makers
d. Market power

21. _____ is a branch of economics that studies how individuals, households and firms and some states make decisions to allocate limited resources, typically in markets where goods or services are being bought and sold. _____ examines how these decisions and behaviours affect the supply and demand for goods and services, which determines prices; and how prices, in turn, determine the supply and demand of goods and services.

Whereas macroeconomics involves the 'sum total of economic activity, dealing with the issues of growth, inflation and unemployment, and with national economic policies relating to these issues' and the effects of government actions on them.

a. Microeconomics
b. New Keynesian economics
c. Countercyclical
d. Recession

22. _____ was a predominant American integrated oil producing, transporting, refining, and marketing company. Established in 1870 as an Ohio Corporation, it was the largest oil refiner in the world and operated as a major company trust and was one of the world's first and largest multinational corporations until it was broken up by the United States Supreme Court in 1911. John D. Rockefeller was a founder, chairman and major shareholder, and the company made him a billionaire and eventually the richest man in history.

a. 1921 recession
b. 130-30 fund
c. 100-year flood
d. Standard Oil

23. _____ is a branch of economics that deals with the performance, structure, and behavior of a national or regional economy as a whole. Along with microeconomics, _____ is one of the two most general fields in economics. It is the study of the behavior and decision-making of entire economies.

a. Macroeconomics
b. New Trade Theory
c. Tobit model
d. Nominal value

24. A _____ is an expression that compares quantities relative to each other. The most common examples involve two quantities, but any number of quantities can be compared. _____s are represented mathematically by separating each quantity with a colon, for example the _____ 2:3, which is read as the _____ 'two to three'.

a. 100-year flood
b. 130-30 fund
c. Y-intercept
d. Ratio

25. To _____ is to impose a financial charge or other levy upon a taxpayer by a state or the functional equivalent of a state.

_____es are also imposed by many subnational entities. _____es consist of direct _____ or indirect _____, and may be paid in money or as its labour equivalent (often but not always unpaid.)

a. 100-year flood
b. 130-30 fund
c. 1921 recession
d. Tax

26. The term _____ refers to an offense under Section 2 of the American Sherman Antitrust Act, passed in 1890. Section 2 states that any person 'who shall monopolize .

Chapter 13. LIMITING MARKET POWER: REGULATION AND ANTITRUST

a. Bilateral monopoly
b. Quasi-rent
c. Monopolization
d. Complementary monopoly

27. The term _____ refers to economy-wide fluctuations in production or economic activity over several months or years. These fluctuations occur around a long-term growth trend, and typically involve shifts over time between periods of relatively rapid economic growth (expansion or boom), and periods of relative stagnation or decline (contraction or recession.)

These fluctuations are often measured using the growth rate of real gross domestic product.

a. Tobit model
b. Consumer theory
c. Business cycle
d. Nominal value

28. _____ is the practice of selling a product or service at a very low price, intending to drive competitors out of the market, or create barriers to entry for potential new competitors. If competitors or potential competitors cannot sustain equal or lower prices without losing money, they go out of business or choose not to enter the business. The predatory merchant then has fewer competitors or is even a de facto monopoly, and can then raise prices above what the market would otherwise bear.

a. Group boycott
b. Restraint of trade
c. Third line forcing
d. Predatory pricing

29. _____ is one of the four Ps of the marketing mix. The other three aspects are product, promotion, and place. It is also a key variable in microeconomic price allocation theory.

a. Pricing
b. Premium pricing
c. Guaranteed Maximum Price
d. Point of total assumption

30. _____ are conceptually similar to economies of scale. Whereas economies of scale primarily refer to efficiencies associated with supply-side changes, such as increasing or decreasing the scale of production, of a single product type, _____ refer to efficiencies primarily associated with demand-side changes, such as increasing or decreasing the scope of marketing and distribution, of different types of products. _____ are one of the main reasons for such marketing strategies as product bundling, product lining, and family branding.

a. Economies of scale
b. Isoquant
c. Economies of scope
d. Economic production quantity

31. _____ is a pejorative term used to refer to the perceived business practice of a company providing a product or a service to only provide it to the high-value or low-cost customers of that product or service. It is considered a type of moral hazard. The term derives from the practice of extracting cream from fresh milk at a dairy, in which a device called a 'separator' draws off the cream (which is lighter, and floats) from fresh or raw milk.

a. 100-year flood
b. 1921 recession
c. 130-30 fund
d. Cream skimming

Chapter 13. LIMITING MARKET POWER: REGULATION AND ANTITRUST

32. _____ is an economic, legal and business term used mostly in regulated industries. Originating in the telecommunications sector of the United States, _____ refers to the practice of providing a baseline level of services to every resident of a country. An example is found in the _____ Telecommunications Act of 1996, whose goals are:

- to promote the availability of quality services at just, reasonable, and affordable rates
- to increase access to advanced telecommunications services throughout the Nation
- to advance the availability of such services to all consumers, including those in low income, rural, insular, and high cost areas at rates that are reasonably comparable to those charged in urban areas

It was widely adopted in legislation in Europe beginning in the 1980s and 1990s. For instance, under the EU Postal Services Directive (97/67/EC), the Electricity Market Directive (2003/54/EC) and the Telecommunications Directive (2002/22/EC.)

a. AD-IA Model
b. ACEA agreement
c. ACCRA Cost of Living Index
d. Universal service

33. In economics, _____ is equal to total cost divided by the number of goods produced (the output quantity, Q.) It is also equal to the sum of average variable costs (total variable costs divided by Q) plus average fixed costs (total fixed costs divided by Q.) _____s may be dependent on the time period considered (increasing production may be expensive or impossible in the short term, for example.)

a. Average fixed cost
b. Average variable cost
c. Average cost
d. Explicit cost

34. In economics and finance, _____ is the change in total cost that arises when the quantity produced changes by one unit. It is the cost of producing one more unit of a good. Mathematically, the _____ function is expressed as the first derivative of the total cost (TC) function with respect to quantity (Q.)

a. Variable cost
b. Khozraschyot
c. Quality costs
d. Marginal cost

35. _____ is one of the ways government regulate a monopoly market. Monopolists tend to produce less than the optimal quantity pushing the prices up. Government may use _____ as a tool to regulate prices monopolists may charge.

a. AD-IA Model
b. ACEA agreement
c. ACCRA Cost of Living Index
d. Average cost pricing

36. In economics and sociology, an _____ is any factor (financial or non-financial) that enables or motivates a particular course of action, or counts as a reason for preferring one choice to the alternatives. It is an expectation that encourages people to behave in a certain way. Since human beings are purposeful creatures, the study of _____ structures is central to the study of all economic activity (both in terms of individual decision-making and in terms of co-operation and competition within a larger institutional structure.)

a. Epstein-Zin preferences
b. Isocost
c. Incentive
d. Economic reform

37. In finance, a _____ is a debt security, in which the authorized issuer owes the holders a debt and, depending on the terms of the _____, is obliged to pay interest (the coupon) and/or to repay the principal at a later date, termed maturity. A _____ is a formal contract to repay borrowed money with interest at fixed intervals.

Thus a _____ is like a loan: the issuer is the borrower (debtor), the holder is the lender (creditor), and the coupon is the interest.

a. Zero-coupon
b. Prize Bond
c. Callable
d. Bond

38. In economics, a _____ is a general slowdown in economic activity over a sustained period of time, or a business cycle contraction. During _____s, many macroeconomic indicators vary in a similar way. Production as measured by Gross Domestic Product (GDP), employment, investment spending, capacity utilization, household incomes and business profits all fall during _____s.

a. Monetary economics
b. Treasury View
c. Leading indicators
d. Recession

39. Economics:

- _____, the desire to own something and the ability to pay for it
- _____ curve, a graphic representation of a _____ schedule
- _____ deposit, the money in checking accounts
- _____ pull theory, the theory that inflation occurs when _____ for goods and services exceeds existing supplies
- _____ schedule, a table that lists the quantity of a good a person will buy it each different price
- _____ side economics, the school of economics at believes government spending and tax cuts open economy by raising _____

a. Variability
b. Production
c. McKesson ' Robbins scandal
d. Demand

40. In economics, the _____ can be defined as the graph depicting the relationship between the price of a certain commodity, and the amount of it that consumers are willing and able to purchase at that given price. It is a graphic representation of a demand schedule. The _____ for all consumers together follows from the _____ of every individual consumer: the individual demands at each price are added together.

a. Cost curve
b. Demand curve
c. Kuznets curve
d. Wage curve

41. In neoclassical economics and microeconomics, _____ describes the perfect being a market in which there are many small firms, all producing homogeneous goods. In the short term, such markets are productively inefficient as output will not occur where mc is equal to ac, but allocatively efficient, as output under _____ will always occur where mc is equal to mr, and therefore where mc equals ar. However, in the long term, such markets are both allocatively and productively efficient.

a. Law of supply
b. General equilibrium
c. Perfect competition
d. Co-operative economics

Chapter 13. LIMITING MARKET POWER: REGULATION AND ANTITRUST

42. _____ is the removal or simplification of government rules and regulations that constrain the operation of market forces. _____ does not mean elimination of laws against fraud, but eliminating or reducing government control of how business is done, thereby moving toward a more free market.

The stated rationale for '_____' is often that fewer and simpler regulations will lead to a raised level of competitiveness, therefore higher productivity, more efficiency and lower prices overall.

- a. Fundamental psychological law
- b. Macroeconomic policy instruments
- c. Deregulation
- d. Secular basis

43. The _____ was a worldwide economic downturn starting in most places in 1929 and ending at different times in the 1930s or early 1940s for different countries. It was the largest and most important economic depression in the 20th century, and is used in the 21st century as an example of how far the world's economy can fall. The _____ originated in the United States; historians most often use as a starting date the stock market crash on October 29, 1929, known as Black Tuesday.

- a. British Empire Economic Conference
- b. Great Depression
- c. Jarrow March
- d. Wall Street Crash of 1929

44. The phrase _____, according to the Organization for Economic Co-operation and Development, refers to 'creative work undertaken on a systematic basis in order to increase the stock of knowledge, including knowledge of man, culture and society, and the use of this stock of knowledge to devise new applications [sic]'

New product design and development is more than often a crucial factor in the survival of a company. In an industry that is fast changing, firms must continually revise their design and range of products. This is necessary due to continuous technology change and development as well as other competitors and the changing preference of customers.

- a. 130-30 fund
- b. 1921 recession
- c. 100-year flood
- d. Research and development

45. An _____ is a person who has possession of an enterprise and assumes significant accountability for the inherent risks and the outcome. It is an ambitious leader who combines land, labor, and capital to create and market new goods or services. The term is a loanword from French and was first defined by the Irish economist Richard Cantillon.

- a. ACEA agreement
- b. ACCRA Cost of Living Index
- c. Expansionary policies
- d. Entrepreneur

46. A trade union or _____ is an organization of workers who have banded together to achieve common goals in key areas and working conditions. The trade union, through its leadership, bargains with the employer on behalf of union members (rank and file members) and negotiates labor contracts (Collective bargaining) with employers. This may include the negotiation of wages, work rules, complaint procedures, rules governing hiring, firing and promotion of workers, benefits, workplace safety and policies.

- a. Business valuation standards
- b. Basis of futures
- c. Demand-side technologies
- d. Labor union

47. In economics, _____ is the ratio of the percent change in one variable to the percent change in another variable. It is a tool for measuring the responsiveness of a function to changes in parameters in a relative way. Commonly analyzed are _____ of substitution, price and wealth.
  a. Elasticity
  b. Elasticity of demand
  c. ACCRA Cost of Living Index
  d. ACEA agreement

Chapter 14. THE CASE FOR FREE MARKETS I: THE PRICE SYSTEM

1. '_____' and 'trickle-down theory' are terms of political rhetoric that refer to the policy of providing tax cuts or other benefits to businesses and rich individuals in the belief that this will indirectly benefit the broad population. The term has been attributed to humorist Will Rogers, who said during the Great Depression that 'money was all appropriated for the top in hopes that it would trickle down to the needy.'

Proponents of these policies claim that if the top income earners invest more into the business infrastructure and equity markets, it will in turn lead to more goods at lower prices, and create more jobs for middle and lower class individuals. Proponents argue economic growth flows down from the top to the bottom, indirectly benefiting those who do not directly benefit from the policy changes.

- a. Learning-by-doing
- b. New classical macroeconomics
- c. Binary economics
- d. Trickle-down economics

2. _____s is the social science that studies the production, distribution, and consumption of goods and services. The term _____s comes from the Ancient Greek οἰκονομῖα from οἶκος (oikos, 'house') + νόμος (nomos, 'custom' or 'law'), hence 'rules of the house(hold)'. Current _____ models developed out of the broader field of political economy in the late 19th century, owing to a desire to use an empirical approach more akin to the physical sciences.
- a. Energy economics
- b. Opportunity cost
- c. Inflation
- d. Economic

3. _____ was a survey conducted by the U.S. Department of Justice to gauge the prevalence of alcohol and illegal drug use among prior arrestees. It was a reformulation of the prior Drug Use Forecasting (DUF) program, focused on five drugs in particular: cocaine, marijuana, methamphetamine, opiates, and PCP.

Participants were randomly selected from arrest records in major metropolitan areas; because no personally identifying information is taken from each record chosen, the resulting data can be correlated to arrest rates, but not to the total population of persons charged.

- a. ACEA agreement
- b. ACCRA Cost of Living Index
- c. Arrestee Drug Abuse Monitoring
- d. AD-IA Model

4. _____ in economics and business is the result of an exchange and from that trade we assign a numerical monetary value to a good, service or asset. If Alice trades Bob 4 apples for an orange, the _____ of an orange is 4 apples. Inversely, the _____ of an apple is 1/4 oranges.
- a. Price book
- b. Premium pricing
- c. Price war
- d. Price

5. In economics, a _____ is any economic system that effects its distribution of goods and services with prices and employing any form of money or debt tokens. Except for possible remote and primitive communities, all modern societies use _____s to allocate resources. However, _____s are not used for all resource allocation decisions today.
- a. Neomercantilism
- b. Hanseatic League
- c. Price system
- d. Family economy

6. _____ is used to assign the available resources in an economic way. It is part of resource management.

In strategic planning,is a plan for using available resources, for example human resources, especially in the near term, to achieve goals for the future.

Chapter 14. THE CASE FOR FREE MARKETS I: THE PRICE SYSTEM

   a. 100-year flood
   b. 130-30 fund
   c. 1921 recession
   d. Resource allocation

7. _____ was a Scottish moral philosopher and a pioneer of political economy. One of the key figures of the Scottish Enlightenment, Smith is the author of The Theory of Moral Sentiments and An Inquiry into the Nature and Causes of the Wealth of Nations. The latter, usually abbreviated as The Wealth of Nations, is considered his magnum opus and the first modern work of economics.
   a. Adam Smith
   b. Adolf Hitler
   c. Alan Greenspan
   d. Adolph Fischer

8. A _____ refers to any program which seeks to provide a minimum level of income, service or other support for many marginalized groups such as the poor, elderly, and disabled people. Social welfare programs are undertaken by governments as well as non-governmental organizations (NGOs.) Social welfare payments and services are typically provided at the expense of taxpayers generally, funded by benefactors, or by compulsory enrollment of the poor themselves.
   a. Social welfare provision
   b. 130-30 fund
   c. 1921 recession
   d. 100-year flood

9. _____ is a fee paid on borrowed assets. It is the price paid for the use of borrowed money, or, money earned by deposited funds. Assets that are sometimes lent with _____ include money, shares, consumer goods through hire purchase, major assets such as aircraft, and even entire factories in finance lease arrangements.
   a. Internal debt
   b. Insolvency
   c. Interest
   d. Asset protection

10. The _____ refers to the 'common well-being' or 'general welfare.' The _____ is central to policy debates, politics, democracy and the nature of government itself. While nearly everyone claims that aiding the common well-being or general welfare is positive, there is little, if any, consensus on what exactly constitutes the _____.

There are different views on how many members of the public must benefit from an action before it can be declared to be in the _____: at one extreme, an action has to benefit every single member of society in order to be truly in the _____; at the other extreme, any action can be in the _____ as long as it benefits some of the population and harms none.

   a. Public interest
   b. Power Elite
   c. Stealth tax
   d. Second-class citizen

11. In economics, the _____ is the term economists use to describe the self-regulating nature of the marketplace. The _____ is a metaphor coined by the economist Adam Smith in The Wealth of Nations.

Adam Smith mentions the metaphor in Book IV of The Wealth of Nations, arguing that people in any society will certainly employ their capital in foreign trading only if the profits available by that method far exceed those available locally, and that in such a case it is better for society as a whole if they so did.

   a. ACCRA Cost of Living Index
   b. AD-IA Model
   c. ACEA agreement
   d. Invisible hand

Chapter 14. THE CASE FOR FREE MARKETS I: THE PRICE SYSTEM

12. In microeconomics, _____ is quite simply the conversion of inputs into outputs. It is an economic process that uses resources to create a good or service that is suitable for exchange. This can include manufacturing, storing, shipping, and packaging.
    a. Red Guards
    b. MET
    c. Solved
    d. Production

13. _____ is that which is owed; usually referencing assets owed, but the term can also cover moral obligations and other interactions not requiring money. In the case of assets, _____ is a means of using future purchasing power in the present before a summation has been earned. Some companies and corporations use _____ as a part of their overall corporate finance strategy.
    a. Debenture
    b. Hard money loan
    c. Collateral Management
    d. Debt

14. _____ is a term used to describe a policy of allowing events to take their own course. The term is a French phrase literally meaning 'let do'. It is a doctrine that states that government generally should not intervene in the marketplace.
    a. Heroic capitalism
    b. Laissez-faire
    c. Theory of Productive Forces
    d. Communization

15. _____ is a socioeconomic structure and political ideology that promotes the establishment of an egalitarian, classless, stateless society based on common ownership and control of the means of production and property in general. In political science, the term '_____' is sometimes used to refer to communist states, a form of government in which the state operates under a one-party system and declares allegiance to Marxism-Leninism or a derivative thereof, even if the party does not actually claim that it has already reached _____.

Forerunners of communist ideas existed in antiquity and particularly in the 18th and early 19th century France, with thinkers such as Jean-Jacques Rousseau and the more radical Gracchus Babeuf.

    a. Social fascism
    b. Democratic centralism
    c. New Communist Movement
    d. Communism

16. The _____ is an economic and political union of 27 member states, located primarily in Europe. It was established by the Treaty of Maastricht on 1 November 1993, upon the foundations of the pre-existing European Economic Community. With a population of almost 500 million, the _____ generates an estimated 30% share (US$18.4 trillion in 2008) of the nominal gross world product.
    a. ACEA agreement
    b. European Union
    c. European Court of Justice
    d. ACCRA Cost of Living Index

17. A _____ or market-based mechanism is any of a wide variety of ways to match up buyers and sellers.

An example of a _____ uses announced bid and ask prices. Generally speaking, when two parties wish to engage in a trade, the purchaser will announce a price he is willing to pay (the bid price) and seller will announce a price he is willing to accept (the ask price.)

    a. Market equilibrium
    b. Marketization
    c. Price mechanism
    d. Horizontal market

Chapter 14. THE CASE FOR FREE MARKETS I: THE PRICE SYSTEM

18. _____ is a broad label that refers to any individuals or households that use goods and services generated within the economy. The concept of a _____ is used in different contexts, so that the usage and significance of the term may vary.

Typically when business people and economists talk of _____s they are talking about person as _____, an aggregated commodity item with little individuality other than that expressed in the buy/not-buy decision.

- a. 100-year flood
- b. 130-30 fund
- c. 1921 recession
- d. Consumer

19. In neoclassical economics and microeconomics, _____ describes the perfect being a market in which there are many small firms, all producing homogeneous goods. In the short term, such markets are productively inefficient as output will not occur where mc is equal to ac, but allocatively efficient, as output under _____ will always occur where mc is equal to mr, and therefore where mc equals ar. However, in the long term, such markets are both allocatively and productively efficient.

- a. General equilibrium
- b. Law of supply
- c. Co-operative economics
- d. Perfect competition

20. In economics and finance, _____ is the change in total cost that arises when the quantity produced changes by one unit. It is the cost of producing one more unit of a good. Mathematically, the _____ function is expressed as the first derivative of the total cost (TC) function with respect to quantity (Q.)

- a. Quality costs
- b. Marginal cost
- c. Khozraschyot
- d. Variable cost

21. In economics, the _____ of a good or of a service is the utility of the specific use to which an agent would put a given increase in that good or service, or of the specific use that would be abandoned in response to a given decrease. In other words, _____ is the utility of the marginal use -- which, on the assumption of economic rationality, would be the least urgent use of the good or service, from the best feasible combination of actions in which its use is included. Under the mainstream assumptions, the _____ of a good or service is the posited quantified change in utility obtained by increasing or by decreasing use of that good or service.

- a. 1921 recession
- b. Marginal utility
- c. 130-30 fund
- d. 100-year flood

22. In economics, _____ is a measure of the relative satisfaction from consumption of various goods and services. Given this measure, one may speak meaningfully of increasing or decreasing _____, and thereby explain economic behavior in terms of attempts to increase one's _____. For illustrative purposes, changes in _____ are sometimes expressed in units called utils.

- a. Utility function
- b. Ordinal utility
- c. Utility
- d. Expected utility hypothesis

23. In economics, _____ is equal to total cost divided by the number of goods produced (the output quantity, Q.) It is also equal to the sum of average variable costs (total variable costs divided by Q) plus average fixed costs (total fixed costs divided by Q.) _____s may be dependent on the time period considered (increasing production may be expensive or impossible in the short term, for example).

Chapter 14. THE CASE FOR FREE MARKETS I: THE PRICE SYSTEM

a. Explicit cost
b. Average cost
c. Average fixed cost
d. Average variable cost

24. _____ is one of the ways government regulate a monopoly market. Monopolists tend to produce less than the optimal quantity pushing the prices up. Government may use _____ as a tool to regulate prices monopolists may charge.
   a. ACEA agreement
   b. ACCRA Cost of Living Index
   c. Average cost pricing
   d. AD-IA Model

25. _____ is one of the four Ps of the marketing mix. The other three aspects are product, promotion, and place. It is also a key variable in microeconomic price allocation theory.
   a. Point of total assumption
   b. Pricing
   c. Premium pricing
   d. Guaranteed Maximum Price

26. The _____ or gross domestic income (GDI), a basic measure of an economy's economic performance, is the market value of all final goods and services produced within the borders of a nation in a year. _____ can be defined in three ways, all of which are conceptually identical. First, it is equal to the total expenditures for all final goods and services produced within the country in a stipulated period of time (usually a 365-day year.)
   a. Countercyclical
   b. Market structure
   c. Gross domestic product
   d. Monopolistic competition

27. In economics, the term _____ of income or _____ refers to a simple economic model which describes the reciprocal circulation of income between producers and consumers. In the _____ model, the inter-dependent entities of producer and consumer are referred to as 'firms' and 'households' respectively and provide each other with factors in order to facilitate the flow of income. Firms provide consumers with goods and services in exchange for consumer expenditure and 'factors of production' from households.
   a. 100-year flood
   b. 130-30 fund
   c. 1921 recession
   d. Circular flow

28. In economics, _____ is how a natione;s total economy is distributed among its population. ._____ has always been a central concern of economic theory and economic policy. Classical economists such as Adam Smith, Thomas Malthus and David Ricardo were mainly concerned with factor _____, that is, the distribution of income between the main factors of production, land, labour and capital.
   a. Income distribution
   b. Eco commerce
   c. Authorised capital
   d. Equipment trust certificate

29. A _____ is a theoretical term that economists use to describe a market which is free from government intervention (i.e. no regulation, no subsidization, no single monetary system and no governmental monopolies.) In a _____, property rights are voluntarily exchanged at a price arranged solely by the mutual consent of sellers and buyers. By definition, buyers and sellers do not coerce each other, in the sense that they obtain each other's property without the use of physical force, threat of physical force, or fraud, nor is the coerced by a third party (such as by government via transfer payments) and they engage in trade simply because they both consent and believe that it is a good enough choice.
   a. Free market
   b. Leninism
   c. Third camp
   d. Delegation

Chapter 14. THE CASE FOR FREE MARKETS I: THE PRICE SYSTEM

30. _____ is a type of trade policy that allows traders to act and transact without interference from government. Thus, the policy permits trading partners mutual gains from trade, with goods and services produced according to the theory of comparative advantage.

Under a _____ policy, prices are a reflection of true supply and demand, and are the sole determinant of resource allocation.

- a. 1921 recession
- b. 130-30 fund
- c. 100-year flood
- d. Free trade

31. A _____ is any systematic process enabling many market players to bid and ask: helping bidders and sellers interact and make deals. It is not just the price mechanism but the entire system of regulation, qualification, credentials, reputations and clearing that surrounds that mechanism and makes it operate in a social context.

Because a _____ relies on the assumption that players are constantly involved and unequally enabled, a _____ is distinguished specifically from a voting system where candidates seek the support of voters on a less regular basis.

- a. Market system
- b. Price mechanism
- c. Competitive equilibrium
- d. Contestable market

32.

_____ was a German philosopher, political economist, historian, political theorist, sociologist, communist and revolutionary credited as the founder of communism.

Marx summarized his approach to history and politics in the opening line of the first chapter of The Communist Manifesto : e;The history of all hitherto existing society is the history of class struggles.e; Marx argued that capitalism, like previous socioeconomic systems, will produce internal tensions which will lead to its destruction. Just as capitalism replaced feudalism, socialism will in its turn replace capitalism and lead to a stateless, classless society which will emerge after a transitional period, the 'dictatorship of the proletariat'.

- a. Adam Smith
- b. Marxism
- c. Karl Heinrich Marx
- d. Neo-Gramscianism

33. A _____ is a charge for the use of a product or service.

A _____ may apply per use of the good or service or charge the user for use of the good or service. The first is a charge for each time while the second is a charge for bulk or time-limited use.

- a. Optimal tax theory
- b. Indirect tax
- c. Ad valorem tax
- d. User charge

34. In finance, the _____s between two currencies specifies how much one currency is worth in terms of the other. It is the value of a foreign natione;s currency in terms of the home natione;s currency. For example an _____ of 102 Japanese yen to the United States dollar means that JPY 102 is worth the same as USD 1.
   a. Exchange rate   b. ACCRA Cost of Living Index
   c. ACEA agreement   d. Interbank market

Chapter 15. THE SHORTCOMINGS OF FREE MARKETS

1. _____ was a survey conducted by the U.S. Department of Justice to gauge the prevalence of alcohol and illegal drug use among prior arrestees. It was a reformulation of the prior Drug Use Forecasting (DUF) program, focused on five drugs in particular: cocaine, marijuana, methamphetamine, opiates, and PCP.

Participants were randomly selected from arrest records in major metropolitan areas; because no personally identifying information is taken from each record chosen, the resulting data can be correlated to arrest rates, but not to the total population of persons charged.

   a. ACCRA Cost of Living Index
   b. Arrestee Drug Abuse Monitoring
   c. AD-IA Model
   d. ACEA agreement

2. In economics, the _____ is the term economists use to describe the self-regulating nature of the marketplace. The _____ is a metaphor coined by the economist Adam Smith in The Wealth of Nations.

Adam Smith mentions the metaphor in Book IV of The Wealth of Nations, arguing that people in any society will certainly employ their capital in foreign trading only if the profits available by that method far exceed those available locally, and that in such a case it is better for society as a whole if they so did.

   a. ACCRA Cost of Living Index
   b. AD-IA Model
   c. ACEA agreement
   d. Invisible hand

3. _____ was a Scottish moral philosopher and a pioneer of political economy. One of the key figures of the Scottish Enlightenment, Smith is the author of The Theory of Moral Sentiments and An Inquiry into the Nature and Causes of the Wealth of Nations. The latter, usually abbreviated as The Wealth of Nations, is considered his magnum opus and the first modern work of economics.

   a. Adolph Fischer
   b. Adolf Hitler
   c. Alan Greenspan
   d. Adam Smith

4. The _____ or gross domestic income (GDI), a basic measure of an economy's economic performance, is the market value of all final goods and services produced within the borders of a nation in a year. _____ can be defined in three ways, all of which are conceptually identical. First, it is equal to the total expenditures for all final goods and services produced within the country in a stipulated period of time (usually a 365-day year.)

   a. Gross domestic product
   b. Countercyclical
   c. Market structure
   d. Monopolistic competition

5. In microeconomics, _____ is quite simply the conversion of inputs into outputs. It is an economic process that uses resources to create a good or service that is suitable for exchange. This can include manufacturing, storing, shipping, and packaging.

   a. Red Guards
   b. Solved
   c. MET
   d. Production

6. _____ is used to assign the available resources in an economic way. It is part of resource management.

In strategic planning,is a plan for using available resources, for example human resources, especially in the near term, to achieve goals for the future.

Chapter 15. THE SHORTCOMINGS OF FREE MARKETS

 a. 100-year flood   b. 1921 recession
 c. 130-30 fund   d. Resource allocation

7. In law and economics, the _____, describes the economic efficiency of an economic allocation or outcome in the presence of externalities. The theorem states that when trade in an externality is possible and there are no transaction costs, bargaining will lead to an efficient outcome regardless of the initial allocation of property rights. In practice, obstacles to bargaining or poorly defined property rights can prevent Coasian bargaining.
 a. General Mining Act of 1872   b. Prior appropriation water rights
 c. Coase theorem   d. Means test

8. In economics, an _____ is any good or commodity, transported from one country to another country in a legitimate fashion, typically for use in trade. _____ goods or services are provided to foreign consumers by domestic producers. _____ is an important part of international trade.
 a. ACCRA Cost of Living Index   b. AD-IA Model
 c. ACEA agreement   d. Export

9. In economics, an _____ or spillover of an economic transaction is an impact on a party that is not directly involved in the transaction. In such a case, prices do not reflect the full costs or benefits in production or consumption of a product or service. A positive impact is called an external benefit, while a negative impact is called an external cost.
 a. Existence value   b. Externality
 c. Environmental impact assessment   d. Environmental tariff

10. _____ is a term from economics referring to the use of money exchanged by buyers and sellers with an open and understood system of value and time trade offs to produce the best distribution of goods and services. The use of the _____ does not imply a free market: there can be captive or controlled markets which seek to use supply and demand, or some other form of charging for scarcity, both in social situations and in engineering.

The _____ assumes perfect competition and is regulated by demand and supply.

 a. Product-Market Growth Matrix   b. Partial equilibrium
 c. Two-sided markets   d. Market mechanism

11. In economics, _____ is equal to total cost divided by the number of goods produced (the output quantity, Q.) It is also equal to the sum of average variable costs (total variable costs divided by Q) plus average fixed costs (total fixed costs divided by Q.) _____s may be dependent on the time period considered (increasing production may be expensive or impossible in the short term, for example.)
 a. Average fixed cost   b. Average variable cost
 c. Explicit cost   d. Average cost

12. In economics and finance, _____ is the change in total cost that arises when the quantity produced changes by one unit. It is the cost of producing one more unit of a good. Mathematically, the _____ function is expressed as the first derivative of the total cost (TC) function with respect to quantity (Q.)
 a. Quality costs   b. Khozraschyot
 c. Variable cost   d. Marginal cost

13. In economics _____ is defined as the sum of private and external costs. Economic theorists ascribe individual decision-making to a calculation costs and benefits. Rational choice theory assumes that individuals only consider their own private costs when making decisions, not the costs that may be borne by others.
    a. Cost-Volume-Profit Analysis
    b. Khozraschyot
    c. Social cost
    d. Psychic cost

14. _____ is a practice of protecting the environment, on individual, organisational or governmental level, for the benefit of the natural environment and (or) humans.

Due to the pressures of population and technology the biophysical environment is being degraded, sometimes permanently. This has been recognised and governments began placing restraints on activities that caused environmental degradation.

    a. AD-IA Model
    b. ACEA agreement
    c. ACCRA Cost of Living Index
    d. Environmental Protection

15. _____ is any (course of) action deliberately taken (or not taken) to manage human activities with a view to prevent, reduce or mitigate harmful effects on nature and natural resources, and ensuring that man-made changes to the environment do not have harmful effects on humans.

It is useful to consider that _____ comprises two major terms: environment and policy. Environment primarily refers to the ecological (ecosystems) dimension, but can also take account of social (quality of life) dimension and an economic (resource management) dimension.

    a. Environmental policy
    b. AD-IA Model
    c. ACCRA Cost of Living Index
    d. ACEA agreement

16. _____ is the increase in the average temperature of the Earth's near-surface air and oceans since the mid-twentieth century and its projected continuation. Global surface temperature increased 0.74 ± 0.18 °C (1.33 ± 0.32 °F) during the last century. The Intergovernmental Panel on Climate Change (IPCC) concludes that anthropogenic greenhouse gases are responsible for most of the observed temperature increase since the middle of the twentieth century, and that natural phenomena such as solar variation and volcanoes probably had a small warming effect from pre-industrial times to 1950 and a small cooling effect afterward.
    a. Controlled Foreign Corporations
    b. Consumer goods
    c. Dividend unit
    d. Global warming

17. A _____ is a legal document that is often passed by the legislature, and approved by the chief executive-or president. For example, only certain types of revenue may be imposed and collected. Property tax is frequently the basis for municipal and county revenues, while sales tax and/or income tax are the basis for state revenues, and income tax and corporate tax are the basis for national revenues.
    a. Structural deficit
    b. Lump-sum tax
    c. Right-financing
    d. Government budget

18. An _____ is any government regulation or law that encourages or discourages foreign investment in the local economy, e.g. currency exchange limits.

Chapter 15. THE SHORTCOMINGS OF FREE MARKETS

As globalization integrates the economies of neighboring and of trading states, they are typically forced to trade off such rules as part of a common tax, tariff and trade regime, e.g. as defined by a free trade pact. _____ favoring local investors over global ones is typically discouraged in such pacts, and the idea of a separate _____ rapidly becomes a fiction or fantasy, as real decisions reflect the real need for nations to compete for investment, even from their own local investors.

- a. International sanctions
- b. Economic liberalization
- c. Electricity liberalization
- d. Investment policy

19. In economics, a _____ is a good that is non-rivaled and non-excludable. This means, respectively, that consumption of the good by one individual does not reduce availability of the good for consumption by others; and that no one can be effectively excluded from using the good. In the real world, there may be no such thing as an absolutely non-rivaled and non-excludable good; but economists think that some goods approximate the concept closely enough for the analysis to be economically useful.
    - a. Demand-pull theory
    - b. Happiness economics
    - c. Public good
    - d. Neoclassical synthesis

20. A _____ is an object whose consumption increases the utility of the consumer, for which the quantity demanded exceeds the quantity supplied at zero price. _____s are usually modeled as having diminishing marginal utility. The first individual purchase has high utility; the second has less.
    - a. Composite good
    - b. Pie method
    - c. Merit good
    - d. Good

21. A _____ is defined in economics as a good that exhibits these properties:

    - Excludable - it is reasonably possible to prevent a class of consumers (e.g. those who have not paid for it) from consuming the good.
    - Rivalrous - consumptions by one consumer prevents simultaneous consumption by other consumers. _____s satisfies an individual want while public good satisfies a collective want of the society.

    A _____ is the opposite of a public good, as they are almost exclusively made for profit.

    An example of the _____ is bread: bread eaten by a given person cannot be consumed by another (rivalry), and it is easy for a baker to refuse to trade a loaf (excludable

    - a. Positional goods
    - b. Pie method
    - c. Demerit good
    - d. Private good

22. _____ is one of the ways government regulate a monopoly market. Monopolists tend to produce less than the optimal quantity pushing the prices up. Government may use _____ as a tool to regulate prices monopolists may charge.
    - a. Average cost pricing
    - b. ACCRA Cost of Living Index
    - c. AD-IA Model
    - d. ACEA agreement

Chapter 15. THE SHORTCOMINGS OF FREE MARKETS

23. _____ is one of the four Ps of the marketing mix. The other three aspects are product, promotion, and place. It is also a key variable in microeconomic price allocation theory.
    a. Point of total assumption
    b. Pricing
    c. Guaranteed Maximum Price
    d. Premium pricing

24. The _____ is the central banking system of the United States. Created in 1913 by the enactment of the Federal Reserve Act (signed by Woodrow Wilson), it is a quasi-public and quasi-private (government entity with private components) banking system that comprises (1) the presidentially appointed Board of Governors of the _____ in Washington, D.C.; (2) the Federal Open Market Committee; (3) twelve regional Federal Reserve Banks located in major cities throughout the nation acting as fiscal agents for the U.S. Treasury, each with its own nine-member board of directors; (4) numerous other private U.S. member banks, which subscribe to required amounts of non-transferable stock in their regional Federal Reserve Banks; and (5) various advisory councils. Since February 2006, Ben Bernanke has served as the Chairman of the Board of Governors of the _____.
    a. Federal Reserve System
    b. Term auction facility
    c. Monetary Policy Report to the Congress
    d. Federal Reserve System Open Market Account

25. _____ or economic opportunity loss is the value of the next best alternative foregone as the result of making a decision. _____ analysis is an important part of a company's decision-making processes but is not treated as an actual cost in any financial statement. The next best thing that a person can engage in is referred to as the _____ of doing the best thing and ignoring the next best thing to be done.
    a. Economic
    b. Industrial organization
    c. Economic ideology
    d. Opportunity cost

26. The _____ is the expected return forgone by bypassing of other potential investment activities for a given capital. It is a rate of return that investors could earn in financial markets.
    a. AD-IA Model
    b. ACCRA Cost of Living Index
    c. Opportunity cost of capital
    d. ACEA agreement

27. The _____ is an expected return that the provider of capital plans to earn on their investment.

    Capital (money) used for funding a business should earn returns for the capital providers who risk their capital. For an investment to be worthwhile, the expected return on capital must be greater than the _____.

    a. Capital expenditure
    b. Modigliani-Miller theorem
    c. Capital intensive
    d. Cost of capital

28. _____ is a fee paid on borrowed assets. It is the price paid for the use of borrowed money, or, money earned by deposited funds. Assets that are sometimes lent with _____ include money, shares, consumer goods through hire purchase, major assets such as aircraft, and even entire factories in finance lease arrangements.
    a. Internal debt
    b. Asset protection
    c. Insolvency
    d. Interest

29. An _____ is the price a borrower pays for the use of money they do not own, for instance a small company might borrow from a bank to kick start their business, and the return a lender receives for deferring the use of funds, by lending it to the borrower. _____s are normally expressed as a percentage rate over the period of one year.

Chapter 15. THE SHORTCOMINGS OF FREE MARKETS 123

_____s targets are also a vital tool of monetary policy and are used to control variables like investment, inflation, and unemployment.

a. ACCRA Cost of Living Index
c. Arrow-Debreu model
b. Enterprise value
d. Interest rate

30. _____s (economically referred to as land or raw materials) occur naturally within environments that exist relatively undisturbed by mankind, in a natural form. A _____'s is often characterized by amounts of biodiversity existent in various ecosystems.

Mining, petroleum extraction, fishing, hunting, and forestry are generally considered natural-resource industries.

a. 1921 recession
c. 100-year flood
b. Natural resource
d. 130-30 fund

31. _____ is Latin for 'Let the buyer beware'. Generally _____ is the property law doctrine that controls the sale of real property after the date of closing.

Under the doctrine of _____, the buyer could not recover from the seller for defects on the property that rendered the property unfit for ordinary purposes.

a. 1921 recession
c. 130-30 fund
b. 100-year flood
d. Caveat emptor

32. A _____ is a theoretical term that economists use to describe a market which is free from government intervention (i.e. no regulation, no subsidization, no single monetary system and no governmental monopolies.) In a _____, property rights are voluntarily exchanged at a price arranged solely by the mutual consent of sellers and buyers. By definition, buyers and sellers do not coerce each other, in the sense that they obtain each other's property without the use of physical force, threat of physical force, or fraud, nor is the coerced by a third party (such as by government via transfer payments) and they engage in trade simply because they both consent and believe that it is a good enough choice.

a. Leninism
c. Third camp
b. Delegation
d. Free market

33. _____ is a type of trade policy that allows traders to act and transact without interference from government. Thus, the policy permits trading partners mutual gains from trade, with goods and services produced according to the theory of comparative advantage.

Under a _____ policy, prices are a reflection of true supply and demand, and are the sole determinant of resource allocation.

a. 130-30 fund
c. 1921 recession
b. 100-year flood
d. Free trade

Chapter 15. THE SHORTCOMINGS OF FREE MARKETS

34. A _____ is any systematic process enabling many market players to bid and ask: helping bidders and sellers interact and make deals. It is not just the price mechanism but the entire system of regulation, qualification, credentials, reputations and clearing that surrounds that mechanism and makes it operate in a social context.

Because a _____ relies on the assumption that players are constantly involved and unequally enabled, a _____ is distinguished specifically from a voting system where candidates seek the support of voters on a less regular basis.

- a. Competitive equilibrium
- b. Contestable market
- c. Price mechanism
- d. Market system

35. _____ is the prospect that a party insulated from risk may behave differently from the way it would behave if it were fully exposed to the risk. In insurance, _____ that occurs without conscious or malicious action is called morale hazard.

_____ is related to information asymmetry, a situation in which one party in a transaction has more information than another.

- a. 100-year flood
- b. 1921 recession
- c. 130-30 fund
- d. Moral hazard

36. _____ in economics and business is the result of an exchange and from that trade we assign a numerical monetary value to a good, service or asset. If Alice trades Bob 4 apples for an orange, the _____ of an orange is 4 apples. Inversely, the _____ of an apple is 1/4 oranges.

- a. Price book
- b. Premium pricing
- c. Price war
- d. Price

37. In economics, a _____ is any economic system that effects its distribution of goods and services with prices and employing any form of money or debt tokens. Except for possible remote and primitive communities, all modern societies use _____s to allocate resources. However, _____s are not used for all resource allocation decisions today.

- a. Neomercantilism
- b. Hanseatic League
- c. Price system
- d. Family economy

38. Economic _____ is defined as an excess distribution to any factor in a production process above that which is required to induce the factor into the process or any excess above that which is necessary to keep the factor in its current use..

Classical Factor _____ is primarily concerned with the fee paid for the use of fixed (e.g. natural) resources. The classical definition is expressed as any excess payment above that required to induce or provide for production.

- a. 130-30 fund
- b. 100-year flood
- c. 1921 recession
- d. Rent

39. In economics, _____ occurs when an individual, organization or firm seeks to make money through economic rent.

Chapter 15. THE SHORTCOMINGS OF FREE MARKETS

_____ generally implies the extraction of uncompensated value from others without making any contribution to productivity, such as by gaining control of land and other pre-existing natural resources, or by imposing burdensome regulations or other government decisions that may affect consumers or businesses. While there may be few people in modern industrialized countries who do not gain something, directly or indirectly, through some form or another of _____, Rent seeking in the aggregate imposes substantial losses on society.

- a. 100-year flood
- b. Rent seeking
- c. Good governance
- d. 130-30 fund

40. In finance, the _____s between two currencies specifies how much one currency is worth in terms of the other. It is the value of a foreign natione;s currency in terms of the home natione;s currency. For example an _____ of 102 Japanese yen to the United States dollar means that JPY 102 is worth the same as USD 1.
- a. Exchange rate
- b. Interbank market
- c. ACEA agreement
- d. ACCRA Cost of Living Index

41. In political science and economics, the _____ or agency dilemma treats the difficulties that arise under conditions of incomplete and asymmetric information when a principal hires an agent, such as the problem that the two may not have the same interests, while the principal is, presumably, hiring the agent to pursue the interests of the former.

Various mechanisms may be used to try to align the interests of the agent with those of the principal, such as piece rates/commissions, profit sharing, efficiency wages, performance measurement (including financial statements), the agent posting a bond, or fear of firing. The _____ is found in most employer/employee relationships, for example, when stockholders hire top executives of corporations.

- a. Principal-agent problem
- b. 100-year flood
- c. 1921 recession
- d. 130-30 fund

42. _____ is the public sector analogy to market failure and occurs when a government intervention causes a more inefficient allocation of goods and resources than would occur without that intervention. Likewise, the government's failure to intervene in a market failure that would result in a socially preferable mix of output is referred to as passive _____ (Weimer and Vining, 2004.) Just as with market failures, there are many different kinds of _____s that describe corresponding distortions.
- a. Government-granted monopoly
- b. Natural monopoly
- c. Privatizing profits and socializing losses
- d. Government failure

43. _____s is the social science that studies the production, distribution, and consumption of goods and services. The term _____s comes from the Ancient Greek oá¼°κονομῖα from oá¼¶κος (oikos, 'house') + νϊŒμος (nomos, 'custom' or 'law'), hence 'rules of the house(hold)'. Current _____ models developed out of the broader field of political economy in the late 19th century, owing to a desire to use an empirical approach more akin to the physical sciences.
- a. Opportunity cost
- b. Economic
- c. Energy economics
- d. Inflation

44. _____ refers to the actions that governments take in the economic field. It covers the systems for setting interest rates and government deficit as well as the labour market, national ownership, and many other areas of government.

Such policies are often influenced by international institutions like the International Monetary Fund or World Bank as well as political beliefs and the consequent policies of parties.

a. ACEA agreement
b. AD-IA Model
c. ACCRA Cost of Living Index
d. Economic policy

45. A _____ occurs when an entity spends more money than it takes in. The opposite of a _____ is a budget surplus. Debt is essentially an accumulated flow of deficits.
a. Public Financial Management
b. Lump-sum tax
c. Funding body
d. Budget deficit

46. In calculus, a function f defined on a subset of the real numbers with real values is called _____, if for all x and y such that x >≤ y one has f(x) >≤ f(y), so f preserves the order. In layman's terms, the sign of the slope is always positive (the curve tending upwards) or zero (i.e., non-decreasing, or asymptotic, or depicted as a horizontal, flat line) Likewise, a function is called monotonically decreasing (non-increasing) if, whenever x >≤ y, then f(x) >≥ f(y), so it reverses the order.
a. 1921 recession
b. 100-year flood
c. 130-30 fund
d. Monotonic

47. A consumer price index (_____) is a measure of the average price of consumer goods and services purchased by households. A consumer price index measures a price change for a constant market basket of goods and services from one period to the next within the same area (city, region, or nation.) It is a price index determined by measuring the price of a standard group of goods meant to represent the typical market basket of a typical urban consumer.
a. Hedonic price index
b. Cost-of-living index
c. Lipstick index
d. CPI

48. _____ is a broad label that refers to any individuals or households that use goods and services generated within the economy. The concept of a _____ is used in different contexts, so that the usage and significance of the term may vary.

Typically when business people and economists talk of _____s they are talking about person as _____, an aggregated commodity item with little individuality other than that expressed in the buy/not-buy decision.

a. 100-year flood
b. 130-30 fund
c. 1921 recession
d. Consumer

49. A _____ is a measure of the average price of consumer goods and services purchased by households. A _____ measures a price change for a constant market basket of goods and services from one period to the next within the same area (city, region, or nation.) It is a price index determined by measuring the price of a standard group of goods meant to represent the typical market basket of a typical urban consumer.
a. CPI
b. Cost-of-living index
c. Lipstick index
d. Consumer Price Index

Chapter 15. THE SHORTCOMINGS OF FREE MARKETS

50. A _____ is a normalized average (typically a weighted average) of prices for a given class of goods or services in a given region, during a given interval of time. It is a statistic designed to help to compare how these prices, taken as a whole, differ between time periods or geographical locations.

Price indices have several potential uses.

- a. Two-part tariff
- b. Transactional Net Margin Method
- c. Product sabotage
- d. Price Index

51. In economics, economic output is divided into physical goods and intangible services. Consumption of _____ is assumed to produce utility. It is often used when referring to a _____ Tax.
- a. Private good
- b. Composite good
- c. Goods and services
- d. Manufactured goods

52. _____ in economics refers to metrics and measures of output from production processes, per unit of input. Labor _____, for example, is typically measured as a ratio of output per labor-hour, an input. _____ may be conceived of as a metrics of the technical or engineering efficiency of production.
- a. Productivity
- b. Piece work
- c. Fordism
- d. Production-possibility frontier

53. In economics, _____ is the total supply of goods and services produced by a national economy during a specific time period. It is the total amount of goods and services in the economy available at all possible price levels.
- a. Aggregation problem
- b. Aggregate supply
- c. Aggregate expenditure
- d. Aggregate demand

Chapter 16. THE MARKET'S PRIME ACHIEVEMENT: INNOVATION AND GROWTH

1. Procter is a surname, and may also refer to:

   - Bryan Waller Procter (pseud. Barry Cornwall), English poet
   - Goodwin Procter, American law firm
   - _____, consumer products multinational

   a. Drawdown
   b. Procter ' Gamble
   c. Tightness
   d. Bucket shop

2. A _____ is any systematic process enabling many market players to bid and ask: helping bidders and sellers interact and make deals. It is not just the price mechanism but the entire system of regulation, qualification, credentials, reputations and clearing that surrounds that mechanism and makes it operate in a social context.

   Because a _____ relies on the assumption that players are constantly involved and unequally enabled, a _____ is distinguished specifically from a voting system where candidates seek the support of voters on a less regular basis.

   a. Price mechanism
   b. Contestable market
   c. Competitive equilibrium
   d. Market system

3. _____ in economics refers to metrics and measures of output from production processes, per unit of input. Labor _____, for example, is typically measured as a ratio of output per labor-hour, an input. _____ may be conceived of as a metrics of the technical or engineering efficiency of production.

   a. Fordism
   b. Production-possibility frontier
   c. Piece work
   d. Productivity

4. In economics, _____ is the total supply of goods and services produced by a national economy during a specific time period. It is the total amount of goods and services in the economy available at all possible price levels.

   a. Aggregation problem
   b. Aggregate demand
   c. Aggregate expenditure
   d. Aggregate supply

5. In economics, the term _____ of income or _____ refers to a simple economic model which describes the reciprocal circulation of income between producers and consumers. In the _____ model, the inter-dependent entities of producer and consumer are referred to as 'firms' and 'households' respectively and provide each other with factors in order to facilitate the flow of income. Firms provide consumers with goods and services in exchange for consumer expenditure and 'factors of production' from households.

   a. 100-year flood
   b. 1921 recession
   c. 130-30 fund
   d. Circular flow

6. In economics, an _____ is any good or commodity, transported from one country to another country in a legitimate fashion, typically for use in trade. _____ goods or services are provided to foreign consumers by domestic producers. _____ is an important part of international trade.

   a. ACCRA Cost of Living Index
   b. ACEA agreement
   c. AD-IA Model
   d. Export

Chapter 16. THE MARKET`S PRIME ACHIEVEMENT: INNOVATION AND GROWTH

7. _____ is a misspelled phrase from Latin 'pro capite' phrase meaning per head with pro meaning 'per' or 'for each' and capite meaning 'head.' Both words together equate to the phrase 'for each head.'

It is usually used in the field of statistics to indicate the average per person for any given concern, such as income, crime rate, etc.

It is also used in wills to indicate that each of the named beneficiaries should receive, by devise or bequest, equal shares of the estate. This is in contrast to a per stirpes division, in which each branch of the inheriting family inherits an equal share of the estate.

- a. Population statistics
- b. False positive rate
- c. Sargan test
- d. Per capita

8. _____ means how much each individual receives, in monetary terms, of the yearly income generated in the country. This is what each citizen is to receive if the yearly national income is divided equally among everyone. _____ is usually reported in units of currency per year.
- a. Per capita Income
- b. Real income
- c. Family income
- d. Lerman ratio

9. _____ is an economic system in which wealth, and the means of producing wealth, are privately owned. Through _____, the land, labor, and capital are owned, operated, and traded for the purpose of generating profits, without force or fraud, by private individuals either singly or jointly, and investments, distribution, income, production, pricing and supply of goods, commodities and services are determined by voluntary private decision in a market economy. A distinguishing feature of _____ is that each person owns his or her own labor and therefore is allowed to sell the use of it to employers.
- a. Late capitalism
- b. Capitalism
- c. Creative capitalism
- d. Socialism for the rich and capitalism for the poor

10. The _____ was a period in the late 18th and early 19th centuries when major changes in agriculture, manufacturing, mining, and transportation had a profound effect on the socioeconomic and cultural conditions in Britain. The changes subsequently spread throughout Europe, North America, and eventually the world. The onset of the _____ marked a major turning point in human society; almost every aspect of daily life was eventually influenced in some way.
- a. Adolf Hitler
- b. Adam Smith
- c. Adolph Fischer
- d. Industrial Revolution

11. _____ is the conformance of a residence or abode to the implied warranty of _____. A residence that complies is said to be 'habitable.' It is an implied warranty or contract, meaning it does not have to be an express contract, covenant, or provision of a contract. It is a common law right of a tenant or Legal doctrine.
- a. Patent portfolio
- b. Misappropriation
- c. Habitability
- d. Clean Air Act Extension of 1970

12. The _____ or gross domestic income (GDI), a basic measure of an economy's economic performance, is the market value of all final goods and services produced within the borders of a nation in a year. _____ can be defined in three ways, all of which are conceptually identical. First, it is equal to the total expenditures for all final goods and services produced within the country in a stipulated period of time (usually a 365-day year.)

a. Monopolistic competition
b. Market structure
c. Countercyclical
d. Gross domestic product

13. An _____, in economics, is the amount by which the real Gross domestic product exceeds potential GDP. The real GDP is also known as GDP 'adjusted for inflation', 'constant prices' GDP or 'constant dollar' GDP, because it measures the aggregate output in a country's income accounts in a given year, expressed in base-year prices. On the other hand, the potential GDP is the quantity of real GDP when a country's economy is at full-employment.
　a. ACEA agreement
　b. Inflationary gap
　c. AD-IA Model
　d. ACCRA Cost of Living Index

14. An _____ is a person who has possession of an enterprise and assumes significant accountability for the inherent risks and the outcome. It is an ambitious leader who combines land, labor, and capital to create and market new goods or services. The term is a loanword from French and was first defined by the Irish economist Richard Cantillon.
　a. Entrepreneur
　b. ACEA agreement
　c. Expansionary policies
　d. ACCRA Cost of Living Index

15. A _____ is a theoretical term that economists use to describe a market which is free from government intervention (i.e. no regulation, no subsidization, no single monetary system and no governmental monopolies.) In a _____, property rights are voluntarily exchanged at a price arranged solely by the mutual consent of sellers and buyers. By definition, buyers and sellers do not coerce each other, in the sense that they obtain each other's property without the use of physical force, threat of physical force, or fraud, nor is the coerced by a third party (such as by government via transfer payments) and they engage in trade simply because they both consent and believe that it is a good enough choice.
　a. Delegation
　b. Third camp
　c. Leninism
　d. Free market

16. _____ is a type of trade policy that allows traders to act and transact without interference from government. Thus, the policy permits trading partners mutual gains from trade, with goods and services produced according to the theory of comparative advantage.

Under a _____ policy, prices are a reflection of true supply and demand, and are the sole determinant of resource allocation.

　a. 1921 recession
　b. 100-year flood
　c. 130-30 fund
　d. Free trade

17. _____ in economics and business is the result of an exchange and from that trade we assign a numerical monetary value to a good, service or asset. If Alice trades Bob 4 apples for an orange, the _____ of an orange is 4 apples. Inversely, the _____ of an apple is 1/4 oranges.
　a. Premium pricing
　b. Price war
　c. Price book
　d. Price

18. In economics, a _____ is any economic system that effects its distribution of goods and services with prices and employing any form of money or debt tokens. Except for possible remote and primitive communities, all modern societies use _____s to allocate resources. However, _____s are not used for all resource allocation decisions today.

Chapter 16. THE MARKET`S PRIME ACHIEVEMENT: INNOVATION AND GROWTH

a. Hanseatic League
b. Family economy
c. Price system
d. Neomercantilism

19. _____ is money accepted for exchange of goods in an economy. The prevalence of one money over another arises, usually, when a government designates through decrees that the government shall accept only particular notes and coins in payment for taxes. Typically, money of _____ consists of stamped coins and minted paper bills.
a. Totnes pound
b. Local currency
c. Currency
d. Security thread

20. In finance, the _____s between two currencies specifies how much one currency is worth in terms of the other. It is the value of a foreign natione;s currency in terms of the home natione;s currency. For example an _____ of 102 Japanese yen to the United States dollar means that JPY 102 is worth the same as USD 1.
a. ACEA agreement
b. Interbank market
c. ACCRA Cost of Living Index
d. Exchange rate

21. _____ is one of the four Ps of the marketing mix. The other three aspects are product, promotion, and place. It is also a key variable in microeconomic price allocation theory.
a. Guaranteed Maximum Price
b. Pricing
c. Point of total assumption
d. Premium pricing

22. The process of _____ involves the introduction of a good or service that is new or substantially improved. This includes, but is not limited to, improvements in functional characteristics, technical abilities, or ease of use.
a. Dogs of the Dow
b. Microcap stock
c. Refusal to deal
d. Product innovation

23. In economics, the _____ can be defined as the graph depicting the relationship between the price of a certain commodity, and the amount of it that consumers are willing and able to purchase at that given price. It is a graphic representation of a demand schedule. The _____ for all consumers together follows from the _____ of every individual consumer: the individual demands at each price are added together.
a. Kuznets curve
b. Cost curve
c. Wage curve
d. Demand curve

24. In economics, the _____ is the term economists use to describe the self-regulating nature of the marketplace. The _____ is a metaphor coined by the economist Adam Smith in The Wealth of Nations.

Adam Smith mentions the metaphor in Book IV of The Wealth of Nations, arguing that people in any society will certainly employ their capital in foreign trading only if the profits available by that method far exceed those available locally, and that in such a case it is better for society as a whole if they so did.

a. ACEA agreement
b. AD-IA Model
c. Invisible hand
d. ACCRA Cost of Living Index

25. _____ is an economic model based on price, utility and quantity in a market. It predicts that in a competitive market, price will function to equalize the quantity demanded by consumers, and the quantity supplied by producers, resulting in an economic equilibrium of price and quantity. The model incorporates other factors changing equilibrium as a shift of demand and/or supply.

Chapter 16. THE MARKET`S PRIME ACHIEVEMENT: INNOVATION AND GROWTH

a. Deferred gratification
b. Rational addiction
c. Joint demand
d. Supply and demand

26. Economics:

- _____, the desire to own something and the ability to pay for it
- _____ curve, a graphic representation of a _____ schedule
- _____ deposit, the money in checking accounts
- _____ pull theory, the theory that inflation occurs when _____ for goods and services exceeds existing supplies
- _____ schedule, a table that lists the quantity of a good a person will buy it each different price
- _____ side economics, the school of economics at believes government spending and tax cuts open economy by raising _____

a. Production
b. McKesson ' Robbins scandal
c. Variability
d. Demand

27. In economics, _____ is the ratio of the percent change in one variable to the percent change in another variable. It is a tool for measuring the responsiveness of a function to changes in parameters in a relative way. Commonly analyzed are _____ of substitution, price and wealth.
a. ACEA agreement
b. Elasticity of demand
c. ACCRA Cost of Living Index
d. Elasticity

28. An _____ is a market form in which a market or industry is dominated by a small number of sellers (oligopolists.) Because there are few participants in this type of market, each oligopolist is aware of the actions of the others. The decisions of one firm influence, and are influenced by, the decisions of other firms.
a. ACEA agreement
b. Oligopsony
c. ACCRA Cost of Living Index
d. Oligopoly

29. The phrase _____, according to the Organization for Economic Co-operation and Development, refers to 'creative work undertaken on a systematic basis in order to increase the stock of knowledge, including knowledge of man, culture and society, and the use of this stock of knowledge to devise new applications [sic]'

New product design and development is more than often a crucial factor in the survival of a company. In an industry that is fast changing, firms must continually revise their design and range of products. This is necessary due to continuous technology change and development as well as other competitors and the changing preference of customers.

a. 100-year flood
b. Research and development
c. 1921 recession
d. 130-30 fund

Chapter 16. THE MARKET`S PRIME ACHIEVEMENT: INNOVATION AND GROWTH

30. An _____ is a manufacturing process in which parts (usually interchangeable parts) are added to a product in a sequential manner using optimally planned logistics to create a finished product much faster than with handcrafting-type methods. The _____ developed by Ford Motor Company between 1908 and 1915 made _____s famous in the following decade through the social ramifications of mass production, such as the affordability of the Ford Model T and the introduction of high wages for Ford workers. However, the various preconditions for the development at Ford stretched far back into the 19th century, from the gradual realization of the dream of interchangeability, to the concept of reinventing workflow and job descriptions using analytical methods.
    a. ACCRA Cost of Living Index
    b. ACEA agreement
    c. Assembly line
    d. AD-IA Model

31. _____, short for _____, was the first general-purpose electronic computer. It was a Turing-complete, digital computer capable of being reprogrammed to solve a full range of computing problems. _____ was designed and built to calculate artillery firing tables for the U.S. Army's Ballistic Research Laboratory.
    a. AD-IA Model
    b. ACCRA Cost of Living Index
    c. ENIAC
    d. ACEA agreement

32. _____ was a writer, management consultant, and self-described 'social ecologist.' Widely considered to be 'the father of modern management,' his 39 books and countless scholarly and popular articles explored how humans are organized across all sectors of society--in business, government and the nonprofit world. His writings have predicted many of the major developments of the late twentieth century, including privatization and decentralization; the rise of Japan to economic world power; the decisive importance of marketing; and the emergence of the information society with its necessity of lifelong learning. In 1959, Drucker coined the term 'knowledge worker' and later in his life considered knowledge work productivity to be the next frontier of management.
    a. Thomas Mun
    b. Werner Sombart
    c. George Cabot Lodge II
    d. Peter Ferdinand Drucker

33. _____ was a survey conducted by the U.S. Department of Justice to gauge the prevalence of alcohol and illegal drug use among prior arrestees. It was a reformulation of the prior Drug Use Forecasting (DUF) program, focused on five drugs in particular: cocaine, marijuana, methamphetamine, opiates, and PCP.

Participants were randomly selected from arrest records in major metropolitan areas; because no personally identifying information is taken from each record chosen, the resulting data can be correlated to arrest rates, but not to the total population of persons charged.

    a. AD-IA Model
    b. ACCRA Cost of Living Index
    c. Arrestee Drug Abuse Monitoring
    d. ACEA agreement

34. _____ was a Scottish moral philosopher and a pioneer of political economy. One of the key figures of the Scottish Enlightenment, Smith is the author of The Theory of Moral Sentiments and An Inquiry into the Nature and Causes of the Wealth of Nations. The latter, usually abbreviated as The Wealth of Nations, is considered his magnum opus and the first modern work of economics.
    a. Adolf Hitler
    b. Adolph Fischer
    c. Adam Smith
    d. Alan Greenspan

Chapter 16. THE MARKET'S PRIME ACHIEVEMENT: INNOVATION AND GROWTH

35. Competition law, known in the United States as _____ law, has three main elements:

- prohibiting agreements or practices that restrict free trading and competition between business entities. This includes in particular the repression of cartels.
- banning abusive behaviour by a firm dominating a market, or anti-competitive practices that tend to lead to such a dominant position. Practices controlled in this way may include predatory pricing, tying, price gouging, refusal to deal, and many others.
- supervising the mergers and acquisitions of large corporations, including some joint ventures. Transactions that are considered to threaten the competitive process can be prohibited altogether, or approved subject to 'remedies' such as an obligation to divest part of the merged business or to offer licences or access to facilities to enable other businesses to continue competing.

The substance and practice of competition law varies from jurisdiction to jurisdiction. Protecting the interests of consumers (consumer welfare) and ensuring that entrepreneurs have an opportunity to compete in the market economy are often treated as important objectives. Competition law is closely connected with law on deregulation of access to markets, state aids and subsidies, the privatisation of state owned assets and the establishment of independent sector regulators. In recent decades, competition law has been viewed as a way to provide better public services.

a. Intellectual property law
b. Anti-Inflation Act
c. United Kingdom competition law
d. Antitrust

36. _____, known in the United States as antitrust law, has three main elements:

- prohibiting agreements or practices that restrict free trading and competition between business entities. This includes in particular the repression of cartels.
- banning abusive behaviour by a firm dominating a market, or anti-competitive practices that tend to lead to such a dominant position. Practices controlled in this way may include predatory pricing, tying, price gouging, refusal to deal, and many others.
- supervising the mergers and acquisitions of large corporations, including some joint ventures. Transactions that are considered to threaten the competitive process can be prohibited altogether, or approved subject to 'remedies' such as an obligation to divest part of the merged business or to offer licences or access to facilities to enable other businesses to continue competing.

The substance and practice of _____ varies from jurisdiction to jurisdiction. Protecting the interests of consumers (consumer welfare) and ensuring that entrepreneurs have an opportunity to compete in the market economy are often treated as important objectives. _____ is closely connected with law on deregulation of access to markets, state aids and subsidies, the privatisation of state owned assets and the establishment of independent sector regulators. In recent decades, _____ has been viewed as a way to provide better public services.

a. Fee simple
b. Due diligence
c. Hostile work environment
d. Competition law

Chapter 16. THE MARKET'S PRIME ACHIEVEMENT: INNOVATION AND GROWTH

37. In economics, _____ is equal to total cost divided by the number of goods produced (the output quantity, Q.) It is also equal to the sum of average variable costs (total variable costs divided by Q) plus average fixed costs (total fixed costs divided by Q.) _____s may be dependent on the time period considered (increasing production may be expensive or impossible in the short term, for example.)
   a. Explicit cost
   b. Average cost
   c. Average fixed cost
   d. Average variable cost

38. In economics and finance, _____ is the change in total cost that arises when the quantity produced changes by one unit. It is the cost of producing one more unit of a good. Mathematically, the _____ function is expressed as the first derivative of the total cost (TC) function with respect to quantity (Q.)
   a. Variable cost
   b. Quality costs
   c. Khozraschyot
   d. Marginal cost

39. In economics, a _____ exists when a specific individual or enterprise has sufficient control over a particular product or service to determine significantly the terms on which other individuals shall have access to it. Monopolies are thus characterized by a lack of economic competition for the good or service that they provide and a lack of viable substitute goods. The verb 'monopolize' refers to the process by which a firm gains persistently greater market share than what is expected under perfect competition.
   a. 130-30 fund
   b. 1921 recession
   c. 100-year flood
   d. Monopoly

40. In economics, a firm is said to reap _____s when a lack of viable market competition allows it to set its prices above the equilibrium price for a good or service without losing profits to competitors. _____ is a type of economic profit, that is, it is a profit greater than the normal profit that is typical in a perfectly competitive industry. The resulting price is known as the monopoly price.
   a. Cleanup clause
   b. Monopoly profit
   c. First-price sealed-bid auction
   d. Borrowing base

41. _____ is a common concept in economics, and gives rise to derived concepts such as consumer debt. Generally _____ is defined by opposition to production. But the precise definition can vary because different schools of economists define production quite differently.
   a. Foreclosure data providers
   b. Federal Reserve Bank Notes
   c. Consumption
   d. Cash or share options

42. In economics, a _____ is a good that is non-rivaled and non-excludable. This means, respectively, that consumption of the good by one individual does not reduce availability of the good for consumption by others; and that no one can be effectively excluded from using the good. In the real world, there may be no such thing as an absolutely non-rivaled and non-excludable good; but economists think that some goods approximate the concept closely enough for the analysis to be economically useful.
   a. Happiness economics
   b. Demand-pull theory
   c. Neoclassical synthesis
   d. Public good

43. A _____ is an object whose consumption increases the utility of the consumer, for which the quantity demanded exceeds the quantity supplied at zero price. _____s are usually modeled as having diminishing marginal utility. The first individual purchase has high utility; the second has less.

a. Good
b. Merit good
c. Pie method
d. Composite good

44. In economics, an _____ or spillover of an economic transaction is an impact on a party that is not directly involved in the transaction. In such a case, prices do not reflect the full costs or benefits in production or consumption of a product or service. A positive impact is called an external benefit, while a negative impact is called an external cost.
    a. Existence value
    b. Environmental impact assessment
    c. Environmental tariff
    d. Externality

45. _____ is research accessing and using some part of the research communities' (the academy's) accumulated theories, knowledge, methods, and techniques, for a specific, often state, commercial, or client driven purpose. _____ is often contrasted with pure research in debates about research ideals, programs, and projects.

Every organizational entity engages in _____.

    a. ACEA agreement
    b. ACCRA Cost of Living Index
    c. Applied research
    d. AD-IA Model

46. _____ or fundamental research (sometimes pure research) is research carried out to increase understanding of fundamental principles. Many times the end results have no direct or immediate commercial benefits: _____ can be thought of as arising out of curiosity. However, in the long term it is the basis for many commercial products and applied research.
    a. 100-year flood
    b. Basic research
    c. 1921 recession
    d. 130-30 fund

47. _____ is a recursive process where two or more people or organizations work together intersection of common goals -- for example, an intellectual endeavor that is creative in nature--by sharing knowledge, learning and building consensus. _____ does not require leadership and can sometimes bring better results through decentralization and egalitarianism. In particular, teams that work collaboratively can obtain greater resources, recognition and reward when facing competition for finite resources. _____ is also present in opposing goals exhibiting the notion of adversarial _____, though this notion is atypical of the annotation that people have given towards their understanding of _____.
    a. 130-30 fund
    b. 1921 recession
    c. 100-year flood
    d. Collaboration

Chapter 17. EXTERNALITIES, THE ENVIRONMENT, AND NATURAL RESOURCES

1. In law and economics, the _____, describes the economic efficiency of an economic allocation or outcome in the presence of externalities. The theorem states that when trade in an externality is possible and there are no transaction costs, bargaining will lead to an efficient outcome regardless of the initial allocation of property rights. In practice, obstacles to bargaining or poorly defined property rights can prevent Coasian bargaining.

   a. Coase theorem
   b. General Mining Act of 1872
   c. Means test
   d. Prior appropriation water rights

2. _____s is the social science that studies the production, distribution, and consumption of goods and services. The term _____s comes from the Ancient Greek οἰκονομῐ́α from οἶκος (oikos, 'house') + νόμος (nomos, 'custom' or 'law'), hence 'rules of the house(hold)'. Current _____ models developed out of the broader field of political economy in the late 19th century, owing to a desire to use an empirical approach more akin to the physical sciences.

   a. Energy economics
   b. Inflation
   c. Opportunity cost
   d. Economic

3. _____ is any (course of) action deliberately taken (or not taken) to manage human activities with a view to prevent, reduce or mitigate harmful effects on nature and natural resources, and ensuring that man-made changes to the environment do not have harmful effects on humans.

   It is useful to consider that _____ comprises two major terms: environment and policy. Environment primarily refers to the ecological (ecosystems) dimension, but can also take account of social (quality of life) dimension and an economic (resource management) dimension.

   a. AD-IA Model
   b. ACCRA Cost of Living Index
   c. Environmental policy
   d. ACEA agreement

4. A _____ is any systematic process enabling many market players to bid and ask: helping bidders and sellers interact and make deals. It is not just the price mechanism but the entire system of regulation, qualification, credentials, reputations and clearing that surrounds that mechanism and makes it operate in a social context.

   Because a _____ relies on the assumption that players are constantly involved and unequally enabled, a _____ is distinguished specifically from a voting system where candidates seek the support of voters on a less regular basis.

   a. Price mechanism
   b. Competitive equilibrium
   c. Contestable market
   d. Market system

5. _____s (economically referred to as land or raw materials) occur naturally within environments that exist relatively undisturbed by mankind, in a natural form. A _____'s is often characterized by amounts of biodiversity existent in various ecosystems.

   Mining, petroleum extraction, fishing, hunting, and forestry are generally considered natural-resource industries.

   a. 130-30 fund
   b. 100-year flood
   c. 1921 recession
   d. Natural resource

Chapter 17. EXTERNALITIES, THE ENVIRONMENT, AND NATURAL RESOURCES

6. In economics, an _____ is any good or commodity, transported from one country to another country in a legitimate fashion, typically for use in trade. _____ goods or services are provided to foreign consumers by domestic producers. _____ is an important part of international trade.
   a. Export
   b. AD-IA Model
   c. ACCRA Cost of Living Index
   d. ACEA agreement

7. In economics, an _____ or spillover of an economic transaction is an impact on a party that is not directly involved in the transaction. In such a case, prices do not reflect the full costs or benefits in production or consumption of a product or service. A positive impact is called an external benefit, while a negative impact is called an external cost.
   a. Environmental tariff
   b. Environmental impact assessment
   c. Existence value
   d. Externality

8. _____ is a term from economics referring to the use of money exchanged by buyers and sellers with an open and understood system of value and time trade offs to produce the best distribution of goods and services. The use of the _____ does not imply a free market: there can be captive or controlled markets which seek to use supply and demand, or some other form of charging for scarcity, both in social situations and in engineering.

   The _____ assumes perfect competition and is regulated by demand and supply.

   a. Product-Market Growth Matrix
   b. Partial equilibrium
   c. Two-sided markets
   d. Market mechanism

9. _____ is a practice of protecting the environment, on individual, organisational or governmental level, for the benefit of the natural environment and (or) humans.

   Due to the pressures of population and technology the biophysical environment is being degraded, sometimes permanently. This has been recognised and governments began placing restraints on activities that caused environmental degradation.

   a. AD-IA Model
   b. ACEA agreement
   c. ACCRA Cost of Living Index
   d. Environmental Protection

10. The _____ Index or Pollutant Standard Index) is a number used by government agencies to characterize the quality of the air at a given location. As the Air qualityI increases, an increasingly large percentage of the population is likely to experience increasingly severe adverse health effects. To compute the Air qualityI requires an air pollutant concentration from a monitor or model.
    a. ACCRA Cost of Living Index
    b. Air quality
    c. ACEA agreement
    d. AD-IA Model

11. A _____ or directed economy is an economic system in which the government or workers' councils manages the economy. It is an economic system in which the central government makes all decisions on the production and consumption of goods and services. Its most extensive form is referred to as a _____, centrally planned economy, or command and control economy.
    a. Transition economy
    b. Subsistence economy
    c. Nutritional Economics
    d. Command economy

Chapter 17. EXTERNALITIES, THE ENVIRONMENT, AND NATURAL RESOURCES

12. _____ is money accepted for exchange of goods in an economy. The prevalence of one money over another arises, usually, when a government designates through decrees that the government shall accept only particular notes and coins in payment for taxes. Typically, money of _____ consists of stamped coins and minted paper bills.
    a. Local currency
    b. Totnes pound
    c. Security thread
    d. Currency

13. _____ is the increase in the average temperature of the Earth's near-surface air and oceans since the mid-twentieth century and its projected continuation. Global surface temperature increased 0.74 ± 0.18 °C (1.33 ± 0.32 °F) during the last century. The Intergovernmental Panel on Climate Change (IPCC) concludes that anthropogenic greenhouse gases are responsible for most of the observed temperature increase since the middle of the twentieth century, and that natural phenomena such as solar variation and volcanoes probably had a small warming effect from pre-industrial times to 1950 and a small cooling effect afterward.
    a. Global warming
    b. Dividend unit
    c. Consumer goods
    d. Controlled Foreign Corporations

14. A _____ is a legal document that is often passed by the legislature, and approved by the chief executive-or president. For example, only certain types of revenue may be imposed and collected. Property tax is frequently the basis for municipal and county revenues, while sales tax and/or income tax are the basis for state revenues, and income tax and corporate tax are the basis for national revenues.
    a. Structural deficit
    b. Right-financing
    c. Lump-sum tax
    d. Government budget

15. In finance, the term _____ describes various legal measures taken to ensure that debtors, whether individuals, businesses honor their debts and make an honest effort to repay the money that they owe. Generally regarded as a subdivision of tax law, _____ is most often enforced through a combination of audits and legal restrictions. For example, a provision of the Federal Debt Collection Procedure Act states that a person or organization indebted to the United States, against whom a judgment lien has been filed, is ineligible to receive a government grant.
    a. Carryback loan
    b. Hard money loan
    c. Microcredit
    d. Debt compliance

16. The _____ or gross domestic income (GDI), a basic measure of an economy's economic performance, is the market value of all final goods and services produced within the borders of a nation in a year. _____ can be defined in three ways, all of which are conceptually identical. First, it is equal to the total expenditures for all final goods and services produced within the country in a stipulated period of time (usually a 365-day year.)
    a. Countercyclical
    b. Gross domestic product
    c. Market structure
    d. Monopolistic competition

17. A _____ refers to any program which seeks to provide a minimum level of income, service or other support for many marginalized groups such as the poor, elderly, and disabled people. Social welfare programs are undertaken by governments as well as non-governmental organizations (NGOs.) Social welfare payments and services are typically provided at the expense of taxpayers generally, funded by benefactors, or by compulsory enrollment of the poor themselves.
    a. Social welfare provision
    b. 1921 recession
    c. 100-year flood
    d. 130-30 fund

Chapter 17. EXTERNALITIES, THE ENVIRONMENT, AND NATURAL RESOURCES

18. _____ involves processing used materials into new products in order to prevent waste of potentially useful materials, reduce the consumption of fresh raw materials, reduce energy usage, reduce air pollution (from incineration) and water pollution (from landfilling) by reducing the need for 'conventional' waste disposal, and lower greenhouse gas emissions as compared to virgin production. _____ is a key component of modern waste management and is the third component of the 'Reduce, Reuse, Recycle' waste hierarchy.

Recyclable materials include many kinds of glass, paper, metal, plastic, textiles, and electronics.

- a. Cash or share options
- b. History of minimum wage
- c. Recycling
- d. 2008 budget crisis

19. The _____ consists of a number of economic theories which describe the nature of the firm, company including its existence, its behaviour, and its relationship with the market.

In simplified terms, the _____ aims to answer these questions:

1. Existence - why do firms emerge, why are not all transactions in the economy mediated over the market?
2. Boundaries - why the boundary between firms and the market is located exactly there? Which transactions are performed internally and which are negotiated on the market?
3. Organization - why are firms structured in such specific way? What is the interplay of formal and informal relationships?

Despite looking simple, these questions are not answered by the established economic theory, which usually views firms as given, and treats them as black boxes without any internal structure.

The First World War period saw a change of emphasis in economic theory away from industry-level analysis which mainly included analysing markets to analysis at the level of the firm, as it became increasingly clear that perfect competition was no longer an adequate model of how firms behaved. Economic theory till then had focussed on trying to understand markets alone and there had been little study on understanding why firms or organisations exist.

- a. Policy Ineffectiveness Proposition
- b. Khazzoom-Brookes postulate
- c. Technology gap
- d. Theory of the firm

20. A _____ describes one of a number of pieces of legislation relating to the reduction of smog and air pollution in general. The use by governments to enforce clean air standards has contributed to an improvement in human health and longer life spans. Critics argue it has also sapped corporate profits and contributed to outsourcing, while defenders counter that improved environmental air quality has generated more jobs than it has eliminated.
- a. 100-year flood
- b. 130-30 fund
- c. Smog
- d. Clean Air Act

21. To _____ is to impose a financial charge or other levy upon a taxpayer by a state or the functional equivalent of a state.

Chapter 17. EXTERNALITIES, THE ENVIRONMENT, AND NATURAL RESOURCES   141

_____es are also imposed by many subnational entities. _____es consist of direct _____ or indirect _____, and may be paid in money or as its labour equivalent (often but not always unpaid.)

a. 130-30 fund
b. 100-year flood
c. Tax
d. 1921 recession

22. To tax is to impose a financial charge or other levy upon a taxpayer by a state or the functional equivalent of a state.

_____ are also imposed by many subnational entities. _____ consist of direct tax or indirect tax, and may be paid in money or as its labour equivalent (often but not always unpaid.)

a. 1921 recession
b. 100-year flood
c. 130-30 fund
d. Taxes

23. The _____ , established in 1848, is the world's oldest futures and options exchange. More than 50 different options and futures contracts are traded by over 3,600 _____ members through open outcry and eTrading. Volumes at the exchange in 2003 were a record breaking 454 million contracts.

a. 130-30 fund
b. 100-year flood
c. New York Mercantile Exchange
d. Chicago Board of Trade

24. The _____ Act of 2001 (Pub.L. 107-110, 115 Stat. 1425, enacted January 8, 2002), often abbreviated in print as _____ and sometimes shortened in pronunciation to 'nicklebee', is a United States Act of Congress that was originally proposed by President George W. Bush immediately after taking office.

a. Community property
b. Due diligence
c. Nexus of contracts
d. No Child Left Behind

25. _____ is the point where a person stops employment completely. A person may also semi-retire and keep some sort of _____ job, out of choice rather than necessity. This usually happens upon reaching a determined age, when physical conditions don't allow the person to work any more (by illness or accident), or even for personal choice (usually in the presence of an adequate pension or personal savings.)

a. 100-year flood
b. Retirement
c. Layoff
d. Termination of employment

26. _____ is a common concept in economics, and gives rise to derived concepts such as consumer debt. Generally _____ is defined by opposition to production. But the precise definition can vary because different schools of economists define production quite differently.

a. Foreclosure data providers
b. Cash or share options
c. Consumption
d. Federal Reserve Bank Notes

27. _____ in economics and business is the result of an exchange and from that trade we assign a numerical monetary value to a good, service or asset. If Alice trades Bob 4 apples for an orange, the _____ of an orange is 4 apples. Inversely, the _____ of an apple is 1/4 oranges.

a. Price
b. Price book
c. Price war
d. Premium pricing

Chapter 17. EXTERNALITIES, THE ENVIRONMENT, AND NATURAL RESOURCES

28. _____ is one of the four Ps of the marketing mix. The other three aspects are product, promotion, and place. It is also a key variable in microeconomic price allocation theory.
   a. Point of total assumption
   b. Guaranteed Maximum Price
   c. Pricing
   d. Premium pricing

29. The Organization of the Petroleum Exporting Countries is a cartel of twelve countries made up of Algeria, Angola, Ecuador, Iran, Iraq, Kuwait, Libya, Nigeria, Qatar, Saudi Arabia, the United Arab Emirates, and Venezuela. The cartel has maintained its headquarters in Vienna since 1965, and hosts regular meetings among the oil ministers of its Member Countries. Indonesia withdrew its membership in _____ in 2008 after it became a net importer of oil, but stated it would likely return if it became a net exporter in the world.
   a. ACEA agreement
   b. AD-IA Model
   c. ACCRA Cost of Living Index
   d. OPEC

Chapter 18. TAXATION AND RESOURCE ALLOCATION

1. A _____ occurs when an entity spends more money than it takes in. The opposite of a _____ is a budget surplus. Debt is essentially an accumulated flow of deficits.
   a. Funding body
   b. Lump-sum tax
   c. Public Financial Management
   d. Budget deficit

2. _____ is any long-term change in the patterns of average weather of a specific region or the Earth as a whole. _____ reflects abnormal variations to the Earth's climate and subsequent effects on other parts of the Earth, such as in the ice caps over durations ranging from decades to millions of years.

   In recent usage, especially in the context of environmental policy, _____ usually refers to changes in modern climate

   a. Climate change
   b. 100-year flood
   c. 1921 recession
   d. 130-30 fund

3. The _____ or gross domestic income (GDI), a basic measure of an economy's economic performance, is the market value of all final goods and services produced within the borders of a nation in a year. _____ can be defined in three ways, all of which are conceptually identical. First, it is equal to the total expenditures for all final goods and services produced within the country in a stipulated period of time (usually a 365-day year.)
   a. Countercyclical
   b. Market structure
   c. Monopolistic competition
   d. Gross domestic product

4. An _____, in economics, is the amount by which the real Gross domestic product exceeds potential GDP. The real GDP is also known as GDP 'adjusted for inflation', 'constant prices' GDP or 'constant dollar' GDP, because it measures the aggregate output in a country's income accounts in a given year, expressed in base-year prices. On the other hand, the potential GDP is the quantity of real GDP when a country's economy is at full-employment.
   a. ACEA agreement
   b. ACCRA Cost of Living Index
   c. AD-IA Model
   d. Inflationary gap

5. _____ was a global military conflict which involved a majority of the world's nations, including all of the great powers, organized into two opposing military alliances: the Allies and the Axis. The war involved the mobilization of over 100 million military personnel, making it the most widespread war in history. In a state of 'total war', the major participants placed their entire economic, industrial, and scientific capabilities at the service of the war effort, erasing the distinction between civilian and military resources.
   a. 100-year flood
   b. 130-30 fund
   c. 1921 recession
   d. World War II

6. _____s is the social science that studies the production, distribution, and consumption of goods and services. The term _____s comes from the Ancient Greek oá¼°κονομῖα from oá¼¶κος (oikos, 'house') + vÏŒμος (nomos, 'custom' or 'law'), hence 'rules of the house(hold)'. Current _____ models developed out of the broader field of political economy in the late 19th century, owing to a desire to use an empirical approach more akin to the physical sciences.
   a. Economic
   b. Inflation
   c. Energy economics
   d. Opportunity cost

7. _____ is a misspelled phrase from Latin 'pro capite' phrase meaning per head with pro meaning 'per' or 'for each' and capite meaning 'head.' Both words together equate to the phrase 'for each head.'

Chapter 18. TAXATION AND RESOURCE ALLOCATION

It is usually used in the field of statistics to indicate the average per person for any given concern, such as income, crime rate, etc.

It is also used in wills to indicate that each of the named beneficiaries should receive, by devise or bequest, equal shares of the estate. This is in contrast to a per stirpes division, in which each branch of the inheriting family inherits an equal share of the estate.

- a. Population statistics
- b. Per capita
- c. False positive rate
- d. Sargan test

8. _____ is the incidence or process of transferring ownership of a business, enterprise, agency or public service from the public sector (government) to the private sector (business.) In a broader sense, _____ refers to transfer of any government function to the private sector including governmental functions like revenue collection and law enforcement.

The term '_____' also has been used to describe two unrelated transactions.

- a. Performance reports
- b. Privatization
- c. Ricardian equivalence
- d. Compound empowerment

9. To _____ is to impose a financial charge or other levy upon a taxpayer by a state or the functional equivalent of a state.

_____es are also imposed by many subnational entities. _____es consist of direct _____ or indirect _____, and may be paid in money or as its labour equivalent (often but not always unpaid.)

- a. 130-30 fund
- b. 100-year flood
- c. 1921 recession
- d. Tax

10. A _____ is a reduction in taxes. Economic stimulus via _____s, along with interest rate intervention and deficit spending, are one of the central tenets of Keynesian economics.

The immediate effects of a _____ are, generally, a decrease in the real income of the government and an increase in the real income of those whose tax rate has been lowered.

- a. Withholding tax
- b. Tax cut
- c. Direct taxes
- d. Popiwek

11. The term direct tax has more than one meaning: a colloquial meaning and, in the United States, a constitutional law meaning. Certain taxes may be _____ in the colloquial sense but indirect taxes in the constitutional sense.

In the UK, direct tax refers to tax levied directly off of an organisation or an individual person, like income tax.

Chapter 18. TAXATION AND RESOURCE ALLOCATION

    a. Taxation as theft

    b. National War Tax Resistance Coordinating Committee

    c. Honorarium

    d. Direct taxes

12. The _____ is an economic and political union of 27 member states, located primarily in Europe. It was established by the Treaty of Maastricht on 1 November 1993, upon the foundations of the pre-existing European Economic Community. With a population of almost 500 million, the _____ generates an estimated 30% share (US$18.4 trillion in 2008) of the nominal gross world product.

    a. ACCRA Cost of Living Index

    b. ACEA agreement

    c. European Court of Justice

    d. European Union

13. A poll tax, _____ fixed amount per individual in accordance with the census (as opposed to a percentage of income.) When a corvée is commuted for cash payment, in effect it becomes a poll tax (and vice versa, if a poll tax obligation can be worked off.) Poll taxes were important sources of revenue for many governments from ancient times until the 19th century.

    a. Cess

    b. Head tax

    c. Tax Executives Institute

    d. Privatized tax collection

14. The term _____ has more than one meaning.

In the colloquial sense, an _____, or goods and services tax (GST)) is a tax collected by an intermediary (such as a retail store) from the person who bears the ultimate economic burden of the tax (such as the customer.) The intermediary later files a tax return and forwards the tax proceeds to government with the return.

    a. Indirect tax

    b. Olivera-Tanzi effect

    c. Optimal tax

    d. User charge

15. Total _____ is defined by the United States' Bureau of Economic Analysis as

income received by persons from all sources. It includes income received from participation in production as well as from government and business transfer payments. It is the sum of compensation of employees (received), supplements to wages and salaries, proprietors' income with inventory valuation adjustment (IVA) and capital consumption adjustment (CCAdj), rental income of persons with CCAdj, _____ receipts on assets, and personal current transfer receipts, less contributions for government social insurance.

    a. Bidding

    b. Greater fool theory

    c. Dividend Discount Model

    d. Personal income

16. A _____ is a tax by which the tax rate increases as the taxable amount increases. 'Progressive' describes a distribution effect on income or expenditure, referring to the way the rate progresses from low to high, where the average tax rate is less than the marginal tax rate. It can be applied to individual taxes or to a tax system as a whole; a year, multi-year, or lifetime.

    a. Progressive tax

    b. 130-30 fund

    c. Proportional tax

    d. 100-year flood

Chapter 18. TAXATION AND RESOURCE ALLOCATION

17. _____ is an ad valorem tax that an owner is required to pay on the value of the property being taxed. _____ can be defined as 'generally, tax imposed by municipalities upon owners of property within their jurisdiction based on the value of such property.' There are three species or types of property: Land, Improvements to Land (immovable manmade objects; i.e., buildings), and Personal (movable manmade objects.) Real estate, real property or realty are all terms for the combination of land and improvements.
   a. Community property
   b. Property tax
   c. Chief Financial Officers Act of 1990
   d. Bank regulation

18. A _____ is a tax imposed so that the tax rate is fixed as the amount subject to taxation increases. In simple terms, it imposes an equal burden (relative to resources) on the rich and poor. 'Proportional' describes a distribution effect on income or expenditure, referring to the way the rate remains consistent (does not progress from 'low to high' or 'high to low' as income or consumption changes), where the marginal tax rate is equal to the average tax rate.
   a. 100-year flood
   b. Regressive tax
   c. Proportional tax
   d. 130-30 fund

19. A _____ is a tax imposed in such a manner that the tax rate decreases as the amount subject to taxation increases. In simple terms, a _____ imposes a greater burden (relative to resources) on the poor than on the rich -- there is an inverse relationship between the tax rate and the taxpayer's ability to pay as measured by assets, consumption, or income. 'Regressive' describes a distribution effect on income or expenditure, referring to the way the rate progresses from high to low, where the average tax rate exceeds the marginal tax rate.
   a. 130-30 fund
   b. Proportional tax
   c. Regressive tax
   d. 100-year flood

20. A _____ is a consumption tax charged at the point of purchase for certain goods and services. The tax is usually set as a percentage by the government charging the tax. There is usually a list of exemptions.
   a. 100-year flood
   b. 1921 recession
   c. 130-30 fund
   d. Sales tax

21. In economics, the term _____ of income or _____ refers to a simple economic model which describes the reciprocal circulation of income between producers and consumers. In the _____ model, the inter-dependent entities of producer and consumer are referred to as 'firms' and 'households' respectively and provide each other with factors in order to facilitate the flow of income. Firms provide consumers with goods and services in exchange for consumer expenditure and 'factors of production' from households.
   a. 130-30 fund
   b. 1921 recession
   c. 100-year flood
   d. Circular flow

22. An _____ is a tax levied on the financial income of people, corporations, or other legal entities. Various _____ systems exist, with varying degrees of tax incidence. Income taxation can be progressive, proportional, or regressive.
   a. ACEA agreement
   b. Income tax
   c. AD-IA Model
   d. ACCRA Cost of Living Index

23. To tax is to impose a financial charge or other levy upon a taxpayer by a state or the functional equivalent of a state. _____ are also imposed by many subnational entities. _____ consist of direct tax or indirect tax, and may be paid in money or as its labour equivalent (often but not always unpaid.)

Chapter 18. TAXATION AND RESOURCE ALLOCATION 147

    a. 1921 recession
    c. 130-30 fund
    b. 100-year flood
    d. Taxes

24. In finance, a _____ is a debt security, in which the authorized issuer owes the holders a debt and, depending on the terms of the _____, is obliged to pay interest (the coupon) and/or to repay the principal at a later date, termed maturity. A _____ is a formal contract to repay borrowed money with interest at fixed intervals.

Thus a _____ is like a loan: the issuer is the borrower (debtor), the holder is the lender (creditor), and the coupon is the interest.

    a. Callable
    c. Zero-coupon
    b. Prize Bond
    d. Bond

25. A municipality is an administrative entity composed of a clearly defined territory and its population and commonly denotes a city, town or a small grouping of them. A municipality is typically governed by a mayor and a city council or _____ council.

The notion of municipality includes townships but is not restricted to them.

    a. 1921 recession
    c. 130-30 fund
    b. 100-year flood
    d. Municipal

26. A _____ is a bond issued by a city or other local government, or their agencies. Potential issuers of _____ s include cities, counties, redevelopment agencies, school districts, publicly owned airports and seaports, and any other governmental entity (or group of governments) below the state level. _____ s may be general obligations of the issuer or secured by specified revenues.

    a. Collectivization of agriculture in Romania
    c. Fixed-income arbitrage
    b. Guaranteed investment contracts
    d. Municipal bond

27. In a company, _____ is the sum of all financial records of salaries, wages, bonuses and deductions.

A paycheck, is traditionally a paper document issued by an employer to pay an employee for services rendered. While most commonly used in the United States, recently the physical paycheck has been increasingly replaced by electronic direct deposit to bank accounts.

    a. Tax expense
    c. 100-year flood
    b. Total Expense Ratio
    d. Payroll

28. The _____ refers to the 'common well-being' or 'general welfare.' The _____ is central to policy debates, politics, democracy and the nature of government itself. While nearly everyone claims that aiding the common well-being or general welfare is positive, there is little, if any, consensus on what exactly constitutes the _____.

There are different views on how many members of the public must benefit from an action before it can be declared to be in the _____: at one extreme, an action has to benefit every single member of society in order to be truly in the _____; at the other extreme, any action can be in the _____ as long as it benefits some of the population and harms none.

Chapter 18. TAXATION AND RESOURCE ALLOCATION

a. Power Elite
c. Stealth tax
b. Second-class citizen
d. Public interest

29. _____ is a fee paid on borrowed assets. It is the price paid for the use of borrowed money, or, money earned by deposited funds. Assets that are sometimes lent with _____ include money, shares, consumer goods through hire purchase, major assets such as aircraft, and even entire factories in finance lease arrangements.
a. Insolvency
c. Asset protection
b. Interest
d. Internal debt

30. The principle that taxes should vary according to an individual's level of wealth or income is the _____ principle.
a. ACCRA Cost of Living Index
c. AD-IA Model
b. Ability-to-pay
d. ACEA agreement

31. _____ is the concept or idea of fairness in economics, particularly as to taxation or welfare economics.

In welfare economics, _____ may be distinguished from economic efficiency in overall evaluation of social welfare. Although '_____' has broader uses, it may be posed as a counterpart to economic inequality in yielding a 'good' distribution of welfare.

a. AD-IA Model
c. Equity
b. ACCRA Cost of Living Index
d. ACEA agreement

32. The term _____ refers to government debt, expenditures and revenues, or to finance (particularly financial revenue) in general.

- _____ deficit is the budget deficit of federal or local government
- _____ policy is the discretionary spending of governments. Contrasts with monetary policy.
- _____ year and _____ quarter are reporting periods for firms and other agencies.

a. Procter ' Gamble
c. Drawdown
b. Fiscal
d. Bucket shop

33. As a subfield of public economics, _____ is concerned with 'understanding which functions and instruments are best centralized and which are best placed in the sphere of decentralized levels of government' (Oates, 1999.) In other words, it is the study of how competencies (expenditure side) and fiscal instruments (revenue side) are allocated across different (vertical) layers of the administration.

An important part of its subject matter is the system of transfer payments or grants by which a central government shares its revenues with lower levels of government.

a. 130-30 fund
c. 1921 recession
b. Fiscal federalism
d. 100-year flood

34. _____ is used to assign the available resources in an economic way. It is part of resource management.

Chapter 18. TAXATION AND RESOURCE ALLOCATION

In strategic planning, is a plan for using available resources, for example human resources, especially in the near term, to achieve goals for the future.

a. 1921 recession
b. Resource allocation
c. 100-year flood
d. 130-30 fund

35. _____ is exchange of capital, goods, and services across international borders or territories. In most countries, it represents a significant share of gross domestic product (GDP.) While _____ has been present throughout much of history, its economic, social, and political importance has been on the rise in recent centuries.

a. Intra-industry trade
b. Import license
c. International trade
d. Incoterms

36. _____ is the process of changing the way taxes are collected or managed by the government.

_____ers have different goals. Some seek to reduce the level of taxation of all people by the government.

a. Tax Reform
b. Nil-rate band
c. Tax break
d. Special-purpose local-option sales tax

37. In economics, _____ is the analysis of the effect of a particular tax on the distribution of economic welfare. _____ is said to 'fall' upon the group that, at the end of the day, bears the burden of the tax. The key concept is that the _____ or tax burden does not depend on where the revenue is collected, but on the price elasticity of demand and price elasticity of supply.

a. 1921 recession
b. 130-30 fund
c. 100-year flood
d. Tax incidence

38. _____ theory is the study of how best to design a tax to avoid distortion and inefficiency. Other things being equal, if a tax-payer must choose between two mutually exclusive economic projects (say investments) that face the same pre-tax risk and returns, the one with the lower tax or with a tax break would be chosen by the rational actor. With that insight, economists argue that generally taxes distort behavior.

a. Optimal tax
b. User charge
c. Olivera-Tanzi effect
d. Optimal tax theory

Chapter 19. PRICING THE FACTORS OF PRODUCTION

1. _____ according to Onuoha (2007) is the practice of starting new organizations or revitalizing mature organizations, particularly new businesses generally in response to identified opportunities. _____ is often a difficult undertaking, as a vast majority of new businesses fail. Entrepreneurial activities are substantially different depending on the type of organization that is being started.
   a. ACCRA Cost of Living Index
   b. ACEA agreement
   c. Intrapreneurship
   d. Entrepreneurship

2. In economics, _____ are the resources employed to produce goods and services. They facilitate production but do not become part of the product (as with raw materials) or significantly transformed by the production process (as with fuel used to power machinery.) To 19th century economists, the _____ were land (natural resources, gifts from nature), labor (the ability to work), and capital goods (human-made tools and equipment.)
   a. Hicks-neutral technical change
   b. Product Pipeline
   c. Long-run
   d. Factors of production

3. In economics, the marginal product or _____ is the extra output produced by one more unit of an input (for instance, the difference in output when a firm's labour is increased from five to six units.) Assuming that no other inputs to production change, the marginal product of a given input (X) can be expressed as:

   $MP = \Delta Y/\Delta X$ = (the change of Y)/(the change of X.)

   In neoclassical economics, this is the mathematical derivative of the production function....

   a. Multifactor productivity
   b. Diseconomies of scale
   c. Marginal physical product
   d. Productive capacity

4. In microeconomics, _____ is the extra revenue that an additional unit of product will bring. It is the additional income from selling one more unit of a good; sometimes equal to price. It can also be described as the change in total revenue/change in number of units sold.
   a. Marginal revenue
   b. Market demand schedule
   c. Long term
   d. Reservation price

5. The marginal revenue productivity theory of wages, also referred to as the _____ of labor, is the change in total revenue earned by a firm that results from employing one more unit of labor. It is a neoclassical model that determines, under some conditions, the optimal number of workers to employ at an exogenously determined market wage rate.

   The _____ of a worker is equal to the product of the marginal product of labor (MP) and the marginal revenue (MR), given by MR×MP = _____.

   a. Marginal revenue productivity theory of wages
   b. Real prices and ideal prices
   c. Coal depletion
   d. Marginal revenue product

6. _____ in economics and business is the result of an exchange and from that trade we assign a numerical monetary value to a good, service or asset. If Alice trades Bob 4 apples for an orange, the _____ of an orange is 4 apples. Inversely, the _____ of an apple is 1/4 oranges.
   a. Price war
   b. Price
   c. Premium pricing
   d. Price book

Chapter 19. PRICING THE FACTORS OF PRODUCTION

7. _____ in economics refers to metrics and measures of output from production processes, per unit of input. Labor _____, for example, is typically measured as a ratio of output per labor-hour, an input. _____ may be conceived of as a metrics of the technical or engineering efficiency of production.
   - a. Fordism
   - b. Piece work
   - c. Productivity
   - d. Production-possibility frontier

8. In economics, _____ is the total supply of goods and services produced by a national economy during a specific time period. It is the total amount of goods and services in the economy available at all possible price levels.
   - a. Aggregate supply
   - b. Aggregate demand
   - c. Aggregation problem
   - d. Aggregate expenditure

9. In economics, the term _____ of income or _____ refers to a simple economic model which describes the reciprocal circulation of income between producers and consumers. In the _____ model, the inter-dependent entities of producer and consumer are referred to as 'firms' and 'households' respectively and provide each other with factors in order to facilitate the flow of income. Firms provide consumers with goods and services in exchange for consumer expenditure and 'factors of production' from households.
   - a. 100-year flood
   - b. 1921 recession
   - c. 130-30 fund
   - d. Circular flow

10. In economics, _____ is how a natione;s total economy is distributed among its population. ._____ has always been a central concern of economic theory and economic policy. Classical economists such as Adam Smith, Thomas Malthus and David Ricardo were mainly concerned with factor _____, that is, the distribution of income between the main factors of production, land, labour and capital.
    - a. Authorised capital
    - b. Eco commerce
    - c. Equipment trust certificate
    - d. Income distribution

11. In microeconomics, _____ is quite simply the conversion of inputs into outputs. It is an economic process that uses resources to create a good or service that is suitable for exchange. This can include manufacturing, storing, shipping, and packaging.
    - a. Red Guards
    - b. MET
    - c. Production
    - d. Solved

12. Economics:

    - _____, the desire to own something and the ability to pay for it
    - _____ curve, a graphic representation of a _____ schedule
    - _____ deposit, the money in checking accounts
    - _____ pull theory, the theory that inflation occurs when _____ for goods and services exceeds existing supplies
    - _____ schedule, a table that lists the quantity of a good a person will buy it each different price
    - _____ side economics, the school of economics at believes government spending and tax cuts open economy by raising _____

Chapter 19. PRICING THE FACTORS OF PRODUCTION

a. Variability
b. Production
c. McKesson ' Robbins scandal
d. Demand

13. In economics, the _____ can be defined as the graph depicting the relationship between the price of a certain commodity, and the amount of it that consumers are willing and able to purchase at that given price. It is a graphic representation of a demand schedule. The _____ for all consumers together follows from the _____ of every individual consumer: the individual demands at each price are added together.
   a. Cost curve
   b. Wage curve
   c. Kuznets curve
   d. Demand curve

14. _____ is a term in economics, where demand for one good or service occurs as a result of demand for another. This may occur as the former is a part of production of the second. For example, demand for coal leads to _____ for mining, as coal must be mined for coal to be consumed.
   a. Days Sales Outstanding
   b. Leontief production function
   c. Derived demand
   d. Rate risk

15. _____ is the term denoting either an entrance or changes which are inserted into a system and which activate/modify a process. It is an abstract concept, used in the modeling, system(s) design and system(s) exploitation. It is usually connected with other terms, e.g., _____ field, _____ variable, _____ parameter, _____ value, _____ signal, _____ device and _____ file.
   a. AD-IA Model
   b. ACCRA Cost of Living Index
   c. Input
   d. ACEA agreement

16. _____ is an economic model based on price, utility and quantity in a market. It predicts that in a competitive market, price will function to equalize the quantity demanded by consumers, and the quantity supplied by producers, resulting in an economic equilibrium of price and quantity. The model incorporates other factors changing equilibrium as a shift of demand and/or supply.
   a. Deferred gratification
   b. Supply and demand
   c. Rational addiction
   d. Joint demand

17. _____ is a broad label that refers to any individuals or households that use goods and services generated within the economy. The concept of a _____ is used in different contexts, so that the usage and significance of the term may vary.

Typically when business people and economists talk of _____s they are talking about person as _____, an aggregated commodity item with little individuality other than that expressed in the buy/not-buy decision.

   a. 1921 recession
   b. 130-30 fund
   c. 100-year flood
   d. Consumer

18. In economics, _____ is the ratio of the percent change in one variable to the percent change in another variable. It is a tool for measuring the responsiveness of a function to changes in parameters in a relative way. Commonly analyzed are _____ of substitution, price and wealth.

Chapter 19. PRICING THE FACTORS OF PRODUCTION

a. ACEA agreement
b. ACCRA Cost of Living Index
c. Elasticity of demand
d. Elasticity

19. In finance, a _____ is a debt security, in which the authorized issuer owes the holders a debt and, depending on the terms of the _____, is obliged to pay interest (the coupon) and/or to repay the principal at a later date, termed maturity. A _____ is a formal contract to repay borrowed money with interest at fixed intervals.

Thus a _____ is like a loan: the issuer is the borrower (debtor), the holder is the lender (creditor), and the coupon is the interest.

a. Prize Bond
b. Callable
c. Bond
d. Zero-coupon

20. _____ is a three-volume work on finance published by Austrian economist Eugen von Böhm-Bawerk.

The first two volumes were published in the 1880s when he was teaching at the University of Innsbruck.

The first volume of _____, titled History and Critique of Interest Theories (1884), is an exhaustive survey of the alternative treatments of the phenomenon of interest: use theories, productivity theories, abstinence theories, and many more.

a. The General Theory of Employment, Interest and Money
b. Development as Freedom
c. The Bell Curve
d. Capital and interest

21. _____ is a fee paid on borrowed assets. It is the price paid for the use of borrowed money , or, money earned by deposited funds . Assets that are sometimes lent with _____ include money, shares, consumer goods through hire purchase, major assets such as aircraft, and even entire factories in finance lease arrangements.

a. Internal debt
b. Insolvency
c. Asset protection
d. Interest

22. An _____ is the price a borrower pays for the use of money they do not own, for instance a small company might borrow from a bank to kick start their business, and the return a lender receives for deferring the use of funds, by lending it to the borrower. _____s are normally expressed as a percentage rate over the period of one year.

_____s targets are also a vital tool of monetary policy and are used to control variables like investment, inflation, and unemployment.

a. ACCRA Cost of Living Index
b. Arrow-Debreu model
c. Interest rate
d. Enterprise value

Chapter 19. PRICING THE FACTORS OF PRODUCTION

23. The Demand side is a term used in economics to refer to a number of things:

   - The demand element of a supply and demand partial equilibrium diagram, in microeconomics
   - The aggregate demand in an economy, in macroeconomics
   - Economic policy actions which are designed to affect aggregate demand.
   - _____ learning referring to the incentive to learn how to use and modify free software as opposed to buying conventional software.

   The term is also used broadly to distinguish supply-side economics from other schools, for instance Keynesian economics.

   a. CPFR
   b. Delayed differentiation
   c. Reverse auction
   d. Demand-side

24. The _____ is the central banking system of the United States. Created in 1913 by the enactment of the Federal Reserve Act (signed by Woodrow Wilson), it is a quasi-public and quasi-private (government entity with private components) banking system that comprises (1) the presidentially appointed Board of Governors of the _____ in Washington, D.C.; (2) the Federal Open Market Committee; (3) twelve regional Federal Reserve Banks located in major cities throughout the nation acting as fiscal agents for the U.S. Treasury, each with its own nine-member board of directors; (4) numerous other private U.S. member banks, which subscribe to required amounts of non-transferable stock in their regional Federal Reserve Banks; and (5) various advisory councils. Since February 2006, Ben Bernanke has served as the Chairman of the Board of Governors of the _____.

   a. Federal Reserve System
   b. Monetary Policy Report to the Congress
   c. Federal Reserve System Open Market Account
   d. Term auction facility

25. Economic _____ is defined as an excess distribution to any factor in a production process above that which is required to induce the factor into the process or any excess above that which is necessary to keep the factor in its current use..

   Classical Factor _____ is primarily concerned with the fee paid for the use of fixed (e.g. natural) resources. The classical definition is expressed as any excess payment above that required to induce or provide for production.

   a. Rent
   b. 100-year flood
   c. 1921 recession
   d. 130-30 fund

26. _____s is the social science that studies the production, distribution, and consumption of goods and services. The term _____s comes from the Ancient Greek oá¼°κονομῖα from oá¼¶κος (oikos, 'house') + vĺŒµος (nomos, 'custom' or 'law'), hence 'rules of the house(hold)'. Current _____ models developed out of the broader field of political economy in the late 19th century, owing to a desire to use an empirical approach more akin to the physical sciences.
   a. Opportunity cost
   b. Inflation
   c. Energy economics
   d. Economic

27. In economics supernormal profit _____ or pure profit or excess profits, is a profit exceeding the normal profit. Normal profit equals the opportunity cost of labour and capital, while supernormal profit is the amount exceeds the normal return from these input factors in production.

Chapter 19. PRICING THE FACTORS OF PRODUCTION

_____ is usually generated by an oligopoly or a monopoly; however, these firms often try to hide this from the market to reduce risk of competition or antitrust investigation.

- a. Economic profit
- c. Abnormal profit
- b. Accounting profit
- d. ACCRA Cost of Living Index

28. _____ was a survey conducted by the U.S. Department of Justice to gauge the prevalence of alcohol and illegal drug use among prior arrestees. It was a reformulation of the prior Drug Use Forecasting (DUF) program, focused on five drugs in particular: cocaine, marijuana, methamphetamine, opiates, and PCP.

Participants were randomly selected from arrest records in major metropolitan areas; because no personally identifying information is taken from each record chosen, the resulting data can be correlated to arrest rates, but not to the total population of persons charged.

- a. AD-IA Model
- c. ACCRA Cost of Living Index
- b. ACEA agreement
- d. Arrestee Drug Abuse Monitoring

29. _____ was a Scottish moral philosopher and a pioneer of political economy. One of the key figures of the Scottish Enlightenment, Smith is the author of The Theory of Moral Sentiments and An Inquiry into the Nature and Causes of the Wealth of Nations. The latter, usually abbreviated as The Wealth of Nations, is considered his magnum opus and the first modern work of economics.
- a. Adolf Hitler
- c. Adolph Fischer
- b. Alan Greenspan
- d. Adam Smith

30. Competition law, known in the United States as _____ law, has three main elements:

- prohibiting agreements or practices that restrict free trading and competition between business entities. This includes in particular the repression of cartels.
- banning abusive behaviour by a firm dominating a market, or anti-competitive practices that tend to lead to such a dominant position. Practices controlled in this way may include predatory pricing, tying, price gouging, refusal to deal, and many others.
- supervising the mergers and acquisitions of large corporations, including some joint ventures. Transactions that are considered to threaten the competitive process can be prohibited altogether, or approved subject to 'remedies' such as an obligation to divest part of the merged business or to offer licences or access to facilities to enable other businesses to continue competing.

The substance and practice of competition law varies from jurisdiction to jurisdiction. Protecting the interests of consumers (consumer welfare) and ensuring that entrepreneurs have an opportunity to compete in the market economy are often treated as important objectives. Competition law is closely connected with law on deregulation of access to markets, state aids and subsidies, the privatisation of state owned assets and the establishment of independent sector regulators. In recent decades, competition law has been viewed as a way to provide better public services.

Chapter 19. PRICING THE FACTORS OF PRODUCTION

a. United Kingdom competition law
b. Anti-Inflation Act
c. Antitrust
d. Intellectual property law

31. _____, known in the United States as antitrust law, has three main elements:

- prohibiting agreements or practices that restrict free trading and competition between business entities. This includes in particular the repression of cartels.
- banning abusive behaviour by a firm dominating a market, or anti-competitive practices that tend to lead to such a dominant position. Practices controlled in this way may include predatory pricing, tying, price gouging, refusal to deal, and many others.
- supervising the mergers and acquisitions of large corporations, including some joint ventures. Transactions that are considered to threaten the competitive process can be prohibited altogether, or approved subject to 'remedies' such as an obligation to divest part of the merged business or to offer licences or access to facilities to enable other businesses to continue competing.

The substance and practice of _____ varies from jurisdiction to jurisdiction. Protecting the interests of consumers (consumer welfare) and ensuring that entrepreneurs have an opportunity to compete in the market economy are often treated as important objectives. _____ is closely connected with law on deregulation of access to markets, state aids and subsidies, the privatisation of state owned assets and the establishment of independent sector regulators. In recent decades, _____ has been viewed as a way to provide better public services.

a. Competition law
b. Hostile work environment
c. Due diligence
d. Fee simple

32. In economics, a _____ exists when a specific individual or enterprise has sufficient control over a particular product or service to determine significantly the terms on which other individuals shall have access to it. Monopolies are thus characterized by a lack of economic competition for the good or service that they provide and a lack of viable substitute goods. The verb 'monopolize' refers to the process by which a firm gains persistently greater market share than what is expected under perfect competition.

a. 100-year flood
b. 1921 recession
c. Monopoly
d. 130-30 fund

33. _____ or economic opportunity loss is the value of the next best alternative foregone as the result of making a decision. _____ analysis is an important part of a company's decision-making processes but is not treated as an actual cost in any financial statement. The next best thing that a person can engage in is referred to as the _____ of doing the best thing and ignoring the next best thing to be done.

a. Economic
b. Economic ideology
c. Industrial organization
d. Opportunity cost

34. The _____ is the expected return forgone by bypassing of other potential investment activities for a given capital. It is a rate of return that investors could earn in financial markets.

a. AD-IA Model
b. Opportunity cost of capital
c. ACCRA Cost of Living Index
d. ACEA agreement

35. The _____ is an expected return that the provider of capital plans to earn on their investment.

Chapter 19. PRICING THE FACTORS OF PRODUCTION

Capital (money) used for funding a business should earn returns for the capital providers who risk their capital. For an investment to be worthwhile, the expected return on capital must be greater than the _____.

a. Modigliani-Miller theorem
b. Capital expenditure
c. Capital intensive
d. Cost of capital

36. _____ refers to laws or ordinances that set price controls on the renting of residential housing. It functions as a price ceiling.

_____ exists in approximately 40 countries around the world.

a. 100-year flood
b. Tenant rights
c. National Housing Conference
d. Rent control

37. In economics, a _____ is a table that lists the quantity of a good a person will buy it each different price See Demand curve.

a. Free contract
b. Rational irrationality
c. Federal Reserve districts
d. Demand schedule

38. In economics, _____ is the difference between a company's total revenue and its opportunity costs. It is the increase in wealth that an investor has from making an investment, taking into consideration all costs associated with that investment including the opportunity cost of capital.

Profit is the factor income of the entrepreneur.

a. Accounting profit
b. ACCRA Cost of Living Index
c. Economic profit
d. Operating profit

39. _____ is a financial mechanism in which a debtor obtains the right to delay payments to a creditor, for a defined period of time, in exchange for a charge or fee. Essentially, the party that owes money in the present purchases the right to delay the payment until some future date. The discount, or charge, is simply the difference between the original amount owed in the present and the amount that has to be paid in the future to settle the debt.

a. Maximum life span
b. Certified Risk Manager
c. Generalized linear model
d. Discounting

40. _____ is the value on a given date of a future payment or series of future payments, discounted to reflect the time value of money and other factors such as investment risk. _____ calculations are widely used in business and economics to provide a means to compare cash flows at different times on a meaningful 'like to like' basis.

Money value fluctuates over time: $100 today are not worth $100 in five years.

a. Future value
b. Tax shield
c. Present value
d. Present value of costs

Chapter 19. PRICING THE FACTORS OF PRODUCTION

41. _____ is the a method of technical and economic research of the systems for purpose to optimize a parity between system's consumer functions or properties and expenses to achieve those functions or properties.

This methodology for continuous perfection of production, industrial technologies, organizational structures was developed by Juryj Sobolev in 1948 at the 'Perm telephone factory'

- 1948 Juryj Sobolev - the first success in application of a method analysis at the 'Perm telephone factory'.
- 1949 - the first application for the invention as result of use of the new method.

Today in economically developed countries practically each enterprise or the company use methodology of the kind of functional-cost analysis as a practice of the quality management, most full satisfying to principles of standards of series ISO 9000.

- Interest of consumer not in products itself, but the advantage which it will receive from its usage.
- The consumer aspires to reduce his expenses
- Functions needed by consumer can be executed in the various ways, and, hence, with various efficiency and expenses. Among possible alternatives of realization of functions exist such in which the parity of quality and the price is the optimal for the consumer.

The goal of _____ is achievement of the highest consumer satisfaction of production at simultaneous decrease in all kinds of industrial expenses Classical _____ has three English synonyms - Value Engineering, Value Management, Value Analysis.

a. Monopoly wage
c. Staple financing
b. Function cost analysis
d. Willingness to pay

Chapter 20. LABOR AND ENTREPRENEURSHIP: THE HUMAN INPUTS

1. _____ is a specific term used in companies' financial reporting from the company-whole point of view. Because that use excludes the effects of changing ownership interest, an economic measure of _____ is necessary for financial analysis from the shareholders' point of view

_____ is defined by the Financial Accounting Standards Board, or FASB, as e;the change in equity [net assets] of a business enterprise during a period from transactions and other events and circumstances from nonowner sources. It includes all changes in equity during a period except those resulting from investments by owners and distributions to owners.e;

_____ is the sum of net income and other items that must bypass the income statement because they have not been realized, including items like an unrealized holding gain or loss from available for sale securities and foreign currency translation gains or losses.

   a. Net national income
   b. Real income
   c. Windfall gain
   d. Comprehensive income

2. An _____ is a person who has possession of an enterprise and assumes significant accountability for the inherent risks and the outcome. It is an ambitious leader who combines land, labor, and capital to create and market new goods or services. The term is a loanword from French and was first defined by the Irish economist Richard Cantillon.
   a. ACCRA Cost of Living Index
   b. ACEA agreement
   c. Expansionary policies
   d. Entrepreneur

3. The _____ or gross domestic income (GDI), a basic measure of an economy's economic performance, is the market value of all final goods and services produced within the borders of a nation in a year. _____ can be defined in three ways, all of which are conceptually identical. First, it is equal to the total expenditures for all final goods and services produced within the country in a stipulated period of time (usually a 365-day year.)
   a. Market structure
   b. Countercyclical
   c. Monopolistic competition
   d. Gross domestic product

4. The _____ was a worldwide economic downturn starting in most places in 1929 and ending at different times in the 1930s or early 1940s for different countries. It was the largest and most important economic depression in the 20th century, and is used in the 21st century as an example of how far the world's economy can fall. The _____ originated in the United States; historians most often use as a starting date the stock market crash on October 29, 1929, known as Black Tuesday.
   a. Jarrow March
   b. Wall Street Crash of 1929
   c. British Empire Economic Conference
   d. Great Depression

5. _____, 1st Baron Keynes was a renowned economist from Britain whose many ideas on economic and political theories as well as on many governments' monetary policies influenced America. He advocated a government that played an active role in the lives of people regarding business, economy, etc. In this role, the government would use fiscal measures to reduce the consequences of recessions, economic depressions and booms.
   a. Adam Smith
   b. Adolf Hitler
   c. John Maynard Keynes
   d. Adolph Fischer

Chapter 20. LABOR AND ENTREPRENEURSHIP: THE HUMAN INPUTS

6. An _____, in economics, is the amount by which the real Gross domestic product exceeds potential GDP. The real GDP is also known as GDP 'adjusted for inflation', 'constant prices' GDP or 'constant dollar' GDP, because it measures the aggregate output in a country's income accounts in a given year, expressed in base-year prices. On the other hand, the potential GDP is the quantity of real GDP when a country's economy is at full-employment.

   a. AD-IA Model
   b. ACCRA Cost of Living Index
   c. ACEA agreement
   d. Inflationary gap

7. The term _____s refers to wages that have been adjusted for inflation. This term is used in contrast to nominal wages or unadjusted wages.

   The use of adjusted figures is in undertaking some form of economic analysis.

   a. Federal Wage System
   b. Profit sharing
   c. Real wage
   d. Living wage

8. _____ was an American inventor best known as the inventor of the cotton gin. This was one of the key inventions of the industrial revolution and shaped the economy of the antebellum South. Whitney's invention made short staple cotton into a profitable crop, which strengthened the economic foundation of slavery.

   a. Oskar Morgenstern
   b. Alfred Marshall
   c. Andrew Carnegie
   d. Eli Whitney

9. _____ was a global military conflict which involved a majority of the world's nations, including all of the great powers, organized into two opposing military alliances: the Allies and the Axis. The war involved the mobilization of over 100 million military personnel, making it the most widespread war in history. In a state of 'total war', the major participants placed their entire economic, industrial, and scientific capabilities at the service of the war effort, erasing the distinction between civilian and military resources.

   a. 130-30 fund
   b. 100-year flood
   c. 1921 recession
   d. World War II

10. In a _____ there is both a monopoly (a single seller) and monopsony (a single buyer) in the same market.

    In such market price and output will be determined by the non economic forces like bargaining power of both buyer and seller. A _____ model is often used in situations where the switching costs of both sides are prohibitively high.

    a. Price takers
    b. Bilateral monopoly
    c. Revenue-cap regulation
    d. Market concentration

11. _____s is the social science that studies the production, distribution, and consumption of goods and services. The term _____s comes from the Ancient Greek οἰκονομία from οἶκος (oikos, 'house') + νόμος (nomos, 'custom' or 'law'), hence 'rules of the house(hold)'. Current _____ models developed out of the broader field of political economy in the late 19th century, owing to a desire to use an empirical approach more akin to the physical sciences.

    a. Inflation
    b. Economic
    c. Energy economics
    d. Opportunity cost

Chapter 20. LABOR AND ENTREPRENEURSHIP: THE HUMAN INPUTS

12. In economics, a _____ exists when a specific individual or enterprise has sufficient control over a particular product or service to determine significantly the terms on which other individuals shall have access to it. Monopolies are thus characterized by a lack of economic competition for the good or service that they provide and a lack of viable substitute goods. The verb 'monopolize' refers to the process by which a firm gains persistently greater market share than what is expected under perfect competition.
    a. 130-30 fund
    b. 100-year flood
    c. 1921 recession
    d. Monopoly

13. _____ is a misspelled phrase from Latin 'pro capite' phrase meaning per head with pro meaning 'per' or 'for each' and capite meaning 'head.' Both words together equate to the phrase 'for each head.'

It is usually used in the field of statistics to indicate the average per person for any given concern, such as income, crime rate, etc.

It is also used in wills to indicate that each of the named beneficiaries should receive, by devise or bequest, equal shares of the estate. This is in contrast to a per stirpes division, in which each branch of the inheriting family inherits an equal share of the estate.

   a. Per capita
   b. Population statistics
   c. False positive rate
   d. Sargan test

14. _____ is one of the four Ps of the marketing mix. The other three aspects are product, promotion, and place. It is also a key variable in microeconomic price allocation theory.
    a. Premium pricing
    b. Guaranteed Maximum Price
    c. Point of total assumption
    d. Pricing

15. Economics:

   - _____ ,the desire to own something and the ability to pay for it
   - _____ curve,a graphic representation of a _____ schedule
   - _____ deposit, the money in checking accounts
   - _____ pull theory,the theory that inflation occurs when _____ for goods and services exceeds existing supplies
   - _____ schedule,a table that lists the quantity of a good a person will buy it each different price
   - _____ side economics,the school of economics at believes government spending and tax cuts open economy by raising _____

   a. Variability
   b. McKesson ' Robbins scandal
   c. Demand
   d. Production

16. In economics, the _____ can be defined as the graph depicting the relationship between the price of a certain commodity, and the amount of it that consumers are willing and able to purchase at that given price. It is a graphic representation of a demand schedule. The _____ for all consumers together follows from the _____ of every individual consumer: the individual demands at each price are added together.

Chapter 20. LABOR AND ENTREPRENEURSHIP: THE HUMAN INPUTS

a. Kuznets curve
c. Cost curve
b. Demand curve
d. Wage curve

17. _____ is a broad label that refers to any individuals or households that use goods and services generated within the economy. The concept of a _____ is used in different contexts, so that the usage and significance of the term may vary.

Typically when business people and economists talk of _____s they are talking about person as _____, an aggregated commodity item with little individuality other than that expressed in the buy/not-buy decision.

a. 130-30 fund
c. 100-year flood
b. 1921 recession
d. Consumer

18. _____ is a term used by economists to refer to the higher wages earned by unionized workers compared to non-unionized workers. It entails the idea that unions act as coercive monopolies by raising wages other than what they would be if there was competition between individual workers.

a. Rate risk
c. Global strategy
b. Seasonal industry
d. Monopoly wage

19. _____ is a term in economics, where demand for one good or service occurs as a result of demand for another. This may occur as the former is a part of production of the second. For example, demand for coal leads to _____ for mining, as coal must be mined for coal to be consumed.

a. Days Sales Outstanding
c. Rate risk
b. Leontief production function
d. Derived demand

20. _____ refers to the stock of skills and knowledge embodied in the ability to perform labor so as to produce economic value. It is the skills and knowledge gained by a worker through education and experience. Many early economic theories refer to it simply as labor, one of three factors of production, and consider it to be a fungible resource -- homogeneous and easily interchangeable. Other conceptions of labor dispense with these assumptions.

a. Human capital
c. Price theory
b. General equilibrium
d. Law of increasing costs

21. In microeconomics, _____ is the extra revenue that an additional unit of product will bring. It is the additional income from selling one more unit of a good; sometimes equal to price. It can also be described as the change in total revenue/change in number of units sold.

a. Reservation price
c. Long term
b. Marginal revenue
d. Market demand schedule

22. The marginal revenue productivity theory of wages, also referred to as the _____ of labor, is the change in total revenue earned by a firm that results from employing one more unit of labor. It is a neoclassical model that determines, under some conditions, the optimal number of workers to employ at an exogenously determined market wage rate.

The _____ of a worker is equal to the product of the marginal product of labor (MP) and the marginal revenue (MR), given by MR×MP = _____.

Chapter 20. LABOR AND ENTREPRENEURSHIP: THE HUMAN INPUTS

a. Marginal revenue productivity theory of wages
b. Coal depletion
c. Marginal revenue product
d. Real prices and ideal prices

23. _____ is an economic model based on price, utility and quantity in a market. It predicts that in a competitive market, price will function to equalize the quantity demanded by consumers, and the quantity supplied by producers, resulting in an economic equilibrium of price and quantity. The model incorporates other factors changing equilibrium as a shift of demand and/or supply.

a. Rational addiction
b. Joint demand
c. Deferred gratification
d. Supply and demand

24. In economics, _____ is the ratio of the percent change in one variable to the percent change in another variable. It is a tool for measuring the responsiveness of a function to changes in parameters in a relative way. Commonly analyzed are _____ of substitution, price and wealth.

a. ACEA agreement
b. ACCRA Cost of Living Index
c. Elasticity of demand
d. Elasticity

25. In economics, the people in the _____ are the suppliers of labor. The _____ is all the nonmilitary people who are employed or unemployed. In 2005, the worldwide _____ was over 3 billion people.

a. Distributed workforce
b. Departmentalization
c. Labor force
d. Grenelle agreements

26. A trade union or _____ is an organization of workers who have banded together to achieve common goals in key areas and working conditions. The trade union, through its leadership, bargains with the employer on behalf of union members (rank and file members) and negotiates labor contracts (Collective bargaining) with employers. This may include the negotiation of wages, work rules, complaint procedures, rules governing hiring, firing and promotion of workers, benefits, workplace safety and policies.

a. Labor union
b. Basis of futures
c. Business valuation standards
d. Demand-side technologies

27. The _____ is the number of total hours that workers wish to work at a given real wage rate.

Labor supply curves are derived from the 'labor-leisure' trade-off. More hours worked earn higher incomes but necessitate a cut in the amount of leisure that workers enjoy.

a. Dual labor market
b. Compound interest
c. De minimis fringe benefits
d. Supply of Labor

28. The supply of labor is the number of total hours that workers wish to work at a given real wage rate.

_____ curves are derived from the 'labor-leisure' trade-off. More hours worked earn higher incomes but necessitate a cut in the amount of leisure that workers enjoy.

a. Human trafficking
b. Creative capitalism
c. Late capitalism
d. Labor supply

29. In economics, the _____ is the change in consumption resulting from a change in real income.

Another important item that can change is the money income of the consumer. The _____ is the phenomenon observed through changes in purchasing power.

a. Export subsidy
c. Inflation hedge
b. Equilibrium wage
d. Income effect

30. In economics, the _____ is the wage rate that produces neither an access supply of workers nor an excess demand for workers and labor market. See economic equilibrium.
a. Effective unemployment rate
c. International free trade agreement
b. Economic stability
d. Equilibrium wage

31. In economics, the marginal product or _____ is the extra output produced by one more unit of an input (for instance, the difference in output when a firm's labour is increased from five to six units.) Assuming that no other inputs to production change, the marginal product of a given input (X) can be expressed as:

$MP = \Delta Y/\Delta X$ = (the change of Y)/(the change of X.)

In neoclassical economics, this is the mathematical derivative of the production function....

a. Productive capacity
c. Multifactor productivity
b. Marginal physical product
d. Diseconomies of scale

32. A _____ is a group of people who share or are motivated by at least one common issue or interest, or work together on a specific project(s) to achieve a common objective. _____s are also characterised by attempts to share and exercise political and social power and to make decisions on a consensus-driven and egalitarian basis. _____s differ from cooperatives in that they are not necessarily focused upon an economic benefit or saving (but can be that as well.)
a. 100-year flood
c. 130-30 fund
b. 1921 recession
d. Collective

33. In organized labor, _____ is the method whereby workers organize together (usually in unions) to meet, converse, and negotiate upon the work conditions with their employers normally resulting in a written contract setting forth the wages, hours, and other conditions to be observed for a stipulated period.It is the practice in which union and company representatives meet to negotiate a new labor contract. In various national labor and employment law contexts, _____ takes on a more specific legal meaning and so, in a broad sense, however, it is the coming together of workers to negotiate their employment.

A collective agreement is a labor contract between an employer and one or more unions.

a. Demarcation dispute
c. Strikebreaker
b. Designated Suppliers Program
d. Collective bargaining

Chapter 20. LABOR AND ENTREPRENEURSHIP: THE HUMAN INPUTS

34. A _____ or labor union is an organization of workers who have banded together to achieve common goals in key areas and working conditions. The _____, through its leadership, bargains with the employer on behalf of union members (rank and file members) and negotiates labor contracts (Collective bargaining) with employers. This may include the negotiation of wages, work rules, complaint procedures, rules governing hiring, firing and promotion of workers, benefits, workplace safety and policies.
   a. Trade union
   b. Consumer goods
   c. Guaranteed investment contracts
   d. Case-Shiller Home Price Indices

35. The term '_____' refers to the concept of collecting information and attempting to spot a pattern in the information. In some fields of study, the term '_____' has more formally-defined meanings.

In project management _____ is a mathematical technique that uses historical results to predict future outcome.

   a. Coefficient of determination
   b. Trend analysis
   c. Quantile regression
   d. Probit model

36. The _____ in New York City on March 25, 1911, was the largest industrial disaster in the history of the city of New York, causing the death of 146 garment workers who either died from the fire or jumped to their deaths. It was the worst workplace disaster in New York City until September 11, 2001. The fire led to legislation requiring improved factory safety standards and helped spur the growth of the International Ladies' Garment Workers' Union, which fought for safer and better working conditions for sweatshop workers in that industry.
   a. Triangle Shirtwaist Factory fire
   b. 130-30 fund
   c. 100-year flood
   d. 1921 recession

37. _____ is a cross-disciplinary area concerned with protecting the safety, health and welfare of people engaged in work or employment. As a secondary effect, it may also protect co-workers, family members, employers, customers, suppliers, nearby communities, and other members of the public who are impacted by the workplace environment. It may involve interactions among many subject areas, including occupational medicine, occupational (or industrial) hygiene, public health, safety engineering, chemistry, health physics, ergonomics, toxicology, epidemiology, environmental health, industrial relations, public policy, sociology, and occupational health psychology.
   a. AD-IA Model
   b. ACEA agreement
   c. ACCRA Cost of Living Index
   d. Occupational safety and health

38. _____ was a survey conducted by the U.S. Department of Justice to gauge the prevalence of alcohol and illegal drug use among prior arrestees. It was a reformulation of the prior Drug Use Forecasting (DUF) program, focused on five drugs in particular: cocaine, marijuana, methamphetamine, opiates, and PCP.

Participants were randomly selected from arrest records in major metropolitan areas; because no personally identifying information is taken from each record chosen, the resulting data can be correlated to arrest rates, but not to the total population of persons charged.

   a. ACEA agreement
   b. Arrestee Drug Abuse Monitoring
   c. ACCRA Cost of Living Index
   d. AD-IA Model

Chapter 20. LABOR AND ENTREPRENEURSHIP: THE HUMAN INPUTS

39. _____ was a Scottish moral philosopher and a pioneer of political economy. One of the key figures of the Scottish Enlightenment, Smith is the author of The Theory of Moral Sentiments and An Inquiry into the Nature and Causes of the Wealth of Nations. The latter, usually abbreviated as The Wealth of Nations, is considered his magnum opus and the first modern work of economics.

   a. Adam Smith
   b. Adolf Hitler
   c. Alan Greenspan
   d. Adolph Fischer

40. Competition law, known in the United States as _____ law, has three main elements:

- prohibiting agreements or practices that restrict free trading and competition between business entities. This includes in particular the repression of cartels.
- banning abusive behaviour by a firm dominating a market, or anti-competitive practices that tend to lead to such a dominant position. Practices controlled in this way may include predatory pricing, tying, price gouging, refusal to deal, and many others.
- supervising the mergers and acquisitions of large corporations, including some joint ventures. Transactions that are considered to threaten the competitive process can be prohibited altogether, or approved subject to 'remedies' such as an obligation to divest part of the merged business or to offer licences or access to facilities to enable other businesses to continue competing.

The substance and practice of competition law varies from jurisdiction to jurisdiction. Protecting the interests of consumers (consumer welfare) and ensuring that entrepreneurs have an opportunity to compete in the market economy are often treated as important objectives. Competition law is closely connected with law on deregulation of access to markets, state aids and subsidies, the privatisation of state owned assets and the establishment of independent sector regulators. In recent decades, competition law has been viewed as a way to provide better public services.

   a. United Kingdom competition law
   b. Antitrust
   c. Intellectual property law
   d. Anti-Inflation Act

41. _____, known in the United States as antitrust law, has three main elements:

- prohibiting agreements or practices that restrict free trading and competition between business entities. This includes in particular the repression of cartels.
- banning abusive behaviour by a firm dominating a market, or anti-competitive practices that tend to lead to such a dominant position. Practices controlled in this way may include predatory pricing, tying, price gouging, refusal to deal, and many others.
- supervising the mergers and acquisitions of large corporations, including some joint ventures. Transactions that are considered to threaten the competitive process can be prohibited altogether, or approved subject to 'remedies' such as an obligation to divest part of the merged business or to offer licences or access to facilities to enable other businesses to continue competing.

Chapter 20. LABOR AND ENTREPRENEURSHIP: THE HUMAN INPUTS

The substance and practice of _____ varies from jurisdiction to jurisdiction. Protecting the interests of consumers (consumer welfare) and ensuring that entrepreneurs have an opportunity to compete in the market economy are often treated as important objectives. _____ is closely connected with law on deregulation of access to markets, state aids and subsidies, the privatisation of state owned assets and the establishment of independent sector regulators. In recent decades, _____ has been viewed as a way to provide better public services.

a. Due diligence
b. Hostile work environment
c. Fee simple
d. Competition law

42. In economics, a _____ 'purchase') is a market form in which only one buyer faces many sellers. It is an example of imperfect competition, similar to a monopoly, in which only one seller faces many buyers. As the only purchaser of a good or service, the 'monopsonist' may dictate terms to its suppliers in the same manner that a monopolist controls the market for its buyers.

a. 100-year flood
b. 1921 recession
c. 130-30 fund
d. Monopsony

43. The International Union, United Automobile, Aerospace and Agricultural Implement Workers of America, better known as the _____ , is a labor union which represents workers in the United States and Puerto Rico. Founded in order to represent workers in the automobile manufacturing industry, _____ members in the 21st century work in industries as diverse as health care, casino gaming and higher education. Headquartered in Detroit, Michigan, the union has approximately 800 local unions, which negotiated 3,100 contracts with some 2,000 employers.

a. ACEA agreement
b. ACCRA Cost of Living Index
c. AD-IA Model
d. United Auto Workers

44. _____ is the term denoting either an entrance or changes which are inserted into a system and which activate/modify a process. It is an abstract concept, used in the modeling, system(s) design and system(s) exploitation. It is usually connected with other terms, e.g., _____ field, _____ variable, _____ parameter, _____ value, _____ signal, _____ device and _____ file.

a. AD-IA Model
b. ACEA agreement
c. ACCRA Cost of Living Index
d. Input

45. The process of _____ involves the introduction of a good or service that is new or substantially improved. This includes, but is not limited to, improvements in functional characteristics, technical abilities, or ease of use.

a. Product innovation
b. Dogs of the Dow
c. Refusal to deal
d. Microcap stock

46. The notion of _____ is found in the writings of Mikhail Bakunin, Friedrich Nietzsche, and in Werner Sombart's Krieg und Kapitalismus (War and Capitalism) (1913, p. 207), where he wrote: 'again out of destruction a new spirit of creativity arises'. In Capitalism, Socialism and Democracy, the Austrian economist Joseph Schumpeter popularized and used the term to describe the process of transformation that accompanies radical innovation.

a. 130-30 fund
b. 1921 recession
c. Creative destruction
d. 100-year flood

Chapter 20. LABOR AND ENTREPRENEURSHIP: THE HUMAN INPUTS

47. _____ according to Onuoha (2007) is the practice of starting new organizations or revitalizing mature organizations, particularly new businesses generally in response to identified opportunities. _____ is often a difficult undertaking, as a vast majority of new businesses fail. Entrepreneurial activities are substantially different depending on the type of organization that is being started.
   a. ACCRA Cost of Living Index
   b. ACEA agreement
   c. Intrapreneurship
   d. Entrepreneurship

48. _____ in economics and business is the result of an exchange and from that trade we assign a numerical monetary value to a good, service or asset. If Alice trades Bob 4 apples for an orange, the _____ of an orange is 4 apples. Inversely, the _____ of an apple is 1/4 oranges.
   a. Premium pricing
   b. Price war
   c. Price book
   d. Price

49. In economics, _____ is equal to total cost divided by the number of goods produced (the output quantity, Q.) It is also equal to the sum of average variable costs (total variable costs divided by Q) plus average fixed costs (total fixed costs divided by Q.) _____s may be dependent on the time period considered (increasing production may be expensive or impossible in the short term, for example.)
   a. Explicit cost
   b. Average variable cost
   c. Average fixed cost
   d. Average cost

50. In economics, _____ are business expenses that are not dependent on the activities of the business They tend to be time-related, such as salaries or rents being paid per month. This is in contrast to variable costs, which are volume-related (and are paid per quantity.)

In management accounting, _____ are defined as expenses that do not change in proportion to the activity of a business, within the relevant period or scale of production.

   a. Cost of poor quality
   b. Fixed costs
   c. Quality costs
   d. Cost-Volume-Profit Analysis

51. In economics and finance, _____ is the change in total cost that arises when the quantity produced changes by one unit. It is the cost of producing one more unit of a good. Mathematically, the _____ function is expressed as the first derivative of the total cost (TC) function with respect to quantity (Q.)
   a. Variable cost
   b. Quality costs
   c. Khozraschyot
   d. Marginal cost

52. In economics, a _____ is a good that is non-rivaled and non-excludable. This means, respectively, that consumption of the good by one individual does not reduce availability of the good for consumption by others; and that no one can be effectively excluded from using the good. In the real world, there may be no such thing as an absolutely non-rivaled and non-excludable good; but economists think that some goods approximate the concept closely enough for the analysis to be economically useful.
   a. Public good
   b. Demand-pull theory
   c. Happiness economics
   d. Neoclassical synthesis

Chapter 20. LABOR AND ENTREPRENEURSHIP: THE HUMAN INPUTS

53. The phrase _____, according to the Organization for Economic Co-operation and Development, refers to 'creative work undertaken on a systematic basis in order to increase the stock of knowledge, including knowledge of man, culture and society, and the use of this stock of knowledge to devise new applications [sic]'

New product design and development is more than often a crucial factor in the survival of a company. In an industry that is fast changing, firms must continually revise their design and range of products. This is necessary due to continuous technology change and development as well as other competitors and the changing preference of customers.

a. 130-30 fund
b. 1921 recession
c. Research and development
d. 100-year flood

54. A _____ is an object whose consumption increases the utility of the consumer, for which the quantity demanded exceeds the quantity supplied at zero price. _____s are usually modeled as having diminishing marginal utility. The first individual purchase has high utility; the second has less.

a. Pie method
b. Good
c. Composite good
d. Merit good

55. Price _____ is defined as the measure of responsiveness in the quantity demanded for a commodity as a result of change in price of the same commodity. It is a measure of how consumers react to a change in price. In other words, it is percentage change in quantity demanded by the percentage change in price of the same commodity.

a. ACEA agreement
b. Elasticity
c. ACCRA Cost of Living Index
d. Elasticity of demand

56. In economics, _____ describes demand that is not very sensitive to a change in price.

a. Effective unemployment rate
b. Export-led growth
c. Inflation hedge
d. Inelastic

57. A _____ is a set of exclusive rights granted by a state to an inventor or his assignee for a limited period of time in exchange for a disclosure of an invention.

The procedure for granting _____s, the requirements placed on the _____ee and the extent of the exclusive rights vary widely between countries according to national laws and international agreements. Typically, however, a _____ application must include one or more claims defining the invention which must be new, inventive, and useful or industrially applicable.

a. Bank regulation
b. Bona fide occupational qualification
c. Long service leave
d. Patent

58. _____ is money accepted for exchange of goods in an economy. The prevalence of one money over another arises, usually, when a government designates through decrees that the government shall accept only particular notes and coins in payment for taxes. Typically, money of _____ consists of stamped coins and minted paper bills.

a. Totnes pound
b. Local currency
c. Security thread
d. Currency

Chapter 21. POVERTY, INEQUALITY, AND DISCRIMINATION

1. _____ in economics and business is the result of an exchange and from that trade we assign a numerical monetary value to a good, service or asset. If Alice trades Bob 4 apples for an orange, the _____ of an orange is 4 apples. Inversely, the _____ of an apple is 1/4 oranges.
   - a. Price war
   - b. Premium pricing
   - c. Price
   - d. Price book

2. In economics, the term _____ of income or _____ refers to a simple economic model which describes the reciprocal circulation of income between producers and consumers. In the _____ model, the inter-dependent entities of producer and consumer are referred to as 'firms' and 'households' respectively and provide each other with factors in order to facilitate the flow of income. Firms provide consumers with goods and services in exchange for consumer expenditure and 'factors of production' from households.
   - a. Circular flow
   - b. 100-year flood
   - c. 130-30 fund
   - d. 1921 recession

3. In economics, _____ is how a natione;s total economy is distributed among its population. ._____ has always been a central concern of economic theory and economic policy. Classical economists such as Adam Smith, Thomas Malthus and David Ricardo were mainly concerned with factor _____, that is, the distribution of income between the main factors of production, land, labour and capital.
   - a. Authorised capital
   - b. Equipment trust certificate
   - c. Eco commerce
   - d. Income distribution

4. In mathematics, an _____ is a statement about the relative size or order of two objects, or about whether they are the same or not

   - The notation a < b means that a is less than b.
   - The notation a > b means that a is greater than b.
   - The notation a ≠ b means that a is not equal to b, but does not say that one is greater than the other or even that they can be compared in size.

   In each statement above, a is not equal to b. These relations are known as strict inequalities. The notation a < b may also be read as 'a is strictly less than b'.

   - a. ACEA agreement
   - b. AD-IA Model
   - c. ACCRA Cost of Living Index
   - d. Inequality

5. _____ is the shortage of common things such as food, clothing, shelter and safe drinking water, all of which determine the quality of life. It may also include the lack of access to opportunities such as education and employment which aid the escape from _____ and/or allow one to enjoy the respect of fellow citizens. According to Mollie Orshansky who developed the _____ measurements used by the U.S. government, 'to be poor is to be deprived of those goods and services and pleasures which others around us take for granted.' Ongoing debates over causes, effects and best ways to measure _____, directly influence the design and implementation of _____-reduction programs and are therefore relevant to the fields of public administration and international development.
   - a. Liberal welfare reforms
   - b. Growth Elasticity of Poverty
   - c. Poverty map
   - d. Poverty

Chapter 21. POVERTY, INEQUALITY, AND DISCRIMINATION

6. _____ is the incidence or process of transferring ownership of a business, enterprise, agency or public service from the public sector (government) to the private sector (business.) In a broader sense, _____ refers to transfer of any government function to the private sector including governmental functions like revenue collection and law enforcement.

The term '_____' also has been used to describe two unrelated transactions.

   a. Privatization
   c. Performance reports
   b. Compound empowerment
   d. Ricardian equivalence

7. To _____ is to impose a financial charge or other levy upon a taxpayer by a state or the functional equivalent of a state.

_____es are also imposed by many subnational entities. _____es consist of direct _____ or indirect _____, and may be paid in money or as its labour equivalent (often but not always unpaid.)

   a. Tax
   c. 100-year flood
   b. 1921 recession
   d. 130-30 fund

8. A _____ is a reduction in taxes. Economic stimulus via _____s, along with interest rate intervention and deficit spending, are one of the central tenets of Keynesian economics.

The immediate effects of a _____ are, generally, a decrease in the real income of the government and an increase in the real income of those whose tax rate has been lowered.

   a. Direct taxes
   c. Withholding tax
   b. Popiwek
   d. Tax cut

9. The _____ is the minimum level of income deemed necessary to achieve an adequate standard of living in a given country. In practice, like the definition of poverty, the official or common understanding of the poverty line is significantly higher in developed countries than in developing countries.

The common international poverty line has been roughly $1 a day, or more precisely $1.08 at 1993 purchasing-power parity (PPP.)

   a. Poverty
   c. Poverty reduction
   b. Poverty threshold
   d. Poverty map

10. The _____ is the name for legislation first introduced by United States President Lyndon B. Johnson during his State of the Union address on January 8, 1964. This legislation was proposed by Johnson in response to a national poverty rate of around nineteen percent. The speech led the United States Congress to pass the Economic Opportunity Act, which established the Office of Economic Opportunity (OEO) to administer the local application of federal funds targeted against poverty.
   a. 130-30 fund
   c. Supplemental Nutrition Assistance Program
   b. 100-year flood
   d. War on Poverty

11. A _____ is the procedure of systematically acquiring and recording information about the members of a given population. It is a regularly occurring and official count of a particular population. The term is used mostly in connection with national 'population and door to door _____ es' (to be taken every 10 years according to United Nations recommendations), agriculture, and business _____ es.

   a. 1921 recession   b. 100-year flood
   c. Census   d. 130-30 fund

12. The _____ is an economic and political union of 27 member states, located primarily in Europe. It was established by the Treaty of Maastricht on 1 November 1993, upon the foundations of the pre-existing European Economic Community. With a population of almost 500 million, the _____ generates an estimated 30% share (US$18.4 trillion in 2008) of the nominal gross world product.

   a. ACCRA Cost of Living Index   b. European Union
   c. European Court of Justice   d. ACEA agreement

13. The _____, asbl is a non-profit project which produces a cross-national database of micro-economic income data for social science research. The project started in 1983 and is headquartered in Luxembourg. In 2006 the database included data from 30 countries on four continents, with some countries represented for over 30 years.

   a. Leading stock   b. Bankruptcy of Lehman Brothers
   c. Deutsche Bank   d. Luxembourg Income Study

14. In a _____ there is both a monopoly (a single seller) and monopsony (a single buyer) in the same market.

In such market price and output will be determined by the non economic forces like bargaining power of both buyer and seller. A _____ model is often used in situations where the switching costs of both sides are prohibitively high.

   a. Price takers   b. Market concentration
   c. Revenue-cap regulation   d. Bilateral monopoly

15. In economics, a _____ exists when a specific individual or enterprise has sufficient control over a particular product or service to determine significantly the terms on which other individuals shall have access to it. Monopolies are thus characterized by a lack of economic competition for the good or service that they provide and a lack of viable substitute goods. The verb 'monopolize' refers to the process by which a firm gains persistently greater market share than what is expected under perfect competition.

   a. 100-year flood   b. Monopoly
   c. 1921 recession   d. 130-30 fund

16. _____ is a term used by economists to refer to the higher wages earned by unionized workers compared to non-unionized workers. It entails the idea that unions act as coercive monopolies by raising wages other than what they would be if there was competition between individual workers.

   a. Seasonal industry   b. Monopoly wage
   c. Global strategy   d. Rate risk

Chapter 21. POVERTY, INEQUALITY, AND DISCRIMINATION

17. _____ refers to the stock of skills and knowledge embodied in the ability to perform labor so as to produce economic value. It is the skills and knowledge gained by a worker through education and experience. Many early economic theories refer to it simply as labor, one of three factors of production, and consider it to be a fungible resource -- homogeneous and easily interchangeable. Other conceptions of labor dispense with these assumptions.

   a. Human capital
   c. General equilibrium
   b. Price theory
   d. Law of increasing costs

18. _____ is a branch of economics that studies how individuals, households and firms and some states make decisions to allocate limited resources, typically in markets where goods or services are being bought and sold. _____ examines how these decisions and behaviours affect the supply and demand for goods and services, which determines prices; and how prices, in turn, determine the supply and demand of goods and services.

   Whereas macroeconomics involves the 'sum total of economic activity, dealing with the issues of growth, inflation and unemployment, and with national economic policies relating to these issues' and the effects of government actions on them.

   a. New Keynesian economics
   c. Recession
   b. Microeconomics
   d. Countercyclical

19. Economics:

   - _____, the desire to own something and the ability to pay for it
   - _____ curve, a graphic representation of a _____ schedule
   - _____ deposit, the money in checking accounts
   - _____ pull theory, the theory that inflation occurs when _____ for goods and services exceeds existing supplies
   - _____ schedule, a table that lists the quantity of a good a person will buy it each different price
   - _____ side economics, the school of economics at believes government spending and tax cuts open economy by raising _____

   a. Variability
   c. McKesson ' Robbins scandal
   b. Production
   d. Demand

20. _____ is a branch of economics that deals with the performance, structure, and behavior of a national or regional economy as a whole. Along with microeconomics, _____ is one of the two most general fields in economics. It is the study of the behavior and decision-making of entire economies.

   a. New Trade Theory
   c. Nominal value
   b. Tobit model
   d. Macroeconomics

21. _____ in economics refers to metrics and measures of output from production processes, per unit of input. Labor _____, for example, is typically measured as a ratio of output per labor-hour, an input. _____ may be conceived of as a metrics of the technical or engineering efficiency of production.

   a. Productivity
   c. Fordism
   b. Piece work
   d. Production-possibility frontier

Chapter 21. POVERTY, INEQUALITY, AND DISCRIMINATION

22. In economics, _____ is the total supply of goods and services produced by a national economy during a specific time period. It is the total amount of goods and services in the economy available at all possible price levels.
    a. Aggregate expenditure
    b. Aggregate demand
    c. Aggregate supply
    d. Aggregation problem

23. _____s is the social science that studies the production, distribution, and consumption of goods and services. The term _____s comes from the Ancient Greek οἰκονομία from οἶκος (oikos, 'house') + νόμος (nomos, 'custom' or 'law'), hence 'rules of the house(hold)'. Current _____ models developed out of the broader field of political economy in the late 19th century, owing to a desire to use an empirical approach more akin to the physical sciences.
    a. Inflation
    b. Opportunity cost
    c. Economic
    d. Energy economics

24. In probability theory and statistics, a _____ is described as the number separating the higher half of a sample, a population from the lower half. The _____ of a finite list of numbers can be found by arranging all the observations from lowest value to highest value and picking the middle one. If there is an even number of observations, the _____ is not unique, so one often takes the mean of the two middle values.
    a. Labour vouchers
    b. Fiscal stimulus plans
    c. First player wins
    d. Median

25. The _____ is a group of three respected economists who advise the President of the United States on economic policy. It is a part of the Executive Office of the President of the United States, and provides much of the economic policy of the White House. The council prepares the annual Economic Report of the President.
    a. Constrained Pareto optimality
    b. Council of Economic Advisers
    c. Hybrid renewable energy systems
    d. Federal Reserve Bank Notes

26. _____ is a voluntary transfer of resources from one country to another, given at least partly with the objective of benefiting the recipient country. It may have other functions as well: it may be given as a signal of diplomatic approval, or to strengthen a military ally, to reward a government for behaviour desired by the donor, to extend the donor's cultural influence, to provide infrastructure needed by the donor for resource extraction from the recipient country, or to gain other kinds of commercial access. Humanitarianism and altruism are, nevertheless, significant motivations for the giving of _____.
    a. ACEA agreement
    b. Aid
    c. ACCRA Cost of Living Index
    d. AD-IA Model

27. _____ was a federal assistance program in effect from 1935 to 1997, which was administered by the United States Department of Health and Human Services. This program provided financial assistance to children whose families had low or no income.

The program was created under the name Aid to Dependent Children (ADC) by the Social Security Act of 1935 as part of the New Deal; the words 'families with' were added to the name in 1960, partly due to concern that the program's rules discouraged marriage.

   a. ACCRA Cost of Living Index
   b. ACEA agreement
   c. AD-IA Model
   d. Aid to Families with Dependent Children

Chapter 21. POVERTY, INEQUALITY, AND DISCRIMINATION

28. _____ refers to the economic policies of United States President Bill Clinton during the 1990s. Clinton assumed office at the tail end of a recession, and the economic theories he utilized and implemented are claimed by his supporters to have eventually led to a strong recovery, though Clinton's opponents deny this.

The strategy was outlined in the following three points:

- Establishing fiscal discipline, eliminating the budget deficit, keeping interest rates low, and spurring private-sector investment.
- Investing in people through education, training, science, and research.
- Opening foreign markets so American workers can compete abroad.

During the 1992 presidential campaign America had undergone twelve years of conservative policies implemented by Ronald Reagan and George Herbert Walker Bush. Clinton ran on the economic platform of balancing the budget, lowering inflation, lowering unemployment, and continuing the traditionally conservative policies of free trade.

- a. Structural equation modeling
- b. Jawboning
- c. Purchasing Managers Index
- d. Clintonomics

29. _____ is the United States of America's federal assistance program, formerly known as 'welfare'. It began on July 1, 1997, and succeeded the Aid to Families with Dependent Children program, providing cash assistance to indigent American families with dependent children through the United States Department of Health and Human Services. Prior to 1997, the federal government designed the overall program requirements and guidelines, while states administered the program and determined eligibility for benefits.
- a. 130-30 fund
- b. 100-year flood
- c. Temporary Assistance for Needy Families
- d. 1921 recession

30. In economics, a _____ is a progressive income tax system where people earning below a certain amount receive supplemental pay from the government instead of paying taxes to the government. Such a system has been discussed by economists but never fully implemented. It was developed by Juliet Rhys-Williams in the 1940s and later by United States economist Milton Friedman in 1962 in Capitalism and Freedom.
- a. 130-30 fund
- b. Negative income tax
- c. 1921 recession
- d. 100-year flood

31. An _____ is a tax levied on the financial income of people, corporations, or other legal entities. Various _____ systems exist, with varying degrees of tax incidence. Income taxation can be progressive, proportional, or regressive.
- a. ACCRA Cost of Living Index
- b. AD-IA Model
- c. ACEA agreement
- d. Income tax

32. A _____ refers to any type debt instrument, such as a loan, bond, mortgage that does not have a fixed rate of interest over the life of the instrument. Such debt typically uses an index or other base rate for establishing the interest rate for each relevant period. One of the most common rates to use as the basis for applying interest rates is the London Inter-bank Offered Rate, or LIBOR

a. Moneylender
b. Disposal tax effect
c. Money market
d. Floating interest rate

33. The United States federal _____ is a refundable tax credit. For tax year 2008, a claimant with one qualifying child can receive a maximum credit of $2,917. For two or more qualifying children, the maximum credit is $4,824.
   a. ACEA agreement
   b. AD-IA Model
   c. ACCRA Cost of Living Index
   d. Earned Income Tax Credit

34. Total _____ is defined by the United States' Bureau of Economic Analysis as

income received by persons from all sources. It includes income received from participation in production as well as from government and business transfer payments. It is the sum of compensation of employees (received), supplements to wages and salaries, proprietors' income with inventory valuation adjustment (IVA) and capital consumption adjustment (CCAdj), rental income of persons with CCAdj, _____ receipts on assets, and personal current transfer receipts, less contributions for government social insurance.

   a. Dividend Discount Model
   b. Greater fool theory
   c. Bidding
   d. Personal income

35. The term _____ describes two different concepts:

   - The first is a recognition of partial payment already made towards taxes due.
   - The second is a state benefit paid to workers through the tax system, which has the effect of increasing (rather than reducing) net income.

Within the Australian, Canadian, United Kingdom, and United States tax systems, a _____ is a recognition of partial payment already made towards taxes due. A similar concept exists (fr:Avoir fiscal) in the French tax system. This situation arises, for example, when standard rate tax has been deducted at source , but the tax-payer is subject to further taxation at a higher rate. It also applies in dividend imputation systems.

   a. 130-30 fund
   b. 100-year flood
   c. Tax Credit
   d. 1921 recession

36. In economics and sociology, an _____ is any factor (financial or non-financial) that enables or motivates a particular course of action, or counts as a reason for preferring one choice to the alternatives. It is an expectation that encourages people to behave in a certain way. Since human beings are purposeful creatures, the study of _____ structures is central to the study of all economic activity (both in terms of individual decision-making and in terms of co-operation and competition within a larger institutional structure.)
   a. Incentive
   b. Epstein-Zin preferences
   c. Economic reform
   d. Isocost

37. The _____ was a landmark piece of legislation in the United States that outlawed racial segregation in schools, public places, and employment.
   a. Postcautionary principle
   b. Patent portfolio
   c. Le Chapelier Law
   d. Civil Rights Act of 1964

Chapter 21. POVERTY, INEQUALITY, AND DISCRIMINATION

38. The U.S. _____ (EEOC) is a federal agency whose goal is ending employment discrimination. The _____ investigates discrimination complaints based on an individual's race, color, national origin, religion, sex, age, disability and retaliation for reporting and/or opposing a discriminatory practice. The Commission is also tasked with filing suits on behalf of alleged victim(s) of discrimination against employers and as an adjudicatory for claims of discrimination brought against federal agencies.
   a. ACEA agreement
   b. AD-IA Model
   c. EEOC
   d. ACCRA Cost of Living Index

39. The U.S. _____ is a federal agency whose goal is ending employment discrimination. The _____ investigates discrimination complaints based on an individual's race, color, national origin, religion, sex, age, disability and retaliation for reporting and/or opposing a discriminatory practice. The Commission is also tasked with filing suits on behalf of alleged victim(s) of discrimination against employers and as an adjudicatory for claims of discrimination brought against federal agencies.
   a. AD-IA Model
   b. ACCRA Cost of Living Index
   c. ACEA agreement
   d. Equal Employment Opportunity Commission

40. _____ is any long-term change in the patterns of average weather of a specific region or the Earth as a whole. _____ reflects abnormal variations to the Earth's climate and subsequent effects on other parts of the Earth, such as in the ice caps over durations ranging from decades to millions of years.

In recent usage, especially in the context of environmental policy, _____ usually refers to changes in modern climate

   a. 1921 recession
   b. 100-year flood
   c. Climate change
   d. 130-30 fund

41. Economic _____ is defined as an excess distribution to any factor in a production process above that which is required to induce the factor into the process or any excess above that which is necessary to keep the factor in its current use..

Classical Factor _____ is primarily concerned with the fee paid for the use of fixed (e.g. natural) resources. The classical definition is expressed as any excess payment above that required to induce or provide for production.

   a. 130-30 fund
   b. 1921 recession
   c. 100-year flood
   d. Rent

42. A _____ is a legal document that is often passed by the legislature, and approved by the chief executive-or president. For example, only certain types of revenue may be imposed and collected. Property tax is frequently the basis for municipal and county revenues, while sales tax and/or income tax are the basis for state revenues, and income tax and corporate tax are the basis for national revenues.
   a. Government budget
   b. Lump-sum tax
   c. Right-financing
   d. Structural deficit

43. A _____ is a theoretical term that economists use to describe a market which is free from government intervention (i.e. no regulation, no subsidization, no single monetary system and no governmental monopolies.) In a _____, property rights are voluntarily exchanged at a price arranged solely by the mutual consent of sellers and buyers. By definition, buyers and sellers do not coerce each other, in the sense that they obtain each other's property without the use of physical force, threat of physical force, or fraud, nor is the coerced by a third party (such as by government via transfer payments) and they engage in trade simply because they both consent and believe that it is a good enough choice.

a. Delegation
b. Third camp
c. Leninism
d. Free market

Chapter 22. AN INTRODUCTION TO MACROECONOMICS

1. _____ is a branch of economics that deals with the performance, structure, and behavior of a national or regional economy as a whole. Along with microeconomics, _____ is one of the two most general fields in economics. It is the study of the behavior and decision-making of entire economies.
    a. Nominal value
    b. Tobit model
    c. New Trade Theory
    d. Macroeconomics

2. _____s is the social science that studies the production, distribution, and consumption of goods and services. The term _____s comes from the Ancient Greek oá¼°κονομῖα from oá¼¶κος (oikos, 'house') + vÏŒμος (nomos, 'custom' or 'law'), hence 'rules of the house(hold)'. Current _____ models developed out of the broader field of political economy in the late 19th century, owing to a desire to use an empirical approach more akin to the physical sciences.
    a. Opportunity cost
    b. Inflation
    c. Energy economics
    d. Economic

3. _____ is a branch of economics that studies how individuals, households and firms and some states make decisions to allocate limited resources, typically in markets where goods or services are being bought and sold. _____ examines how these decisions and behaviours affect the supply and demand for goods and services, which determines prices; and how prices, in turn , determine the supply and demand of goods and services.

   Whereas macroeconomics involves the 'sum total of economic activity, dealing with the issues of growth, inflation and unemployment, and with national economic policies relating to these issues' and the effects of government actions on them.

    a. New Keynesian economics
    b. Countercyclical
    c. Microeconomics
    d. Recession

4. _____ is the shortage of common things such as food, clothing, shelter and safe drinking water, all of which determine the quality of life. It may also include the lack of access to opportunities such as education and employment which aid the escape from _____ and/or allow one to enjoy the respect of fellow citizens. According to Mollie Orshansky who developed the _____ measurements used by the U.S. government, 'to be poor is to be deprived of those goods and services and pleasures which others around us take for granted.' Ongoing debates over causes, effects and best ways to measure _____, directly influence the design and implementation of _____-reduction programs and are therefore relevant to the fields of public administration and international development.
    a. Growth Elasticity of Poverty
    b. Poverty map
    c. Poverty
    d. Liberal welfare reforms

5. In economics, the _____ can be defined as the graph depicting the relationship between the price of a certain commodity, and the amount of it that consumers are willing and able to purchase at that given price. It is a graphic representation of a demand schedule. The _____ for all consumers together follows from the _____ of every individual consumer: the individual demands at each price are added together.
    a. Kuznets curve
    b. Wage curve
    c. Cost curve
    d. Demand curve

Chapter 22. AN INTRODUCTION TO MACROECONOMICS

6. Economics:

   - _____,the desire to own something and the ability to pay for it
   - _____ curve,a graphic representation of a _____ schedule
   - _____ deposit, the money in checking accounts
   - _____ pull theory,the theory that inflation occurs when _____ for goods and services exceeds existing supplies
   - _____ schedule,a table that lists the quantity of a good a person will buy it each different price
   - _____ side economics,the school of economics at believes government spending and tax cuts open economy by raising _____

   a. Production
   b. McKesson ' Robbins scandal
   c. Demand
   d. Variability

7. In economics, a _____ is a table that lists the quantity of a good a person will buy it each different price See Demand curve.
   a. Rational irrationality
   b. Federal Reserve districts
   c. Free contract
   d. Demand schedule

8. _____ is an economic model based on price, utility and quantity in a market. It predicts that in a competitive market, price will function to equalize the quantity demanded by consumers, and the quantity supplied by producers, resulting in an economic equilibrium of price and quantity. The model incorporates other factors changing equilibrium as a shift of demand and/or supply.
   a. Joint demand
   b. Rational addiction
   c. Supply and demand
   d. Deferred gratification

9. In economics, _____ is the total demand for final goods and services in the economy (Y) at a given time and price level. It is the amount of goods and services in the economy that will be purchased at all possible price levels. This is the demand for the gross domestic product of a country when inventory levels are static.
   a. Aggregation problem
   b. Aggregate expenditure
   c. Aggregate supply
   d. Aggregate demand

10. In economics, _____ is the total supply of goods and services produced by a national economy during a specific time period. It is the total amount of goods and services in the economy available at all possible price levels.
    a. Aggregate demand
    b. Aggregate expenditure
    c. Aggregate supply
    d. Aggregation problem

11. _____ is a broad label that refers to any individuals or households that use goods and services generated within the economy. The concept of a _____ is used in different contexts, so that the usage and significance of the term may vary.

Typically when business people and economists talk of _____s they are talking about person as _____, an aggregated commodity item with little individuality other than that expressed in the buy/not-buy decision.

Chapter 22. AN INTRODUCTION TO MACROECONOMICS

a. 1921 recession
b. 100-year flood
c. 130-30 fund
d. Consumer

12. A _____ is a measure of the average price of consumer goods and services purchased by households. A _____ measures a price change for a constant market basket of goods and services from one period to the next within the same area (city, region, or nation.) It is a price index determined by measuring the price of a standard group of goods meant to represent the typical market basket of a typical urban consumer.

a. Cost-of-living index
b. Consumer Price Index
c. Lipstick index
d. CPI

13. The _____ or gross domestic income (GDI), a basic measure of an economy's economic performance, is the market value of all final goods and services produced within the borders of a nation in a year. _____ can be defined in three ways, all of which are conceptually identical. First, it is equal to the total expenditures for all final goods and services produced within the country in a stipulated period of time (usually a 365-day year.)

a. Monopolistic competition
b. Market structure
c. Gross domestic product
d. Countercyclical

14. _____ and Keynesian Theory) is a macroeconomic theory based on the ideas of 20th-century British economist John Maynard Keynes. _____ argues that private sector decisions sometimes lead to inefficient macroeconomic outcomes and therefore advocates active policy responses by the public sector, including monetary policy actions by the central bank and fiscal policy actions by the government to stabilize output over the business cycle.

The theories forming the basis of _____ were first presented in The General Theory of Employment, Interest and Money, published in 1936.

a. Rational choice theory
b. Deflation
c. Market failure
d. Keynesian economics

15. _____ in economics and business is the result of an exchange and from that trade we assign a numerical monetary value to a good, service or asset. If Alice trades Bob 4 apples for an orange, the _____ of an orange is 4 apples. Inversely, the _____ of an apple is 1/4 oranges.

a. Price war
b. Price book
c. Premium pricing
d. Price

16. A _____ is a normalized average (typically a weighted average) of prices for a given class of goods or services in a given region, during a given interval of time. It is a statistic designed to help to compare how these prices, taken as a whole, differ between time periods or geographical locations.

Price indices have several potential uses.

a. Two-part tariff
b. Product sabotage
c. Transactional Net Margin Method
d. Price Index

17. An _____, in economics, is the amount by which the real Gross domestic product exceeds potential GDP. The real GDP is also known as GDP 'adjusted for inflation', 'constant prices' GDP or 'constant dollar' GDP, because it measures the aggregate output in a country's income accounts in a given year, expressed in base-year prices. On the other hand, the potential GDP is the quantity of real GDP when a country's economy is at full-employment.
- a. AD-IA Model
- b. Inflationary gap
- c. ACCRA Cost of Living Index
- d. ACEA agreement

18. In economics, a _____ is a general slowdown in economic activity over a sustained period of time, or a business cycle contraction. During _____s, many macroeconomic indicators vary in a similar way. Production as measured by Gross Domestic Product (GDP), employment, investment spending, capacity utilization, household incomes and business profits all fall during _____s.
- a. Monetary economics
- b. Leading indicators
- c. Treasury View
- d. Recession

19. The _____ is the largest national economy in the world. Its gross domestic product (GDP) was estimated as $14.2 trillion in 2008. The U.S. economy maintains a high level of output per person (GDP per capita, $46,800 in 2008, ranked at around number ten in the world.)
- a. ACCRA Cost of Living Index
- b. ACEA agreement
- c. AD-IA Model
- d. Economy of the United States

20. In finance, the _____s between two currencies specifies how much one currency is worth in terms of the other. It is the value of a foreign natione;s currency in terms of the home natione;s currency. For example an _____ of 102 Japanese yen to the United States dollar means that JPY 102 is worth the same as USD 1.
- a. ACCRA Cost of Living Index
- b. ACEA agreement
- c. Interbank market
- d. Exchange rate

21. _____ is a misspelled phrase from Latin 'pro capite' phrase meaning per head with pro meaning 'per' or 'for each' and capite meaning 'head.' Both words together equate to the phrase 'for each head.'

It is usually used in the field of statistics to indicate the average per person for any given concern, such as income, crime rate, etc.

It is also used in wills to indicate that each of the named beneficiaries should receive, by devise or bequest, equal shares of the estate. This is in contrast to a per stirpes division, in which each branch of the inheriting family inherits an equal share of the estate.

- a. Sargan test
- b. False positive rate
- c. Per capita
- d. Population statistics

22. In economics _____s are goods that are ultimately consumed rather than used in the production of another good. For example, a car sold to a consumer is a _____; the components such as tires sold to the car manufacturer are not; they are intermediate goods used to make the _____.

When used in measures of national income and output the term _____s only includes new goods.

Chapter 22. AN INTRODUCTION TO MACROECONOMICS

a. Luxury good
b. Substitute good
c. Final good
d. Goods and services

23. A _____ is an object whose consumption increases the utility of the consumer, for which the quantity demanded exceeds the quantity supplied at zero price. _____s are usually modeled as having diminishing marginal utility. The first individual purchase has high utility; the second has less.
   a. Composite good
   b. Merit good
   c. Good
   d. Pie method

24. _____ or producer goods are goods used as inputs in the production of other goods, such as partly finished goods. They are goods used in production of final goods. A firm may make then use _____, or make then sell, or buy then use them.
   a. Intermediate goods
   b. Economic forecasting
   c. Inflation adjustment
   d. Income distribution

25. In economics, economic output is divided into physical goods and intangible services. Consumption of _____ is assumed to produce utility. It is often used when referring to a _____ Tax.
   a. Composite good
   b. Private good
   c. Manufactured goods
   d. Goods and services

26. In economics, _____ is equal to total cost divided by the number of goods produced (the output quantity, Q.) It is also equal to the sum of average variable costs (total variable costs divided by Q) plus average fixed costs (total fixed costs divided by Q.) _____s may be dependent on the time period considered (increasing production may be expensive or impossible in the short term, for example.)
   a. Average cost
   b. Average fixed cost
   c. Explicit cost
   d. Average variable cost

27. _____ is any (course of) action deliberately taken (or not taken) to manage human activities with a view to prevent, reduce or mitigate harmful effects on nature and natural resources, and ensuring that man-made changes to the environment do not have harmful effects on humans.

It is useful to consider that _____ comprises two major terms: environment and policy. Environment primarily refers to the ecological (ecosystems) dimension, but can also take account of social (quality of life) dimension and an economic (resource management) dimension.

   a. AD-IA Model
   b. ACCRA Cost of Living Index
   c. Environmental policy
   d. ACEA agreement

28. In economics and finance, _____ is the change in total cost that arises when the quantity produced changes by one unit. It is the cost of producing one more unit of a good. Mathematically, the _____ function is expressed as the first derivative of the total cost (TC) function with respect to quantity (Q.)
   a. Variable cost
   b. Marginal cost
   c. Quality costs
   d. Khozraschyot

29. _____ refers to a business or organization attempting to acquire goods or services to accomplish the goals of the enterprise. Though there are several organizations that attempt to set standards in the _____ process, processes can vary greatly between organizations. Typically the word '_____' is not used interchangeably with the word 'procurement', since procurement typically includes Expediting, Supplier Quality, and Traffic and Logistics (T'L) in addition to _____.
   a. Free port
   b. 100-year flood
   c. 130-30 fund
   d. Purchasing

30. _____ is the number of goods/services that can be purchased with a unit of currency. For example, if you had taken one dollar to a store in the 1950s, you would have been able to buy a greater number of items than you would today, indicating that you would have had a greater _____ in the 1950s. Currency can be either a commodity money, like gold or silver, or fiat currency like US dollars.
   a. Purchasing power
   b. Compliance cost
   c. Human Poverty Index
   d. Genuine progress indicator

31. _____ refers to the economic policies of United States President Bill Clinton during the 1990s. Clinton assumed office at the tail end of a recession, and the economic theories he utilized and implemented are claimed by his supporters to have eventually led to a strong recovery, though Clinton's opponents deny this.

The strategy was outlined in the following three points:

- Establishing fiscal discipline, eliminating the budget deficit, keeping interest rates low, and spurring private-sector investment.
- Investing in people through education, training, science, and research.
- Opening foreign markets so American workers can compete abroad.

During the 1992 presidential campaign America had undergone twelve years of conservative policies implemented by Ronald Reagan and George Herbert Walker Bush. Clinton ran on the economic platform of balancing the budget, lowering inflation, lowering unemployment, and continuing the traditionally conservative policies of free trade.

   a. Jawboning
   b. Structural equation modeling
   c. Clintonomics
   d. Purchasing Managers Index

32. In economics, _____ is a sustained decrease in the general price level of goods and services. _____ occurs when the annual inflation rate falls below zero percent, resulting in an increase in the real value of money -- a negative inflation rate. This should not be confused with disinflation, a slow-down in the inflation rate (i.e. when the inflation decreases, but still remains positive.)
   a. Deflation
   b. Price revolution
   c. Tobit model
   d. Literacy rate

33. A _____ occurs when an entity spends more money than it takes in. The opposite of a _____ is a budget surplus. Debt is essentially an accumulated flow of deficits.
   a. Funding body
   b. Lump-sum tax
   c. Public Financial Management
   d. Budget deficit

Chapter 22. AN INTRODUCTION TO MACROECONOMICS

34. _____ is the increase in the amount of the goods and services produced by an economy over time. It is conventionally measured as the percent rate of increase in real gross domestic product, or real GDP. Growth is usually calculated in real terms, i.e. inflation-adjusted terms, in order to net out the effect of inflation on the price of the goods and services produced.
   a. ACEA agreement
   b. Economic growth
   c. ACCRA Cost of Living Index
   d. AD-IA Model

35. In economics, _____ is a rise in the general level of prices of goods and services in an economy over a period of time. When the general price level rises, each unit of currency buys fewer goods and services; consequently, _____ is also a decline in the real value of money--a loss of purchasing power in the medium of exchange which is also the monetary unit of account in the economy. A chief measure of general price-level _____ is the general _____ rate, which is the percentage change in a general price index (normally the Consumer Price Index) over time.
   a. Opportunity cost
   b. Energy economics
   c. Economic
   d. Inflation

36. The _____ was a worldwide economic downturn starting in most places in 1929 and ending at different times in the 1930s or early 1940s for different countries. It was the largest and most important economic depression in the 20th century, and is used in the 21st century as an example of how far the world's economy can fall. The _____ originated in the United States; historians most often use as a starting date the stock market crash on October 29, 1929, known as Black Tuesday.
   a. Jarrow March
   b. Great Depression
   c. British Empire Economic Conference
   d. Wall Street Crash of 1929

37. _____ was the 31st President of the United States (1929-1933.) Besides his political career, Hoover was a professional mining engineer and author. As the United States Secretary of Commerce in the 1920s under Presidents Warren Harding and Calvin Coolidge, he promoted government intervention under the rubric 'economic modernization'.
   a. Adolph Fischer
   b. Herbert Hoover
   c. Adam Smith
   d. Adolf Hitler

38. A _____ was the popular name for shanty towns built by homeless people during the Great Depression. They were named after the President at the time, Herbert Hoover, because he allegedly let the nation slide into depression. The term was coined by Charles Michelson, publicity chief of the Democratic National Committee.
   a. 1921 recession
   b. 100-year flood
   c. Hooverville
   d. 130-30 fund

39. The term _____ refers to government debt, expenditures and revenues, or to finance (particularly financial revenue) in general.

   - _____ deficit is the budget deficit of federal or local government
   - _____ policy is the discretionary spending of governments. Contrasts with monetary policy.
   - _____ year and _____ quarter are reporting periods for firms and other agencies.

a. Procter ' Gamble
c. Drawdown
b. Fiscal
d. Bucket shop

40. In economics, _____ is the use of government spending and revenue collection to influence the economy.

_____ can be contrasted with the other main type of economic policy, monetary policy, which attempts to stabilize the economy by controlling interest rates and the supply of money. The two main instruments of _____ are government spending and taxation.

a. 100-year flood
c. Sustainable investment rule
b. Fiscalism
d. Fiscal policy

41. _____ was written by the English economist John Maynard Keynes. The book, generally considered to be his magnum opus, is largely credited with creating the terminology and shape of modern macroeconomics. Published in February 1936 it sought to bring about a revolution, commonly referred to as the 'Keynesian Revolution', in the way economists thought - especially in relation to the proposition that a market economy tends naturally to restore itself to full employment after temporary shocks.

a. Principles of Political Economy
c. Wealth of Nations
b. General Theory of Employment, Interest and Money
d. The General Theory of Employment, Interest and Money

42. _____ is a fee paid on borrowed assets. It is the price paid for the use of borrowed money , or, money earned by deposited funds . Assets that are sometimes lent with _____ include money, shares, consumer goods through hire purchase, major assets such as aircraft, and even entire factories in finance lease arrangements.

a. Internal debt
c. Asset protection
b. Insolvency
d. Interest

43. _____ was a global military conflict which involved a majority of the world's nations, including all of the great powers, organized into two opposing military alliances: the Allies and the Axis. The war involved the mobilization of over 100 million military personnel, making it the most widespread war in history. In a state of 'total war', the major participants placed their entire economic, industrial, and scientific capabilities at the service of the war effort, erasing the distinction between civilian and military resources.

a. 1921 recession
c. 100-year flood
b. World War II
d. 130-30 fund

44. _____s (economically referred to as land or raw materials) occur naturally within environments that exist relatively undisturbed by mankind, in a natural form. A _____'s is often characterized by amounts of biodiversity existent in various ecosystems.

Mining, petroleum extraction, fishing, hunting, and forestry are generally considered natural-resource industries.

a. 100-year flood
c. Natural resource
b. 130-30 fund
d. 1921 recession

Chapter 22. AN INTRODUCTION TO MACROECONOMICS

45. The Organization of the Petroleum Exporting Countries is a cartel of twelve countries made up of Algeria, Angola, Ecuador, Iran, Iraq, Kuwait, Libya, Nigeria, Qatar, Saudi Arabia, the United Arab Emirates, and Venezuela. The cartel has maintained its headquarters in Vienna since 1965, and hosts regular meetings among the oil ministers of its Member Countries. Indonesia withdrew its membership in _____ in 2008 after it became a net importer of oil, but stated it would likely return if it became a net exporter in the world.

  a. ACEA agreement
  b. AD-IA Model
  c. ACCRA Cost of Living Index
  d. OPEC

46. _____ is an economic situation in which inflation and economic stagnation occur simultaneously and remain unchecked for a period of time. The portmanteau _____ is generally attributed to British politician Iain Macleod, who coined the term in a speech to Parliament in 1965. The concept is notable partly because, in postwar macroeconomic theory, inflation and recession were regarded as mutually exclusive, and also because _____ has generally proven to be difficult and costly to eradicate once it gets started.

  a. Real interest rate
  b. Chronic inflation
  c. Price/wage spiral
  d. Stagflation

47. _____ is any long-term change in the patterns of average weather of a specific region or the Earth as a whole. _____ reflects abnormal variations to the Earth's climate and subsequent effects on other parts of the Earth, such as in the ice caps over durations ranging from decades to millions of years.

In recent usage, especially in the context of environmental policy, _____ usually refers to changes in modern climate

  a. 1921 recession
  b. 130-30 fund
  c. 100-year flood
  d. Climate change

48. The _____ is the central banking system of the United States. Created in 1913 by the enactment of the Federal Reserve Act (signed by Woodrow Wilson), it is a quasi-public and quasi-private (government entity with private components) banking system that comprises (1) the presidentially appointed Board of Governors of the _____ in Washington, D.C.; (2) the Federal Open Market Committee; (3) twelve regional Federal Reserve Banks located in major cities throughout the nation acting as fiscal agents for the U.S. Treasury, each with its own nine-member board of directors; (4) numerous other private U.S. member banks, which subscribe to required amounts of non-transferable stock in their regional Federal Reserve Banks; and (5) various advisory councils. Since February 2006, Ben Bernanke has served as the Chairman of the Board of Governors of the _____.

  a. Monetary Policy Report to the Congress
  b. Federal Reserve System Open Market Account
  c. Term auction facility
  d. Federal Reserve System

49. _____ is an economic policy in which a central bank estimates and makes public a projected, or 'target,' inflation rate and then attempts to steer actual inflation towards the target through the use of interest rate changes and other monetary tools.

Because interest rates and the inflation rate tend to be inversely related, the likely moves of the central bank to raise or lower interest rates become more transparent under the policy of _____. Examples:

- if inflation appears to be above the target, the bank is likely to raise interest rates. This usually (but not always) has the effect over time of cooling the economy and bringing down inflation.

- if inflation appears to be below the target, the bank is likely to lower interest rates. This usually (again, not always) has the effect over time of accelerating the economy and raising inflation.

a. Employment Cost Index
b. Incomes policies
c. Inflation swap
d. Inflation targeting

50.   The _____ was an evolution of developed countries from an industrial/manufacturing-based wealth producing economy into a service sector asset based economy, brought about by globalization and currency manipulation by governments and their central banks. Some analysts claimed that this change in the economic structure of the United States had created a state of permanent steady growth, low unemployment, and immunity to boom and bust macroeconomic cycles. They believed that the change rendered obsolete many business practices.

a. 1921 recession
b. New Economy
c. 100-year flood
d. 130-30 fund

51.   _____ refers to the economic policies promoted by United States President Ronald Reagan during the 1980s. The four pillars of Reagan's economic policy were to:

1. reduce the growth of government spending,
2. reduce income and capital gains marginal tax rates,
3. reduce government regulation of the economy,
4. control the money supply to reduce inflation.

In attempting to cut back on domestic spending while lowering taxes, Reagan's approach was a departure from his immediate predecessors.

Reagan became president during a period of high inflation and unemployment (commonly referred to as stagflation), which had largely abated by the time he left office eight years later.

Prior to the Reagan Administration was a roughly ten year period of economic stagnation and inflation, known as stagflation.

a. Social savings
b. Business sector
c. Happiness economics
d. Reaganomics

52.   An _____ is the price a borrower pays for the use of money they do not own, for instance a small company might borrow from a bank to kick start their business, and the return a lender receives for deferring the use of funds, by lending it to the borrower. _____s are normally expressed as a percentage rate over the period of one year.

Chapter 22. AN INTRODUCTION TO MACROECONOMICS

_____s targets are also a vital tool of monetary policy and are used to control variables like investment, inflation, and unemployment.

a. Enterprise value
c. ACCRA Cost of Living Index
b. Arrow-Debreu model
d. Interest rate

53. _____ is a policy or ideology of violence intended to intimidate or cause terror for the purpose of 'exerting pressure on decision making by state bodies.' The term 'terror' is largely used to indicate clandestine, low-intensity violence that targets civilians and generates public fear. Thus 'terror' is distinct from asymmetric warfare, and violates the concept of a common law of war in which civilian life is regarded. The term '-ism' is used to indicate an ideology --typically one that claims its attacks are in the domain of a 'just war' concept, though most condemn such as crimes against humanity.

a. 130-30 fund
c. Terrorism
b. 1921 recession
d. 100-year flood

54. _____ is the incidence or process of transferring ownership of a business, enterprise, agency or public service from the public sector (government) to the private sector (business.) In a broader sense, _____ refers to transfer of any government function to the private sector including governmental functions like revenue collection and law enforcement.

The term '_____' also has been used to describe two unrelated transactions.

a. Privatization
c. Performance reports
b. Ricardian equivalence
d. Compound empowerment

55. To _____ is to impose a financial charge or other levy upon a taxpayer by a state or the functional equivalent of a state.

_____es are also imposed by many subnational entities. _____es consist of direct _____ or indirect _____, and may be paid in money or as its labour equivalent (often but not always unpaid.)

a. 100-year flood
c. 130-30 fund
b. 1921 recession
d. Tax

56. A _____ is a reduction in taxes. Economic stimulus via _____s, along with interest rate intervention and deficit spending, are one of the central tenets of Keynesian economics.

The immediate effects of a _____ are, generally, a decrease in the real income of the government and an increase in the real income of those whose tax rate has been lowered.

a. Popiwek
c. Direct taxes
b. Withholding tax
d. Tax cut

57. A _____ is a package or set of measures introduced to stabilise a financial system or economy. The term can refer to policies in two distinct sets of circumstances: business cycle stabilization and crisis stabilization.

Stabilization can refer to correcting the normal behavior of the business cycle.

a. Capacity Development
c. New International Economic Order
b. Volunteers for Economic Growth Alliance
d. Stabilization policy

58. _____ is the process by which the government, central bank (ii) availability of money, and (iii) cost of money or rate of interest, in order to attain a set of objectives oriented towards the growth and stability of the economy. Monetary theory provides insight into how to craft optimal _____.

_____ is referred to as either being an expansionary policy where an expansionary policy increases the total supply of money in the economy, and a contractionary policy decreases the total money supply.

a. 1921 recession
c. Monetary policy
b. 100-year flood
d. 130-30 fund

Chapter 23. THE GOALS OF MACROECONOMIC POLICY

1. In economics, _____ is the total demand for final goods and services in the economy (Y) at a given time and price level. It is the amount of goods and services in the economy that will be purchased at all possible price levels. This is the demand for the gross domestic product of a country when inventory levels are static.
   a. Aggregate expenditure
   b. Aggregation problem
   c. Aggregate supply
   d. Aggregate demand

2. In economics, _____ is the total supply of goods and services produced by a national economy during a specific time period. It is the total amount of goods and services in the economy available at all possible price levels.
   a. Aggregation problem
   b. Aggregate demand
   c. Aggregate expenditure
   d. Aggregate supply

3. _____ is the term denoting either an entrance or changes which are inserted into a system and which activate/modify a process. It is an abstract concept, used in the modeling, system(s) design and system(s) exploitation. It is usually connected with other terms, e.g., _____ field, _____ variable, _____ parameter, _____ value, _____ signal, _____ device and _____ file.
   a. ACEA agreement
   b. AD-IA Model
   c. ACCRA Cost of Living Index
   d. Input

4. _____ is a branch of economics that deals with the performance, structure, and behavior of a national or regional economy as a whole. Along with microeconomics, _____ is one of the two most general fields in economics. It is the study of the behavior and decision-making of entire economies.
   a. New Trade Theory
   b. Tobit model
   c. Nominal value
   d. Macroeconomics

5. Economics:

   - _____, the desire to own something and the ability to pay for it
   - _____ curve, a graphic representation of a _____ schedule
   - _____ deposit, the money in checking accounts
   - _____ pull theory, the theory that inflation occurs when _____ for goods and services exceeds existing supplies
   - _____ schedule, a table that lists the quantity of a good a person will buy it each different price
   - _____ side economics, the school of economics at believes government spending and tax cuts open economy by raising _____

   a. Demand
   b. Production
   c. McKesson ' Robbins scandal
   d. Variability

6. In economics, the _____ can be defined as the graph depicting the relationship between the price of a certain commodity, and the amount of it that consumers are willing and able to purchase at that given price. It is a graphic representation of a demand schedule. The _____ for all consumers together follows from the _____ of every individual consumer: the individual demands at each price are added together.
   a. Wage curve
   b. Cost curve
   c. Kuznets curve
   d. Demand curve

Chapter 23. THE GOALS OF MACROECONOMIC POLICY

7. The _____ or gross domestic income (GDI), a basic measure of an economy's economic performance, is the market value of all final goods and services produced within the borders of a nation in a year. _____ can be defined in three ways, all of which are conceptually identical. First, it is equal to the total expenditures for all final goods and services produced within the country in a stipulated period of time (usually a 365-day year.)

 a. Market structure
 b. Countercyclical
 c. Monopolistic competition
 d. Gross domestic product

8. In economics, the _____ is a historical inverse relation between the rate of unemployment and the rate of inflation in an economy. Stated simply, the lower the unemployment in an economy, the higher the rate of increase in nominal wages in the economy. Rate of Change of Wages against Unemployment, United Kingdom 1913-1948 from Phillips (1958)

William Phillips, a New Zealand born economist, wrote a paper in 1958 titled The Relationship between Unemployment and the Rate of Change of Money Wages in the United Kingdom 1861-1957, which was published in the quarterly journal Economica.

 a. Cost curve
 b. Demand curve
 c. Lorenz curve
 d. Phillips curve

9. _____ in economics refers to metrics and measures of output from production processes, per unit of input. Labor _____, for example, is typically measured as a ratio of output per labor-hour, an input. _____ may be conceived of as a metrics of the technical or engineering efficiency of production.

 a. Productivity
 b. Piece work
 c. Fordism
 d. Production-possibility frontier

10. _____ is a term used in national accounts statistics and macroeconomics. It basically refers to the net additions to the (physical) capital stock in an accounting period, or, to the value of the increase of the capital stock; though it may occasionally also refer to the (growth of the) total stock of capital formed.

Thus, in UNSNA, _____ equals fixed capital investment, the increase in the value of inventories held, plus (net) lending to foreign countries, during an accounting period.

 a. Capital flight
 b. Consumption of fixed capital
 c. Capital intensity
 d. Capital formation

11. _____s is the social science that studies the production, distribution, and consumption of goods and services. The term _____s comes from the Ancient Greek oá¼°κονομῖα from oá¼¶κος (oikos, 'house') + vĺŒµος (nomos, 'custom' or 'law'), hence 'rules of the house(hold)'. Current _____ models developed out of the broader field of political economy in the late 19th century, owing to a desire to use an empirical approach more akin to the physical sciences.

 a. Inflation
 b. Opportunity cost
 c. Economic
 d. Energy economics

12. _____ is the increase in the amount of the goods and services produced by an economy over time. It is conventionally measured as the percent rate of increase in real gross domestic product, or real GDP. Growth is usually calculated in real terms, i.e. inflation-adjusted terms, in order to net out the effect of inflation on the price of the goods and services produced.

Chapter 23. THE GOALS OF MACROECONOMIC POLICY

a. ACEA agreement
b. ACCRA Cost of Living Index
c. AD-IA Model
d. Economic growth

13. _____ is the concept of adding accumulated interest back to the principal, so that interest is earned on interest from that moment on. The act of declaring interest to be principal is called compounding (i.e., interest is compounded.) A loan, for example, may have its interest compounded every month: in this case, a loan with $100 principal and 1% interest per month would have a balance of $101 at the end of the first month.
  a. Foreclosure data providers
  b. General purpose technologies
  c. Fama-French three factor model
  d. Compound interest

14. _____ is a fee paid on borrowed assets. It is the price paid for the use of borrowed money, or, money earned by deposited funds. Assets that are sometimes lent with _____ include money, shares, consumer goods through hire purchase, major assets such as aircraft, and even entire factories in finance lease arrangements.
  a. Internal debt
  b. Asset protection
  c. Insolvency
  d. Interest

15. An _____ is the price a borrower pays for the use of money they do not own, for instance a small company might borrow from a bank to kick start their business, and the return a lender receives for deferring the use of funds, by lending it to the borrower. _____s are normally expressed as a percentage rate over the period of one year.

_____s targets are also a vital tool of monetary policy and are used to control variables like investment, inflation, and unemployment.
  a. ACCRA Cost of Living Index
  b. Enterprise value
  c. Arrow-Debreu model
  d. Interest rate

16. In economics, the people in the _____ are the suppliers of labor. The _____ is all the nonmilitary people who are employed or unemployed. In 2005, the worldwide _____ was over 3 billion people.
  a. Distributed workforce
  b. Departmentalization
  c. Grenelle agreements
  d. Labor force

17. In microeconomics, _____ is quite simply the conversion of inputs into outputs. It is an economic process that uses resources to create a good or service that is suitable for exchange. This can include manufacturing, storing, shipping, and packaging.
  a. Solved
  b. Red Guards
  c. MET
  d. Production

18. In economics, a _____ is a function that specifies the output of a firm, an industry, or an entire economy for all combinations of inputs. A meta-_____ compares the practice of the existing entities converting inputs X into output y to determine the most efficient practice _____ of the existing entities, whether the most efficient feasible practice production or the most efficient actual practice production. In either case, the maximum output of a technologically-determined production process is a mathematical function of input factors of production.
  a. Production function
  b. Post-Fordism
  c. Short-run
  d. Constant elasticity of substitution

Chapter 23. THE GOALS OF MACROECONOMIC POLICY

19. _____ was a global military conflict which involved a majority of the world's nations, including all of the great powers, organized into two opposing military alliances: the Allies and the Axis. The war involved the mobilization of over 100 million military personnel, making it the most widespread war in history. In a state of 'total war', the major participants placed their entire economic, industrial, and scientific capabilities at the service of the war effort, erasing the distinction between civilian and military resources.
   - a. World War II
   - b. 100-year flood
   - c. 1921 recession
   - d. 130-30 fund

20. Unemployment occurs when a person is available to work and seeking work but currently without work. The prevalence of unemployment is usually measured using the _____, which is defined as the percentage of those in the labor force who are unemployed. The _____ is also used in economic studies and economic indexes such as the United States' Conference Board's Index of Leading Indicators as a measure of the state of the macroeconomics.
   - a. ACCRA Cost of Living Index
   - b. ACEA agreement
   - c. AD-IA Model
   - d. Unemployment rate

21. The _____ was a worldwide economic downturn starting in most places in 1929 and ending at different times in the 1930s or early 1940s for different countries. It was the largest and most important economic depression in the 20th century, and is used in the 21st century as an example of how far the world's economy can fall. The _____ originated in the United States; historians most often use as a starting date the stock market crash on October 29, 1929, known as Black Tuesday.
   - a. Great Depression
   - b. Jarrow March
   - c. British Empire Economic Conference
   - d. Wall Street Crash of 1929

22. _____, 1st Baron Keynes was a renowned economist from Britain whose many ideas on economic and political theories as well as on many governments' monetary policies influenced America. He advocated a government that played an active role in the lives of people regarding business, economy, etc. In this role, the government would use fiscal measures to reduce the consequences of recessions, economic depressions and booms.
   - a. Adolph Fischer
   - b. Adam Smith
   - c. Adolf Hitler
   - d. John Maynard Keynes

23. The _____, a unit of the United States Department of Labor, is the principal fact-finding agency for the U.S. government in the broad field of labor economics and statistics. The BLS is an independent national statistical agency that collects, processes, analyzes, and disseminates essential statistical data to the American public, the U.S. Congress, other Federal agencies, State and local governments, business, and labor representatives. The BLS also serves as a statistical resource to the Department of Labor.
   - a. Gross world product
   - b. Bureau of Labor Statistics
   - c. Gross Regional Product
   - d. Gross national product

24. _____ was an American clergyman, activist and prominent leader in the African-American civil rights movement. His main legacy was to secure progress on civil rights in the United States and he is frequently referenced as a human rights icon today.
   - a. Adolf Hitler
   - b. Wang Laboratories
   - c. Martin Luther King, Jr.
   - d. Adam Smith

Chapter 23. THE GOALS OF MACROECONOMIC POLICY

25. _____ changed the course of Western civilization by initiating the Protestant Reformation. As a priest and theology professor, he confronted indulgence salesmen with his 95 Theses in 1517. Luther strongly disputed their claim that freedom from God's punishment of sin could be purchased with money.
   a. Martin Luther
   b. George Cabot Lodge II
   c. Maximilian Carl Emil Weber
   d. Henry Ford

26. Wisconsin originated the idea of _____ in the U.S. in 1932. In the United States, there are 50 state _____ programs plus one each in the District of Columbia and Puerto Rico. Through the Social Security Act of 1935, the Federal Government of the United States effectively coerced the individual states into adopting _____ plans.
   a. ACCRA Cost of Living Index
   b. AD-IA Model
   c. ACEA agreement
   d. Unemployment insurance

27. _____, in law and economics, is a form of risk management primarily used to hedge against the risk of a contingent loss. _____ is defined as the equitable transfer of the risk of a loss, from one entity to another, in exchange for a premium, and can be thought of as a guaranteed small loss to prevent a large, possibly devastating loss. An insurer is a company selling the _____; an insured or policyholder is the person or entity buying the _____.
   a. ACCRA Cost of Living Index
   b. AD-IA Model
   c. ACEA agreement
   d. Insurance

28. Economists distinguish between various types of unemployment, including _____, frictional unemployment, structural unemployment and classical unemployment. Some additional types of unemployment that are occasionally mentioned are seasonal unemployment, hardcore unemployment, and hidden unemployment. Real-world unemployment may combine different types.
   a. Cyclical unemployment
   b. Types of unemployment
   c. Seasonal unemployment
   d. Structural unemployment

29. In economics, a _____ is a person of legal employment age who is not actively seeking employment. This is usually due to the fact that an individual has given up looking or has had no success in finding a job, hence the term 'discouraged.' Their belief may derive from a variety of factors including: a shortage of jobs in their locality or line of work; perceived discrimination for reasons such as age, race, sex and religion; a lack of necessary skills, training or experience; or, a chronic illness or disability. Some _____s, however, are voluntarily unemployed such as stay-at-home parents, pregnant mothers, and will beneficiaries.
   a. Discouraged worker
   b. Relative income hypothesis
   c. Demand side economics
   d. Hedonimetry

30. Economists distinguish between various types of unemployment, including cyclical unemployment, _____, structural unemployment and classical unemployment. Some additional types of unemployment that are occasionally mentioned are seasonal unemployment, hardcore unemployment, and hidden unemployment. Real-world unemployment may combine different types.
   a. Frictional unemployment
   b. Types of unemployment
   c. Seasonal unemployment
   d. Structural unemployment

31. _____ is long-term and chronic unemployment arising from imbalances between the skills and other characteristics of workers in the market and the needs of employers. It involves a mismatch between workers looking for jobs and the vacancies available often despite the number of vacancies being similar to the number of unemployed people. In this case, the unemployed workers lack the specific skills required for the jobs, or are located in a different geographical region to the vacant jobs.

   a. Seasonal unemployment
   b. Frictional unemployment
   c. Types of unemployment
   d. Structural unemployment

32. Economists distinguish between various _____, including cyclical unemployment, frictional unemployment, structural unemployment and classical unemployment. Some additional _____ that are occasionally mentioned are seasonal unemployment, hardcore unemployment, and hidden unemployment. Real-world unemployment may combine different types.

   a. Frictional unemployment
   b. Structural unemployment
   c. Types of Unemployment
   d. Graduate unemployment

33. _____ refers to the economic policies of United States President Bill Clinton during the 1990s. Clinton assumed office at the tail end of a recession, and the economic theories he utilized and implemented are claimed by his supporters to have eventually led to a strong recovery, though Clinton's opponents deny this.

The strategy was outlined in the following three points:

- Establishing fiscal discipline, eliminating the budget deficit, keeping interest rates low, and spurring private-sector investment.
- Investing in people through education, training, science, and research.
- Opening foreign markets so American workers can compete abroad.

During the 1992 presidential campaign America had undergone twelve years of conservative policies implemented by Ronald Reagan and George Herbert Walker Bush. Clinton ran on the economic platform of balancing the budget, lowering inflation, lowering unemployment, and continuing the traditionally conservative policies of free trade.

   a. Clintonomics
   b. Jawboning
   c. Structural equation modeling
   d. Purchasing Managers Index

34. In macroeconomics, _____ is a condition of the national economy, where all or nearly all persons willing and able to work at the prevailing wages and working conditions are able to do so. It is defined either as 0% unemployment, literally, no unemployment (the rate of unemployment is the fraction of the work force unable to find work), as by James Tobin, or as the level of employment rates when there is no cyclical unemployment. It is defined by the majority of mainstream economists as being an acceptable level of natural unemployment above 0%, the discrepancy from 0% being due to non-cyclical types of unemployment.

   a. Full employment
   b. Marginal propensity to consume
   c. Demand shock
   d. Harrod-Johnson diagram

35. A _____ is the lowest hourly, daily or monthly wage that employers may legally pay to employees or workers. Equivalently, it is the lowest wage at which workers may sell their labor. Although _____ laws are in effect in a great many jurisdictions, there are differences of opinion about the benefits and drawbacks of a _____.

Chapter 23. THE GOALS OF MACROECONOMIC POLICY

a. Microfoundations
b. Minimum wage
c. Permanent war economy
d. Marginal propensity to consume

36. _____ is a broad label that refers to any individuals or households that use goods and services generated within the economy. The concept of a _____ is used in different contexts, so that the usage and significance of the term may vary.

Typically when business people and economists talk of _____s they are talking about person as _____, an aggregated commodity item with little individuality other than that expressed in the buy/not-buy decision.

a. Consumer
b. 130-30 fund
c. 1921 recession
d. 100-year flood

37. A _____ is a measure of the average price of consumer goods and services purchased by households. A _____ measures a price change for a constant market basket of goods and services from one period to the next within the same area (city, region, or nation.) It is a price index determined by measuring the price of a standard group of goods meant to represent the typical market basket of a typical urban consumer.

a. CPI
b. Cost-of-living index
c. Lipstick index
d. Consumer Price Index

38. _____ in economics and business is the result of an exchange and from that trade we assign a numerical monetary value to a good, service or asset. If Alice trades Bob 4 apples for an orange, the _____ of an orange is 4 apples. Inversely, the _____ of an apple is 1/4 oranges.

a. Price war
b. Premium pricing
c. Price book
d. Price

39. A _____ is a normalized average (typically a weighted average) of prices for a given class of goods or services in a given region, during a given interval of time. It is a statistic designed to help to compare how these prices, taken as a whole, differ between time periods or geographical locations.

Price indices have several potential uses.

a. Product sabotage
b. Two-part tariff
c. Transactional Net Margin Method
d. Price Index

40. In economics, _____ is a rise in the general level of prices of goods and services in an economy over a period of time. When the general price level rises, each unit of currency buys fewer goods and services; consequently, _____ is also a decline in the real value of money--a loss of purchasing power in the medium of exchange which is also the monetary unit of account in the economy. A chief measure of general price-level _____ is the general _____ rate, which is the percentage change in a general price index (normally the Consumer Price Index) over time.

a. Economic
b. Energy economics
c. Inflation
d. Opportunity cost

Chapter 23. THE GOALS OF MACROECONOMIC POLICY

41. _____ refers to a business or organization attempting to acquire goods or services to accomplish the goals of the enterprise. Though there are several organizations that attempt to set standards in the _____ process, processes can vary greatly between organizations. Typically the word '_____' is not used interchangeably with the word 'procurement', since procurement typically includes Expediting, Supplier Quality, and Traffic and Logistics (T'L) in addition to _____.
   a. 130-30 fund
   b. 100-year flood
   c. Free port
   d. Purchasing

42. _____ is the number of goods/services that can be purchased with a unit of currency. For example, if you had taken one dollar to a store in the 1950s, you would have been able to buy a greater number of items than you would today, indicating that you would have had a greater _____ in the 1950s. Currency can be either a commodity money, like gold or silver, or fiat currency like US dollars.
   a. Human Poverty Index
   b. Compliance cost
   c. Purchasing power
   d. Genuine progress indicator

43. The term _____s refers to wages that have been adjusted for inflation. This term is used in contrast to nominal wages or unadjusted wages.

The use of adjusted figures is in undertaking some form of economic analysis.

   a. Living wage
   b. Federal Wage System
   c. Profit sharing
   d. Real wage

44. A consumer price index (_____) is a measure of the average price of consumer goods and services purchased by households. A consumer price index measures a price change for a constant market basket of goods and services from one period to the next within the same area (city, region, or nation.) It is a price index determined by measuring the price of a standard group of goods meant to represent the typical market basket of a typical urban consumer.
   a. Hedonic price index
   b. Lipstick index
   c. Cost-of-living index
   d. CPI

45. _____ is the price of a commodity such as a good or service in terms of another; ie, the ratio of two prices. A _____ may be expressed in terms of a ratio between any two prices or the ratio between the price of one particular good and a weighted average of all other goods available in the market. A _____ is an opportunity cost.
   a. Relative price
   b. Food cooperative
   c. False economy
   d. False shortage

46. The _____ is the central banking system of the United States. Created in 1913 by the enactment of the Federal Reserve Act (signed by Woodrow Wilson), it is a quasi-public and quasi-private (government entity with private components) banking system that comprises (1) the presidentially appointed Board of Governors of the _____ in Washington, D.C.; (2) the Federal Open Market Committee; (3) twelve regional Federal Reserve Banks located in major cities throughout the nation acting as fiscal agents for the U.S. Treasury, each with its own nine-member board of directors; (4) numerous other private U.S. member banks, which subscribe to required amounts of non-transferable stock in their regional Federal Reserve Banks; and (5) various advisory councils. Since February 2006, Ben Bernanke has served as the Chairman of the Board of Governors of the _____.
   a. Term auction facility
   b. Federal Reserve System Open Market Account
   c. Monetary Policy Report to the Congress
   d. Federal Reserve System

Chapter 23. THE GOALS OF MACROECONOMIC POLICY

47. In economics, the term _____ of income or _____ refers to a simple economic model which describes the reciprocal circulation of income between producers and consumers. In the _____ model, the inter-dependent entities of producer and consumer are referred to as 'firms' and 'households' respectively and provide each other with factors in order to facilitate the flow of income. Firms provide consumers with goods and services in exchange for consumer expenditure and 'factors of production' from households.
- a. 130-30 fund
- b. 1921 recession
- c. 100-year flood
- d. Circular flow

48. In finance and economics _____ or nominal rate of interest refers to the rate of interest before adjustment for inflation (in contrast with the real interest rate); or, for interest rates 'as stated' without adjustment for the full effect of compounding (also referred to as the nominal annual rate.) An interest rate is called nominal if the frequency of compounding (e.g. a month) is not identical to the basic time unit (normally a year.)

The real interest rate includes compensation for the lender's lost value due to inflation, whereas the _____ excludes inflation.

- a. London Interbank Offered Rate
- b. Risk-free interest rate
- c. Fixed interest
- d. Nominal interest rate

49. In economics, _____ is equal to total cost divided by the number of goods produced (the output quantity, Q.) It is also equal to the sum of average variable costs (total variable costs divided by Q) plus average fixed costs (total fixed costs divided by Q.) _____s may be dependent on the time period considered (increasing production may be expensive or impossible in the short term, for example.)
- a. Average variable cost
- b. Average fixed cost
- c. Explicit cost
- d. Average cost

50. In economics and finance, _____ is the change in total cost that arises when the quantity produced changes by one unit. It is the cost of producing one more unit of a good. Mathematically, the _____ function is expressed as the first derivative of the total cost (TC) function with respect to quantity (Q.)
- a. Khozraschyot
- b. Variable cost
- c. Quality costs
- d. Marginal cost

51. In economics, _____ is inflation that is very high or 'out of control', a condition in which prices increase rapidly as a currency loses its value. Definitions used by the media vary from a cumulative inflation rate over three years approaching 100% to 'inflation exceeding 50% a month.' In informal usage the term is often applied to much lower rates. As a rule of thumb, normal inflation is reported per year, but _____ is often reported for much shorter intervals, often per month.
- a. 100-year flood
- b. Hyperinflation
- c. 1921 recession
- d. 130-30 fund

52. An _____, in economics, is the amount by which the real Gross domestic product exceeds potential GDP. The real GDP is also known as GDP 'adjusted for inflation', 'constant prices' GDP or 'constant dollar' GDP, because it measures the aggregate output in a country's income accounts in a given year, expressed in base-year prices. On the other hand, the potential GDP is the quantity of real GDP when a country's economy is at full-employment.
- a. ACEA agreement
- b. Inflationary gap
- c. AD-IA Model
- d. ACCRA Cost of Living Index

Chapter 23. THE GOALS OF MACROECONOMIC POLICY

53. The term _____, 'the state or characteristic of being variable', _____ describes how spread out or closely clustered a set of data is. may be applied to many different subjects:

- Climate _____
- Genetic _____
- Heart rate _____
- Human _____
- Solar van
- Spatial _____
- Statistical _____
- _____

a. Characteristic
c. Total product

b. Variability
d. Demand

54. The _____ is an international organization that oversees the global financial system by following the macroeconomic policies of its member countries, in particular those with an impact on exchange rates and the balance of payments. It is an organization formed to stabilize international exchange rates and facilitate development. It also offers financial and technical assistance to its members, making it an international lender of last resort.

a. ACCRA Cost of Living Index
c. ACEA agreement

b. Office of Thrift Supervision
d. International Monetary Fund

55. In economics, _____ is a measure of the relative satisfaction from consumption of various goods and services. Given this measure, one may speak meaningfully of increasing or decreasing _____, and thereby explain economic behavior in terms of attempts to increase one's _____. For illustrative purposes, changes in _____ are sometimes expressed in units called utils.

a. Ordinal utility
c. Utility function

b. Utility
d. Expected utility hypothesis

Chapter 23. THE GOALS OF MACROECONOMIC POLICY

56. A _____ is:

- Rewrite _____, in generative grammar and computer science
- Standardization, a formal and widely-accepted statement, fact, definition, or qualification
- Operation, a determinate _____ for performing a mathematical operation and obtaining a certain result (Mathematics, Logic)
    - Unary operation
    - Binary operation
- _____ of inference, a function from sets of formulae to formulae (Mathematics, Logic)
- _____ of thumb, principle with broad application that is not intended to be strictly accurate or reliable for every situation. Also often simply referred to as a _____
- Moral, an atomic element of a moral code for guiding choices in human behavior
- Heuristic, a quantized '_____' which shows a tendency or probability for successful function
- A regulation, as in sports
- A Production _____, as in computer science
- Procedural law, a _____ set governing the application of laws to cases
    - A law, which may informally be called a '_____'
    - A court ruling, a decision by a court
- In the U.S. Government, a regulation mandated by Congress, but written or expanded upon by the Executive Branch.
- Norm (sociology), an informal but widely accepted _____, concept, truth, definition, or qualification (social norms, legal norms, coding norms)
- Norm (philosophy), a kind of sentence or a reason to act, feel or believe
- 'Rulership' is the concept of governance by a government:
    - Military _____, governance by a military body
    - Monastic _____, a collection of precepts that guides the life of monks or nuns in a religious order where the superior holds the place of Christ
- Slide _____

- '_____,' a song by Ayumi Hamasaki
- '_____,' a song by rapper Nas
- '_____s,' an album by the band The Whitest Boy Alive
- _____s: Pyaar Ka Superhit Formula, a 2003 Bollywood film
- ruler, an instrument for measuring lengths
- _____, a component of an astrolabe, circumferator or similar instrument
- The _____s, a bestselling self-help book
- _____ Project (Run Up-to-date Linux Everywhere), a project that aims to use up-to-date Linux software on old PCs
- _____ engine, a software system that helps managing business _____s
- Ja _____, a hip hop artist
    - R.U.L.E., a 2005 greatest hits album by rapper Ja _____
- '_____s,' a KMFDM song

a. Procter ' Gamble
b. Technocracy
c. Rule
d. Demand

57. An _____ is an economic data figure reflecting price or quantity compared with a standard or base value. The base usually equals 100 and the _____ is usually expressed as 100 times the ratio to the base value. For example, if a commodity costs twice as much in 1970 as it did in 1960, its _____ would be 200 relative to 1960.
   a. Index number
   b. Economic depreciation
   c. International economics
   d. ACCRA Cost of Living Index

Chapter 24. ECONOMIC GROWTH: THEORY AND POLICY

1. A _____ is a package or set of measures introduced to stabilise a financial system or economy. The term can refer to policies in two distinct sets of circumstances: business cycle stabilization and crisis stabilization.

Stabilization can refer to correcting the normal behavior of the business cycle.

   a. New International Economic Order
   b. Capacity Development
   c. Volunteers for Economic Growth Alliance
   d. Stabilization policy

2. The _____ is an international financial institution that provides financial and technical assistance to developing countries for development programs (e.g. bridges, roads, schools, etc.) with the stated goal of reducing poverty.

The _____ differs from the _____ Group, in that the _____ comprises only two institutions:

   - International Bank for Reconstruction and Development (IBRD)
   - International Development Association (IDA)

Whereas the latter incorporates these two in addition to three more:

   - International Finance Corporation (IFC)
   - Multilateral Investment Guarantee Agency (MIGA)
   - International Centre for Settlement of Investment Disputes (ICSID)

John Maynard Keynes (right) represented the UK at the conference, and Harry Dexter White represented the US.

The _____ is one of two major financial institutions created as a result of the Bretton Woods Conference in 1944. The International Monetary Fund, a related but separate institution, is the second.

   a. Flow to Equity-Approach
   b. Financial costs of the 2003 Iraq War
   c. Bank-State-Branch
   d. World Bank

3. In economics, _____ is the total supply of goods and services produced by a national economy during a specific time period. It is the total amount of goods and services in the economy available at all possible price levels.
   a. Aggregation problem
   b. Aggregate supply
   c. Aggregate expenditure
   d. Aggregate demand

4. _____ is a term used in national accounts statistics and macroeconomics. It basically refers to the net additions to the (physical) capital stock in an accounting period, or, to the value of the increase of the capital stock; though it may occasionally also refer to the (growth of the) total stock of capital formed.

Thus, in UNSNA, _____ equals fixed capital investment, the increase in the value of inventories held, plus (net) lending to foreign countries, during an accounting period.

   a. Capital intensity
   b. Consumption of fixed capital
   c. Capital flight
   d. Capital formation

Chapter 24. ECONOMIC GROWTH: THEORY AND POLICY

5. _____ is money accepted for exchange of goods in an economy. The prevalence of one money over another arises, usually, when a government designates through decrees that the government shall accept only particular notes and coins in payment for taxes. Typically, money of _____ consists of stamped coins and minted paper bills.
   a. Currency
   b. Totnes pound
   c. Local currency
   d. Security thread

6. A consumer price index (_____) is a measure of the average price of consumer goods and services purchased by households. A consumer price index measures a price change for a constant market basket of goods and services from one period to the next within the same area (city, region, or nation.) It is a price index determined by measuring the price of a standard group of goods meant to represent the typical market basket of a typical urban consumer.
   a. Lipstick index
   b. CPI
   c. Hedonic price index
   d. Cost-of-living index

7. _____ is a broad label that refers to any individuals or households that use goods and services generated within the economy. The concept of a _____ is used in different contexts, so that the usage and significance of the term may vary.

   Typically when business people and economists talk of _____s they are talking about person as _____, an aggregated commodity item with little individuality other than that expressed in the buy/not-buy decision.

   a. 100-year flood
   b. Consumer
   c. 1921 recession
   d. 130-30 fund

8. A _____ is a measure of the average price of consumer goods and services purchased by households. A _____ measures a price change for a constant market basket of goods and services from one period to the next within the same area (city, region, or nation.) It is a price index determined by measuring the price of a standard group of goods meant to represent the typical market basket of a typical urban consumer.
   a. Cost-of-living index
   b. Consumer Price Index
   c. CPI
   d. Lipstick index

9. A trade union or _____ is an organization of workers who have banded together to achieve common goals in key areas and working conditions. The trade union, through its leadership, bargains with the employer on behalf of union members (rank and file members) and negotiates labor contracts (Collective bargaining) with employers. This may include the negotiation of wages, work rules, complaint procedures, rules governing hiring, firing and promotion of workers, benefits, workplace safety and policies.
   a. Demand-side technologies
   b. Basis of futures
   c. Business valuation standards
   d. Labor union

10. _____ in economics and business is the result of an exchange and from that trade we assign a numerical monetary value to a good, service or asset. If Alice trades Bob 4 apples for an orange, the _____ of an orange is 4 apples. Inversely, the _____ of an apple is 1/4 oranges.
    a. Price war
    b. Premium pricing
    c. Price
    d. Price book

Chapter 24. ECONOMIC GROWTH: THEORY AND POLICY

11. A _____ is a normalized average (typically a weighted average) of prices for a given class of goods or services in a given region, during a given interval of time. It is a statistic designed to help to compare how these prices, taken as a whole, differ between time periods or geographical locations.

Price indices have several potential uses.

    a. Transactional Net Margin Method   b. Two-part tariff
    c. Product sabotage   d. Price Index

12. _____ in economics refers to metrics and measures of output from production processes, per unit of input. Labor _____, for example, is typically measured as a ratio of output per labor-hour, an input. _____ may be conceived of as a metrics of the technical or engineering efficiency of production.

    a. Production-possibility frontier   b. Piece work
    c. Fordism   d. Productivity

13. _____ is a type of private equity investment, most often a minority investment, in relatively mature companies that are looking for capital to expand or restructure operations, enter new markets or finance a significant acquisition without a change of control of the business.

Companies that seek _____, will often do so in order to finance a transformational event in their lifecycle. These companies are likely to be more mature than venture capital funded companies, able to generate revenue and operating profits but unable to generate sufficient cash to fund major expansions, acquisitions or other investments.

    a. Startup company   b. Growth Capital
    c. Club deal   d. Seed money

14. The _____ or gross domestic income (GDI), a basic measure of an economy's economic performance, is the market value of all final goods and services produced within the borders of a nation in a year. _____ can be defined in three ways, all of which are conceptually identical. First, it is equal to the total expenditures for all final goods and services produced within the country in a stipulated period of time (usually a 365-day year.)

    a. Gross domestic product   b. Market structure
    c. Countercyclical   d. Monopolistic competition

15. _____ refers to the stock of skills and knowledge embodied in the ability to perform labor so as to produce economic value. It is the skills and knowledge gained by a worker through education and experience.Many early economic theories refer to it simply as labor, one of three factors of production, and consider it to be a fungible resource -- homogeneous and easily interchangeable. Other conceptions of labor dispense with these assumptions.

    a. Price theory   b. Law of increasing costs
    c. Human capital   d. General equilibrium

16. The _____ is the labour pool in employment. It is generally used to describe those working for a single company or industry, but can also apply to a geographic region like a city, country, state, etc. The term generally excludes the employers or management, and implies those involved in manual labour.

a. Collective bargaining
b. Workforce
c. Grenelle agreements
d. Departmentalization

17. In a _____ there is both a monopoly (a single seller) and monopsony (a single buyer) in the same market.

In such market price and output will be determined by the non economic forces like bargaining power of both buyer and seller. A _____ model is often used in situations where the switching costs of both sides are prohibitively high.

a. Revenue-cap regulation
b. Market concentration
c. Bilateral monopoly
d. Price takers

18. In economics, a _____ exists when a specific individual or enterprise has sufficient control over a particular product or service to determine significantly the terms on which other individuals shall have access to it. Monopolies are thus characterized by a lack of economic competition for the good or service that they provide and a lack of viable substitute goods. The verb 'monopolize' refers to the process by which a firm gains persistently greater market share than what is expected under perfect competition.

a. Monopoly
b. 100-year flood
c. 1921 recession
d. 130-30 fund

19. In finance, a _____ is a debt security, in which the authorized issuer owes the holders a debt and, depending on the terms of the _____, is obliged to pay interest (the coupon) and/or to repay the principal at a later date, termed maturity. A _____ is a formal contract to repay borrowed money with interest at fixed intervals.

Thus a _____ is like a loan: the issuer is the borrower (debtor), the holder is the lender (creditor), and the coupon is the interest.

a. Bond
b. Zero-coupon
c. Prize Bond
d. Callable

20. The _____ is the central banking system of the United States. Created in 1913 by the enactment of the Federal Reserve Act (signed by Woodrow Wilson), it is a quasi-public and quasi-private (government entity with private components) banking system that comprises (1) the presidentially appointed Board of Governors of the _____ in Washington, D.C.; (2) the Federal Open Market Committee; (3) twelve regional Federal Reserve Banks located in major cities throughout the nation acting as fiscal agents for the U.S. Treasury, each with its own nine-member board of directors; (4) numerous other private U.S. member banks, which subscribe to required amounts of non-transferable stock in their regional Federal Reserve Banks; and (5) various advisory councils. Since February 2006, Ben Bernanke has served as the Chairman of the Board of Governors of the _____.

a. Term auction facility
b. Federal Reserve System
c. Monetary Policy Report to the Congress
d. Federal Reserve System Open Market Account

21. In microeconomics, _____ is quite simply the conversion of inputs into outputs. It is an economic process that uses resources to create a good or service that is suitable for exchange. This can include manufacturing, storing, shipping, and packaging.

Chapter 24. ECONOMIC GROWTH: THEORY AND POLICY

a. Red Guards
b. Solved
c. Production
d. MET

22. A _____, reserve bank, or monetary authority is the entity responsible for the monetary policy of a country or of a group of member states. It is a bank that can lend money to other banks in times of need. Its primary responsibility is to maintain the stability of the national currency and money supply, but more active duties include controlling subsidized-loan interest rates, and acting as a lender of last resort to the banking sector during times of financial crisis (private banks often being integral to the national financial system.)
   a. 130-30 fund
   b. 100-year flood
   c. 1921 recession
   d. Central bank

23. _____ is a fee paid on borrowed assets. It is the price paid for the use of borrowed money, or, money earned by deposited funds. Assets that are sometimes lent with _____ include money, shares, consumer goods through hire purchase, major assets such as aircraft, and even entire factories in finance lease arrangements.
   a. Insolvency
   b. Internal debt
   c. Asset protection
   d. Interest

24. A _____ is a tax charged on capital gains, the profit realized on the sale of a non-inventory asset that was purchased at a lower price. The most common capital gains are realized from the sale of stocks, bonds, precious metals and property. Not all countries implement a _____ and most have different rates of taxation for individuals and corporations.
   a. Potentially dangerous taxpayer
   b. Tax deferral
   c. Capital gains tax
   d. Tax resistance

25. In economics, the _____ can be defined as the graph depicting the relationship between the price of a certain commodity, and the amount of it that consumers are willing and able to purchase at that given price. It is a graphic representation of a demand schedule. The _____ for all consumers together follows from the _____ of every individual consumer: the individual demands at each price are added together.
   a. Cost curve
   b. Wage curve
   c. Kuznets curve
   d. Demand curve

26. _____ is an economic model based on price, utility and quantity in a market. It predicts that in a competitive market, price will function to equalize the quantity demanded by consumers, and the quantity supplied by producers, resulting in an economic equilibrium of price and quantity. The model incorporates other factors changing equilibrium as a shift of demand and/or supply.
   a. Deferred gratification
   b. Rational addiction
   c. Joint demand
   d. Supply and demand

Chapter 24. ECONOMIC GROWTH: THEORY AND POLICY

27. Economics:

    - _____,the desire to own something and the ability to pay for it
    - _____ curve,a graphic representation of a _____ schedule
    - _____ deposit, the money in checking accounts
    - _____ pull theory,the theory that inflation occurs when _____ for goods and services exceeds existing supplies
    - _____ schedule,a table that lists the quantity of a good a person will buy it each different price
    - _____ side economics,the school of economics at believes government spending and tax cuts open economy by raising _____

    a. Demand
    b. Production
    c. Variability
    d. McKesson ' Robbins scandal

28. In economics, _____ is the ratio of the percent change in one variable to the percent change in another variable. It is a tool for measuring the responsiveness of a function to changes in parameters in a relative way. Commonly analyzed are _____ of substitution, price and wealth.
    a. Elasticity of demand
    b. ACEA agreement
    c. ACCRA Cost of Living Index
    d. Elasticity

29. To _____ is to impose a financial charge or other levy upon a taxpayer by a state or the functional equivalent of a state.

    _____es are also imposed by many subnational entities. _____es consist of direct _____ or indirect _____, and may be paid in money or as its labour equivalent (often but not always unpaid.)

    a. 1921 recession
    b. 100-year flood
    c. 130-30 fund
    d. Tax

30. A _____ is the exclusive authority to determine how a resource is used, whether that resource is owned by government or by individuals. All economic goods have a _____s attribute. This attribute has three broad components

    1. The right to use the good
    2. The right to earn income from the good
    3. The right to transfer the good to others

    The concept of _____s as used by economists and legal scholars are related but distinct. The distinction is largely seen in the economists' focus on the ability of an individual or collective to control the use of the good.

    a. Post-sale restraint
    b. Property right
    c. High-reeve
    d. Holder in due course

31. Economic _____ is defined as an excess distribution to any factor in a production process above that which is required to induce the factor into the process or any excess above that which is necessary to keep the factor in its current use..

Chapter 24. ECONOMIC GROWTH: THEORY AND POLICY

Classical Factor _____ is primarily concerned with the fee paid for the use of fixed (e.g. natural) resources. The classical definition is expressed as any excess payment above that required to induce or provide for production.

a. 130-30 fund
c. 100-year flood
b. 1921 recession
d. Rent

32. _____ refers to the collection of laws and rules that govern the operation of education systems.

Education occurs in many forms for many purposes through many institutions. Examples include early childhood education, kindergarten through to 12th grade, two and four year colleges or universities, graduate and professional education, adult education and job training.

a. ACCRA Cost of Living Index
c. Education policy
b. AD-IA Model
d. ACEA agreement

33. The _____ Act of 2001 (Pub.L. 107-110, 115 Stat. 1425, enacted January 8, 2002), often abbreviated in print as _____ and sometimes shortened in pronunciation to 'nicklebee', is a United States Act of Congress that was originally proposed by President George W. Bush immediately after taking office.

a. No Child Left Behind
c. Due diligence
b. Nexus of contracts
d. Community property

34. The phrase _____, according to the Organization for Economic Co-operation and Development, refers to 'creative work undertaken on a systematic basis in order to increase the stock of knowledge, including knowledge of man, culture and society, and the use of this stock of knowledge to devise new applications [sic]'

New product design and development is more than often a crucial factor in the survival of a company. In an industry that is fast changing, firms must continually revise their design and range of products. This is necessary due to continuous technology change and development as well as other competitors and the changing preference of customers.

a. 100-year flood
c. 1921 recession
b. 130-30 fund
d. Research and development

35. _____, in microeconomics, are the cost advantages that a business obtains due to expansion. They are factors that cause a producere;s average cost per unit to fall as scale is increased. _____ is a long run concept and refers to reductions in unit cost as the size of a facility, or scale, increases.

a. Isoquant
c. Underinvestment employment relationship
b. Economic production quantity
d. Economies of scale

36. _____ is a term that is used to describe the overall process of invention, innovation and diffusion of technology or processes. The term is redundant with technological development, technological achievement, and technological progress. In essence _____ is the invention of a technology (or a process), the continuous process of improving a technology (in which it often becomes cheaper) and its diffusion throughout industry or society.

Chapter 24. ECONOMIC GROWTH: THEORY AND POLICY

a. 1921 recession
c. 130-30 fund
b. Technological change
d. 100-year flood

37. A _____ refers to any type debt instrument, such as a loan, bond, mortgage that does not have a fixed rate of interest over the life of the instrument. Such debt typically uses an index or other base rate for establishing the interest rate for each relevant period. One of the most common rates to use as the basis for applying interest rates is the London Inter-bank Offered Rate, or LIBOR
   a. Disposal tax effect
   c. Money market
   b. Moneylender
   d. Floating interest rate

38. The _____ is an agency of the United States government, responsible for the nation's public space program. NASA was established on July 29, 1958, by the National Aeronautics and Space Act.

In addition to the space program, it is also responsible for long-term civilian and military aerospace research.

   a. H.R. 5405
   c. Consumption
   b. Commodity trading advisors
   d. National Aeronautics and Space Administration

39. The _____ is an agency of the United States Department of Health and Human Services and is the primary agency of the United States government responsible for biomedical and health-related research. It consists of 27 separate institutes and centers plus the Office of the Director. Its science and engineering counterpart is the National Science Foundation.
   a. 100-year flood
   c. 130-30 fund
   b. 1921 recession
   d. National Institutes of Health

40. The _____ is a United States government agency that supports fundamental research and education in all the non-medical fields of science and engineering. Its medical counterpart is the National Institutes of Health. With an annual budget of about $6.02 billion (fiscal year 2008), _____ funds approximately 20 percent of all federally supported basic research conducted by the United States' colleges and universities.
   a. 1921 recession
   c. 100-year flood
   b. National Science Foundation
   d. 130-30 fund

41. _____ refers to the movement of cash into or out of a business or financial product. It is usually measured during a specified, finite period of time. Measurement of _____ can be used

- to determine a project's rate of return or value. The time of _____s into and out of projects are used as inputs in financial models such as internal rate of return, and net present value.
- to determine problems with a business's liquidity. Being profitable does not necessarily mean being liquid. A company can fail because of a shortage of cash, even while profitable.
- as an alternate measure of a business's profits when it is believed that accrual accounting concepts do not represent economic realities. For example, a company may be notionally profitable but generating little operational cash (as may be the case for a company that barters its products rather than selling for cash.) In such a case, the company may be deriving additional operating cash by issuing shares evaluating default risk, re-investment requirements, etc.

_____ is a generic term used differently depending on the context. It may be defined by users for their own purposes.

Chapter 24. ECONOMIC GROWTH: THEORY AND POLICY 211

a. Second lien loan
b. Restricted stock
c. Strip financing
d. Cash flow

42. The term _____ describes two different concepts:

- The first is a recognition of partial payment already made towards taxes due.
- The second is a state benefit paid to workers through the tax system, which has the effect of increasing (rather than reducing) net income.

Within the Australian, Canadian, United Kingdom, and United States tax systems, a _____ is a recognition of partial payment already made towards taxes due. A similar concept exists (fr:Avoir fiscal) in the French tax system. This situation arises, for example, when standard rate tax has been deducted at source, but the tax-payer is subject to further taxation at a higher rate. It also applies in dividend imputation systems.

a. 1921 recession
b. Tax Credit
c. 100-year flood
d. 130-30 fund

43. _____ , as defined by the _____ Association of America (Information technologyAA), is 'the study, design, development, implementation, support or management of computer-based information systems, particularly software applications and computer hardware.' _____ deals with the use of electronic computers and computer software to convert, store, protect, process, transmit, and securely retrieve information.

Today, the term _____ has ballooned to encompass many aspects of computing and technology, and the term has become very recognizable. The _____ umbrella can be quite large, covering many fields.

a. Information technology
b. ACCRA Cost of Living Index
c. AD-IA Model
d. ACEA agreement

44. In economics, an _____ is a contour line drawn through the set of points at which the same quantity of output is produced while changing the quantities of two or more inputs. While an indifference curve helps to answer the utility-maximizing problem of consumers, the _____ deals with the cost-minimization problem of producers. _____s are typically drawn on capital-labor graphs, showing the tradeoff between capital and labor in the production function, and the decreasing marginal returns of both inputs.

a. Isoquant
b. Economies of scale
c. Economic production quantity
d. Underinvestment employment relationship

45. The Organization of the Petroleum Exporting Countries is a cartel of twelve countries made up of Algeria, Angola, Ecuador, Iran, Iraq, Kuwait, Libya, Nigeria, Qatar, Saudi Arabia, the United Arab Emirates, and Venezuela. The cartel has maintained its headquarters in Vienna since 1965, and hosts regular meetings among the oil ministers of its Member Countries. Indonesia withdrew its membership in _____ in 2008 after it became a net importer of oil, but stated it would likely return if it became a net exporter in the world.

a. AD-IA Model
b. ACEA agreement
c. ACCRA Cost of Living Index
d. OPEC

Chapter 24. ECONOMIC GROWTH: THEORY AND POLICY

46. The _____, also commonly known as the Computer Age or Information Era, is an idea that the current age will be characterised by the ability of individuals to transfer information freely, and to have instant access to knowledge that would have been difficult or impossible to find previously. The idea is heavily linked to the concept of a Digital Age or Digital Revolution, and carries the ramifications of a shift from traditional industry that the Industrial Revolution brought through industrialisation, to an economy based around the manipulation of information. The period is generally said to have begun in the latter half of the 20th century, though the particular date varies.

a. ACEA agreement
b. ACCRA Cost of Living Index
c. Information Age
d. AD-IA Model

47. The term _____s refers to wages that have been adjusted for inflation. This term is used in contrast to nominal wages or unadjusted wages.

The use of adjusted figures is in undertaking some form of economic analysis.

a. Profit sharing
b. Living wage
c. Federal Wage System
d. Real wage

48. The _____ consists of a number of economic theories which describe the nature of the firm, company including its existence, its behaviour, and its relationship with the market.

In simplified terms, the _____ aims to answer these questions:

1. Existence - why do firms emerge, why are not all transactions in the economy mediated over the market?
2. Boundaries - why the boundary between firms and the market is located exactly there? Which transactions are performed internally and which are negotiated on the market?
3. Organization - why are firms structured in such specific way? What is the interplay of formal and informal relationships?

Despite looking simple, these questions are not answered by the established economic theory, which usually views firms as given, and treats them as black boxes without any internal structure.

The First World War period saw a change of emphasis in economic theory away from industry-level analysis which mainly included analysing markets to analysis at the level of the firm, as it became increasingly clear that perfect competition was no longer an adequate model of how firms behaved. Economic theory till then had focussed on trying to understand markets alone and there had been little study on understanding why firms or organisations exist.

a. Theory of the firm
b. Khazzoom-Brookes postulate
c. Technology gap
d. Policy Ineffectiveness Proposition

49. _____ in its classic form is defined as a company from one country making a physical investment into building a factory in another country. It is the establishment of an enterprise by a foreigner. Its definition can be extended to include investments made to acquire lasting interest in enterprises operating outside of the economy of the investor.

Chapter 24. ECONOMIC GROWTH: THEORY AND POLICY

a. Non-governmental organization
b. Federal Deposit Insurance Corporation
c. Financial Stability Forum
d. Foreign direct investment

50. A _____ or transnational corporation is a corporation or enterprise that manages production or delivers services in more than one country. It can also be referred to as an international corporation.

The first modern MNC is generally thought to be the Dutch East India Company, established in 1602.

a. Rakon
b. Multinational corporation
c. Luxembourg Income Study
d. Foreign direct investment

51. _____ is a voluntary transfer of resources from one country to another, given at least partly with the objective of benefiting the recipient country. It may have other functions as well: it may be given as a signal of diplomatic approval, or to strengthen a military ally, to reward a government for behaviour desired by the donor, to extend the donor's cultural influence, to provide infrastructure needed by the donor for resource extraction from the recipient country, or to gain other kinds of commercial access. Humanitarianism and altruism are, nevertheless, significant motivations for the giving of _____.

a. Aid
b. AD-IA Model
c. ACCRA Cost of Living Index
d. ACEA agreement

52. _____ is a term used to collectively describe topics relating to the operations of firms with interests in multiple countries. Such firms are sometimes called multinational corporations . Well known MNCs include fast food companies McDonald's and Yum Brands, vehicle manufacturers such as General Motors and Toyota, consumer electronics companies like Samsung, LG and Sony, and energy companies such as ExxonMobil and BP.

a. AD-IA Model
b. ACEA agreement
c. ACCRA Cost of Living Index
d. International Business

53. _____ relates to decisions that define expectations, grant power, or verify performance. It consists either of a separate process or of a specific part of management or leadership processes. Sometimes people set up a government to administer these processes and systems.

a. 130-30 fund
b. 1921 recession
c. 100-year flood
d. Governance

54. In economics, a _____ is a general slowdown in economic activity over a sustained period of time, or a business cycle contraction. During _____s, many macroeconomic indicators vary in a similar way. Production as measured by Gross Domestic Product (GDP), employment, investment spending, capacity utilization, household incomes and business profits all fall during _____s.

a. Leading indicators
b. Monetary economics
c. Treasury View
d. Recession

Chapter 25. AGGREGATE DEMAND AND THE POWERFUL CONSUMER

1. In economics, _____ is the total demand for final goods and services in the economy (Y) at a given time and price level. It is the amount of goods and services in the economy that will be purchased at all possible price levels. This is the demand for the gross domestic product of a country when inventory levels are static.
   - a. Aggregate supply
   - b. Aggregation problem
   - c. Aggregate expenditure
   - d. Aggregate demand

2. The _____ or gross domestic income (GDI), a basic measure of an economy's economic performance, is the market value of all final goods and services produced within the borders of a nation in a year. _____ can be defined in three ways, all of which are conceptually identical. First, it is equal to the total expenditures for all final goods and services produced within the country in a stipulated period of time (usually a 365-day year.)
   - a. Market structure
   - b. Monopolistic competition
   - c. Countercyclical
   - d. Gross domestic product

3. _____, 1st Baron Keynes was a renowned economist from Britain whose many ideas on economic and political theories as well as on many governments' monetary policies influenced America. He advocated a government that played an active role in the lives of people regarding business, economy, etc. In this role, the government would use fiscal measures to reduce the consequences of recessions, economic depressions and booms.
   - a. Adolf Hitler
   - b. Adolph Fischer
   - c. Adam Smith
   - d. John Maynard Keynes

4. A variety of measures of _____ and output are used in economics to estimate total economic activity in a country or region, including gross domestic product (GDP), gross national product (GNP), and net _____

   There are three main ways of calculating these numbers; the output approach, the income approach and the expenditure approach. In theory, the three must yield the same, because total expenditures on goods and services must equal the total income paid to the producers (Gnational income), and that must also equal the total value of the output of goods and services (GNP.)
   - a. National income
   - b. Gross world product
   - c. Volume index
   - d. GNI per capita

5. An _____, in economics, is the amount by which the real Gross domestic product exceeds potential GDP. The real GDP is also known as GDP 'adjusted for inflation', 'constant prices' GDP or 'constant dollar' GDP, because it measures the aggregate output in a country's income accounts in a given year, expressed in base-year prices. On the other hand, the potential GDP is the quantity of real GDP when a country's economy is at full-employment.
   - a. Inflationary gap
   - b. AD-IA Model
   - c. ACCRA Cost of Living Index
   - d. ACEA agreement

6. In economics, the term _____ of income or _____ refers to a simple economic model which describes the reciprocal circulation of income between producers and consumers. In the _____ model, the inter-dependent entities of producer and consumer are referred to as 'firms' and 'households' respectively and provide each other with factors in order to facilitate the flow of income. Firms provide consumers with goods and services in exchange for consumer expenditure and 'factors of production' from households.
   - a. Circular flow
   - b. 100-year flood
   - c. 1921 recession
   - d. 130-30 fund

Chapter 25. AGGREGATE DEMAND AND THE POWERFUL CONSUMER

7. Economics:

    - _____, the desire to own something and the ability to pay for it
    - _____ curve, a graphic representation of a _____ schedule
    - _____ deposit, the money in checking accounts
    - _____ pull theory, the theory that inflation occurs when _____ for goods and services exceeds existing supplies
    - _____ schedule, a table that lists the quantity of a good a person will buy it each different price
    - _____ side economics, the school of economics at believes government spending and tax cuts open economy by raising _____

    a. Variability
    c. Demand
    b. Production
    d. McKesson ' Robbins scandal

8. In economics, the _____ can be defined as the graph depicting the relationship between the price of a certain commodity, and the amount of it that consumers are willing and able to purchase at that given price. It is a graphic representation of a demand schedule. The _____ for all consumers together follows from the _____ of every individual consumer: the individual demands at each price are added together.

    a. Demand curve
    c. Wage curve
    b. Kuznets curve
    d. Cost curve

9. _____ is a misspelled phrase from Latin 'pro capite' phrase meaning per head with pro meaning 'per' or 'for each' and capite meaning 'head.' Both words together equate to the phrase 'for each head.'

    It is usually used in the field of statistics to indicate the average per person for any given concern, such as income, crime rate, etc.

    It is also used in wills to indicate that each of the named beneficiaries should receive, by devise or bequest, equal shares of the estate. This is in contrast to a per stirpes division, in which each branch of the inheriting family inherits an equal share of the estate.

    a. Sargan test
    c. False positive rate
    b. Population statistics
    d. Per capita

10. _____ is a broad label that refers to any individuals or households that use goods and services generated within the economy. The concept of a _____ is used in different contexts, so that the usage and significance of the term may vary.

    Typically when business people and economists talk of _____s they are talking about person as _____, an aggregated commodity item with little individuality other than that expressed in the buy/not-buy decision.

    a. 130-30 fund
    c. 100-year flood
    b. 1921 recession
    d. Consumer

Chapter 25. AGGREGATE DEMAND AND THE POWERFUL CONSUMER

11. _____ is an economic model based on price, utility and quantity in a market. It predicts that in a competitive market, price will function to equalize the quantity demanded by consumers, and the quantity supplied by producers, resulting in an economic equilibrium of price and quantity. The model incorporates other factors changing equilibrium as a shift of demand and/or supply.

   a. Joint demand
   b. Supply and demand
   c. Rational addiction
   d. Deferred gratification

12. In economics, _____ is the ratio of the percent change in one variable to the percent change in another variable. It is a tool for measuring the responsiveness of a function to changes in parameters in a relative way. Commonly analyzed are _____ of substitution, price and wealth.

   a. ACEA agreement
   b. Elasticity of demand
   c. ACCRA Cost of Living Index
   d. Elasticity

13. _____ is the incidence or process of transferring ownership of a business, enterprise, agency or public service from the public sector (government) to the private sector (business.) In a broader sense, _____ refers to transfer of any government function to the private sector including governmental functions like revenue collection and law enforcement.

   The term '_____' also has been used to describe two unrelated transactions.

   a. Ricardian equivalence
   b. Compound empowerment
   c. Performance reports
   d. Privatization

14. To _____ is to impose a financial charge or other levy upon a taxpayer by a state or the functional equivalent of a state.

   _____es are also imposed by many subnational entities. _____es consist of direct _____ or indirect _____, and may be paid in money or as its labour equivalent (often but not always unpaid.)

   a. 130-30 fund
   b. 1921 recession
   c. 100-year flood
   d. Tax

15. A _____ product is a product designed for cheapness and short-term convenience rather than medium to long-term durability, with most products only intended for single use. The term is also sometimes used for products that may last several months (ex. _____ air filters) to distinguish from similar products that last indefinitely (ex.

   a. 130-30 fund
   b. 100-year flood
   c. 1921 recession
   d. Disposable

16. _____ is gross income minus income tax on that income.

Discretionary income is income after subtracting taxes and normal expenses (such as rent or mortgage, utilities, insurance, medical, transportation, property maintenance, child support, inflation, food and sundries, 'c.) to maintain a certain standard of living.

   a. Stamp Act
   b. Disposable income
   c. Disposable personal income
   d. Taxation as theft

Chapter 25. AGGREGATE DEMAND AND THE POWERFUL CONSUMER   217

17. In microeconomics, _____ is quite simply the conversion of inputs into outputs. It is an economic process that uses resources to create a good or service that is suitable for exchange. This can include manufacturing, storing, shipping, and packaging.
    a. Solved
    b. Production
    c. MET
    d. Red Guards

18. _____ is a common concept in economics, and gives rise to derived concepts such as consumer debt. Generally _____ is defined by opposition to production. But the precise definition can vary because different schools of economists define production quite differently.
    a. Foreclosure data providers
    b. Cash or share options
    c. Consumption
    d. Federal Reserve Bank Notes

19. In business and accounting, _____ are everything of value that is owned by a person or company. It is a claim on the property your income of a borrower. The balance sheet of a firm records the monetary value of the _____ owned by the firm.
    a. Assets
    b. ACCRA Cost of Living Index
    c. Amortization schedule
    d. ACEA agreement

20. In economics, an _____ is any good or commodity, transported from one country to another country in a legitimate fashion, typically for use in trade. _____ goods or services are provided to foreign consumers by domestic producers. _____ is an important part of international trade.
    a. AD-IA Model
    b. ACEA agreement
    c. ACCRA Cost of Living Index
    d. Export

21. _____ is the production of large amounts of standardized products, including and especially on assembly lines. The concepts of _____ are applied to various kinds of products, from fluids and particulates handled in bulk to discrete solid parts to assemblies of such parts

    _____ of assemblies typically uses electric-motor-powered moving tracks or conveyor belts to move partially complete products to workers, who perform simple repetitive tasks.

    a. 1921 recession
    b. 100-year flood
    c. Mass production
    d. 130-30 fund

22. _____ refers to a business or organization attempting to acquire goods or services to accomplish the goals of the enterprise. Though there are several organizations that attempt to set standards in the _____ process, processes can vary greatly between organizations. Typically the word '_____' is not used interchangeably with the word 'procurement', since procurement typically includes Expediting, Supplier Quality, and Traffic and Logistics (T'L) in addition to _____.
    a. Purchasing
    b. 130-30 fund
    c. Free port
    d. 100-year flood

23. _____ comprises the total value produced within a country (i.e. its gross domestic product), together with its income received from other countries (notably interest and dividends), less similar payments made to other countries.

218 *Chapter 25. AGGREGATE DEMAND AND THE POWERFUL CONSUMER*

The _____ consists of: the personal consumption expenditures, the gross private investment, the government consumption expenditures, the net income from assets abroad (net income receipts), and the gross exports of goods and services, after deducting two components: the gross imports of goods and services, and the indirect business taxes. The _____ is similar to the gross national product (GNP), except that in measuring the GNP one does not deduct the indirect business taxes.

    a. Gross national income
    b. Central limit order book
    c. Base period
    d. Market-based instruments

24. _____ or consumer demand or consumption is also known as personal consumption expenditure. It is the largest part of aggregate demand or effective demand at the macroeconomic level. There are two variants of consumption in the aggregate demand model, including induced consumption and autonomous consumption.
    a. Dishoarding
    b. Complex multiplier
    c. Potential output
    d. Consumer spending

25. A _____ is a legal document that is often passed by the legislature, and approved by the chief executive-or president. For example, only certain types of revenue may be imposed and collected. Property tax is frequently the basis for municipal and county revenues, while sales tax and/or income tax are the basis for state revenues, and income tax and corporate tax are the basis for national revenues.
    a. Structural deficit
    b. Government budget
    c. Lump-sum tax
    d. Right-financing

26. In economics, a _____ is a redistribution of income in the market system. These payments are considered to be nonexhaustive because they do not directly absorb resources or create output. Examples of certain _____s include welfare (financial aid), social security, and government subsidies for certain businesses (firms.)
    a. 1921 recession
    b. 100-year flood
    c. 130-30 fund
    d. Transfer payment

27. Wisconsin originated the idea of _____ in the U.S. in 1932. In the United States, there are 50 state _____ programs plus one each in the District of Columbia and Puerto Rico. Through the Social Security Act of 1935, the Federal Government of the United States effectively coerced the individual states into adopting _____ plans.
    a. ACEA agreement
    b. AD-IA Model
    c. ACCRA Cost of Living Index
    d. Unemployment insurance

28. _____, in law and economics, is a form of risk management primarily used to hedge against the risk of a contingent loss. _____ is defined as the equitable transfer of the risk of a loss, from one entity to another, in exchange for a premium, and can be thought of as a guaranteed small loss to prevent a large, possibly devastating loss. An insurer is a company selling the _____; an insured or policyholder is the person or entity buying the _____.
    a. ACEA agreement
    b. ACCRA Cost of Living Index
    c. AD-IA Model
    d. Insurance

29. A _____ is the transfer of wealth from one party (such as a person or company) to another. A _____ is usually made in exchange for the provision of goods, services or both, or to fulfill a legal obligation.

The simplest and oldest form of _____ is barter, the exchange of one good or service for another.

Chapter 25. AGGREGATE DEMAND AND THE POWERFUL CONSUMER

a. Going concern
b. Soft count
c. Payment
d. Social gravity

30. To tax is to impose a financial charge or other levy upon a taxpayer by a state or the functional equivalent of a state. _____ are also imposed by many subnational entities. _____ consist of direct tax or indirect tax, and may be paid in money or as its labour equivalent (often but not always unpaid.)

a. 130-30 fund
b. 1921 recession
c. 100-year flood
d. Taxes

31. The _____ is the multiple by which Aggregate demand will increase, when there is an increase in transfer payments (e.g. welfare spending, unemployment payments.) Changes in spending usually lead to a larger than one for one increase in Aggregate demand, because any increase in household incomes caused by the increase in spending also increases in consumption spending, which further increases Aggregate demand.

a. Market-based instruments
b. Cost-effectiveness analysis
c. Legal monopoly
d. Transfer payments Multiplier

32. _____ is the a method of technical and economic research of the systems for purpose to optimize a parity between system's consumer functions or properties and expenses to achieve those functions or properties.

This methodology for continuous perfection of production, industrial technologies, organizational structures was developed by Juryj Sobolev in 1948 at the 'Perm telephone factory'

- 1948 Juryj Sobolev - the first success in application of a method analysis at the 'Perm telephone factory' .
- 1949 - the first application for the invention as result of use of the new method.

Today in economically developed countries practically each enterprise or the company use methodology of the kind of functional-cost analysis as a practice of the quality management, most full satisfying to principles of standards of series ISO 9000.

- Interest of consumer not in products itself, but the advantage which it will receive from its usage.
- The consumer aspires to reduce his expenses
- Functions needed by consumer can be executed in the various ways, and, hence, with various efficiency and expenses. Among possible alternatives of realization of functions exist such in which the parity of quality and the price is the optimal for the consumer.

The goal of _____ is achievement of the highest consumer satisfaction of production at simultaneous decrease in all kinds of industrial expenses Classical _____ has three English synonyms - Value Engineering, Value Management, Value Analysis.

a. Monopoly wage
b. Willingness to pay
c. Staple financing
d. Function cost analysis

Chapter 25. AGGREGATE DEMAND AND THE POWERFUL CONSUMER

33. In economics, the _____ is a single mathematical function used to express consumer spending. It was developed by John Maynard Keynes and detailed most famously in his book The General Theory of Employment, Interest, and Money. The function is used to calculate the amount of total consumption in an economy.
   a. Liquidity preference
   b. Procyclical
   c. DAD-SAS model
   d. Consumption function

34. In economics, the _____ is an empirical metric that quantifies induced consumption, the concept that the increase in personal consumer spending (consumption) that occurs with an increase in disposable income (income after taxes and transfers.) For example, if a household earns one extra dollar of disposable income, and the _____ is 0.65, then of that dollar, the household will spend 65 cents and save 35 cents.

Mathematically, the _____ (MPC) function is expressed as the derivative of the consumption (C) function with respect to disposable income (Y.)

   a. Technology shock
   b. Marginal propensity to import
   c. Supply shock
   d. Marginal propensity to consume

35. In finance, a _____ is a debt security, in which the authorized issuer owes the holders a debt and, depending on the terms of the _____, is obliged to pay interest (the coupon) and/or to repay the principal at a later date, termed maturity. A _____ is a formal contract to repay borrowed money with interest at fixed intervals.

Thus a _____ is like a loan: the issuer is the borrower (debtor), the holder is the lender (creditor), and the coupon is the interest.

   a. Zero-coupon
   b. Prize Bond
   c. Callable
   d. Bond

36. The _____ is the central banking system of the United States. Created in 1913 by the enactment of the Federal Reserve Act (signed by Woodrow Wilson), it is a quasi-public and quasi-private (government entity with private components) banking system that comprises (1) the presidentially appointed Board of Governors of the _____ in Washington, D.C.; (2) the Federal Open Market Committee; (3) twelve regional Federal Reserve Banks located in major cities throughout the nation acting as fiscal agents for the U.S. Treasury, each with its own nine-member board of directors; (4) numerous other private U.S. member banks, which subscribe to required amounts of non-transferable stock in their regional Federal Reserve Banks; and (5) various advisory councils. Since February 2006, Ben Bernanke has served as the Chairman of the Board of Governors of the _____.

   a. Federal Reserve System
   b. Federal Reserve System Open Market Account
   c. Term auction facility
   d. Monetary Policy Report to the Congress

37. _____ in economics and business is the result of an exchange and from that trade we assign a numerical monetary value to a good, service or asset. If Alice trades Bob 4 apples for an orange, the _____ of an orange is 4 apples. Inversely, the _____ of an apple is 1/4 oranges.
   a. Premium pricing
   b. Price book
   c. Price
   d. Price war

38. A _____ is a hypothetical measure of overall prices for some set of goods and services, in a given region during a given interval, normalized relative to some base set. Typically, a _____ is approximated with a price index.

Chapter 25. AGGREGATE DEMAND AND THE POWERFUL CONSUMER

The classical dichotomy is the assumption that there is a relatively clean distinction between overall increases or decreases in prices and underlying, e;reale; economic variables.

a. Price elasticity of supply
c. Discretionary spending
b. Discouraged worker
d. Price level

39. _____ is a fee paid on borrowed assets. It is the price paid for the use of borrowed money , or, money earned by deposited funds . Assets that are sometimes lent with _____ include money, shares, consumer goods through hire purchase, major assets such as aircraft, and even entire factories in finance lease arrangements.
a. Internal debt
c. Asset protection
b. Insolvency
d. Interest

40. An _____ is a retirement plan account that provides some tax advantages for retirement savings in the United States.

There are a number of different types of _____s, which may be either employer-provided or self-provided plans. The types include:

- Roth _____ - contributions are made with after-tax assets, all transactions within the _____ have no tax impact, and withdrawals are usually tax-free. Named for Senator William Roth.
- Traditional _____ - contributions are often tax-deductible (often simplified as 'money is deposited before tax' or 'contributions are made with pre-tax assets'), all transactions and earnings within the _____ have no tax impact, and withdrawals at retirement are taxed as income (except for those portions of the withdrawal corresponding to contributions that were not deducted.) Depending upon the nature of the contribution, a traditional _____ may be referred to as a 'deductible _____' or a 'non-deductible _____.'
- SEP _____ - a provision that allows an employer (typically a small business or self-employed individual) to make retirement plan contributions into a Traditional _____ established in the employee's name, instead of to a pension fund account in the company's name.
- SIMPLE _____ - a simplified employee pension plan that allows both employer and employee contributions, similar to a 401(k) plan, but with lower contribution limits and simpler (and thus less costly) administration. Although it is termed an _____, it is treated separately.
- Self-Directed _____ - a self-directed _____ that permits the account holder to make investments on behalf of the retirement plan.

There are two other subtypes of _____, named Rollover _____ and Conduit _____, that are viewed as obsolete under current tax law (their functions have been subsumed by the Traditional _____) by some; but this tax law is set to expire unless extended. However, some individuals still maintain these accounts in order to keep track of the source of these assets.

a. ACEA agreement
c. Individual Retirement Arrangement
b. AD-IA Model
d. ACCRA Cost of Living Index

Chapter 25. AGGREGATE DEMAND AND THE POWERFUL CONSUMER

41. _____ is the point where a person stops employment completely. A person may also semi-retire and keep some sort of _____ job, out of choice rather than necessity. This usually happens upon reaching a determined age, when physical conditions don't allow the person to work any more (by illness or accident), or even for personal choice (usually in the presence of an adequate pension or personal savings.)
   a. 100-year flood
   b. Termination of employment
   c. Layoff
   d. Retirement

42. A _____ is an aspect of the tax code designed to incentivize a certain type of behavior. This may be accomplished through means including tax holidays or tax deductions.
   a. Nil-rate band
   b. General nondiscrimination
   c. Current use
   d. Tax incentive

43. The term _____, 'the state or characteristic of being variable', _____ describes how spread out or closely clustered a set of data is. may be applied to many different subjects:

   - Climate _____
   - Genetic _____
   - Heart rate _____
   - Human _____
   - Solar van
   - Spatial _____
   - Statistical _____
   - _____

   a. Demand
   b. Total product
   c. Characteristic
   d. Variability

44. _____ is the price of a commodity such as a good or service in terms of another; ie, the ratio of two prices. A _____ may be expressed in terms of a ratio between any two prices or the ratio between the price of one particular good and a weighted average of all other goods available in the market. A _____ is an opportunity cost.
   a. Food cooperative
   b. False shortage
   c. False economy
   d. Relative price

45. _____ was written by the English economist John Maynard Keynes. The book, generally considered to be his magnum opus, is largely credited with creating the terminology and shape of modern macroeconomics. Published in February 1936 it sought to bring about a revolution, commonly referred to as the 'Keynesian Revolution', in the way economists thought - especially in relation to the proposition that a market economy tends naturally to restore itself to full employment after temporary shocks.
   a. Principles of Political Economy
   b. Wealth of Nations
   c. General Theory of Employment, Interest and Money
   d. The General Theory of Employment, Interest and Money

Chapter 25. AGGREGATE DEMAND AND THE POWERFUL CONSUMER 223

46. A _____ is:

- Rewrite _____, in generative grammar and computer science
- Standardization, a formal and widely-accepted statement, fact, definition, or qualification
- Operation, a determinate _____ for performing a mathematical operation and obtaining a certain result (Mathematics, Logic)
    - Unary operation
    - Binary operation
- _____ of inference, a function from sets of formulae to formulae (Mathematics, Logic)
- _____ of thumb, principle with broad application that is not intended to be strictly accurate or reliable for every situation. Also often simply referred to as a _____
- Moral, an atomic element of a moral code for guiding choices in human behavior
- Heuristic, a quantized '_____' which shows a tendency or probability for successful function
- A regulation, as in sports
- A Production _____, as in computer science
- Procedural law, a _____ set governing the application of laws to cases
    - A law, which may informally be called a '_____'
    - A court ruling, a decision by a court
- In the U.S. Government, a regulation mandated by Congress, but written or expanded upon by the Executive Branch.
- Norm (sociology), an informal but widely accepted _____, concept, truth, definition, or qualification (social norms, legal norms, coding norms)
- Norm (philosophy), a kind of sentence or a reason to act, feel or believe
- 'Rulership' is the concept of governance by a government:
    - Military _____, governance by a military body
    - Monastic _____, a collection of precepts that guides the life of monks or nuns in a religious order where the superior holds the place of Christ
- Slide _____

- '_____,' a song by Ayumi Hamasaki
- '_____,' a song by rapper Nas
- '_____s,' an album by the band The Whitest Boy Alive
- _____s: Pyaar Ka Superhit Formula, a 2003 Bollywood film
- ruler, an instrument for measuring lengths
- _____, a component of an astrolabe, circumferator or similar instrument
- The _____s, a bestselling self-help book
- _____ Project (Run Up-to-date Linux Everywhere), a project that aims to use up-to-date Linux software on old PCs
- _____ engine, a software system that helps managing business _____s
- Ja _____, a hip hop artist
    - R.U.L.E., a 2005 greatest hits album by rapper Ja _____
- '_____s,' a KMFDM song

a. Demand
b. Technocracy
c. Procter ' Gamble
d. Rule

Chapter 25. AGGREGATE DEMAND AND THE POWERFUL CONSUMER

47. In economics _____s are goods that are ultimately consumed rather than used in the production of another good. For example, a car sold to a consumer is a _____; the components such as tires sold to the car manufacturer are not; they are intermediate goods used to make the _____.

When used in measures of national income and output the term _____s only includes new goods.

   a. Substitute good
   b. Luxury good
   c. Goods and services
   d. Final good

48. _____ is the measure of investment used to compute GDP. This is an important component of GDP because it provides an indicator of the future productive capacity of the economy. It includes replacement purchases plus net additions to capital assets plus investments in inventories.

   a. Compensation of employees
   b. Current account
   c. National Income and Product Accounts
   d. Gross private domestic investment

49. A _____ is an object whose consumption increases the utility of the consumer, for which the quantity demanded exceeds the quantity supplied at zero price. _____s are usually modeled as having diminishing marginal utility. The first individual purchase has high utility; the second has less.

   a. Pie method
   b. Good
   c. Merit good
   d. Composite good

50. In economics, economic output is divided into physical goods and intangible services. Consumption of _____ is assumed to produce utility. It is often used when referring to a _____ Tax.

   a. Private good
   b. Goods and services
   c. Manufactured goods
   d. Composite good

51. _____ or producer goods are goods used as inputs in the production of other goods, such as partly finished goods. They are goods used in production of final goods. A firm may make then use _____, or make then sell, or buy then use them.

   a. Intermediate goods
   b. Economic forecasting
   c. Inflation adjustment
   d. Income distribution

52. _____ is the total market value of all final goods and services produced by citizens of an economy during a given period of time (gross national product or GNP) minus depreciation. The _____ can be similarly applied at a country's domestic output level. The net domestic product (NDP) is the equivalent application of _____ within macroeconomics, and NDP is equal to gross domestic product (GDP) minus depreciation: NDP = GDP - depreciation.

   a. Gross private domestic investment
   b. Compensation of employees
   c. Current account
   d. Net national product

53. _____ is a term used in accounting, economics and finance to spread the cost of an asset over the span of several years.

In simple words we can say that _____ is the reduction in the value of an asset due to usage, passage of time, wear and tear, technological outdating or obsolescence, depletion, inadequacy, rot, rust, decay or other such factors.

Chapter 25. AGGREGATE DEMAND AND THE POWERFUL CONSUMER

In accounting, _____ is a term used to describe any method of attributing the historical or purchase cost of an asset across its useful life, roughly corresponding to normal wear and tear.

a. Depreciation
b. Net income per employee
c. Salvage value
d. Historical cost

54. In finance, the _____s between two currencies specifies how much one currency is worth in terms of the other. It is the value of a foreign natione;s currency in terms of the home natione;s currency. For example an _____ of 102 Japanese yen to the United States dollar means that JPY 102 is worth the same as USD 1.

a. ACCRA Cost of Living Index
b. Interbank market
c. Exchange rate
d. ACEA agreement

55. A variety of measures of national income and output are used in economics to estimate total economic activity in a country or region, including gross domestic product (GDP), _____ , and net national income (NNI.)

There are three main ways of calculating these numbers; the output approach, the income approach and the expenditure approach. In theory, the three must yield the same, because total expenditures on goods and services must equal the total income paid to the producers (GNI), and that must also equal the total value of the output of goods and services (_____.)

a. Household final consumption expenditure
b. Purchasing power parity
c. Gross world product
d. Gross national product

56. _____ is exchange of capital, goods, and services across international borders or territories. In most countries, it represents a significant share of gross domestic product (GDP.) While _____ has been present throughout much of history , its economic, social, and political importance has been on the rise in recent centuries.

a. Incoterms
b. Import license
c. Intra-industry trade
d. International trade

57. _____ refers to the additional value of a commodity over the cost of commodities used to produce it from the previous stage of production. An example is the price of gasoline at the pump over the price of the oil in it. In national accounts used in macroeconomics, it refers to the contribution of the factors of production, i.e., land, labor, and capital goods, to raising the value of a product and corresponds to the incomes received by the owners of these factors.

a. Value added
b. Solow residual
c. Full employment
d. Hodrick-Prescott filter

58. The Demand side is a term used in economics to refer to a number of things:

- The demand element of a supply and demand partial equilibrium diagram, in microeconomics
- The aggregate demand in an economy, in macroeconomics
- Economic policy actions which are designed to affect aggregate demand.
- _____ learning referring to the incentive to learn how to use and modify free software as opposed to buying conventional software.

The term is also used broadly to distinguish supply-side economics from other schools, for instance Keynesian economics.

a. Demand-side
b. Reverse auction
c. CPFR
d. Delayed differentiation

Chapter 26. DEMAND-SIDE EQUILIBRIUM: UNEMPLOYMENT OR INFLATION?

1. The _____ of monetary management established the rules for commercial and financial relations among the world's major industrial states in the mid 20th Century. The _____ was the first example of a fully negotiated monetary order intended to govern monetary relations among independent nation-states.

Preparing to rebuild the international economic system as World War II was still raging, 730 delegates from all 44 Allied nations gathered at the Mount Washington Hotel in Bretton Woods, New Hampshire, United States, for the United Nations Monetary and Financial Conference.

   a. 100-year flood
   c. 1921 recession
   b. 130-30 fund
   d. Bretton Woods system

2. The Demand side is a term used in economics to refer to a number of things:

   - The demand element of a supply and demand partial equilibrium diagram, in microeconomics
   - The aggregate demand in an economy, in macroeconomics
   - Economic policy actions which are designed to affect aggregate demand.
   - _____ learning referring to the incentive to learn how to use and modify free software as opposed to buying conventional software.

The term is also used broadly to distinguish supply-side economics from other schools, for instance Keynesian economics.

   a. CPFR
   c. Reverse auction
   b. Delayed differentiation
   d. Demand-side

3. The _____ or gross domestic income (GDI), a basic measure of an economy's economic performance, is the market value of all final goods and services produced within the borders of a nation in a year. _____ can be defined in three ways, all of which are conceptually identical. First, it is equal to the total expenditures for all final goods and services produced within the country in a stipulated period of time (usually a 365-day year.)
   a. Countercyclical
   c. Monopolistic competition
   b. Gross domestic product
   d. Market structure

4. _____ and Keynesian Theory) is a macroeconomic theory based on the ideas of 20th-century British economist John Maynard Keynes. _____ argues that private sector decisions sometimes lead to inefficient macroeconomic outcomes and therefore advocates active policy responses by the public sector, including monetary policy actions by the central bank and fiscal policy actions by the government to stabilize output over the business cycle.

The theories forming the basis of _____ were first presented in The General Theory of Employment, Interest and Money, published in 1936.

   a. Deflation
   c. Keynesian economics
   b. Market failure
   d. Rational choice theory

5. An _____, in economics, is the amount by which the real Gross domestic product exceeds potential GDP. The real GDP is also known as GDP 'adjusted for inflation', 'constant prices' GDP or 'constant dollar' GDP, because it measures the aggregate output in a country's income accounts in a given year, expressed in base-year prices. On the other hand, the potential GDP is the quantity of real GDP when a country's economy is at full-employment.

Chapter 26. DEMAND-SIDE EQUILIBRIUM: UNEMPLOYMENT OR INFLATION?

a. Inflationary gap
b. ACCRA Cost of Living Index
c. AD-IA Model
d. ACEA agreement

6. In economics, _____ is the total demand for final goods and services in the economy (Y) at a given time and price level. It is the amount of goods and services in the economy that will be purchased at all possible price levels. This is the demand for the gross domestic product of a country when inventory levels are static.
a. Aggregate expenditure
b. Aggregation problem
c. Aggregate supply
d. Aggregate demand

7. In economics, _____ is the total supply of goods and services produced by a national economy during a specific time period. It is the total amount of goods and services in the economy available at all possible price levels.
a. Aggregation problem
b. Aggregate supply
c. Aggregate expenditure
d. Aggregate demand

8. Economics:

- _____, the desire to own something and the ability to pay for it
- _____ curve, a graphic representation of a _____ schedule
- _____ deposit, the money in checking accounts
- _____ pull theory, the theory that inflation occurs when _____ for goods and services exceeds existing supplies
- _____ schedule, a table that lists the quantity of a good a person will buy it each different price
- _____ side economics, the school of economics at believes government spending and tax cuts open economy by raising _____

a. Production
b. Demand
c. Variability
d. McKesson ' Robbins scandal

9. In economics, the _____ can be defined as the graph depicting the relationship between the price of a certain commodity, and the amount of it that consumers are willing and able to purchase at that given price. It is a graphic representation of a demand schedule. The _____ for all consumers together follows from the _____ of every individual consumer: the individual demands at each price are added together.
a. Kuznets curve
b. Demand curve
c. Wage curve
d. Cost curve

10. _____ is a misspelled phrase from Latin 'pro capite' phrase meaning per head with pro meaning 'per' or 'for each' and capite meaning 'head.' Both words together equate to the phrase 'for each head.'

It is usually used in the field of statistics to indicate the average per person for any given concern, such as income, crime rate, etc.

It is also used in wills to indicate that each of the named beneficiaries should receive, by devise or bequest, equal shares of the estate. This is in contrast to a per stirpes division, in which each branch of the inheriting family inherits an equal share of the estate.

Chapter 26. DEMAND-SIDE EQUILIBRIUM: UNEMPLOYMENT OR INFLATION?

   a. False positive rate
   c. Sargan test
   b. Population statistics
   d. Per capita

11. In economics, a _____ is a general slowdown in economic activity over a sustained period of time, or a business cycle contraction. During _____s, many macroeconomic indicators vary in a similar way. Production as measured by Gross Domestic Product (GDP), employment, investment spending, capacity utilization, household incomes and business profits all fall during _____s.
   a. Monetary economics
   c. Leading indicators
   b. Treasury View
   d. Recession

12. _____ is an economic model based on price, utility and quantity in a market. It predicts that in a competitive market, price will function to equalize the quantity demanded by consumers, and the quantity supplied by producers, resulting in an economic equilibrium of price and quantity. The model incorporates other factors changing equilibrium as a shift of demand and/or supply.
   a. Deferred gratification
   c. Supply and demand
   b. Rational addiction
   d. Joint demand

13. In economics, the term _____ of income or _____ refers to a simple economic model which describes the reciprocal circulation of income between producers and consumers. In the _____ model, the inter-dependent entities of producer and consumer are referred to as 'firms' and 'households' respectively and provide each other with factors in order to facilitate the flow of income. Firms provide consumers with goods and services in exchange for consumer expenditure and 'factors of production' from households.
   a. Circular flow
   c. 1921 recession
   b. 130-30 fund
   d. 100-year flood

14. In finance, a _____ is a debt security, in which the authorized issuer owes the holders a debt and, depending on the terms of the _____, is obliged to pay interest (the coupon) and/or to repay the principal at a later date, termed maturity. A _____ is a formal contract to repay borrowed money with interest at fixed intervals.

Thus a _____ is like a loan: the issuer is the borrower (debtor), the holder is the lender (creditor), and the coupon is the interest.

   a. Prize Bond
   c. Zero-coupon
   b. Callable
   d. Bond

15. In algebra, a _____ is a function depending on n that associates a scalar, det(A), to an n×n square matrix A. The fundamental geometric meaning of a _____ is a scale factor for measure when A is regarded as a linear transformation. _____s are important both in calculus, where they enter the substitution rule for several variables, and in multilinear algebra.

For a fixed nonnegative integer n, there is a unique _____ function for the n×n matrices over any commutative ring R. In particular, this function exists when R is the field of real or complex numbers.

   a. 130-30 fund
   c. 1921 recession
   b. 100-year flood
   d. Determinant

Chapter 26. DEMAND-SIDE EQUILIBRIUM: UNEMPLOYMENT OR INFLATION?

16. In business and accounting, _____ are everything of value that is owned by a person or company. It is a claim on the property your income of a borrower. The balance sheet of a firm records the monetary value of the _____ owned by the firm.

   a. ACCRA Cost of Living Index
   b. Amortization schedule
   c. ACEA agreement
   d. Assets

17. _____ is a broad label that refers to any individuals or households that use goods and services generated within the economy. The concept of a _____ is used in different contexts, so that the usage and significance of the term may vary.

   Typically when business people and economists talk of _____s they are talking about person as _____, an aggregated commodity item with little individuality other than that expressed in the buy/not-buy decision.

   a. 1921 recession
   b. 130-30 fund
   c. 100-year flood
   d. Consumer

18. _____ is a common concept in economics, and gives rise to derived concepts such as consumer debt. Generally _____ is defined by opposition to production. But the precise definition can vary because different schools of economists define production quite differently.

   a. Federal Reserve Bank Notes
   b. Cash or share options
   c. Foreclosure data providers
   d. Consumption

19. In economics, the _____ is a single mathematical function used to express consumer spending. It was developed by John Maynard Keynes and detailed most famously in his book The General Theory of Employment, Interest, and Money. The function is used to calculate the amount of total consumption in an economy.

   a. Procyclical
   b. Liquidity preference
   c. DAD-SAS model
   d. Consumption function

20. In macroeconomics, _____ is a condition of the national economy, where all or nearly all persons willing and able to work at the prevailing wages and working conditions are able to do so. It is defined either as 0% unemployment, literally, no unemployment (the rate of unemployment is the fraction of the work force unable to find work), as by James Tobin, or as the level of employment rates when there is no cyclical unemployment. It is defined by the majority of mainstream economists as being an acceptable level of natural unemployment above 0%, the discrepancy from 0% being due to non-cyclical types of unemployment.

   a. Marginal propensity to consume
   b. Harrod-Johnson diagram
   c. Demand shock
   d. Full employment

21. _____ was written by the English economist John Maynard Keynes. The book, generally considered to be his magnum opus, is largely credited with creating the terminology and shape of modern macroeconomics. Published in February 1936 it sought to bring about a revolution, commonly referred to as the 'Keynesian Revolution', in the way economists thought - especially in relation to the proposition that a market economy tends naturally to restore itself to full employment after temporary shocks.

Chapter 26. DEMAND-SIDE EQUILIBRIUM: UNEMPLOYMENT OR INFLATION?

a. The General Theory of Employment, Interest and Money
b. General Theory of Employment, Interest and Money
c. Wealth of Nations
d. Principles of Political Economy

22. The _____ was a worldwide economic downturn starting in most places in 1929 and ending at different times in the 1930s or early 1940s for different countries. It was the largest and most important economic depression in the 20th century, and is used in the 21st century as an example of how far the world's economy can fall. The _____ originated in the United States; historians most often use as a starting date the stock market crash on October 29, 1929, known as Black Tuesday.
  a. Great Depression
  b. Jarrow March
  c. Wall Street Crash of 1929
  d. British Empire Economic Conference

23. _____ is a fee paid on borrowed assets. It is the price paid for the use of borrowed money , or, money earned by deposited funds . Assets that are sometimes lent with _____ include money, shares, consumer goods through hire purchase, major assets such as aircraft, and even entire factories in finance lease arrangements.
  a. Insolvency
  b. Internal debt
  c. Asset protection
  d. Interest

24. _____, 1st Baron Keynes was a renowned economist from Britain whose many ideas on economic and political theories as well as on many governments' monetary policies influenced America. He advocated a government that played an active role in the lives of people regarding business, economy, etc. In this role, the government would use fiscal measures to reduce the consequences of recessions, economic depressions and booms.
  a. Adolf Hitler
  b. Adolph Fischer
  c. John Maynard Keynes
  d. Adam Smith

25. The GDP gap or the output gap is the difference between potential GDP and actual GDP or actual output. The calculation for the output gap is Y-Y* where Y* is potential output and Y is actual output. If this calculation yields a positive number it is called an expansionary gap and indicates an economy in expansion; if the calculation yields a negative number it is called a _____ and indicates an economy in recession.
  a. Recessionary gap
  b. 1921 recession
  c. 130-30 fund
  d. 100-year flood

26. A _____ is a package or set of measures introduced to stabilise a financial system or economy. The term can refer to policies in two distinct sets of circumstances: business cycle stabilization and crisis stabilization.

Stabilization can refer to correcting the normal behavior of the business cycle.

  a. New International Economic Order
  b. Volunteers for Economic Growth Alliance
  c. Stabilization policy
  d. Capacity Development

27. A _____ is a measure of the average price of consumer goods and services purchased by households. A _____ measures a price change for a constant market basket of goods and services from one period to the next within the same area (city, region, or nation.) It is a price index determined by measuring the price of a standard group of goods meant to represent the typical market basket of a typical urban consumer.

Chapter 26. DEMAND-SIDE EQUILIBRIUM: UNEMPLOYMENT OR INFLATION?

a. Lipstick index
b. Consumer Price Index
c. Cost-of-living index
d. CPI

28. _____ is the electoral problem resulting from competition between two or more candidates or political parties from the same or approximate location in the political ideological spectrum or space against an opposing candidate or political party from the other side of the political ideological spectrum or space. The resulting fragmentation of political support may result in electoral defeat. _____s, and thus political calculations attempting to avoid them, appear most frequently in elections involving executives and representatives from single member districts.

a. 130-30 fund
b. 1921 recession
c. 100-year flood
d. Coordination failure

29. _____ in economics and business is the result of an exchange and from that trade we assign a numerical monetary value to a good, service or asset. If Alice trades Bob 4 apples for an orange, the _____ of an orange is 4 apples. Inversely, the _____ of an apple is 1/4 oranges.

a. Price book
b. Price war
c. Premium pricing
d. Price

30. A _____ is a normalized average (typically a weighted average) of prices for a given class of goods or services in a given region, during a given interval of time. It is a statistic designed to help to compare how these prices, taken as a whole, differ between time periods or geographical locations.

Price indices have several potential uses.

a. Transactional Net Margin Method
b. Two-part tariff
c. Product sabotage
d. Price Index

31. _____ is a concept found in moral, political, and bioethical philosophy. Within these contexts, it refers to the capacity of a rational individual to make an informed, un-coerced decision. In moral and political philosophy, _____ is often used as the basis for determining moral responsibility for one's actions.

a. ACCRA Cost of Living Index
b. ACEA agreement
c. Autonomy
d. AD-IA Model

32. The term _____ refers to economy-wide fluctuations in production or economic activity over several months or years. These fluctuations occur around a long-term growth trend, and typically involve shifts over time between periods of relatively rapid economic growth (expansion or boom), and periods of relative stagnation or decline (contraction or recession.)

These fluctuations are often measured using the growth rate of real gross domestic product.

a. Consumer theory
b. Nominal value
c. Tobit model
d. Business cycle

33. In economics, an _____ is any good (e.g. a commodity) or service brought into one country from another country in a legitimate fashion, typically for use in trade. It is a good that is brought in from another country for sale. _____ goods or services are provided to domestic consumers by foreign producers. An _____ in the receiving country is an export to the sending country.

Chapter 26. DEMAND-SIDE EQUILIBRIUM: UNEMPLOYMENT OR INFLATION?   233

a. Import quota
c. Incoterms
b. Economic integration
d. Import

34. In economics, an _____ is any good or commodity, transported from one country to another country in a legitimate fashion, typically for use in trade. _____ goods or services are provided to foreign consumers by domestic producers. _____ is an important part of international trade.
  a. Export
  c. ACEA agreement
  b. ACCRA Cost of Living Index
  d. AD-IA Model

35. _____ is exchange of capital, goods, and services across international borders or territories. In most countries, it represents a significant share of gross domestic product (GDP.) While _____ has been present throughout much of history , its economic, social, and political importance has been on the rise in recent centuries.
  a. Incoterms
  c. Import license
  b. Intra-industry trade
  d. International trade

Chapter 27. BRINGING IN THE SUPPLY-SIDE: UNEMPLOYMENT AND INFLATION?

1. _____ is a broad label that refers to any individuals or households that use goods and services generated within the economy. The concept of a _____ is used in different contexts, so that the usage and significance of the term may vary.

   Typically when business people and economists talk of _____s they are talking about person as _____, an aggregated commodity item with little individuality other than that expressed in the buy/not-buy decision.

   a. 130-30 fund
   b. 100-year flood
   c. 1921 recession
   d. Consumer

2. A _____ is a measure of the average price of consumer goods and services purchased by households. A _____ measures a price change for a constant market basket of goods and services from one period to the next within the same area (city, region, or nation.) It is a price index determined by measuring the price of a standard group of goods meant to represent the typical market basket of a typical urban consumer.

   a. CPI
   b. Cost-of-living index
   c. Consumer Price Index
   d. Lipstick index

3. A _____ is a theoretical term that economists use to describe a market which is free from government intervention (i.e. no regulation, no subsidization, no single monetary system and no governmental monopolies.) In a _____, property rights are voluntarily exchanged at a price arranged solely by the mutual consent of sellers and buyers. By definition, buyers and sellers do not coerce each other, in the sense that they obtain each other's property without the use of physical force, threat of physical force, or fraud, nor is the coerced by a third party (such as by government via transfer payments) and they engage in trade simply because they both consent and believe that it is a good enough choice.

   a. Leninism
   b. Third camp
   c. Delegation
   d. Free market

4. _____ in economics and business is the result of an exchange and from that trade we assign a numerical monetary value to a good, service or asset. If Alice trades Bob 4 apples for an orange, the _____ of an orange is 4 apples. Inversely, the _____ of an apple is 1/4 oranges.

   a. Price book
   b. Price war
   c. Premium pricing
   d. Price

5. A _____ is a normalized average (typically a weighted average) of prices for a given class of goods or services in a given region, during a given interval of time. It is a statistic designed to help to compare how these prices, taken as a whole, differ between time periods or geographical locations.

   Price indices have several potential uses.

   a. Price Index
   b. Product sabotage
   c. Two-part tariff
   d. Transactional Net Margin Method

6. The GDP gap or the output gap is the difference between potential GDP and actual GDP or actual output. The calculation for the output gap is Y-Y* where Y* is potential output and Y is actual output. If this calculation yields a positive number it is called an expansionary gap and indicates an economy in expansion; if the calculation yields a negative number it is called a _____ and indicates an economy in recession.

Chapter 27. BRINGING IN THE SUPPLY-SIDE: UNEMPLOYMENT AND INFLATION? 235

a. 100-year flood
b. 130-30 fund
c. Recessionary gap
d. 1921 recession

7. _____ is an economic situation in which inflation and economic stagnation occur simultaneously and remain unchecked for a period of time. The portmanteau _____ is generally attributed to British politician Iain Macleod, who coined the term in a speech to Parliament in 1965. The concept is notable partly because, in postwar macroeconomic theory, inflation and recession were regarded as mutually exclusive, and also because _____ has generally proven to be difficult and costly to eradicate once it gets started.
a. Real interest rate
b. Chronic inflation
c. Stagflation
d. Price/wage spiral

8. The _____ is the largest national economy in the world. Its gross domestic product (GDP) was estimated as $14.2 trillion in 2008. The U.S. economy maintains a high level of output per person (GDP per capita, $46,800 in 2008, ranked at around number ten in the world.)
a. ACCRA Cost of Living Index
b. Economy of the United States
c. ACEA agreement
d. AD-IA Model

9. In economics, _____ is a rise in the general level of prices of goods and services in an economy over a period of time. When the general price level rises, each unit of currency buys fewer goods and services; consequently, _____ is also a decline in the real value of money--a loss of purchasing power in the medium of exchange which is also the monetary unit of account in the economy. A chief measure of general price-level _____ is the general _____ rate, which is the percentage change in a general price index (normally the Consumer Price Index) over time.
a. Energy economics
b. Opportunity cost
c. Economic
d. Inflation

10. In economics, _____ is the total demand for final goods and services in the economy (Y) at a given time and price level. It is the amount of goods and services in the economy that will be purchased at all possible price levels. This is the demand for the gross domestic product of a country when inventory levels are static.
a. Aggregate supply
b. Aggregation problem
c. Aggregate expenditure
d. Aggregate demand

11. In economics, _____ is the total supply of goods and services produced by a national economy during a specific time period. It is the total amount of goods and services in the economy available at all possible price levels.
a. Aggregate demand
b. Aggregation problem
c. Aggregate expenditure
d. Aggregate supply

12. The _____ or gross domestic income (GDI), a basic measure of an economy's economic performance, is the market value of all final goods and services produced within the borders of a nation in a year. _____ can be defined in three ways, all of which are conceptually identical. First, it is equal to the total expenditures for all final goods and services produced within the country in a stipulated period of time (usually a 365-day year.)
a. Gross domestic product
b. Monopolistic competition
c. Countercyclical
d. Market structure

Chapter 27. BRINGING IN THE SUPPLY-SIDE: UNEMPLOYMENT AND INFLATION?

13. An _____, in economics, is the amount by which the real Gross domestic product exceeds potential GDP. The real GDP is also known as GDP 'adjusted for inflation', 'constant prices' GDP or 'constant dollar' GDP, because it measures the aggregate output in a country's income accounts in a given year, expressed in base-year prices. On the other hand, the potential GDP is the quantity of real GDP when a country's economy is at full-employment.
   a. AD-IA Model
   b. ACEA agreement
   c. ACCRA Cost of Living Index
   d. Inflationary gap

14. Economics:

   - _____, the desire to own something and the ability to pay for it
   - _____ curve, a graphic representation of a _____ schedule
   - _____ deposit, the money in checking accounts
   - _____ pull theory, the theory that inflation occurs when _____ for goods and services exceeds existing supplies
   - _____ schedule, a table that lists the quantity of a good a person will buy it each different price
   - _____ side economics, the school of economics at believes government spending and tax cuts open economy by raising _____

   a. Production
   b. Demand
   c. McKesson ' Robbins scandal
   d. Variability

15. In economics, the _____ can be defined as the graph depicting the relationship between the price of a certain commodity, and the amount of it that consumers are willing and able to purchase at that given price. It is a graphic representation of a demand schedule. The _____ for all consumers together follows from the _____ of every individual consumer: the individual demands at each price are added together.
   a. Kuznets curve
   b. Cost curve
   c. Demand curve
   d. Wage curve

16. The International Union, United Automobile, Aerospace and Agricultural Implement Workers of America, better known as the _____ , is a labor union which represents workers in the United States and Puerto Rico. Founded in order to represent workers in the automobile manufacturing industry, _____ members in the 21st century work in industries as diverse as health care, casino gaming and higher education. Headquartered in Detroit, Michigan, the union has approximately 800 local unions, which negotiated 3,100 contracts with some 2,000 employers.
   a. ACCRA Cost of Living Index
   b. ACEA agreement
   c. AD-IA Model
   d. United Auto Workers

17. _____ in economics refers to metrics and measures of output from production processes, per unit of input. Labor _____, for example, is typically measured as a ratio of output per labor-hour, an input. _____ may be conceived of as a metrics of the technical or engineering efficiency of production.
   a. Piece work
   b. Production-possibility frontier
   c. Fordism
   d. Productivity

18. In a _____ there is both a monopoly (a single seller) and monopsony (a single buyer) in the same market.

Chapter 27. BRINGING IN THE SUPPLY-SIDE: UNEMPLOYMENT AND INFLATION? 237

In such market price and output will be determined by the non economic forces like bargaining power of both buyer and seller. A _____ model is often used in situations where the switching costs of both sides are prohibitively high.

a. Price takers
c. Revenue-cap regulation
b. Market concentration
d. Bilateral monopoly

19. In economics, a _____ exists when a specific individual or enterprise has sufficient control over a particular product or service to determine significantly the terms on which other individuals shall have access to it. Monopolies are thus characterized by a lack of economic competition for the good or service that they provide and a lack of viable substitute goods. The verb 'monopolize' refers to the process by which a firm gains persistently greater market share than what is expected under perfect competition.

a. 130-30 fund
c. 100-year flood
b. 1921 recession
d. Monopoly

20. The _____ is the number of total hours that workers wish to work at a given real wage rate.

Labor supply curves are derived from the 'labor-leisure' trade-off. More hours worked earn higher incomes but necessitate a cut in the amount of leisure that workers enjoy.

a. Dual labor market
c. De minimis fringe benefits
b. Compound interest
d. Supply of Labor

21. The Demand side is a term used in economics to refer to a number of things:

- The demand element of a supply and demand partial equilibrium diagram, in microeconomics
- The aggregate demand in an economy, in macroeconomics
- Economic policy actions which are designed to affect aggregate demand.
- _____ learning referring to the incentive to learn how to use and modify free software as opposed to buying conventional software.

The term is also used broadly to distinguish supply-side economics from other schools, for instance Keynesian economics.

a. Delayed differentiation
c. CPFR
b. Reverse auction
d. Demand-side

22. _____ is an economic model based on price, utility and quantity in a market. It predicts that in a competitive market, price will function to equalize the quantity demanded by consumers, and the quantity supplied by producers, resulting in an economic equilibrium of price and quantity. The model incorporates other factors changing equilibrium as a shift of demand and/or supply.

a. Supply and demand
c. Joint demand
b. Rational addiction
d. Deferred gratification

Chapter 27. BRINGING IN THE SUPPLY-SIDE: UNEMPLOYMENT AND INFLATION?

23. Economists distinguish between various types of unemployment, including _____, frictional unemployment, structural unemployment and classical unemployment. Some additional types of unemployment that are occasionally mentioned are seasonal unemployment, hardcore unemployment, and hidden unemployment. Real-world unemployment may combine different types.
   - a. Structural unemployment
   - b. Seasonal unemployment
   - c. Types of unemployment
   - d. Cyclical unemployment

24. In economics, _____ is a sustained decrease in the general price level of goods and services. _____ occurs when the annual inflation rate falls below zero percent, resulting in an increase in the real value of money -- a negative inflation rate. This should not be confused with disinflation, a slow-down in the inflation rate (i.e. when the inflation decreases, but still remains positive.)
   - a. Deflation
   - b. Price revolution
   - c. Tobit model
   - d. Literacy rate

25. _____, 1st Baron Keynes was a renowned economist from Britain whose many ideas on economic and political theories as well as on many governments' monetary policies influenced America. He advocated a government that played an active role in the lives of people regarding business, economy, etc. In this role, the government would use fiscal measures to reduce the consequences of recessions, economic depressions and booms.
   - a. Adolph Fischer
   - b. John Maynard Keynes
   - c. Adolf Hitler
   - d. Adam Smith

26. A _____, reserve bank, or monetary authority is the entity responsible for the monetary policy of a country or of a group of member states. It is a bank that can lend money to other banks in times of need. Its primary responsibility is to maintain the stability of the national currency and money supply, but more active duties include controlling subsidized-loan interest rates, and acting as a lender of last resort to the banking sector during times of financial crisis (private banks often being integral to the national financial system.)
   - a. 100-year flood
   - b. 130-30 fund
   - c. Central bank
   - d. 1921 recession

27. The Organization of the Petroleum Exporting Countries is a cartel of twelve countries made up of Algeria, Angola, Ecuador, Iran, Iraq, Kuwait, Libya, Nigeria, Qatar, Saudi Arabia, the United Arab Emirates, and Venezuela. The cartel has maintained its headquarters in Vienna since 1965, and hosts regular meetings among the oil ministers of its Member Countries. Indonesia withdrew its membership in _____ in 2008 after it became a net importer of oil, but stated it would likely return if it became a net exporter in the world.
   - a. ACEA agreement
   - b. AD-IA Model
   - c. ACCRA Cost of Living Index
   - d. OPEC

28. A _____ is an event that suddenly changes the price of a commodity or service. It may be caused by a sudden increase or decrease in the supply of a particular good. This sudden change affects the equilibrium price.
   - a. Friedman rule
   - b. Supply shock
   - c. SIMIC
   - d. Demand shock

Chapter 27. BRINGING IN THE SUPPLY-SIDE: UNEMPLOYMENT AND INFLATION?

29. _____ describes a deliberate attempt to interfere with the free and fair operation of the market and create artificial, false or misleading appearances with respect to the price of a security, commodity or currency. _____ is prohibited under Section 9(a)(2) of the Securities Exchange Act of 1934, and in Australia under Section s 1041A of the Corporations Act 2001. The Act defines _____ as transactions which create an artificial price or maintain an artificial price for a tradable security.

a. Legal monopoly
b. Managerial economics
c. Net domestic product
d. Market manipulation

30. A _____ is a hypothetical measure of overall prices for some set of goods and services, in a given region during a given interval, normalized relative to some base set. Typically, a _____ is approximated with a price index.

The classical dichotomy is the assumption that there is a relatively clean distinction between overall increases or decreases in prices and underlying, e;reale; economic variables.

a. Price level
b. Discouraged worker
c. Discretionary spending
d. Price elasticity of supply

31. _____ refers to the economic policies of United States President Bill Clinton during the 1990s. Clinton assumed office at the tail end of a recession, and the economic theories he utilized and implemented are claimed by his supporters to have eventually led to a strong recovery, though Clinton's opponents deny this.

The strategy was outlined in the following three points:

- Establishing fiscal discipline, eliminating the budget deficit, keeping interest rates low, and spurring private-sector investment.
- Investing in people through education, training, science, and research.
- Opening foreign markets so American workers can compete abroad.

During the 1992 presidential campaign America had undergone twelve years of conservative policies implemented by Ronald Reagan and George Herbert Walker Bush. Clinton ran on the economic platform of balancing the budget, lowering inflation, lowering unemployment, and continuing the traditionally conservative policies of free trade.

a. Clintonomics
b. Jawboning
c. Structural equation modeling
d. Purchasing Managers Index

32. The term _____ refers to government debt, expenditures and revenues, or to finance (particularly financial revenue) in general.

- _____ deficit is the budget deficit of federal or local government
- _____ policy is the discretionary spending of governments. Contrasts with monetary policy.
- _____ year and _____ quarter are reporting periods for firms and other agencies.

Chapter 27. BRINGING IN THE SUPPLY-SIDE: UNEMPLOYMENT AND INFLATION?

a. Procter ' Gamble
b. Bucket shop
c. Drawdown
d. Fiscal

33. In economics, _____ is the use of government spending and revenue collection to influence the economy.

_____ can be contrasted with the other main type of economic policy, monetary policy, which attempts to stabilize the economy by controlling interest rates and the supply of money. The two main instruments of _____ are government spending and taxation.

a. 100-year flood
b. Fiscalism
c. Sustainable investment rule
d. Fiscal policy

34. In economics, the _____ is a historical inverse relation between the rate of unemployment and the rate of inflation in an economy. Stated simply, the lower the unemployment in an economy, the higher the rate of increase in nominal wages in the economy. Rate of Change of Wages against Unemployment, United Kingdom 1913-1948 from Phillips (1958)

William Phillips, a New Zealand born economist, wrote a paper in 1958 titled The Relationship between Unemployment and the Rate of Change of Money Wages in the United Kingdom 1861-1957, which was published in the quarterly journal Economica.

a. Demand curve
b. Phillips curve
c. Cost curve
d. Lorenz curve

35. _____ refers to the economic policies promoted by United States President Ronald Reagan during the 1980s. The four pillars of Reagan's economic policy were to:

1. reduce the growth of government spending,
2. reduce income and capital gains marginal tax rates,
3. reduce government regulation of the economy,
4. control the money supply to reduce inflation.

In attempting to cut back on domestic spending while lowering taxes, Reagan's approach was a departure from his immediate predecessors.

Reagan became president during a period of high inflation and unemployment (commonly referred to as stagflation), which had largely abated by the time he left office eight years later.

Prior to the Reagan Administration was a roughly ten year period of economic stagnation and inflation, known as stagflation.

a. Business sector
b. Happiness economics
c. Reaganomics
d. Social savings

Chapter 27. BRINGING IN THE SUPPLY-SIDE: UNEMPLOYMENT AND INFLATION? 241

36. _____ is a school of macroeconomic thought that argues that economic growth can be most effectively created using incentives for people to produce (supply) goods and services, such as adjusting income tax and capital gains tax rates, and by allowing greater flexibility by reducing regulation. Consumers will then benefit from a greater supply of goods and services at lower prices.

The term _____ was coined by journalist Jude Wanniski in 1975, and popularized the ideas of economists Robert Mundell and Arthur Laffer.

a. Clap note
b. Fiscal stimulus plans
c. Commodity trading advisors
d. Supply-side economics

37. _____ are banks' holdings of deposits in accounts with their central bank (for instance the European Central Bank or the Federal Reserve, in the latter case including federal funds), plus currency that is physically held in bank vaults (vault cash.) The central banks of some nations set minimum reserve requirements. Even when no requirements are set, banks commonly wish to hold some reserves, called desired reserves, against unexpected events.

a. Sweep account
b. Structuring
c. Bilateral netting
d. Bank reserves

38. A _____ is a package or set of measures introduced to stabilise a financial system or economy. The term can refer to policies in two distinct sets of circumstances: business cycle stabilization and crisis stabilization.

Stabilization can refer to correcting the normal behavior of the business cycle.

a. Volunteers for Economic Growth Alliance
b. Stabilization policy
c. New International Economic Order
d. Capacity Development

Chapter 28. MANAGING AGGREGATE DEMAND: FISCAL POLICY

1. The term _____ refers to government debt, expenditures and revenues, or to finance (particularly financial revenue) in general.

   - _____ deficit is the budget deficit of federal or local government
   - _____ policy is the discretionary spending of governments. Contrasts with monetary policy.
   - _____ year and _____ quarter are reporting periods for firms and other agencies.

   a. Bucket shop
   b. Drawdown
   c. Procter ' Gamble
   d. Fiscal

2. In economics, _____ is the use of government spending and revenue collection to influence the economy.

   _____ can be contrasted with the other main type of economic policy, monetary policy, which attempts to stabilize the economy by controlling interest rates and the supply of money. The two main instruments of _____ are government spending and taxation.

   a. Fiscal policy
   b. Sustainable investment rule
   c. 100-year flood
   d. Fiscalism

3. In economics, _____ is the total demand for final goods and services in the economy (Y) at a given time and price level. It is the amount of goods and services in the economy that will be purchased at all possible price levels. This is the demand for the gross domestic product of a country when inventory levels are static.

   a. Aggregate expenditure
   b. Aggregate demand
   c. Aggregate supply
   d. Aggregation problem

4. Economics:

   - _____, the desire to own something and the ability to pay for it
   - _____ curve, a graphic representation of a _____ schedule
   - _____ deposit, the money in checking accounts
   - _____ pull theory, the theory that inflation occurs when _____ for goods and services exceeds existing supplies
   - _____ schedule, a table that lists the quantity of a good a person will buy it each different price
   - _____ side economics, the school of economics at believes government spending and tax cuts open economy by raising _____

   a. Demand
   b. McKesson ' Robbins scandal
   c. Production
   d. Variability

5. In economics, _____ is the total supply of goods and services produced by a national economy during a specific time period. It is the total amount of goods and services in the economy available at all possible price levels.

   a. Aggregate supply
   b. Aggregate expenditure
   c. Aggregation problem
   d. Aggregate demand

Chapter 28. MANAGING AGGREGATE DEMAND: FISCAL POLICY

6. _____ is a common concept in economics, and gives rise to derived concepts such as consumer debt. Generally _____ is defined by opposition to production. But the precise definition can vary because different schools of economists define production quite differently.

   a. Federal Reserve Bank Notes
   b. Foreclosure data providers
   c. Consumption
   d. Cash or share options

7. In economics, the term _____ of income or _____ refers to a simple economic model which describes the reciprocal circulation of income between producers and consumers. In the _____ model, the inter-dependent entities of producer and consumer are referred to as 'firms' and 'households' respectively and provide each other with factors in order to facilitate the flow of income. Firms provide consumers with goods and services in exchange for consumer expenditure and 'factors of production' from households.

   a. Circular flow
   b. 1921 recession
   c. 100-year flood
   d. 130-30 fund

8. In economics, the _____ can be defined as the graph depicting the relationship between the price of a certain commodity, and the amount of it that consumers are willing and able to purchase at that given price. It is a graphic representation of a demand schedule. The _____ for all consumers together follows from the _____ of every individual consumer: the individual demands at each price are added together.

   a. Cost curve
   b. Kuznets curve
   c. Wage curve
   d. Demand curve

9. An _____ is a tax levied on the financial income of people, corporations, or other legal entities. Various _____ systems exist, with varying degrees of tax incidence. Income taxation can be progressive, proportional, or regressive.

   a. ACEA agreement
   b. ACCRA Cost of Living Index
   c. AD-IA Model
   d. Income tax

10. _____ is the incidence or process of transferring ownership of a business, enterprise, agency or public service from the public sector (government) to the private sector (business.) In a broader sense, _____ refers to transfer of any government function to the private sector including governmental functions like revenue collection and law enforcement.

    The term '_____' also has been used to describe two unrelated transactions.

    a. Performance reports
    b. Ricardian equivalence
    c. Compound empowerment
    d. Privatization

11. To _____ is to impose a financial charge or other levy upon a taxpayer by a state or the functional equivalent of a state.

    _____es are also imposed by many subnational entities. _____es consist of direct _____ or indirect _____, and may be paid in money or as its labour equivalent (often but not always unpaid.)

    a. Tax
    b. 100-year flood
    c. 130-30 fund
    d. 1921 recession

12. A _____ is a reduction in taxes. Economic stimulus via _____s, along with interest rate intervention and deficit spending, are one of the central tenets of Keynesian economics.

The immediate effects of a _____ are, generally, a decrease in the real income of the government and an increase in the real income of those whose tax rate has been lowered.

a. Tax cut
c. Withholding tax
b. Popiwek
d. Direct taxes

13. To tax is to impose a financial charge or other levy upon a taxpayer by a state or the functional equivalent of a state.

_____ are also imposed by many subnational entities. _____ consist of direct tax or indirect tax, and may be paid in money or as its labour equivalent (often but not always unpaid.)

a. 1921 recession
c. 100-year flood
b. 130-30 fund
d. Taxes

14. The _____ or gross domestic income (GDI), a basic measure of an economy's economic performance, is the market value of all final goods and services produced within the borders of a nation in a year. _____ can be defined in three ways, all of which are conceptually identical. First, it is equal to the total expenditures for all final goods and services produced within the country in a stipulated period of time (usually a 365-day year.)

a. Countercyclical
c. Market structure
b. Monopolistic competition
d. Gross domestic product

15. An _____, in economics, is the amount by which the real Gross domestic product exceeds potential GDP. The real GDP is also known as GDP 'adjusted for inflation', 'constant prices' GDP or 'constant dollar' GDP, because it measures the aggregate output in a country's income accounts in a given year, expressed in base-year prices. On the other hand, the potential GDP is the quantity of real GDP when a country's economy is at full-employment.

a. AD-IA Model
c. ACCRA Cost of Living Index
b. Inflationary gap
d. ACEA agreement

16. _____ is a misspelled phrase from Latin 'pro capite' phrase meaning per head with pro meaning 'per' or 'for each' and capite meaning 'head.' Both words together equate to the phrase 'for each head.'

It is usually used in the field of statistics to indicate the average per person for any given concern, such as income, crime rate, etc.

It is also used in wills to indicate that each of the named beneficiaries should receive, by devise or bequest, equal shares of the estate. This is in contrast to a per stirpes division, in which each branch of the inheriting family inherits an equal share of the estate.

a. False positive rate
c. Sargan test
b. Population statistics
d. Per capita

17. A _____ occurs when an entity spends more money than it takes in. The opposite of a _____ is a budget surplus. Debt is essentially an accumulated flow of deficits.

a. Funding body
b. Lump-sum tax
c. Public Financial Management
d. Budget deficit

18. A _____ is a legal document that is often passed by the legislature, and approved by the chief executive-or president. For example, only certain types of revenue may be imposed and collected. Property tax is frequently the basis for municipal and county revenues, while sales tax and/or income tax are the basis for state revenues, and income tax and corporate tax are the basis for national revenues.
a. Structural deficit
b. Government budget
c. Lump-sum tax
d. Right-financing

19. A _____ is a package or set of measures introduced to stabilise a financial system or economy. The term can refer to policies in two distinct sets of circumstances: business cycle stabilization and crisis stabilization.

Stabilization can refer to correcting the normal behavior of the business cycle.

a. New International Economic Order
b. Volunteers for Economic Growth Alliance
c. Capacity Development
d. Stabilization policy

20. In economics, a _____ is a redistribution of income in the market system. These payments are considered to be nonexhaustive because they do not directly absorb resources or create output. Examples of certain _____s include welfare (financial aid), social security, and government subsidies for certain businesses (firms.)
a. 1921 recession
b. 100-year flood
c. Transfer payment
d. 130-30 fund

21. A _____ is the transfer of wealth from one party (such as a person or company) to another. A _____ is usually made in exchange for the provision of goods, services or both, or to fulfill a legal obligation.

The simplest and oldest form of _____ is barter, the exchange of one good or service for another.

a. Going concern
b. Payment
c. Soft count
d. Social gravity

22. The _____ is the multiple by which Aggregate demand will increase, when there is an increase in transfer payments (e.g. welfare spending, unemployment payments.) Changes in spending usually lead to a larger than one for one increase in Aggregate demand, because any increase in household incomes caused by the increase in spending also increases in consumption spending, which further increases Aggregate demand.
a. Market-based instruments
b. Transfer payments Multiplier
c. Cost-effectiveness analysis
d. Legal monopoly

23. In economics, a _____ is a progressive income tax system where people earning below a certain amount receive supplemental pay from the government instead of paying taxes to the government. Such a system has been discussed by economists but never fully implemented. It was developed by Juliet Rhys-Williams in the 1940s and later by United States economist Milton Friedman in 1962 in Capitalism and Freedom.
a. Negative income tax
b. 100-year flood
c. 1921 recession
d. 130-30 fund

Chapter 28. MANAGING AGGREGATE DEMAND: FISCAL POLICY

24. _____ is the shortage of common things such as food, clothing, shelter and safe drinking water, all of which determine the quality of life. It may also include the lack of access to opportunities such as education and employment which aid the escape from _____ and/or allow one to enjoy the respect of fellow citizens. According to Mollie Orshansky who developed the _____ measurements used by the U.S. government, 'to be poor is to be deprived of those goods and services and pleasures which others around us take for granted.' Ongoing debates over causes, effects and best ways to measure _____, directly influence the design and implementation of _____-reduction programs and are therefore relevant to the fields of public administration and international development.
   a. Growth Elasticity of Poverty
   b. Liberal welfare reforms
   c. Poverty map
   d. Poverty

25. The GDP gap or the output gap is the difference between potential GDP and actual GDP or actual output. The calculation for the output gap is Y-Y* where Y* is potential output and Y is actual output. If this calculation yields a positive number it is called an expansionary gap and indicates an economy in expansion; if the calculation yields a negative number it is called a _____ and indicates an economy in recession.
   a. 130-30 fund
   b. 100-year flood
   c. Recessionary gap
   d. 1921 recession

26. _____ is the government's approach to taxation, both from the practical and normative side of the question.

Policymakers debate the nature of the tax structure they plan to implement (i.e., how progressive or regressive) and how they might affect individuals and businesses (i.e., tax incidence.)

The reason for such focus is economic efficiency as advisor to the Stuart King of England Richard Petty had noted that the government does not want to kill the goose that lays the golden egg.

   a. Tax-allocation district
   b. Partnership taxation
   c. Commuter tax
   d. Tax policy

27. _____ in economics and business is the result of an exchange and from that trade we assign a numerical monetary value to a good, service or asset. If Alice trades Bob 4 apples for an orange, the _____ of an orange is 4 apples. Inversely, the _____ of an apple is 1/4 oranges.
   a. Price war
   b. Price book
   c. Premium pricing
   d. Price

28. _____ is a broad label that refers to any individuals or households that use goods and services generated within the economy. The concept of a _____ is used in different contexts, so that the usage and significance of the term may vary.

Typically when business people and economists talk of _____s they are talking about person as _____, an aggregated commodity item with little individuality other than that expressed in the buy/not-buy decision.

   a. 130-30 fund
   b. 100-year flood
   c. 1921 recession
   d. Consumer

Chapter 28. MANAGING AGGREGATE DEMAND: FISCAL POLICY   247

29. _____ or consumer demand or consumption is also known as personal consumption expenditure. It is the largest part of aggregate demand or effective demand at the macroeconomic level. There are two variants of consumption in the aggregate demand model, including induced consumption and autonomous consumption.
   a. Potential output
   b. Complex multiplier
   c. Dishoarding
   d. Consumer spending

30. _____s is the social science that studies the production, distribution, and consumption of goods and services. The term _____s comes from the Ancient Greek oá¼°κονομῖα from oá¼¶κος (oikos, 'house') + vÏŒμος (nomos, 'custom' or 'law'), hence 'rules of the house(hold)'. Current _____ models developed out of the broader field of political economy in the late 19th century, owing to a desire to use an empirical approach more akin to the physical sciences.
   a. Economic
   b. Energy economics
   c. Inflation
   d. Opportunity cost

31. In macroeconomics, _____ is a condition of the national economy, where all or nearly all persons willing and able to work at the prevailing wages and working conditions are able to do so. It is defined either as 0% unemployment, literally, no unemployment (the rate of unemployment is the fraction of the work force unable to find work), as by James Tobin, or as the level of employment rates when there is no cyclical unemployment. It is defined by the majority of mainstream economists as being an acceptable level of natural unemployment above 0%, the discrepancy from 0% being due to non-cyclical types of unemployment.
   a. Full employment
   b. Marginal propensity to consume
   c. Demand shock
   d. Harrod-Johnson diagram

32. _____ refers to the economic policies promoted by United States President Ronald Reagan during the 1980s. The four pillars of Reagan's economic policy were to:

   1. reduce the growth of government spending,
   2. reduce income and capital gains marginal tax rates,
   3. reduce government regulation of the economy,
   4. control the money supply to reduce inflation.

In attempting to cut back on domestic spending while lowering taxes, Reagan's approach was a departure from his immediate predecessors.

Reagan became president during a period of high inflation and unemployment (commonly referred to as stagflation), which had largely abated by the time he left office eight years later.

Prior to the Reagan Administration was a roughly ten year period of economic stagnation and inflation, known as stagflation.

   a. Reaganomics
   b. Social savings
   c. Business sector
   d. Happiness economics

33. _____ is a school of macroeconomic thought that argues that economic growth can be most effectively created using incentives for people to produce (supply) goods and services, such as adjusting income tax and capital gains tax rates, and by allowing greater flexibility by reducing regulation. Consumers will then benefit from a greater supply of goods and services at lower prices.

Chapter 28. MANAGING AGGREGATE DEMAND: FISCAL POLICY

The term _____ was coined by journalist Jude Wanniski in 1975, and popularized the ideas of economists Robert Mundell and Arthur Laffer.

a. Commodity trading advisors
c. Clap note
b. Fiscal stimulus plans
d. Supply-side economics

34. The _____ is the largest national economy in the world. Its gross domestic product (GDP) was estimated as $14.2 trillion in 2008. The U.S. economy maintains a high level of output per person (GDP per capita, $46,800 in 2008, ranked at around number ten in the world.)

a. ACEA agreement
c. AD-IA Model
b. ACCRA Cost of Living Index
d. Economy of the United States

35. The term _____, 'the state or characteristic of being variable',_____ describes how spread out or closely clustered a set of data is. may be applied to many different subjects:

- Climate _____
- Genetic _____
- Heart rate _____
- Human _____
- Solar van
- Spatial _____
- Statistical _____
- _____

a. Total product
c. Demand
b. Characteristic
d. Variability

36. Total _____ is defined by the United States' Bureau of Economic Analysis as

income received by persons from all sources. It includes income received from participation in production as well as from government and business transfer payments. It is the sum of compensation of employees (received), supplements to wages and salaries, proprietors' income with inventory valuation adjustment (IVA) and capital consumption adjustment (CCAdj), rental income of persons with CCAdj, _____ receipts on assets, and personal current transfer receipts, less contributions for government social insurance.

a. Dividend Discount Model
c. Greater fool theory
b. Bidding
d. Personal income

37. In economics, _____ is how a natione;s total economy is distributed among its population. ._____ has always been a central concern of economic theory and economic policy. Classical economists such as Adam Smith, Thomas Malthus and David Ricardo were mainly concerned with factor _____, that is, the distribution of income between the main factors of production, land, labour and capital.

Chapter 28. MANAGING AGGREGATE DEMAND: FISCAL POLICY

a. Equipment trust certificate
c. Income distribution
b. Authorised capital
d. Eco commerce

38. _____ refers to the economic policies of United States President Bill Clinton during the 1990s. Clinton assumed office at the tail end of a recession, and the economic theories he utilized and implemented are claimed by his supporters to have eventually led to a strong recovery, though Clinton's opponents deny this.

The strategy was outlined in the following three points:

- Establishing fiscal discipline, eliminating the budget deficit, keeping interest rates low, and spurring private-sector investment.
- Investing in people through education, training, science, and research.
- Opening foreign markets so American workers can compete abroad.

During the 1992 presidential campaign America had undergone twelve years of conservative policies implemented by Ronald Reagan and George Herbert Walker Bush. Clinton ran on the economic platform of balancing the budget, lowering inflation, lowering unemployment, and continuing the traditionally conservative policies of free trade.

a. Jawboning
c. Purchasing Managers Index
b. Structural equation modeling
d. Clintonomics

39. A _____ is a consumption tax charged at the point of purchase for certain goods and services. The tax is usually set as a percentage by the government charging the tax. There is usually a list of exemptions.
a. 1921 recession
c. Sales tax
b. 100-year flood
d. 130-30 fund

40. A _____ is one scenario provided for evaluation by respondents in a Choice Experiment. Responses are collected and used to create a Choice Model. Respondents are usually provided with a series of differing _____s for evaluation.
a. 130-30 fund
c. 1921 recession
b. 100-year flood
d. Choice Set

Chapter 29. MONEY AND THE BANKING SYSTEM

1. The _____ was a worldwide economic downturn starting in most places in 1929 and ending at different times in the 1930s or early 1940s for different countries. It was the largest and most important economic depression in the 20th century, and is used in the 21st century as an example of how far the world's economy can fall. The _____ originated in the United States; historians most often use as a starting date the stock market crash on October 29, 1929, known as Black Tuesday.

   a. Jarrow March
   b. Wall Street Crash of 1929
   c. British Empire Economic Conference
   d. Great Depression

2. In economics, _____ is the total amount of money available in an economy at a particular point in time. There are several ways to define 'money', but standard measures usually include currency in circulation and demand deposits.

   _____ data are recorded and published, usually by the government or the central bank of the country.

   a. Neutrality of money
   b. Money supply
   c. Velocity of money
   d. Veil of money

3. Bartering is a medium in which goods or services are directly exchanged for other goods and/or services, without the use of money. It can be bilateral or multilateral, and usually exists parallel to monetary systems in most developed countries, though to a very limited extent. _____ usually replaces money as the method of exchange in times of monetary crisis, when the currency is unstable and devalued by hyperinflation.

   a. Barter
   b. Community-based economics
   c. Meitheal
   d. New Economics Foundation

4. The _____ is the largest national economy in the world. Its gross domestic product (GDP) was estimated as $14.2 trillion in 2008. The U.S. economy maintains a high level of output per person (GDP per capita, $46,800 in 2008, ranked at around number ten in the world.)

   a. AD-IA Model
   b. ACEA agreement
   c. ACCRA Cost of Living Index
   d. Economy of the United States

5. A _____ occurs when a bank is unable to meet its obligations to its depositors or other creditors. More specifically, a bank fails economically when the market value of its assets declines to a value that is less than the market value of its liabilities. As such, the bank is unable to fulfill the demands of all of its depositors on time.

   a. Concentration account
   b. Bank failure
   c. Transactional account
   d. Lombard Club

6. The _____ problem (often 'double _____') is an important category of transaction costs that impose severe limitations on economies lacking money and thus dominated by barter or other in-kind transactions. The problem is caused by the improbability of the wants, needs or events that cause or motivate a transaction occurring at the same time and the same place.

   In-kind transactions have several problems, most notably timing constraints.

   a. Going concern
   b. RFM
   c. Buy-sell agreement
   d. Coincidence of wants

7. A _____ is an intermediary used in trade to avoid the inconveniences of a pure barter system.

Chapter 29. MONEY AND THE BANKING SYSTEM

By contrast, as William Stanley Jevons argued, in a barter system there must be a coincidence of wants before two people can trade - one must want exactly what the other has to offer, when and where it is offered, so that the exchange can occur. A _____ permits the value of goods to be assessed and rendered in terms of the intermediary, most often, a form of money widely accepted to buy any other good.

a. Labour economics
c. Consumer theory
b. Price revolution
d. Medium of exchange

8. To act as a _____, a commodity, a form of money stored, and retrieved - and be predictably useful when it is so retrieved.

This is distinct from the standard of deferred payment function which requires acceptability to parties one owes a debt to and a minimum of opportunity to cheat others.

a. Fiat money
c. Store of value
b. World currency
d. Petrodollar

9. A _____ is a standard monetary unit of measurement of the market value/cost of goods, services, or assets. It is one of three well-known functions of money. It lends meaning to profits, losses, liability, or assets.

a. ACCRA Cost of Living Index
c. AD-IA Model
b. Unit of account
d. ACEA agreement

10. _____ is the a method of technical and economic research of the systems for purpose to optimize a parity between system's consumer functions or properties and expenses to achieve those functions or properties.

This methodology for continuous perfection of production, industrial technologies, organizational structures was developed by Juryj Sobolev in 1948 at the 'Perm telephone factory'

- 1948 Juryj Sobolev - the first success in application of a method analysis at the 'Perm telephone factory'.
- 1949 - the first application for the invention as result of use of the new method.

Today in economically developed countries practically each enterprise or the company use methodology of the kind of functional-cost analysis as a practice of the quality management, most full satisfying to principles of standards of series ISO 9000.

- Interest of consumer not in products itself, but the advantage which it will receive from its usage.
- The consumer aspires to reduce his expenses
- Functions needed by consumer can be executed in the various ways, and, hence, with various efficiency and expenses. Among possible alternatives of realization of functions exist such in which the parity of quality and the price is the optimal for the consumer.

The goal of _____ is achievement of the highest consumer satisfaction of production at simultaneous decrease in all kinds of industrial expenses Classical _____ has three English synonyms - Value Engineering, Value Management, Value Analysis.

Chapter 29. MONEY AND THE BANKING SYSTEM

a. Willingness to pay
b. Staple financing
c. Monopoly wage
d. Function cost analysis

11. _____ is money declared by a government to be legal tender. The term derives from the Latin fiat, meaning 'let it be done'. _____ achieves value because a government accepts it in payment of taxes and says it can be used within the country as a 'tender' to pay all debts.
  a. Currency board
  b. Devaluation
  c. World currency
  d. Fiat money

12. A _____ is a kind of negotiable instrument, a promissory note made by a bank payable to the bearer on demand, used as money, and in many jurisdictions is legal tender. Along with coins, _____s make up the cash or bearer forms of all modern money. With the exception of non-circulating high-value or precious metal commemorative issues, coins are generally used for lower valued monetary units, while _____s are used for higher values.
  a. Local currency
  b. Microprinting
  c. Security thread
  d. Banknote

13. Market _____ is a business, economics or investment term that refers to an asset's ability to be easily converted through an act of buying or selling without causing a significant movement in the price and with minimum loss of value. Money, or cash on hand, is the most liquid asset. An act of exchange of a less liquid asset with a more liquid asset is called liquidation.
  a. Liquidity
  b. 1921 recession
  c. 100-year flood
  d. 130-30 fund

14. In finance, the _____ is the global financial market for short-term borrowing and lending. It provides short-term liquidity funding for the global financial system. The _____ is where short-term obligations such as Treasury bills, commercial paper and bankers' acceptances are bought and sold.
  a. T-Model
  b. Deferred compensation
  c. Money market
  d. Consignment stock

15. _____ is a term used in economics to describe highly liquid assets that can easily be converted into cash.

Various sources provide the following examples of _____:

- Savings account
- Money funds
- Bank time deposits (Certificates of deposit)
- Government treasury securities (such as T-bills)
- Bonds near their redemption date
- Foreign currencies, especially widely traded ones such as the US dollar, euro or yen.
- list of countries by stocks of quasi money.

a. Monetary base
b. Veil of money
c. Silver standard
d. Near money

Chapter 29. MONEY AND THE BANKING SYSTEM

16. _____s are accounts maintained by retail financial institutions that pay interest but can not be used directly as money (for example, by writing a cheque.) These accounts let customers set aside a portion of their liquid assets while earning a monetary return.

_____s are offered by commercial banks, savings and loan associations, credit unions, building societies and mutual savings banks.

   a. Lombard Club
   b. Savings account
   c. Fractional-reserve banking
   d. Fair Finance Watch

17. A _____ is a current account at a banking institution that allows money to be deposited and withdrawn by the account holder, with the transactions and resulting balance being recorded on the bank's books. Some banks charge a fee for this service, while others may pay the customer interest on the funds deposited.

Although restrictions placed on access depend upon the terms and conditions of the account and the provider, the account holder retains rights to have their funds repaid on demand.

   a. Bank statement
   b. Stated income loan
   c. Large Value Transfer System
   d. Deposit account

18. A _____ is a professionally managed type of collective investment scheme that pools money from many investors and invests it in stocks, bonds, short-term money market instruments, and/or other securities. The _____ will have a fund manager that trades the pooled money on a regular basis. As of early 2008, the worldwide value of all _____s totals more than $26 trillion.
   a. Dark pools of liquidity
   b. Self-invested personal pension
   c. Mutual fund
   d. Participating policy

19. _____ is the revenue to a brokerage firm when commissioned securities and insurance salespeople sell a product, whether it is an investment like stocks, bonds or insurance like life insurance or long term care insurance. The commission that the agent receives is usually a percentage of this figure, although some firms like Merrill Lynch use figures called Production Credits, usually smaller than _____, to determine payouts and retain more revenue.

For example, a mutual fund with a 5.75% sales charge is sold to someone who invests $10,000.

   a. Discretionary policy
   b. Monopoly price
   c. Gross Dealer Concession
   d. Number of Shares

20. Fractional-reserve banking is the banking practice in which banks keep only a fraction of their deposits in reserve (as cash and other highly liquid assets) and lend out the remainder, while maintaining the simultaneous obligation to redeem all these deposits upon demand. _____ necessarily occurs when banks lend out any fraction of the funds received from demand deposits. This practice is universal in modern banking.
   a. Prime rate
   b. Narrow banking
   c. Private money
   d. Fractional reserve banking

Chapter 29. MONEY AND THE BANKING SYSTEM

21. A _____, reserve bank, or monetary authority is the entity responsible for the monetary policy of a country or of a group of member states. It is a bank that can lend money to other banks in times of need. Its primary responsibility is to maintain the stability of the national currency and money supply, but more active duties include controlling subsidized-loan interest rates, and acting as a lender of last resort to the banking sector during times of financial crisis (private banks often being integral to the national financial system.)

   a. 130-30 fund
   b. 100-year flood
   c. Central bank
   d. 1921 recession

22. A _____ is a theoretical term that economists use to describe a market which is free from government intervention (i.e. no regulation, no subsidization, no single monetary system and no governmental monopolies.) In a _____, property rights are voluntarily exchanged at a price arranged solely by the mutual consent of sellers and buyers. By definition, buyers and sellers do not coerce each other, in the sense that they obtain each other's property without the use of physical force, threat of physical force, or fraud, nor is the coerced by a third party (such as by government via transfer payments) and they engage in trade simply because they both consent and believe that it is a good enough choice.

   a. Leninism
   b. Delegation
   c. Third camp
   d. Free market

23. A _____ is any systematic process enabling many market players to bid and ask: helping bidders and sellers interact and make deals. It is not just the price mechanism but the entire system of regulation, qualification, credentials, reputations and clearing that surrounds that mechanism and makes it operate in a social context.

Because a _____ relies on the assumption that players are constantly involved and unequally enabled, a _____ is distinguished specifically from a voting system where candidates seek the support of voters on a less regular basis.

   a. Competitive equilibrium
   b. Contestable market
   c. Market system
   d. Price mechanism

24. The _____ consists of a number of economic theories which describe the nature of the firm, company including its existence, its behaviour, and its relationship with the market.

In simplified terms, the _____ aims to answer these questions:

1. Existence - why do firms emerge, why are not all transactions in the economy mediated over the market?
2. Boundaries - why the boundary between firms and the market is located exactly there? Which transactions are performed internally and which are negotiated on the market?
3. Organization - why are firms structured in such specific way? What is the interplay of formal and informal relationships?

Despite looking simple, these questions are not answered by the established economic theory, which usually views firms as given, and treats them as black boxes without any internal structure.

Chapter 29. MONEY AND THE BANKING SYSTEM

The First World War period saw a change of emphasis in economic theory away from industry-level analysis which mainly included analysing markets to analysis at the level of the firm, as it became increasingly clear that perfect competition was no longer an adequate model of how firms behaved. Economic theory till then had focussed on trying to understand markets alone and there had been little study on understanding why firms or organisations exist.

- a. Technology gap
- b. Khazzoom-Brookes postulate
- c. Theory of the firm
- d. Policy Ineffectiveness Proposition

25. The _____ is an economic and political union of 27 member states, located primarily in Europe. It was established by the Treaty of Maastricht on 1 November 1993, upon the foundations of the pre-existing European Economic Community. With a population of almost 500 million, the _____ generates an estimated 30% share (US$18.4 trillion in 2008) of the nominal gross world product.
- a. ACCRA Cost of Living Index
- b. European Court of Justice
- c. ACEA agreement
- d. European Union

26. The _____ is a United States government corporation created by the Glass-Steagall Act of 1933. It provides deposit insurance, which guarantees the safety of deposits in member banks, currently up to $250,000 per depositor per bank. Funds in non-interest bearing transaction accounts are fully insured, with no limit, under the temporary Transaction Account Guarantee Program.
- a. Great Leap Forward
- b. Federal Deposit Insurance Corporation
- c. Foreign direct investment
- d. Luxembourg Income Study

27. _____ is a type of trade policy that allows traders to act and transact without interference from government. Thus, the policy permits trading partners mutual gains from trade, with goods and services produced according to the theory of comparative advantage.

Under a _____ policy, prices are a reflection of true supply and demand, and are the sole determinant of resource allocation.

- a. Free trade
- b. 1921 recession
- c. 100-year flood
- d. 130-30 fund

28. _____, in law and economics, is a form of risk management primarily used to hedge against the risk of a contingent loss. _____ is defined as the equitable transfer of the risk of a loss, from one entity to another, in exchange for a premium, and can be thought of as a guaranteed small loss to prevent a large, possibly devastating loss. An insurer is a company selling the _____; an insured or policyholder is the person or entity buying the _____.
- a. ACCRA Cost of Living Index
- b. AD-IA Model
- c. ACEA agreement
- d. Insurance

29. _____ is the prospect that a party insulated from risk may behave differently from the way it would behave if it were fully exposed to the risk. In insurance, _____ that occurs without conscious or malicious action is called morale hazard.

_____ is related to information asymmetry, a situation in which one party in a transaction has more information than another.

a. Moral hazard
b. 1921 recession
c. 100-year flood
d. 130-30 fund

30. _____ in economics and business is the result of an exchange and from that trade we assign a numerical monetary value to a good, service or asset. If Alice trades Bob 4 apples for an orange, the _____ of an orange is 4 apples. Inversely, the _____ of an apple is 1/4 oranges.

a. Price book
b. Premium pricing
c. Price war
d. Price

31. In economics, a _____ is any economic system that effects its distribution of goods and services with prices and employing any form of money or debt tokens. Except for possible remote and primitive communities, all modern societies use _____s to allocate resources. However, _____s are not used for all resource allocation decisions today.

a. Neomercantilism
b. Hanseatic League
c. Price system
d. Family economy

32. In finance, the _____s between two currencies specifies how much one currency is worth in terms of the other. It is the value of a foreign natione;s currency in terms of the home natione;s currency. For example an _____ of 102 Japanese yen to the United States dollar means that JPY 102 is worth the same as USD 1.

a. Exchange rate
b. Interbank market
c. ACEA agreement
d. ACCRA Cost of Living Index

33. In business and accounting, _____ are everything of value that is owned by a person or company. It is a claim on the property your income of a borrower. The balance sheet of a firm records the monetary value of the _____ owned by the firm.

a. Assets
b. ACCRA Cost of Living Index
c. ACEA agreement
d. Amortization schedule

34. The _____ is a bank regulation that sets the minimum reserves each bank must hold to customer deposits and notes. It would normally be in the form of fiat currency stored in a bank vault (vault cash), or with a central bank.

The reserve ratio is sometimes used as a tool in the monetary policy, influencing the country's economy, borrowing, and interest rates.

a. Fractional-reserve banking
b. Private money
c. Probability of default
d. Reserve requirement

35. In financial accounting, a _____ or statement of financial position is a summary of a person's or organization's balances. Assets, liabilities and ownership equity are listed as of a specific date, such as the end of its financial year. A _____ is often described as a snapshot of a company's financial condition.

a. 100-year flood
b. 130-30 fund
c. 1921 recession
d. Balance sheet

36. In banking, _____ are bank reserves in excess of the reserve requirement set by a central bank (in the United States, the Federal Reserve System, called the Fed; in Canada, the Bank of Canada.) They are reserves of cash more than the required amounts. Holding _____ is generally considered costly and uneconomical as no interest is earned on the excess amount.

Chapter 29. MONEY AND THE BANKING SYSTEM

a. Origination fee
b. Annual percentage rate
c. Universal bank
d. Excess reserves

37. In business, _____ is the total liabilitiess minus total outside assets of an individual or a company. For a company, this is called shareholders' prefernce and may be referred to as book value. _____ is stated as at a particular year in time.
   a. Post earnings announcement drift
   b. Bond credit rating
   c. Sinking fund
   d. Net worth

38. _____ is the process by which money is produced or issued. There are three different ways to create money:

   - manufacturing a new monetary unit, such as paper currency or metal coins (_____)
   - loaning out a physical monetary unit multiple times through fractional-reserve lending (credit creation)
   - buying of government securities or other financial instruments by central bank through Open market operations (electronic creation)

Coins are produced by manufacturing metal in a factory called a mint.

Banknotes and bank account balances are financial securities issued by a bank.

Similarly, money destruction, i.e., the reverse of _____, can occur in two different ways, depending on how the money was created.

   a. Monetary policy of Sweden
   b. Second-round effect
   c. Shadow Open Market Committee
   d. Money creation

39. The most common mechanism used to measure this increase in the money supply is typically called the _____. It calculates the maximum amount of money that an initial deposit can be expanded to with a given reserve ratio - such a factor is called a multiplier.

The _____, m, is the inverse of the reserve requirement, R:

$$m = \frac{1}{R}$$

This formula stems from the fact that the sum of the 'amount loaned out' column above can be expressed mathematically as a geometric series with a common ratio of 1 − R.

   a. Flow to Equity-Approach
   b. Money multiplier
   c. Kibbutz volunteers
   d. Fixed-income arbitrage

40. _____ and Keynesian Theory) is a macroeconomic theory based on the ideas of 20th-century British economist John Maynard Keynes. _____ argues that private sector decisions sometimes lead to inefficient macroeconomic outcomes and therefore advocates active policy responses by the public sector, including monetary policy actions by the central bank and fiscal policy actions by the government to stabilize output over the business cycle.

The theories forming the basis of _____ were first presented in The General Theory of Employment, Interest and Money, published in 1936.

a. Deflation
c. Keynesian economics

b. Rational choice theory
d. Market failure

Chapter 30. MANAGING AGGREGATE DEMAND: MONETARY POLICY

1. The _____ is the central banking system of the United States. Created in 1913 by the enactment of the Federal Reserve Act (signed by Woodrow Wilson), it is a quasi-public and quasi-private (government entity with private components) banking system that comprises (1) the presidentially appointed Board of Governors of the _____ in Washington, D.C.; (2) the Federal Open Market Committee; (3) twelve regional Federal Reserve Banks located in major cities throughout the nation acting as fiscal agents for the U.S. Treasury, each with its own nine-member board of directors; (4) numerous other private U.S. member banks, which subscribe to required amounts of non-transferable stock in their regional Federal Reserve Banks; and (5) various advisory councils. Since February 2006, Ben Bernanke has served as the Chairman of the Board of Governors of the _____.

   a. Federal Reserve System Open Market Account
   b. Federal Reserve System
   c. Monetary Policy Report to the Congress
   d. Term auction facility

2. The term _____ is applied broadly to a variety of situations in which some financial institutions or assets suddenly lose a large part of their value. In the 19th and early 20th centuries, many financial crises were associated with banking panics, and many recessions coincided with these panics. Other situations that are often called financial crises include stock market crashes and the bursting of other financial bubbles, currency crises, and sovereign defaults.

   a. Co-operative economics
   b. Financial crisis
   c. Macroeconomics
   d. Market failure

3. _____ and Keynesian Theory) is a macroeconomic theory based on the ideas of 20th-century British economist John Maynard Keynes. _____ argues that private sector decisions sometimes lead to inefficient macroeconomic outcomes and therefore advocates active policy responses by the public sector, including monetary policy actions by the central bank and fiscal policy actions by the government to stabilize output over the business cycle.

   The theories forming the basis of _____ were first presented in The General Theory of Employment, Interest and Money, published in 1936.

   a. Deflation
   b. Keynesian economics
   c. Market failure
   d. Rational choice theory

4. In economics, _____ is the total amount of money available in an economy at a particular point in time. There are several ways to define 'money', but standard measures usually include currency in circulation and demand deposits.

   _____ data are recorded and published, usually by the government or the central bank of the country.

   a. Veil of money
   b. Velocity of money
   c. Neutrality of money
   d. Money supply

5. In economics, the term _____ of income or _____ refers to a simple economic model which describes the reciprocal circulation of income between producers and consumers. In the _____ model, the inter-dependent entities of producer and consumer are referred to as 'firms' and 'households' respectively and provide each other with factors in order to facilitate the flow of income. Firms provide consumers with goods and services in exchange for consumer expenditure and 'factors of production' from households.

   a. 130-30 fund
   b. 1921 recession
   c. Circular flow
   d. 100-year flood

Chapter 30. MANAGING AGGREGATE DEMAND: MONETARY POLICY

6. A _____, reserve bank, or monetary authority is the entity responsible for the monetary policy of a country or of a group of member states. It is a bank that can lend money to other banks in times of need. Its primary responsibility is to maintain the stability of the national currency and money supply, but more active duties include controlling subsidized-loan interest rates, and acting as a lender of last resort to the banking sector during times of financial crisis (private banks often being integral to the national financial system.)

   a. 130-30 fund   b. 1921 recession

   c. 100-year flood   d. Central bank

7. The _____ , a component of the Federal Reserve System, is charged under United States law with overseeing the nation's open market operations. It is the Federal Reserve Committee that makes key decisions about interest rates and the growth jam of the United States money supply. It is the principal organ of United States national monetary policy.

   a. Federal Reserve Transparency Act   b. Primary Dealer Credit Facility

   c. Fed Funds Probability   d. Federal Open Market Committee

8. The _____ was a worldwide economic downturn starting in most places in 1929 and ending at different times in the 1930s or early 1940s for different countries. It was the largest and most important economic depression in the 20th century, and is used in the 21st century as an example of how far the world's economy can fall. The _____ originated in the United States; historians most often use as a starting date the stock market crash on October 29, 1929, known as Black Tuesday.

   a. British Empire Economic Conference   b. Jarrow March

   c. Great Depression   d. Wall Street Crash of 1929

9. In economics, the _____ is the term used to refer to the environment in which bonds are bought and sold between a central bank ' its regulated banks. It is not a free market process.

- To intervene in the 'business cycle', a central bank may choose to go into the _____ and buy or sell government bonds, which is known as _____ operations to increase reserves.

   a. Outside money   b. Inside money

   c. Open Market   d. ACCRA Cost of Living Index

10. _____ is the process by which the government, central bank (ii) availability of money, and (iii) cost of money or rate of interest, in order to attain a set of objectives oriented towards the growth and stability of the economy. Monetary theory provides insight into how to craft optimal _____.

_____ is referred to as either being an expansionary policy where an expansionary policy increases the total supply of money in the economy, and a contractionary policy decreases the total money supply.

   a. 100-year flood   b. Monetary policy

   c. 130-30 fund   d. 1921 recession

11. The _____ is an economic and political union of 27 member states, located primarily in Europe. It was established by the Treaty of Maastricht on 1 November 1993, upon the foundations of the pre-existing European Economic Community. With a population of almost 500 million, the _____ generates an estimated 30% share (US$18.4 trillion in 2008) of the nominal gross world product.

Chapter 30. MANAGING AGGREGATE DEMAND: MONETARY POLICY

a. ACCRA Cost of Living Index
b. ACEA agreement
c. European Court of Justice
d. European Union

12. The _____ was signed on 7 February 1992 in Maastricht, the Netherlands after final negotiations on 9 December 1991 between the members of the European Community and entered into force on 1 November 1993 during the Delors Commission. It created the European Union and led to the creation of the euro. The _____ has been amended to a degree by later treaties.
    a. Treaties of Rome
    b. 100-year flood
    c. Treaty of Amsterdam
    d. Maastricht Treaty

13. _____ are banks' holdings of deposits in accounts with their central bank (for instance the European Central Bank or the Federal Reserve, in the latter case including federal funds), plus currency that is physically held in bank vaults (vault cash.) The central banks of some nations set minimum reserve requirements. Even when no requirements are set, banks commonly wish to hold some reserves, called desired reserves, against unexpected events.
    a. Bilateral netting
    b. Sweep account
    c. Bank reserves
    d. Structuring

14. A United States Treasury security is a government debt issued by the United States Department of the Treasury through the Bureau of the Public Debt. Treasury securities are the debt financing instruments of the United States Federal government, and they are often referred to simply as Treasuries. There are four types of marketable treasury securities: _____, Treasury notes, Treasury bonds, and Treasury Inflation Protected Securities (TIPS.)
    a. Lawcards
    b. Treasury bills
    c. Labour battalions
    d. Debt to Assets

15. A _____ occurs when a bank is unable to meet its obligations to its depositors or other creditors. More specifically, a bank fails economically when the market value of its assets declines to a value that is less than the market value of its liabilities. As such, the bank is unable to fulfill the demands of all of its depositors on time.
    a. Transactional account
    b. Concentration account
    c. Lombard Club
    d. Bank failure

16. In the United States, _____ are overnight borrowings by banks to maintain their bank reserves at the Federal Reserve. Banks keep reserves at Federal Reserve Banks to meet their reserve requirements and to clear financial transactions. Transactions in the _____ market enable depository institutions with reserve balances in excess of reserve requirements to lend reserves to institutions with reserve deficiencies.
    a. Federal funds
    b. Federal funds rate
    c. Federal Reserve Transparency Act
    d. Term auction facility

17. In the United States, the _____ is the interest rate at which private depository institutions (mostly banks) lend balances (federal funds) at the Federal Reserve to other depository institutions, usually overnight. It is the interest rate banks charge each other for loans. Changing the target rate is one way the Chairman of the Federal Reserve can influence the supply of money in the U.S. economy..
    a. Term auction facility
    b. Monetary Policy Report to the Congress
    c. Federal banking
    d. Federal funds rate

Chapter 30. MANAGING AGGREGATE DEMAND: MONETARY POLICY

18. In finance, a _____ is a debt security, in which the authorized issuer owes the holders a debt and, depending on the terms of the _____, is obliged to pay interest (the coupon) and/or to repay the principal at a later date, termed maturity. A _____ is a formal contract to repay borrowed money with interest at fixed intervals.

Thus a _____ is like a loan: the issuer is the borrower (debtor), the holder is the lender (creditor), and the coupon is the interest.

a. Zero-coupon
b. Callable
c. Prize Bond
d. Bond

19. _____ is a fee paid on borrowed assets. It is the price paid for the use of borrowed money, or, money earned by deposited funds. Assets that are sometimes lent with _____ include money, shares, consumer goods through hire purchase, major assets such as aircraft, and even entire factories in finance lease arrangements.

a. Interest
b. Asset protection
c. Insolvency
d. Internal debt

20. An _____ is the price a borrower pays for the use of money they do not own, for instance a small company might borrow from a bank to kick start their business, and the return a lender receives for deferring the use of funds, by lending it to the borrower. _____s are normally expressed as a percentage rate over the period of one year.

_____s targets are also a vital tool of monetary policy and are used to control variables like investment, inflation, and unemployment.

a. Arrow-Debreu model
b. ACCRA Cost of Living Index
c. Enterprise value
d. Interest rate

21. _____ in economics and business is the result of an exchange and from that trade we assign a numerical monetary value to a good, service or asset. If Alice trades Bob 4 apples for an orange, the _____ of an orange is 4 apples. Inversely, the _____ of an apple is 1/4 oranges.

a. Premium pricing
b. Price
c. Price book
d. Price war

22. In banking, _____ are bank reserves in excess of the reserve requirement set by a central bank (in the United States, the Federal Reserve System, called the Fed; in Canada, the Bank of Canada.) They are reserves of cash more than the required amounts. Holding _____ is generally considered costly and uneconomical as no interest is earned on the excess amount.

a. Annual percentage rate
b. Universal bank
c. Origination fee
d. Excess reserves

23. A security is a fungible, negotiable instrument representing financial value. _____ are broadly categorized into debt _____; equity _____, e.g., common stocks; and derivative (finance) contracts such as forwards, futures, options and swaps. The company or other entity issuing the security is called the issuer.

a. Red herring prospectus
b. Pass-Through Certificates
c. Settlement risk
d. Securities

Chapter 30. MANAGING AGGREGATE DEMAND: MONETARY POLICY

24. Discounting is a financial mechanism in which a debtor obtains the right to delay payments to a creditor, for a defined period of time, in exchange for a charge or fee. Essentially, the party that owes money in the present purchases the right to delay the payment until some future date. The _____, or charge, is simply the difference between the original amount owed in the present and the amount that has to be paid in the future to settle the debt.

   a. Reinsurance
   b. Certified Risk Manager
   c. Reliability theory
   d. Discount

25. The _____ is an interest rate a central bank charges depository institutions that borrow reserves from it.

The term _____ has two meanings:

- the same as interest rate; the term 'discount' does not refer to the meaning of the word, but to the purpose of using the quantity, such as computations of present value, e.g. net present value or discounted cash flow

- the annual effective _____, which is the annual interest divided by the capital including that interest; this rate is lower than the interest rate; it corresponds to using the value after a year as the nominal value, and seeing the initial value as the nominal value minus a discount; it is used for Treasury Bills and similar financial instruments

The annual effective _____ is the annual interest divided by the capital including that interest, which is the interest rate divided by 100% plus the interest rate. It is the annual discount factor to be applied to the future cash flow, to find the discount, subtracted from a future value to find the value one year earlier.

For example, suppose there is a government bond that sells for $95 and pays $100 in a year's time.

   a. Johansen test
   b. Stochastic volatility
   c. Discount rate
   d. Perpetuity

26. The term _____ refers to government debt, expenditures and revenues, or to finance (particularly financial revenue) in general.

- _____ deficit is the budget deficit of federal or local government
- _____ policy is the discretionary spending of governments. Contrasts with monetary policy.
- _____ year and _____ quarter are reporting periods for firms and other agencies.

   a. Procter ' Gamble
   b. Drawdown
   c. Bucket shop
   d. Fiscal

27. In economics, _____ is the use of government spending and revenue collection to influence the economy.

_____ can be contrasted with the other main type of economic policy, monetary policy, which attempts to stabilize the economy by controlling interest rates and the supply of money. The two main instruments of _____ are government spending and taxation.

Chapter 30. MANAGING AGGREGATE DEMAND: MONETARY POLICY

a. 100-year flood
b. Sustainable investment rule
c. Fiscalism
d. Fiscal policy

28. The _____ is a bank regulation that sets the minimum reserves each bank must hold to customer deposits and notes. It would normally be in the form of fiat currency stored in a bank vault (vault cash), or with a central bank.

The reserve ratio is sometimes used as a tool in the monetary policy, influencing the country's economy, borrowing, and interest rates.

a. Probability of default
b. Private money
c. Fractional-reserve banking
d. Reserve requirement

29. In economics, _____ is the total demand for final goods and services in the economy (Y) at a given time and price level. It is the amount of goods and services in the economy that will be purchased at all possible price levels. This is the demand for the gross domestic product of a country when inventory levels are static.

a. Aggregation problem
b. Aggregate supply
c. Aggregate expenditure
d. Aggregate demand

30. Economics:

- _____, the desire to own something and the ability to pay for it
- _____ curve, a graphic representation of a _____ schedule
- _____ deposit, the money in checking accounts
- _____ pull theory, the theory that inflation occurs when _____ for goods and services exceeds existing supplies
- _____ schedule, a table that lists the quantity of a good a person will buy it each different price
- _____ side economics, the school of economics at believes government spending and tax cuts open economy by raising _____

a. Demand
b. Variability
c. McKesson ' Robbins scandal
d. Production

31. In economics, the _____ can be defined as the graph depicting the relationship between the price of a certain commodity, and the amount of it that consumers are willing and able to purchase at that given price. It is a graphic representation of a demand schedule. The _____ for all consumers together follows from the _____ of every individual consumer: the individual demands at each price are added together.

a. Kuznets curve
b. Cost curve
c. Demand curve
d. Wage curve

32. A _____ is a hypothetical measure of overall prices for some set of goods and services, in a given region during a given interval, normalized relative to some base set. Typically, a _____ is approximated with a price index.

The classical dichotomy is the assumption that there is a relatively clean distinction between overall increases or decreases in prices and underlying, e;reale; economic variables.

Chapter 30. MANAGING AGGREGATE DEMAND: MONETARY POLICY

a. Discouraged worker
c. Discretionary spending
b. Price elasticity of supply
d. Price level

33. In economics, _____ is the total supply of goods and services produced by a national economy during a specific time period. It is the total amount of goods and services in the economy available at all possible price levels.
a. Aggregation problem
c. Aggregate expenditure
b. Aggregate demand
d. Aggregate supply

34. _____ is a broad label that refers to any individuals or households that use goods and services generated within the economy. The concept of a _____ is used in different contexts, so that the usage and significance of the term may vary.

Typically when business people and economists talk of _____s they are talking about person as _____, an aggregated commodity item with little individuality other than that expressed in the buy/not-buy decision.

a. 130-30 fund
c. 100-year flood
b. Consumer
d. 1921 recession

35. A _____ is a measure of the average price of consumer goods and services purchased by households. A _____ measures a price change for a constant market basket of goods and services from one period to the next within the same area (city, region, or nation.) It is a price index determined by measuring the price of a standard group of goods meant to represent the typical market basket of a typical urban consumer.
a. CPI
c. Cost-of-living index
b. Consumer Price Index
d. Lipstick index

36. In economics, _____ is a rise in the general level of prices of goods and services in an economy over a period of time. When the general price level rises, each unit of currency buys fewer goods and services; consequently, _____ is also a decline in the real value of money--a loss of purchasing power in the medium of exchange which is also the monetary unit of account in the economy. A chief measure of general price-level _____ is the general _____ rate, which is the percentage change in a general price index (normally the Consumer Price Index) over time.
a. Opportunity cost
c. Economic
b. Energy economics
d. Inflation

37. An _____, in economics, is the amount by which the real Gross domestic product exceeds potential GDP. The real GDP is also known as GDP 'adjusted for inflation', 'constant prices' GDP or 'constant dollar' GDP, because it measures the aggregate output in a country's income accounts in a given year, expressed in base-year prices. On the other hand, the potential GDP is the quantity of real GDP when a country's economy is at full-employment.
a. ACCRA Cost of Living Index
c. Inflationary gap
b. AD-IA Model
d. ACEA agreement

38. A _____ is a normalized average (typically a weighted average) of prices for a given class of goods or services in a given region, during a given interval of time. It is a statistic designed to help to compare how these prices, taken as a whole, differ between time periods or geographical locations.

Price indices have several potential uses.

a. Transactional Net Margin Method
b. Two-part tariff
c. Product sabotage
d. Price Index

39. _____ or economic opportunity loss is the value of the next best alternative foregone as the result of making a decision. _____ analysis is an important part of a company's decision-making processes but is not treated as an actual cost in any financial statement. The next best thing that a person can engage in is referred to as the _____ of doing the best thing and ignoring the next best thing to be done.

a. Economic
b. Industrial organization
c. Economic ideology
d. Opportunity cost

40. The _____ is the expected return forgone by bypassing of other potential investment activities for a given capital. It is a rate of return that investors could earn in financial markets.

a. AD-IA Model
b. Opportunity cost of capital
c. ACCRA Cost of Living Index
d. ACEA agreement

41. The _____ is an expected return that the provider of capital plans to earn on their investment.

Capital (money) used for funding a business should earn returns for the capital providers who risk their capital. For an investment to be worthwhile, the expected return on capital must be greater than the _____.

a. Modigliani-Miller theorem
b. Capital expenditure
c. Capital intensive
d. Cost of capital

Chapter 31. THE DEBATE OVER MONETARY AND FISCAL POLICY

1. _____ is the view within monetary economics that variation in the money supply has major influences on national output in the short run and the price level over longer periods and that objectives of monetary policy are best met by targeting the growth rate of the money supply.

_____ today is mainly associated with the work of Milton Friedman, who was among the generation of economists to accept Keynesian economics and then criticize it on his own terms. Friedman and Anna Schwartz wrote an influential book, Monetary History of the United States 1867-1960, and argued that 'inflation is always and everywhere a monetary phenomenon.' Friedman advocated a central bank policy aimed at keeping the supply and demand for money at equilibrium, as measured by growth in productivity and demand.

   a. Marginal revenue productivity theory of wages
   b. Historical school of economics
   c. Complexity economics
   d. Monetarism

2. In economics, the _____ is the relation:

$$M \cdot V = P \cdot Q$$

where, for a given period,

M is the total amount of money in circulation on average in an economy.
V is the velocity of money, that is the average frequency with which a unit of money is spent.
P is the price level.

   a. Open market
   b. ACCRA Cost of Living Index
   c. Outside money
   d. Equation of exchange

3. The _____ is the central banking system of the United States. Created in 1913 by the enactment of the Federal Reserve Act (signed by Woodrow Wilson), it is a quasi-public and quasi-private (government entity with private components) banking system that comprises (1) the presidentially appointed Board of Governors of the _____ in Washington, D.C.; (2) the Federal Open Market Committee; (3) twelve regional Federal Reserve Banks located in major cities throughout the nation acting as fiscal agents for the U.S. Treasury, each with its own nine-member board of directors; (4) numerous other private U.S. member banks, which subscribe to required amounts of non-transferable stock in their regional Federal Reserve Banks; and (5) various advisory councils. Since February 2006, Ben Bernanke has served as the Chairman of the Board of Governors of the _____.

   a. Federal Reserve System Open Market Account
   b. Term auction facility
   c. Federal Reserve System
   d. Monetary Policy Report to the Congress

4. In economics, _____ is the total amount of money available in an economy at a particular point in time. There are several ways to define 'money', but standard measures usually include currency in circulation and demand deposits.

_____ data are recorded and published, usually by the government or the central bank of the country.

a. Money supply
b. Neutrality of money
c. Velocity of money
d. Veil of money

5. In economics, the _____ of money is a theory emphasizing the positive relationship of overall prices or the nominal value of expenditures to the quantity of money.

It is the mainstream economic theory of the price level. Alternative theories include the real bills doctrine and the more recent fiscal theory of the price level.

a. Dishoarding
b. Romer Model
c. Real business cycle
d. Quantity theory

6. In economics, the _____ is a theory emphasizing the positive relationship of overall prices or the nominal value of expenditures to the quantity of money.

It is the mainstream economic theory of the price level. Alternative theories include the real bills doctrine and the more recent fiscal theory of the price level.

a. Quantity theory of money
b. Microsimulation
c. Fundamental psychological law
d. Consumer spending

7. A _____ is a package or set of measures introduced to stabilise a financial system or economy. The term can refer to policies in two distinct sets of circumstances: business cycle stabilization and crisis stabilization.

Stabilization can refer to correcting the normal behavior of the business cycle.

a. Volunteers for Economic Growth Alliance
b. Stabilization policy
c. New International Economic Order
d. Capacity Development

8. In economics, _____ is the total supply of goods and services produced by a national economy during a specific time period. It is the total amount of goods and services in the economy available at all possible price levels.

a. Aggregate demand
b. Aggregation problem
c. Aggregate expenditure
d. Aggregate supply

9. _____ and Keynesian Theory) is a macroeconomic theory based on the ideas of 20th-century British economist John Maynard Keynes. _____ argues that private sector decisions sometimes lead to inefficient macroeconomic outcomes and therefore advocates active policy responses by the public sector, including monetary policy actions by the central bank and fiscal policy actions by the government to stabilize output over the business cycle.

The theories forming the basis of _____ were first presented in The General Theory of Employment, Interest and Money, published in 1936.

a. Deflation
b. Rational choice theory
c. Market failure
d. Keynesian economics

Chapter 31. THE DEBATE OVER MONETARY AND FISCAL POLICY

10. In economics, _____ is the total demand for final goods and services in the economy (Y) at a given time and price level. It is the amount of goods and services in the economy that will be purchased at all possible price levels. This is the demand for the gross domestic product of a country when inventory levels are static.
   a. Aggregate supply
   b. Aggregate expenditure
   c. Aggregation problem
   d. Aggregate demand

11. Economics:

   - _____, the desire to own something and the ability to pay for it
   - _____ curve, a graphic representation of a _____ schedule
   - _____ deposit, the money in checking accounts
   - _____ pull theory, the theory that inflation occurs when _____ for goods and services exceeds existing supplies
   - _____ schedule, a table that lists the quantity of a good a person will buy it each different price
   - _____ side economics, the school of economics at believes government spending and tax cuts open economy by raising _____

   a. Production
   b. Demand
   c. McKesson ' Robbins scandal
   d. Variability

12. In economics, the _____ can be defined as the graph depicting the relationship between the price of a certain commodity, and the amount of it that consumers are willing and able to purchase at that given price. It is a graphic representation of a demand schedule. The _____ for all consumers together follows from the _____ of every individual consumer: the individual demands at each price are added together.
   a. Cost curve
   b. Wage curve
   c. Kuznets curve
   d. Demand curve

13. The term _____ refers to government debt, expenditures and revenues, or to finance (particularly financial revenue) in general.

   - _____ deficit is the budget deficit of federal or local government
   - _____ policy is the discretionary spending of governments. Contrasts with monetary policy.
   - _____ year and _____ quarter are reporting periods for firms and other agencies.

   a. Drawdown
   b. Bucket shop
   c. Procter ' Gamble
   d. Fiscal

14. In economics, _____ is the use of government spending and revenue collection to influence the economy.

   _____ can be contrasted with the other main type of economic policy, monetary policy, which attempts to stabilize the economy by controlling interest rates and the supply of money. The two main instruments of _____ are government spending and taxation.

Chapter 31. THE DEBATE OVER MONETARY AND FISCAL POLICY

    a. 100-year flood
    b. Fiscalism
    c. Sustainable investment rule
    d. Fiscal policy

15. _____ is a fee paid on borrowed assets. It is the price paid for the use of borrowed money, or, money earned by deposited funds. Assets that are sometimes lent with _____ include money, shares, consumer goods through hire purchase, major assets such as aircraft, and even entire factories in finance lease arrangements.
    a. Internal debt
    b. Asset protection
    c. Insolvency
    d. Interest

16. An _____ is the price a borrower pays for the use of money they do not own, for instance a small company might borrow from a bank to kick start their business, and the return a lender receives for deferring the use of funds, by lending it to the borrower. _____s are normally expressed as a percentage rate over the period of one year.

_____s targets are also a vital tool of monetary policy and are used to control variables like investment, inflation, and unemployment.

    a. Enterprise value
    b. Interest rate
    c. ACCRA Cost of Living Index
    d. Arrow-Debreu model

17. _____ is the process by which the government, central bank (ii) availability of money, and (iii) cost of money or rate of interest, in order to attain a set of objectives oriented towards the growth and stability of the economy. Monetary theory provides insight into how to craft optimal _____.

_____ is referred to as either being an expansionary policy where an expansionary policy increases the total supply of money in the economy, and a contractionary policy decreases the total money supply.

    a. 1921 recession
    b. 100-year flood
    c. 130-30 fund
    d. Monetary policy

18. A consumer price index (_____) is a measure of the average price of consumer goods and services purchased by households. A consumer price index measures a price change for a constant market basket of goods and services from one period to the next within the same area (city, region, or nation.) It is a price index determined by measuring the price of a standard group of goods meant to represent the typical market basket of a typical urban consumer.
    a. Hedonic price index
    b. Lipstick index
    c. CPI
    d. Cost-of-living index

19. _____ is a broad label that refers to any individuals or households that use goods and services generated within the economy. The concept of a _____ is used in different contexts, so that the usage and significance of the term may vary.

Typically when business people and economists talk of _____s they are talking about person as _____, an aggregated commodity item with little individuality other than that expressed in the buy/not-buy decision.

a. 1921 recession
b. 130-30 fund
c. 100-year flood
d. Consumer

20. A _____ is a measure of the average price of consumer goods and services purchased by households. A _____ measures a price change for a constant market basket of goods and services from one period to the next within the same area (city, region, or nation.) It is a price index determined by measuring the price of a standard group of goods meant to represent the typical market basket of a typical urban consumer.
    a. Consumer Price Index
    b. Lipstick index
    c. CPI
    d. Cost-of-living index

21. _____ was an American economist, statistician and public intellectual, and a recipient of the Nobel Memorial Prize in Economic Sciences. He is best known among scholars for his theoretical and empirical research, especially consumption analysis, monetary history and theory, and for his demonstration of the complexity of stabilization policy. A global public followed his restatement of a political philosophy that insisted on minimizing the role of government in favor of the private sector.
    a. Milton Friedman
    b. Adolph Fischer
    c. Adam Smith
    d. Adolf Hitler

22. The _____ or gross domestic income (GDI), a basic measure of an economy's economic performance, is the market value of all final goods and services produced within the borders of a nation in a year. _____ can be defined in three ways, all of which are conceptually identical. First, it is equal to the total expenditures for all final goods and services produced within the country in a stipulated period of time (usually a 365-day year.)
    a. Gross domestic product
    b. Market structure
    c. Countercyclical
    d. Monopolistic competition

23. In economics, _____ is inflation that is very high or 'out of control', a condition in which prices increase rapidly as a currency loses its value. Definitions used by the media vary from a cumulative inflation rate over three years approaching 100% to 'inflation exceeding 50% a month.' In informal usage the term is often applied to much lower rates. As a rule of thumb, normal inflation is reported per year, but _____ is often reported for much shorter intervals, often per month.
    a. 1921 recession
    b. 130-30 fund
    c. Hyperinflation
    d. 100-year flood

24. _____ in economics and business is the result of an exchange and from that trade we assign a numerical monetary value to a good, service or asset. If Alice trades Bob 4 apples for an orange, the _____ of an orange is 4 apples. Inversely, the _____ of an apple is 1/4 oranges.
    a. Price book
    b. Premium pricing
    c. Price war
    d. Price

25. A _____ is a normalized average (typically a weighted average) of prices for a given class of goods or services in a given region, during a given interval of time. It is a statistic designed to help to compare how these prices, taken as a whole, differ between time periods or geographical locations.

Price indices have several potential uses.

Chapter 31. THE DEBATE OVER MONETARY AND FISCAL POLICY

a. Transactional Net Margin Method
b. Two-part tariff
c. Product sabotage
d. Price Index

26. In economics, _____ is a rise in the general level of prices of goods and services in an economy over a period of time. When the general price level rises, each unit of currency buys fewer goods and services; consequently, _____ is also a decline in the real value of money--a loss of purchasing power in the medium of exchange which is also the monetary unit of account in the economy. A chief measure of general price-level _____ is the general _____ rate, which is the percentage change in a general price index (normally the Consumer Price Index) over time.

a. Economic
b. Energy economics
c. Inflation
d. Opportunity cost

27. In finance, a _____ is a debt security, in which the authorized issuer owes the holders a debt and, depending on the terms of the _____, is obliged to pay interest (the coupon) and/or to repay the principal at a later date, termed maturity. A _____ is a formal contract to repay borrowed money with interest at fixed intervals.

Thus a _____ is like a loan: the issuer is the borrower (debtor), the holder is the lender (creditor), and the coupon is the interest.

a. Zero-coupon
b. Prize Bond
c. Callable
d. Bond

28. A _____ is a legal document that is often passed by the legislature, and approved by the chief executive-or president. For example, only certain types of revenue may be imposed and collected. Property tax is frequently the basis for municipal and county revenues, while sales tax and/or income tax are the basis for state revenues, and income tax and corporate tax are the basis for national revenues.

a. Structural deficit
b. Right-financing
c. Lump-sum tax
d. Government budget

29. A _____, reserve bank, or monetary authority is the entity responsible for the monetary policy of a country or of a group of member states. It is a bank that can lend money to other banks in times of need. Its primary responsibility is to maintain the stability of the national currency and money supply, but more active duties include controlling subsidized-loan interest rates, and acting as a lender of last resort to the banking sector during times of financial crisis (private banks often being integral to the national financial system.)

a. 100-year flood
b. 130-30 fund
c. Central Bank
d. 1921 recession

30. The _____ is one of the world's most important central banks, responsible for monetary policy covering the 16 member States of the Eurozone. It was established by the European Union (EU) in 1998 with its headquarters in Frankfurt, Germany.

The predecessor to the _____ was the European Monetary Institute .

a. ACEA agreement
b. AD-IA Model
c. ACCRA Cost of Living Index
d. European Central Bank

Chapter 31. THE DEBATE OVER MONETARY AND FISCAL POLICY

31. The _____ is an economic and political union of 27 member states, located primarily in Europe. It was established by the Treaty of Maastricht on 1 November 1993, upon the foundations of the pre-existing European Economic Community. With a population of almost 500 million, the _____ generates an estimated 30% share (US$18.4 trillion in 2008) of the nominal gross world product.
   a. European Court of Justice
   b. ACCRA Cost of Living Index
   c. ACEA agreement
   d. European Union

32. _____ is an American economist and was the Chairman of the Federal Reserve of the United States from 1987 to 2006. He currently works as a private advisor and providing consulting for firms through his company, Greenspan Associates LLC.

First appointed Federal Reserve chairman by President Ronald Reagan in August 1987, he was reappointed at successive four-year intervals until retiring on January 31, 2006 after the second-longest tenure in the position.

   a. Adolph Fischer
   b. Adam Smith
   c. Adolf Hitler
   d. Alan Greenspan

33. The _____ is the largest national economy in the world. Its gross domestic product (GDP) was estimated as $14.2 trillion in 2008. The U.S. economy maintains a high level of output per person (GDP per capita, $46,800 in 2008, ranked at around number ten in the world.)
   a. ACEA agreement
   b. AD-IA Model
   c. ACCRA Cost of Living Index
   d. Economy of the United States

34. In economics, a _____ is a general slowdown in economic activity over a sustained period of time, or a business cycle contraction. During _____s, many macroeconomic indicators vary in a similar way. Production as measured by Gross Domestic Product (GDP), employment, investment spending, capacity utilization, household incomes and business profits all fall during _____s.
   a. Recession
   b. Treasury View
   c. Leading indicators
   d. Monetary economics

35. _____s is the social science that studies the production, distribution, and consumption of goods and services. The term _____s comes from the Ancient Greek οἰκονομία from οἶκος (oikos, 'house') + νόμος (nomos, 'custom' or 'law'), hence 'rules of the house(hold)'. Current _____ models developed out of the broader field of political economy in the late 19th century, owing to a desire to use an empirical approach more akin to the physical sciences.
   a. Energy economics
   b. Opportunity cost
   c. Inflation
   d. Economic

36. _____ is the incidence or process of transferring ownership of a business, enterprise, agency or public service from the public sector (government) to the private sector (business.) In a broader sense, _____ refers to transfer of any government function to the private sector including governmental functions like revenue collection and law enforcement.

The term '_____' also has been used to describe two unrelated transactions.

   a. Performance reports
   b. Privatization
   c. Compound empowerment
   d. Ricardian equivalence

Chapter 31. THE DEBATE OVER MONETARY AND FISCAL POLICY

37. To _____ is to impose a financial charge or other levy upon a taxpayer by a state or the functional equivalent of a state.

_____es are also imposed by many subnational entities. _____es consist of direct _____ or indirect _____, and may be paid in money or as its labour equivalent (often but not always unpaid.)

   a. Tax
   b. 1921 recession
   c. 100-year flood
   d. 130-30 fund

38. A _____ is a reduction in taxes. Economic stimulus via _____s, along with interest rate intervention and deficit spending, are one of the central tenets of Keynesian economics.

The immediate effects of a _____ are, generally, a decrease in the real income of the government and an increase in the real income of those whose tax rate has been lowered.

   a. Popiwek
   b. Tax cut
   c. Withholding tax
   d. Direct taxes

39. The _____ is the central bank of the United Kingdom and is the model on which most modern, large central banks have been based. Since 1946 it has been a state-owned institution. It was established in 1694 to act as the English Government's banker, and to this day it still acts as the banker for the UK Government.
   a. 130-30 fund
   b. Bank of England
   c. 100-year flood
   d. 1921 recession

40. A _____ occurs when an entity spends more money than it takes in. The opposite of a _____ is a budget surplus. Debt is essentially an accumulated flow of deficits.
   a. Public Financial Management
   b. Budget deficit
   c. Funding body
   d. Lump-sum tax

41. The term _____ refers to economy-wide fluctuations in production or economic activity over several months or years. These fluctuations occur around a long-term growth trend, and typically involve shifts over time between periods of relatively rapid economic growth (expansion or boom), and periods of relative stagnation or decline (contraction or recession.)

These fluctuations are often measured using the growth rate of real gross domestic product.

   a. Consumer theory
   b. Tobit model
   c. Nominal value
   d. Business cycle

42. _____ is an economic policy in which a central bank estimates and makes public a projected, or 'target,' inflation rate and then attempts to steer actual inflation towards the target through the use of interest rate changes and other monetary tools.

Chapter 31. THE DEBATE OVER MONETARY AND FISCAL POLICY

Because interest rates and the inflation rate tend to be inversely related, the likely moves of the central bank to raise or lower interest rates become more transparent under the policy of _____. Examples:

- if inflation appears to be above the target, the bank is likely to raise interest rates. This usually (but not always) has the effect over time of cooling the economy and bringing down inflation.

- if inflation appears to be below the target, the bank is likely to lower interest rates. This usually (again, not always) has the effect over time of accelerating the economy and raising inflation.

a. Incomes policies
b. Employment Cost Index
c. Inflation swap
d. Inflation targeting

43. In economics, the _____ is a historical inverse relation between the rate of unemployment and the rate of inflation in an economy. Stated simply, the lower the unemployment in an economy, the higher the rate of increase in nominal wages in the economy. Rate of Change of Wages against Unemployment, United Kingdom 1913-1948 from Phillips (1958)

William Phillips, a New Zealand born economist, wrote a paper in 1958 titled The Relationship between Unemployment and the Rate of Change of Money Wages in the United Kingdom 1861-1957, which was published in the quarterly journal Economica.

a. Demand curve
b. Lorenz curve
c. Cost curve
d. Phillips curve

44. In economics, a _____ is a monetary-policy rule that stipulates how much the central bank would or should change the nominal interest rate in response to divergences of actual inflation rates from target inflation rates and of actual Gross Domestic Product (GDP) from potential GDP. It was first proposed by the by U.S. economist John B. Taylor in 1993. The rule can be written as follows:

$$i_t = \pi_t + r_t^* + a_\pi(\pi_t - \pi_t^*) + a_y(y_t - \bar{y}_t).$$

In this equation, i_t is the target short-term nominal interest rate (e.g. the federal funds rate in the US), π_t is the rate of inflation as measured by the GDP deflator, π_t^* is the desired rate of inflation, r_t^* is the assumed equilibrium real interest rate, y_t is the logarithm of real GDP, and $\bar{y}_t$ is the logarithm of potential output, as determined by a linear trend.

a. Fed Funds Probability
b. Term Securities Lending Facility
c. Federal Reserve Banks
d. Taylor rule

45. An _____ is any government regulation or law that encourages or discourages foreign investment in the local economy, e.g. currency exchange limits.

Chapter 31. THE DEBATE OVER MONETARY AND FISCAL POLICY

As globalization integrates the economies of neighboring and of trading states, they are typically forced to trade off such rules as part of a common tax, tariff and trade regime, e.g. as defined by a free trade pact. _____ favoring local investors over global ones is typically discouraged in such pacts, and the idea of a separate _____ rapidly becomes a fiction or fantasy, as real decisions reflect the real need for nations to compete for investment, even from their own local investors.

a. Investment policy
b. International sanctions
c. Economic liberalization
d. Electricity liberalization

Chapter 31. THE DEBATE OVER MONETARY AND FISCAL POLICY   277

46. A _____ is:

- Rewrite _____, in generative grammar and computer science
- Standardization, a formal and widely-accepted statement, fact, definition, or qualification
- Operation, a determinate _____ for performing a mathematical operation and obtaining a certain result (Mathematics, Logic)
    - Unary operation
    - Binary operation
- _____ of inference, a function from sets of formulae to formulae (Mathematics, Logic)
- _____ of thumb, principle with broad application that is not intended to be strictly accurate or reliable for every situation. Also often simply referred to as a _____
- Moral, an atomic element of a moral code for guiding choices in human behavior
- Heuristic, a quantized '_____' which shows a tendency or probability for successful function
- A regulation, as in sports
- A Production _____, as in computer science
- Procedural law, a _____ set governing the application of laws to cases
    - A law, which may informally be called a '_____'
    - A court ruling, a decision by a court
- In the U.S. Government, a regulation mandated by Congress, but written or expanded upon by the Executive Branch.
- Norm (sociology), an informal but widely accepted _____, concept, truth, definition, or qualification (social norms, legal norms, coding norms)
- Norm (philosophy), a kind of sentence or a reason to act, feel or believe
- 'Rulership' is the concept of governance by a government:
    - Military _____, governance by a military body
    - Monastic _____, a collection of precepts that guides the life of monks or nuns in a religious order where the superior holds the place of Christ
- Slide _____

- '_____,' a song by Ayumi Hamasaki
- '_____,' a song by rapper Nas
- '_____s,' an album by the band The Whitest Boy Alive
- _____s: Pyaar Ka Superhit Formula, a 2003 Bollywood film
- ruler, an instrument for measuring lengths
- _____, a component of an astrolabe, circumferator or similar instrument
- The _____s, a bestselling self-help book
- _____ Project (Run Up-to-date Linux Everywhere), a project that aims to use up-to-date Linux software on old PCs
- _____ engine, a software system that helps managing business _____s
- Ja _____, a hip hop artist
    - R.U.L.E., a 2005 greatest hits album by rapper Ja _____
- '_____s,' a KMFDM song

a. Procter ' Gamble   b. Technocracy
c. Demand   d. Rule

47. In economics, _____ describes a situation where a decision-maker's preferences change over time, such that what is preferred at one point in time is inconsistent with what is preferred at another point in time. It is often easiest to think about preferences over time in this context by thinking of decision-makers as being made up of many different 'selves', with each self representing the decision-maker at a different point in time. So, for example, there is my today self, my tomorrow self, my next Tuesday self, my year from now self, etc.

   a. Cheap talk

   b. Graph continuous

   c. Bondareva-Shapley theorem

   d. Dynamic inconsistency

Chapter 32. BUDGET DEFICITS IN THE SHORT AND LONG RUN

1. _____ was the 31st President of the United States (1929-1933.) Besides his political career, Hoover was a professional mining engineer and author. As the United States Secretary of Commerce in the 1920s under Presidents Warren Harding and Calvin Coolidge, he promoted government intervention under the rubric 'economic modernization'.
   - a. Adolf Hitler
   - b. Adam Smith
   - c. Adolph Fischer
   - d. Herbert Hoover

2. In economics, _____ is the total demand for final goods and services in the economy (Y) at a given time and price level. It is the amount of goods and services in the economy that will be purchased at all possible price levels. This is the demand for the gross domestic product of a country when inventory levels are static.
   - a. Aggregation problem
   - b. Aggregate expenditure
   - c. Aggregate supply
   - d. Aggregate demand

3. In economics, _____ is the total supply of goods and services produced by a national economy during a specific time period. It is the total amount of goods and services in the economy available at all possible price levels.
   - a. Aggregate demand
   - b. Aggregation problem
   - c. Aggregate expenditure
   - d. Aggregate supply

4. A _____ occurs when an entity spends more money than it takes in. The opposite of a _____ is a budget surplus. Debt is essentially an accumulated flow of deficits.
   - a. Funding body
   - b. Lump-sum tax
   - c. Public Financial Management
   - d. Budget deficit

5. A _____ is a situation in which the government takes in more than it spends.
   - a. 100-year flood
   - b. 130-30 fund
   - c. Budget set
   - d. Budget surplus

6. The _____ or gross domestic income (GDI), a basic measure of an economy's economic performance, is the market value of all final goods and services produced within the borders of a nation in a year. _____ can be defined in three ways, all of which are conceptually identical. First, it is equal to the total expenditures for all final goods and services produced within the country in a stipulated period of time (usually a 365-day year.)
   - a. Gross domestic product
   - b. Monopolistic competition
   - c. Countercyclical
   - d. Market structure

7. Economics:

   - _____ ,the desire to own something and the ability to pay for it
   - _____ curve,a graphic representation of a _____ schedule
   - _____ deposit, the money in checking accounts
   - _____ pull theory,the theory that inflation occurs when _____ for goods and services exceeds existing supplies
   - _____ schedule,a table that lists the quantity of a good a person will buy it each different price
   - _____ side economics,the school of economics at believes government spending and tax cuts open economy by raising _____

a. Variability	b. Production
c. Demand	d. McKesson ' Robbins scandal

8. In economics, the _____ can be defined as the graph depicting the relationship between the price of a certain commodity, and the amount of it that consumers are willing and able to purchase at that given price. It is a graphic representation of a demand schedule. The _____ for all consumers together follows from the _____ of every individual consumer: the individual demands at each price are added together.

a. Demand curve	b. Cost curve
c. Wage curve	d. Kuznets curve

9. _____ is the incidence or process of transferring ownership of a business, enterprise, agency or public service from the public sector (government) to the private sector (business.) In a broader sense, _____ refers to transfer of any government function to the private sector including governmental functions like revenue collection and law enforcement.

The term '_____' also has been used to describe two unrelated transactions.

a. Performance reports	b. Compound empowerment
c. Privatization	d. Ricardian equivalence

10. To _____ is to impose a financial charge or other levy upon a taxpayer by a state or the functional equivalent of a state.

_____es are also imposed by many subnational entities. _____es consist of direct _____ or indirect _____, and may be paid in money or as its labour equivalent (often but not always unpaid.)

a. 100-year flood	b. 130-30 fund
c. 1921 recession	d. Tax

11. A _____ is a reduction in taxes. Economic stimulus via _____s, along with interest rate intervention and deficit spending, are one of the central tenets of Keynesian economics.

The immediate effects of a _____ are, generally, a decrease in the real income of the government and an increase in the real income of those whose tax rate has been lowered.

a. Withholding tax	b. Direct taxes
c. Tax cut	d. Popiwek

12. The _____ is the central banking system of the United States. Created in 1913 by the enactment of the Federal Reserve Act (signed by Woodrow Wilson), it is a quasi-public and quasi-private (government entity with private components) banking system that comprises (1) the presidentially appointed Board of Governors of the _____ in Washington, D.C.; (2) the Federal Open Market Committee; (3) twelve regional Federal Reserve Banks located in major cities throughout the nation acting as fiscal agents for the U.S. Treasury, each with its own nine-member board of directors; (4) numerous other private U.S. member banks, which subscribe to required amounts of non-transferable stock in their regional Federal Reserve Banks; and (5) various advisory councils. Since February 2006, Ben Bernanke has served as the Chairman of the Board of Governors of the _____.

Chapter 32. BUDGET DEFICITS IN THE SHORT AND LONG RUN

a. Term auction facility
b. Federal Reserve System
c. Monetary Policy Report to the Congress
d. Federal Reserve System Open Market Account

13. The term _____ refers to government debt, expenditures and revenues, or to finance (particularly financial revenue) in general.

- _____ deficit is the budget deficit of federal or local government
- _____ policy is the discretionary spending of governments. Contrasts with monetary policy.
- _____ year and _____ quarter are reporting periods for firms and other agencies.

a. Bucket shop
b. Procter ' Gamble
c. Drawdown
d. Fiscal

14. In economics, _____ is the use of government spending and revenue collection to influence the economy.

_____ can be contrasted with the other main type of economic policy, monetary policy, which attempts to stabilize the economy by controlling interest rates and the supply of money. The two main instruments of _____ are government spending and taxation.

a. Fiscal policy
b. Sustainable investment rule
c. 100-year flood
d. Fiscalism

15. _____ is the process by which the government, central bank (ii) availability of money, and (iii) cost of money or rate of interest, in order to attain a set of objectives oriented towards the growth and stability of the economy. Monetary theory provides insight into how to craft optimal _____.

_____ is referred to as either being an expansionary policy where an expansionary policy increases the total supply of money in the economy, and a contractionary policy decreases the total money supply.

a. 130-30 fund
b. Monetary policy
c. 100-year flood
d. 1921 recession

16. In finance, a _____ is a debt security, in which the authorized issuer owes the holders a debt and, depending on the terms of the _____, is obliged to pay interest (the coupon) and/or to repay the principal at a later date, termed maturity. A _____ is a formal contract to repay borrowed money with interest at fixed intervals.

Thus a _____ is like a loan: the issuer is the borrower (debtor), the holder is the lender (creditor), and the coupon is the interest.

a. Callable
b. Zero-coupon
c. Prize Bond
d. Bond

17. In algebra, a _____ is a function depending on n that associates a scalar, det(A), to an n×n square matrix A. The fundamental geometric meaning of a _____ is a scale factor for measure when A is regarded as a linear transformation. _____s are important both in calculus, where they enter the substitution rule for several variables, and in multilinear algebra.

For a fixed nonnegative integer n, there is a unique _____ function for the n×n matrices over any commutative ring R. In particular, this function exists when R is the field of real or complex numbers.

   a. Determinant
   b. 100-year flood
   c. 1921 recession
   d. 130-30 fund

18. _____ is that which is owed; usually referencing assets owed, but the term can also cover moral obligations and other interactions not requiring money. In the case of assets, _____ is a means of using future purchasing power in the present before a summation has been earned. Some companies and corporations use _____ as a part of their overall corporate finance strategy.
   a. Hard money loan
   b. Debenture
   c. Collateral Management
   d. Debt

19. _____ is a fee paid on borrowed assets. It is the price paid for the use of borrowed money , or, money earned by deposited funds . Assets that are sometimes lent with _____ include money, shares, consumer goods through hire purchase, major assets such as aircraft, and even entire factories in finance lease arrangements.
   a. Insolvency
   b. Interest
   c. Asset protection
   d. Internal debt

20. An _____ is the price a borrower pays for the use of money they do not own, for instance a small company might borrow from a bank to kick start their business, and the return a lender receives for deferring the use of funds, by lending it to the borrower. _____s are normally expressed as a percentage rate over the period of one year.

_____s targets are also a vital tool of monetary policy and are used to control variables like investment, inflation, and unemployment.

   a. ACCRA Cost of Living Index
   b. Interest rate
   c. Enterprise value
   d. Arrow-Debreu model

21. An _____, in economics, is the amount by which the real Gross domestic product exceeds potential GDP. The real GDP is also known as GDP 'adjusted for inflation', 'constant prices' GDP or 'constant dollar' GDP, because it measures the aggregate output in a country's income accounts in a given year, expressed in base-year prices. On the other hand, the potential GDP is the quantity of real GDP when a country's economy is at full-employment.
   a. ACEA agreement
   b. AD-IA Model
   c. ACCRA Cost of Living Index
   d. Inflationary gap

22. _____ is a misspelled phrase from Latin 'pro capite' phrase meaning per head with pro meaning 'per' or 'for each' and capite meaning 'head.' Both words together equate to the phrase 'for each head.'

It is usually used in the field of statistics to indicate the average per person for any given concern, such as income, crime rate, etc.

It is also used in wills to indicate that each of the named beneficiaries should receive, by devise or bequest, equal shares of the estate. This is in contrast to a per stirpes division, in which each branch of the inheriting family inherits an equal share of the estate.

a. Population statistics
b. False positive rate
c. Sargan test
d. Per capita

23. From a Keynesian point of view, a _____ in the public sector is achieved when the government equates the revenues with expenditure over the business cycles. In other words, a government's budget is balanced if its income is equal to its expenditure. It is a budget in which revenues are equal to spending.

a. Budget support
b. Budget crisis
c. Budget theory
d. Balanced budget

24. _____ is any long-term change in the patterns of average weather of a specific region or the Earth as a whole. _____ reflects abnormal variations to the Earth's climate and subsequent effects on other parts of the Earth, such as in the ice caps over durations ranging from decades to millions of years.

In recent usage, especially in the context of environmental policy, _____ usually refers to changes in modern climate

a. 1921 recession
b. Climate change
c. 100-year flood
d. 130-30 fund

25. _____ refers to the economic policies promoted by United States President Ronald Reagan during the 1980s. The four pillars of Reagan's economic policy were to:

1. reduce the growth of government spending,
2. reduce income and capital gains marginal tax rates,
3. reduce government regulation of the economy,
4. control the money supply to reduce inflation.

In attempting to cut back on domestic spending while lowering taxes, Reagan's approach was a departure from his immediate predecessors.

Reagan became president during a period of high inflation and unemployment (commonly referred to as stagflation), which had largely abated by the time he left office eight years later.

Prior to the Reagan Administration was a roughly ten year period of economic stagnation and inflation, known as stagflation.

a. Business sector
b. Reaganomics
c. Happiness economics
d. Social savings

Chapter 32. BUDGET DEFICITS IN THE SHORT AND LONG RUN

26. _____ is a policy or ideology of violence intended to intimidate or cause terror for the purpose of 'exerting pressure on decision making by state bodies.' The term 'terror' is largely used to indicate clandestine, low-intensity violence that targets civilians and generates public fear. Thus 'terror' is distinct from asymmetric warfare, and violates the concept of a common law of war in which civilian life is regarded. The term '-ism' is used to indicate an ideology --typically one that claims its attacks are in the domain of a 'just war' concept, though most condemn such as crimes against humanity.
   - a. 1921 recession
   - b. 130-30 fund
   - c. 100-year flood
   - d. Terrorism

27. The _____ is the largest national economy in the world. Its gross domestic product (GDP) was estimated as $14.2 trillion in 2008. The U.S. economy maintains a high level of output per person (GDP per capita, $46,800 in 2008, ranked at around number ten in the world.)
   - a. AD-IA Model
   - b. Economy of the United States
   - c. ACCRA Cost of Living Index
   - d. ACEA agreement

28. In economics, _____ is a rise in the general level of prices of goods and services in an economy over a period of time. When the general price level rises, each unit of currency buys fewer goods and services; consequently, _____ is also a decline in the real value of money--a loss of purchasing power in the medium of exchange which is also the monetary unit of account in the economy. A chief measure of general price-level _____ is the general _____ rate, which is the percentage change in a general price index (normally the Consumer Price Index) over time.
   - a. Energy economics
   - b. Economic
   - c. Opportunity cost
   - d. Inflation

29. _____ is a broad label that refers to any individuals or households that use goods and services generated within the economy. The concept of a _____ is used in different contexts, so that the usage and significance of the term may vary.

Typically when business people and economists talk of _____s they are talking about person as _____, an aggregated commodity item with little individuality other than that expressed in the buy/not-buy decision.

   - a. 100-year flood
   - b. Consumer
   - c. 1921 recession
   - d. 130-30 fund

30. A _____ is a measure of the average price of consumer goods and services purchased by households. A _____ measures a price change for a constant market basket of goods and services from one period to the next within the same area (city, region, or nation.) It is a price index determined by measuring the price of a standard group of goods meant to represent the typical market basket of a typical urban consumer.
   - a. Consumer Price Index
   - b. CPI
   - c. Lipstick index
   - d. Cost-of-living index

31. _____ in economics and business is the result of an exchange and from that trade we assign a numerical monetary value to a good, service or asset. If Alice trades Bob 4 apples for an orange, the _____ of an orange is 4 apples. Inversely, the _____ of an apple is 1/4 oranges.
   - a. Price war
   - b. Price book
   - c. Premium pricing
   - d. Price

Chapter 32. BUDGET DEFICITS IN THE SHORT AND LONG RUN

32. A _____ is a normalized average (typically a weighted average) of prices for a given class of goods or services in a given region, during a given interval of time. It is a statistic designed to help to compare how these prices, taken as a whole, differ between time periods or geographical locations.

Price indices have several potential uses.

a. Price Index
c. Product sabotage
b. Two-part tariff
d. Transactional Net Margin Method

33. _____ is the amount by which a government, private company' the opposite of budget surplus.

When the expenditures of a government to individuals and corporations) are greater than its tax revenues, it creates a deficit in the government budget; such a deficit is known as _____. This causes the government to borrow capital from the 'world market', increasing further debt, debt service and interest rates

a. Deficit spending
c. 1921 recession
b. 130-30 fund
d. 100-year flood

34. _____ is a common concept in economics, and gives rise to derived concepts such as consumer debt. Generally _____ is defined by opposition to production. But the precise definition can vary because different schools of economists define production quite differently.

a. Cash or share options
c. Foreclosure data providers
b. Federal Reserve Bank Notes
d. Consumption

35. _____ is an urban planning and transportation theory that concentrates growth in the center of a city to avoid urban sprawl; and advocates compact, transit-oriented, walkable, bicycle-friendly land use, including neighborhood schools, complete streets, mixed-use development with a range of housing choices.

_____ values long-range, regional considerations of sustainability over a short-term focus. Its goals are to achieve a unique sense of community and place; expand the range of transportation, employment, and housing choices; equitably distribute the costs and benefits of development; preserve and enhance natural and cultural resources; and promote public health.

a. Smart growth
c. 130-30 fund
b. 1921 recession
d. 100-year flood

36. _____ and Keynesian Theory) is a macroeconomic theory based on the ideas of 20th-century British economist John Maynard Keynes. _____ argues that private sector decisions sometimes lead to inefficient macroeconomic outcomes and therefore advocates active policy responses by the public sector, including monetary policy actions by the central bank and fiscal policy actions by the government to stabilize output over the business cycle.

The theories forming the basis of _____ were first presented in The General Theory of Employment, Interest and Money, published in 1936.

a. Market failure
b. Rational choice theory
c. Deflation
d. Keynesian economics

37. _____ was a global military conflict which involved a majority of the world's nations, including all of the great powers, organized into two opposing military alliances: the Allies and the Axis. The war involved the mobilization of over 100 million military personnel, making it the most widespread war in history. In a state of 'total war', the major participants placed their entire economic, industrial, and scientific capabilities at the service of the war effort, erasing the distinction between civilian and military resources.

a. 1921 recession
b. 130-30 fund
c. 100-year flood
d. World War II

38. _____s is the social science that studies the production, distribution, and consumption of goods and services. The term _____s comes from the Ancient Greek oá¼°κονομῖα from oá¼¶κος (oikos, 'house') + vÍŒμος (nomos, 'custom' or 'law'), hence 'rules of the house(hold)'. Current _____ models developed out of the broader field of political economy in the late 19th century, owing to a desire to use an empirical approach more akin to the physical sciences.

a. Inflation
b. Economic
c. Energy economics
d. Opportunity cost

39. A _____ is a legal document that is often passed by the legislature, and approved by the chief executive-or president. For example, only certain types of revenue may be imposed and collected. Property tax is frequently the basis for municipal and county revenues, while sales tax and/or income tax are the basis for state revenues, and income tax and corporate tax are the basis for national revenues.

a. Lump-sum tax
b. Government budget
c. Right-financing
d. Structural deficit

40. In economics, a _____ is a general slowdown in economic activity over a sustained period of time, or a business cycle contraction. During _____s, many macroeconomic indicators vary in a similar way. Production as measured by Gross Domestic Product (GDP), employment, investment spending, capacity utilization, household incomes and business profits all fall during _____s.

a. Recession
b. Monetary economics
c. Leading indicators
d. Treasury View

Chapter 33. THE TRADE-OFF BETWEEN INFLATION AND UNEMPLOYMENT

1. _____ is a broad label that refers to any individuals or households that use goods and services generated within the economy. The concept of a _____ is used in different contexts, so that the usage and significance of the term may vary.

Typically when business people and economists talk of _____s they are talking about person as _____, an aggregated commodity item with little individuality other than that expressed in the buy/not-buy decision.

   a. 130-30 fund
   b. 1921 recession
   c. 100-year flood
   d. Consumer

2. A _____ is a measure of the average price of consumer goods and services purchased by households. A _____ measures a price change for a constant market basket of goods and services from one period to the next within the same area (city, region, or nation.) It is a price index determined by measuring the price of a standard group of goods meant to represent the typical market basket of a typical urban consumer.
   a. Lipstick index
   b. Cost-of-living index
   c. CPI
   d. Consumer Price Index

3. In economics, the _____ is a historical inverse relation between the rate of unemployment and the rate of inflation in an economy. Stated simply, the lower the unemployment in an economy, the higher the rate of increase in nominal wages in the economy. Rate of Change of Wages against Unemployment, United Kingdom 1913-1948 from Phillips (1958)

William Phillips, a New Zealand born economist, wrote a paper in 1958 titled The Relationship between Unemployment and the Rate of Change of Money Wages in the United Kingdom 1861-1957, which was published in the quarterly journal Economica.

   a. Demand curve
   b. Cost curve
   c. Lorenz curve
   d. Phillips curve

4. _____ in economics and business is the result of an exchange and from that trade we assign a numerical monetary value to a good, service or asset. If Alice trades Bob 4 apples for an orange, the _____ of an orange is 4 apples. Inversely, the _____ of an apple is 1/4 oranges.
   a. Price war
   b. Premium pricing
   c. Price book
   d. Price

5. A _____ is a normalized average (typically a weighted average) of prices for a given class of goods or services in a given region, during a given interval of time. It is a statistic designed to help to compare how these prices, taken as a whole, differ between time periods or geographical locations.

Price indices have several potential uses.

   a. Product sabotage
   b. Two-part tariff
   c. Transactional Net Margin Method
   d. Price Index

Chapter 33. THE TRADE-OFF BETWEEN INFLATION AND UNEMPLOYMENT

6. In economics, _____ is a rise in the general level of prices of goods and services in an economy over a period of time. When the general price level rises, each unit of currency buys fewer goods and services; consequently, _____ is also a decline in the real value of money--a loss of purchasing power in the medium of exchange which is also the monetary unit of account in the economy. A chief measure of general price-level _____ is the general _____ rate, which is the percentage change in a general price index (normally the Consumer Price Index) over time.

a. Inflation
b. Energy economics
c. Economic
d. Opportunity cost

7. A _____ is a situation that involves losing one quality or aspect of something in return for gaining another quality or aspect. It implies a decision to be made with full comprehension of both the upside and downside of a particular choice.

In economics the term is expressed as opportunity cost, referring the most preferred alternative given up.

a. Trade-off
b. Whitemail
c. Nonmarket
d. Friedman-Savage utility function

8. In economics, _____ is the total demand for final goods and services in the economy (Y) at a given time and price level. It is the amount of goods and services in the economy that will be purchased at all possible price levels. This is the demand for the gross domestic product of a country when inventory levels are static.

a. Aggregate demand
b. Aggregation problem
c. Aggregate supply
d. Aggregate expenditure

9. The Demand side is a term used in economics to refer to a number of things:

- The demand element of a supply and demand partial equilibrium diagram, in microeconomics
- The aggregate demand in an economy, in macroeconomics
- Economic policy actions which are designed to affect aggregate demand.
- _____ learning referring to the incentive to learn how to use and modify free software as opposed to buying conventional software.

The term is also used broadly to distinguish supply-side economics from other schools, for instance Keynesian economics.

a. CPFR
b. Delayed differentiation
c. Reverse auction
d. Demand-side

10. The _____ was an evolution of developed countries from an industrial/manufacturing-based wealth producing economy into a service sector asset based economy, brought about by globalization and currency manipulation by governments and their central banks. Some analysts claimed that this change in the economic structure of the United States had created a state of permanent steady growth, low unemployment, and immunity to boom and bust macroeconomic cycles. They believed that the change rendered obsolete many business practices.

a. 130-30 fund
b. 1921 recession
c. 100-year flood
d. New Economy

Chapter 33. THE TRADE-OFF BETWEEN INFLATION AND UNEMPLOYMENT

11. _____ refers to the economic policies promoted by United States President Ronald Reagan during the 1980s. The four pillars of Reagan's economic policy were to:

    1. reduce the growth of government spending,
    2. reduce income and capital gains marginal tax rates,
    3. reduce government regulation of the economy,
    4. control the money supply to reduce inflation.

In attempting to cut back on domestic spending while lowering taxes, Reagan's approach was a departure from his immediate predecessors.

Reagan became president during a period of high inflation and unemployment (commonly referred to as stagflation), which had largely abated by the time he left office eight years later.

Prior to the Reagan Administration was a roughly ten year period of economic stagnation and inflation, known as stagflation.

a. Social savings
b. Business sector
c. Happiness economics
d. Reaganomics

12. _____ is a school of macroeconomic thought that argues that economic growth can be most effectively created using incentives for people to produce (supply) goods and services, such as adjusting income tax and capital gains tax rates, and by allowing greater flexibility by reducing regulation. Consumers will then benefit from a greater supply of goods and services at lower prices.

The term _____ was coined by journalist Jude Wanniski in 1975, and popularized the ideas of economists Robert Mundell and Arthur Laffer.

a. Clap note
b. Commodity trading advisors
c. Fiscal stimulus plans
d. Supply-side economics

13. Economics:

- _____, the desire to own something and the ability to pay for it
- _____ curve, a graphic representation of a _____ schedule
- _____ deposit, the money in checking accounts
- _____ pull theory, the theory that inflation occurs when _____ for goods and services exceeds existing supplies
- _____ schedule, a table that lists the quantity of a good a person will buy it each different price
- _____ side economics, the school of economics at believes government spending and tax cuts open economy by raising _____

a. McKesson ' Robbins scandal
b. Variability
c. Production
d. Demand

Chapter 33. THE TRADE-OFF BETWEEN INFLATION AND UNEMPLOYMENT

14. In economics, the _____ can be defined as the graph depicting the relationship between the price of a certain commodity, and the amount of it that consumers are willing and able to purchase at that given price. It is a graphic representation of a demand schedule. The _____ for all consumers together follows from the _____ of every individual consumer: the individual demands at each price are added together.
    a. Kuznets curve
    b. Wage curve
    c. Cost curve
    d. Demand curve

15. _____s is the social science that studies the production, distribution, and consumption of goods and services. The term _____s comes from the Ancient Greek οἰκονομῐ́α from οἶκος (oikos, 'house') + νόμος (nomos, 'custom' or 'law'), hence 'rules of the house(hold)'. Current _____ models developed out of the broader field of political economy in the late 19th century, owing to a desire to use an empirical approach more akin to the physical sciences.
    a. Opportunity cost
    b. Energy economics
    c. Inflation
    d. Economic

16. In economics, _____ is the total supply of goods and services produced by a national economy during a specific time period. It is the total amount of goods and services in the economy available at all possible price levels.
    a. Aggregate expenditure
    b. Aggregate supply
    c. Aggregation problem
    d. Aggregate demand

17. A _____ is an event that suddenly changes the price of a commodity or service. It may be caused by a sudden increase or decrease in the supply of a particular good. This sudden change affects the equilibrium price.
    a. Friedman rule
    b. Demand shock
    c. SIMIC
    d. Supply shock

18. An _____, in economics, is the amount by which the real Gross domestic product exceeds potential GDP. The real GDP is also known as GDP 'adjusted for inflation', 'constant prices' GDP or 'constant dollar' GDP, because it measures the aggregate output in a country's income accounts in a given year, expressed in base-year prices. On the other hand, the potential GDP is the quantity of real GDP when a country's economy is at full-employment.
    a. AD-IA Model
    b. ACCRA Cost of Living Index
    c. Inflationary gap
    d. ACEA agreement

19. The _____ is a concept of economic activity developed in particular by Milton Friedman and Edmund Phelps in the 1960s, both recipients of the Nobel prize in economics. In both cases, the development of the concept is cited as a main motivation behind the prize. It represents the hypothetical unemployment rate consistent with aggregate production being at the 'long-run' level.
    a. Romer Model
    b. Robertson lag
    c. Natural rate of unemployment
    d. Real Business Cycle Theory

20. In economic models, the _____ time frame assumes no fixed factors of production. Firms can enter or leave the marketplace, and the cost (and availability) of land, labor, raw materials, and capital goods can be assumed to vary. In contrast, in the short-run time frame, certain factors are assumed to be fixed, because there is not sufficient time for them to change.
    a. Diseconomies of scale
    b. Long-run
    c. Price/performance ratio
    d. Productivity world

Chapter 33. THE TRADE-OFF BETWEEN INFLATION AND UNEMPLOYMENT

21. _____ and Keynesian Theory) is a macroeconomic theory based on the ideas of 20th-century British economist John Maynard Keynes. _____ argues that private sector decisions sometimes lead to inefficient macroeconomic outcomes and therefore advocates active policy responses by the public sector, including monetary policy actions by the central bank and fiscal policy actions by the government to stabilize output over the business cycle.

The theories forming the basis of _____ were first presented in The General Theory of Employment, Interest and Money, published in 1936.

a. Rational choice theory
b. Deflation
c. Market failure
d. Keynesian economics

22. The term _____ refers to government debt, expenditures and revenues, or to finance (particularly financial revenue) in general.

- _____ deficit is the budget deficit of federal or local government
- _____ policy is the discretionary spending of governments. Contrasts with monetary policy.
- _____ year and _____ quarter are reporting periods for firms and other agencies.

a. Bucket shop
b. Procter ' Gamble
c. Drawdown
d. Fiscal

23. In economics, _____ is the use of government spending and revenue collection to influence the economy.

_____ can be contrasted with the other main type of economic policy, monetary policy, which attempts to stabilize the economy by controlling interest rates and the supply of money. The two main instruments of _____ are government spending and taxation.

a. Sustainable investment rule
b. Fiscal policy
c. 100-year flood
d. Fiscalism

24. _____ is the process by which the government, central bank (ii) availability of money, and (iii) cost of money or rate of interest, in order to attain a set of objectives oriented towards the growth and stability of the economy. Monetary theory provides insight into how to craft optimal _____.

_____ is referred to as either being an expansionary policy where an expansionary policy increases the total supply of money in the economy, and a contractionary policy decreases the total money supply.

a. Monetary policy
b. 130-30 fund
c. 100-year flood
d. 1921 recession

25. In economics, the concept of the _____ refers to the decision-making time frame of a firm in which at least one factor of production is fixed. Costs which are fixed in the _____ have no impact on a firms decisions. For example a firm can raise output by increasing the amount of labour through overtime.

Chapter 33. THE TRADE-OFF BETWEEN INFLATION AND UNEMPLOYMENT

a. Productivity model
b. Short-run
c. Hicks-neutral technical change
d. Product Pipeline

26. In economics, _____ is equal to total cost divided by the number of goods produced (the output quantity, Q.) It is also equal to the sum of average variable costs (total variable costs divided by Q) plus average fixed costs (total fixed costs divided by Q.) _____s may be dependent on the time period considered (increasing production may be expensive or impossible in the short term, for example.)
a. Explicit cost
b. Average variable cost
c. Average fixed cost
d. Average cost

27. The _____ is the central banking system of the United States. Created in 1913 by the enactment of the Federal Reserve Act (signed by Woodrow Wilson), it is a quasi-public and quasi-private (government entity with private components) banking system that comprises (1) the presidentially appointed Board of Governors of the _____ in Washington, D.C.; (2) the Federal Open Market Committee; (3) twelve regional Federal Reserve Banks located in major cities throughout the nation acting as fiscal agents for the U.S. Treasury, each with its own nine-member board of directors; (4) numerous other private U.S. member banks, which subscribe to required amounts of non-transferable stock in their regional Federal Reserve Banks; and (5) various advisory councils. Since February 2006, Ben Bernanke has served as the Chairman of the Board of Governors of the _____.
a. Term auction facility
b. Federal Reserve System Open Market Account
c. Monetary Policy Report to the Congress
d. Federal Reserve System

28. _____ is an economic policy in which a central bank estimates and makes public a projected, or 'target,' inflation rate and then attempts to steer actual inflation towards the target through the use of interest rate changes and other monetary tools.

Because interest rates and the inflation rate tend to be inversely related, the likely moves of the central bank to raise or lower interest rates become more transparent under the policy of _____. Examples:

- if inflation appears to be above the target, the bank is likely to raise interest rates. This usually (but not always) has the effect over time of cooling the economy and bringing down inflation.

- if inflation appears to be below the target, the bank is likely to lower interest rates. This usually (again, not always) has the effect over time of accelerating the economy and raising inflation.

a. Incomes policies
b. Employment Cost Index
c. Inflation swap
d. Inflation targeting

29. In economics and finance, _____ is the change in total cost that arises when the quantity produced changes by one unit. It is the cost of producing one more unit of a good. Mathematically, the _____ function is expressed as the first derivative of the total cost (TC) function with respect to quantity (Q.)
a. Marginal cost
b. Variable cost
c. Quality costs
d. Khozraschyot

30. In economics, _____ is the total amount of money available in an economy at a particular point in time. There are several ways to define 'money', but standard measures usually include currency in circulation and demand deposits.

Chapter 33. THE TRADE-OFF BETWEEN INFLATION AND UNEMPLOYMENT

_____ data are recorded and published, usually by the government or the central bank of the country.

a. Money supply
c. Veil of money

b. Velocity of money
d. Neutrality of money

31. _____ is an assumption used in many contemporary macroeconomic models, and also in other areas of contemporary economics and game theory and in other applications of rational choice theory.

Since most macroeconomic models today study decisions over many periods, the expectations of workers, consumers, and firms about future economic conditions are an essential part of the model. How to model these expectations has long been controversial, and it is well known that the macroeconomic predictions of the model may differ depending on the assumptions made about expectations

a. Minimum wage
c. Balanced-growth equilibrium

b. Potential output
d. Rational expectations

32. A _____ is a package or set of measures introduced to stabilise a financial system or economy. The term can refer to policies in two distinct sets of circumstances: business cycle stabilization and crisis stabilization.

Stabilization can refer to correcting the normal behavior of the business cycle.

a. Volunteers for Economic Growth Alliance
c. Capacity Development

b. New International Economic Order
d. Stabilization policy

33. In economics, a _____ is a general slowdown in economic activity over a sustained period of time, or a business cycle contraction. During _____s, many macroeconomic indicators vary in a similar way. Production as measured by Gross Domestic Product (GDP), employment, investment spending, capacity utilization, household incomes and business profits all fall during _____s.

a. Treasury View
c. Leading indicators

b. Monetary economics
d. Recession

34. _____ is an economic model based on price, utility and quantity in a market. It predicts that in a competitive market, price will function to equalize the quantity demanded by consumers, and the quantity supplied by producers, resulting in an economic equilibrium of price and quantity. The model incorporates other factors changing equilibrium as a shift of demand and/or supply.

a. Deferred gratification
c. Rational addiction

b. Supply and demand
d. Joint demand

35. In economics, _____ is the ratio of the percent change in one variable to the percent change in another variable. It is a tool for measuring the responsiveness of a function to changes in parameters in a relative way. Commonly analyzed are _____ of substitution, price and wealth.

a. ACEA agreement
c. Elasticity of demand

b. ACCRA Cost of Living Index
d. Elasticity

Chapter 33. THE TRADE-OFF BETWEEN INFLATION AND UNEMPLOYMENT

36. An _____ is a clause in a lease or contract that guarantees a change in the agreement price once a particular factor beyond control of either party affecting the value has been determined.

_____s are quite common in construction contracts to cover unexpected costs due to fluctuations in the prices for raw materials, fuel, and labor during the course of the construction project.

    a. Importation right
    c. Escalator clause
    b. Employment protection legislation
    d. Equal opportunity

37. A _____ is a legal document that is often passed by the legislature, and approved by the chief executive-or president. For example, only certain types of revenue may be imposed and collected. Property tax is frequently the basis for municipal and county revenues, while sales tax and/or income tax are the basis for state revenues, and income tax and corporate tax are the basis for national revenues.
    a. Government budget
    c. Lump-sum tax
    b. Structural deficit
    d. Right-financing

38. In economics, a _____ is a redistribution of income in the market system. These payments are considered to be nonexhaustive because they do not directly absorb resources or create output. Examples of certain _____s include welfare (financial aid), social security, and government subsidies for certain businesses (firms.)
    a. 1921 recession
    c. Transfer payment
    b. 100-year flood
    d. 130-30 fund

39. A _____ is the transfer of wealth from one party (such as a person or company) to another. A _____ is usually made in exchange for the provision of goods, services or both, or to fulfill a legal obligation.

The simplest and oldest form of _____ is barter, the exchange of one good or service for another.

    a. Soft count
    c. Payment
    b. Social gravity
    d. Going concern

40. To _____ is to impose a financial charge or other levy upon a taxpayer by a state or the functional equivalent of a state.

_____es are also imposed by many subnational entities. _____es consist of direct _____ or indirect _____, and may be paid in money or as its labour equivalent (often but not always unpaid.)

    a. Tax
    c. 100-year flood
    b. 130-30 fund
    d. 1921 recession

41. To tax is to impose a financial charge or other levy upon a taxpayer by a state or the functional equivalent of a state.

_____ are also imposed by many subnational entities. _____ consist of direct tax or indirect tax, and may be paid in money or as its labour equivalent (often but not always unpaid.)

a. 130-30 fund
b. 1921 recession
c. 100-year flood
d. Taxes

42. The _____ is the multiple by which Aggregate demand will increase, when there is an increase in transfer payments (e.g. welfare spending, unemployment payments.) Changes in spending usually lead to a larger than one for one increase in Aggregate demand, because any increase in household incomes caused by the increase in spending also increases in consumption spending, which further increases Aggregate demand.

a. Market-based instruments
b. Legal monopoly
c. Transfer payments Multiplier
d. Cost-effectiveness analysis

Chapter 34. INTERNATIONAL TRADE AND COMPARATIVE ADVANTAGE

1. In economics, _____ refers to the ability of a person or a country to produce a particular good at a lower marginal cost and opportunity cost than another person or country. It is the ability to produce a product most efficiently given all the other products that could be produced. It can be contrasted with absolute advantage which refers to the ability of a person or a country to produce a particular good at a lower absolute cost than another.
    a. Triffin dilemma
    b. Gravity model of trade
    c. Hot money
    d. Comparative advantage

2. _____ in its literal sense is the process of transformation of local or regional phenomena into global ones. It can be described as a process by which the people of the world are unified into a single society and function together.

This process is a combination of economic, technological, sociocultural and political forces.

    a. Globally Integrated Enterprise
    b. Helsinki Process on Globalisation and Democracy
    c. Globalization
    d. Global Cosmopolitanism

3. In economics, an _____ is any good (e.g. a commodity) or service brought into one country from another country in a legitimate fashion, typically for use in trade. It is a good that is brought in from another country for sale. _____ goods or services are provided to domestic consumers by foreign producers. An _____ in the receiving country is an export to the sending country.
    a. Economic integration
    b. Import quota
    c. Incoterms
    d. Import

4. _____ is exchange of capital, goods, and services across international borders or territories. In most countries, it represents a significant share of gross domestic product (GDP.) While _____ has been present throughout much of history, its economic, social, and political importance has been on the rise in recent centuries.
    a. Incoterms
    b. Import license
    c. Intra-industry trade
    d. International trade

5. _____ is a type of trade policy that allows traders to act and transact without interference from government. Thus, the policy permits trading partners mutual gains from trade, with goods and services produced according to the theory of comparative advantage.

Under a _____ policy, prices are a reflection of true supply and demand, and are the sole determinant of resource allocation.

    a. 100-year flood
    b. 1921 recession
    c. 130-30 fund
    d. Free Trade

6. The _____ is a trilateral trade bloc in North America created by the governments of the United States, Canada, and Mexico. The agreement creating the trade bloc came into force on January 1, 1994. It superseded the Canada-United States Free Trade Agreement between the U.S. and Canada.
    a. Demand-side technologies
    b. Case-Shiller Home Price Indices
    c. North American Free Trade Agreement
    d. Federal Reserve Bank Notes

7. _____ describes the relocation by a company of a business process from one country to another -- typically an operational process, such as manufacturing such as accounting. Even state governments employ _____.

Chapter 34. INTERNATIONAL TRADE AND COMPARATIVE ADVANTAGE

The term is in use in several distinct but closely related ways.

a. Offshore outsourcing
b. Offshoring
c. ACEA agreement
d. ACCRA Cost of Living Index

8. A _____, reserve bank, or monetary authority is the entity responsible for the monetary policy of a country or of a group of member states. It is a bank that can lend money to other banks in times of need. Its primary responsibility is to maintain the stability of the national currency and money supply, but more active duties include controlling subsidized-loan interest rates, and acting as a lender of last resort to the banking sector during times of financial crisis (private banks often being integral to the national financial system.)

a. Central bank
b. 100-year flood
c. 1921 recession
d. 130-30 fund

9. The _____ or gross domestic income (GDI), a basic measure of an economy's economic performance, is the market value of all final goods and services produced within the borders of a nation in a year. _____ can be defined in three ways, all of which are conceptually identical. First, it is equal to the total expenditures for all final goods and services produced within the country in a stipulated period of time (usually a 365-day year.)

a. Market structure
b. Monopolistic competition
c. Countercyclical
d. Gross domestic product

10. In economics, the _____ is a historical inverse relation between the rate of unemployment and the rate of inflation in an economy. Stated simply, the lower the unemployment in an economy, the higher the rate of increase in nominal wages in the economy. Rate of Change of Wages against Unemployment, United Kingdom 1913-1948 from Phillips (1958)

William Phillips, a New Zealand born economist, wrote a paper in 1958 titled The Relationship between Unemployment and the Rate of Change of Money Wages in the United Kingdom 1861-1957, which was published in the quarterly journal Economica.

a. Demand curve
b. Cost curve
c. Phillips curve
d. Lorenz curve

11. An _____, in economics, is the amount by which the real Gross domestic product exceeds potential GDP. The real GDP is also known as GDP 'adjusted for inflation', 'constant prices' GDP or 'constant dollar' GDP, because it measures the aggregate output in a country's income accounts in a given year, expressed in base-year prices. On the other hand, the potential GDP is the quantity of real GDP when a country's economy is at full-employment.

a. AD-IA Model
b. ACEA agreement
c. ACCRA Cost of Living Index
d. Inflationary gap

12. In a _____ there is both a monopoly (a single seller) and monopsony (a single buyer) in the same market.

In such market price and output will be determined by the non economic forces like bargaining power of both buyer and seller. A _____ model is often used in situations where the switching costs of both sides are prohibitively high.

Chapter 34. INTERNATIONAL TRADE AND COMPARATIVE ADVANTAGE

a. Market concentration
b. Bilateral monopoly
c. Revenue-cap regulation
d. Price takers

13. In economics, a _____ exists when a specific individual or enterprise has sufficient control over a particular product or service to determine significantly the terms on which other individuals shall have access to it. Monopolies are thus characterized by a lack of economic competition for the good or service that they provide and a lack of viable substitute goods. The verb 'monopolize' refers to the process by which a firm gains persistently greater market share than what is expected under perfect competition.
   a. 100-year flood
   b. 1921 recession
   c. 130-30 fund
   d. Monopoly

14. _____ is a misspelled phrase from Latin 'pro capite' phrase meaning per head with pro meaning 'per' or 'for each' and capite meaning 'head.' Both words together equate to the phrase 'for each head.'

It is usually used in the field of statistics to indicate the average per person for any given concern, such as income, crime rate, etc.

It is also used in wills to indicate that each of the named beneficiaries should receive, by devise or bequest, equal shares of the estate. This is in contrast to a per stirpes division, in which each branch of the inheriting family inherits an equal share of the estate.

   a. Population statistics
   b. Sargan test
   c. Per capita
   d. False positive rate

15. In finance, the _____s between two currencies specifies how much one currency is worth in terms of the other. It is the value of a foreign natione;s currency in terms of the home natione;s currency. For example an _____ of 102 Japanese yen to the United States dollar means that JPY 102 is worth the same as USD 1.
   a. Exchange rate
   b. Interbank market
   c. ACCRA Cost of Living Index
   d. ACEA agreement

16. In economics, _____ refers to the ability of a party to produce a good or service using fewer real resources than another entity producing the same good or service..A party has an _____ when using the same input as another party, it can produce a greater output. Since _____ is determined by a simple comparison of labor productivities, it is possible for a a party to have no _____ in anything. It can be contrasted with the concept of comparative advantage which refers to the ability to produce a particular good at a lower opportunity cost.
   a. ACCRA Cost of Living Index
   b. International economics
   c. Absolute advantage
   d. Index number

17. _____ is a common concept in economics, and gives rise to derived concepts such as consumer debt. Generally _____ is defined by opposition to production. But the precise definition can vary because different schools of economists define production quite differently.
   a. Consumption
   b. Cash or share options
   c. Foreclosure data providers
   d. Federal Reserve Bank Notes

Chapter 34. INTERNATIONAL TRADE AND COMPARATIVE ADVANTAGE

18. _____ in economics and business is the result of an exchange and from that trade we assign a numerical monetary value to a good, service or asset. If Alice trades Bob 4 apples for an orange, the _____ of an orange is 4 apples. Inversely, the _____ of an apple is 1/4 oranges.
    a. Price war
    b. Price book
    c. Price
    d. Premium pricing

19. _____ is money accepted for exchange of goods in an economy. The prevalence of one money over another arises, usually, when a government designates through decrees that the government shall accept only particular notes and coins in payment for taxes. Typically, money of _____ consists of stamped coins and minted paper bills.
    a. Totnes pound
    b. Security thread
    c. Local currency
    d. Currency

20. A _____ is an expression that compares quantities relative to each other. The most common examples involve two quantities, but any number of quantities can be compared. _____s are represented mathematically by separating each quantity with a colon, for example the _____ 2:3, which is read as the _____ 'two to three'.
    a. 100-year flood
    b. 130-30 fund
    c. Y-intercept
    d. Ratio

21. In microeconomics, _____ is quite simply the conversion of inputs into outputs. It is an economic process that uses resources to create a good or service that is suitable for exchange. This can include manufacturing, storing, shipping, and packaging.
    a. MET
    b. Solved
    c. Production
    d. Red Guards

22. _____ was a survey conducted by the U.S. Department of Justice to gauge the prevalence of alcohol and illegal drug use among prior arrestees. It was a reformulation of the prior Drug Use Forecasting (DUF) program, focused on five drugs in particular: cocaine, marijuana, methamphetamine, opiates, and PCP.

Participants were randomly selected from arrest records in major metropolitan areas; because no personally identifying information is taken from each record chosen, the resulting data can be correlated to arrest rates, but not to the total population of persons charged.

    a. ACCRA Cost of Living Index
    b. Arrestee Drug Abuse Monitoring
    c. AD-IA Model
    d. ACEA agreement

23. _____ is an economic theory that holds that the prosperity of a nation is dependent upon its supply of capital, and that the global volume of international trade is 'unchangeable.' Economic assets or capital, are represented by bullion (gold, silver, and trade value) held by the state, which is best increased through a positive balance of trade with other nations (exports minus imports.) _____ suggests that the ruling government should advance these goals by playing a protectionist role in the economy; by encouraging exports and discouraging imports, notably through the use of tariffs and subsidies.

_____ was the dominant school of thought throughout the early modern period (from the 16th to the 18th century.)

a. Nominal value
b. Consumer theory
c. General equilibrium theory
d. Mercantilism

24. _____ was a Scottish moral philosopher and a pioneer of political economy. One of the key figures of the Scottish Enlightenment, Smith is the author of The Theory of Moral Sentiments and An Inquiry into the Nature and Causes of the Wealth of Nations. The latter, usually abbreviated as The Wealth of Nations, is considered his magnum opus and the first modern work of economics.
   a. Adolf Hitler
   b. Alan Greenspan
   c. Adolph Fischer
   d. Adam Smith

25. A _____ is a duty imposed on goods when they are moved across a political boundary. They are usually associated with protectionism, the economic policy of restraining trade between nations. For political reasons, _____s are usually imposed on imported goods, although they may also be imposed on exported goods.
   a. Tariff
   b. 1921 recession
   c. 100-year flood
   d. 130-30 fund

26. The _____ commenced in September 1986 and continued until April 1994. The round, based on the General Agreement on Tariffs and Trade (GATT) ministerial meeting in Geneva (1982), was launched in Punta del Este in Uruguay (hence the name), followed by negotiations in Montreal, Geneva, Brussels, Washington, D.C., and Tokyo, with the 20 agreements finally being signed in Marrakech - the Marrakesh Agreement. The Round transformed the GATT into the World Trade Organization.
   a. ACCRA Cost of Living Index
   b. AD-IA Model
   c. Uruguay Round
   d. ACEA agreement

27. In economics, a _____ is any economic system that effects its distribution of goods and services with prices and employing any form of money or debt tokens. Except for possible remote and primitive communities, all modern societies use _____s to allocate resources. However, _____s are not used for all resource allocation decisions today.
   a. Hanseatic League
   b. Price system
   c. Neomercantilism
   d. Family economy

28. The _____ consists of a number of economic theories which describe the nature of the firm, company including its existence, its behaviour, and its relationship with the market.

In simplified terms, the _____ aims to answer these questions:

1. Existence - why do firms emerge, why are not all transactions in the economy mediated over the market?
2. Boundaries - why the boundary between firms and the market is located exactly there? Which transactions are performed internally and which are negotiated on the market?
3. Organization - why are firms structured in such specific way? What is the interplay of formal and informal relationships?

Despite looking simple, these questions are not answered by the established economic theory, which usually views firms as given, and treats them as black boxes without any internal structure.

Chapter 34. INTERNATIONAL TRADE AND COMPARATIVE ADVANTAGE 301

The First World War period saw a change of emphasis in economic theory away from industry-level analysis which mainly included analysing markets to analysis at the level of the firm, as it became increasingly clear that perfect competition was no longer an adequate model of how firms behaved. Economic theory till then had focussed on trying to understand markets alone and there had been little study on understanding why firms or organisations exist.

- a. Technology gap
- b. Theory of the firm
- c. Policy Ineffectiveness Proposition
- d. Khazzoom-Brookes postulate

29. In economics, an _____ is any good or commodity, transported from one country to another country in a legitimate fashion, typically for use in trade. _____ goods or services are provided to foreign consumers by domestic producers. _____ is an important part of international trade.
- a. Export
- b. ACEA agreement
- c. AD-IA Model
- d. ACCRA Cost of Living Index

30. _____ is a government policy to encourage export of goods and discourage sale of goods on the domestic market through low-cost loans or tax relief for exporters, or government financed international advertising or R'D. An _____ reduces the price paid by foreign importers, which means domestic consumers pay more than foreign consumers. The WTO prohibits most subsidies directly linked to the volume of exports.
- a. Economic activity rate
- b. Illicit financial flows
- c. Economic repression
- d. Export subsidy

31. The _____ is an important selective, mainly private, international organization designed by its founders to supervise and liberalize international trade. The organization officially commenced on 1 January 1995, under the Marrakesh Agreement, succeeding the 1947 General Agreement on Tariffs and Trade (GATT.)

The _____ deals with regulation of trade between participating countries; it provides a framework for negotiating and formalising trade agreements, and a dispute resolution process aimed at enforcing participants' adherence to _____ agreements which are signed by representatives of member governments and ratified by their parliaments.

- a. Backus-Kehoe-Kydland consumption correlation puzzle
- b. 2009 G-20 London summit protests
- c. World Trade Organization
- d. Bio-energy village

32. In finance, a _____ is a debt security, in which the authorized issuer owes the holders a debt and, depending on the terms of the _____, is obliged to pay interest (the coupon) and/or to repay the principal at a later date, termed maturity. A _____ is a formal contract to repay borrowed money with interest at fixed intervals.

Thus a _____ is like a loan: the issuer is the borrower (debtor), the holder is the lender (creditor), and the coupon is the interest.

- a. Callable
- b. Prize Bond
- c. Zero-coupon
- d. Bond

Chapter 34. INTERNATIONAL TRADE AND COMPARATIVE ADVANTAGE

33. _____ is the economic policy of restraining trade between states, through methods such as tariffs on imported goods, restrictive quotas, and a variety of other restrictive government regulations designed to discourage imports, and prevent foreign take-over of local markets and companies. This policy is closely aligned with anti-globalization, and contrasts with free trade, where government barriers to trade are kept to a minimum. The term is mostly used in the context of economics, where _____ refers to policies or doctrines which 'protect' businesses and workers within a country by restricting or regulating trade with foreign nations.
- a. Google economy
- b. Knowledge economy
- c. Digital economy
- d. Protectionism

34. In economics, a _____ is a general slowdown in economic activity over a sustained period of time, or a business cycle contraction. During _____s, many macroeconomic indicators vary in a similar way. Production as measured by Gross Domestic Product (GDP), employment, investment spending, capacity utilization, household incomes and business profits all fall during _____s.
- a. Treasury View
- b. Recession
- c. Leading indicators
- d. Monetary economics

35. Economics:

- _____,the desire to own something and the ability to pay for it
- _____ curve,a graphic representation of a _____ schedule
- _____ deposit, the money in checking accounts
- _____ pull theory,the theory that inflation occurs when _____ for goods and services exceeds existing supplies
- _____ schedule,a table that lists the quantity of a good a person will buy it each different price
- _____ side economics,the school of economics at believes government spending and tax cuts open economy by raising _____

- a. Variability
- b. Production
- c. McKesson ' Robbins scandal
- d. Demand

36. In economics, the _____ can be defined as the graph depicting the relationship between the price of a certain commodity, and the amount of it that consumers are willing and able to purchase at that given price. It is a graphic representation of a demand schedule. The _____ for all consumers together follows from the _____ of every individual consumer: the individual demands at each price are added together.
- a. Demand curve
- b. Wage curve
- c. Cost curve
- d. Kuznets curve

37. In neoclassical economics and microeconomics, _____ describes the perfect being a market in which there are many small firms, all producing homogeneous goods. In the short term, such markets are productively inefficient as output will not occur where mc is equal to ac, but allocatively efficient, as output under _____ will always occur where mc is equal to mr, and therefore where mc equals ar. However, in the long term, such markets are both allocatively and productively efficient.
- a. Perfect competition
- b. Law of supply
- c. Co-operative economics
- d. General equilibrium

Chapter 34. INTERNATIONAL TRADE AND COMPARATIVE ADVANTAGE

38. _____ is a program of the United States Department of Labor that provides a variety of reemployment services and benefits to workers who have lost their jobs or suffered a reduction of hours and wages as a result of increased imports or shifts in production outside the United States. The _____ program aims to help program participants obtain new jobs, ensuring they retain employment and earn wages comparable to their prior employment.

_____ was established as part of the Trade Expansion Act in 1962, during the Presidency of John F. Kennedy.

a. New Economic Policy
b. Financial Crimes Enforcement Network
c. Delancey Street Foundation
d. Trade adjustment assistance

39. _____ was the first United States Secretary of the Treasury, a Founding Father, economist, and political philosopher. He led calls for the Philadelphia Convention, was one of America's first Constitutional lawyers, and cowrote the Federalist Papers, a primary source for Constitutional interpretation.

Born on the British West Indian island of Nevis, Hamilton was educated in the Thirteen Colonies.

a. Adam Smith
b. American exceptionalism
c. Economic impact of immigration
d. Alexander Hamilton

40. The _____ is an economic and political union of 27 member states, located primarily in Europe. It was established by the Treaty of Maastricht on 1 November 1993, upon the foundations of the pre-existing European Economic Community. With a population of almost 500 million, the _____ generates an estimated 30% share (US$18.4 trillion in 2008) of the nominal gross world product.

a. ACEA agreement
b. ACCRA Cost of Living Index
c. European Court of Justice
d. European Union

41. In economics, a _____ is a table that lists the quantity of a good a person will buy it each different price See Demand curve.

a. Demand schedule
b. Federal Reserve districts
c. Rational irrationality
d. Free contract

42. The supply of labor is the number of total hours that workers wish to work at a given real wage rate.

_____ curves are derived from the 'labor-leisure' trade-off. More hours worked earn higher incomes but necessitate a cut in the amount of leisure that workers enjoy.

a. Human trafficking
b. Creative capitalism
c. Late capitalism
d. Labor supply

43. _____ is one of the four Ps of the marketing mix. The other three aspects are product, promotion, and place. It is also a key variable in microeconomic price allocation theory.

a. Premium pricing
b. Pricing
c. Point of total assumption
d. Guaranteed Maximum Price

Chapter 35. THE INTERNATIONAL MONETARY SYSTEM: ORDER OR DISORDER?

1. A _____ secures the proper functioning of money by regulating economic agents, transaction types, and money supply.

_____s are traditionally formed by the policy decisions of individual governments and administrated as a domestic economic issue.

The current trend, however, is to use international trade and investment to alter the policy and legislation of individual governments.

 a. Financial rand
 b. Monetary system
 c. Consumer basket
 d. Netting

2. _____ refers to the theory that the United States occupies a special niche among developed nations in terms of its national credo, historical evolution, political and religious institutions and unique origins. The roots of the term are attributed to Alexis de Tocqueville, who noted that the then-50-year-old United States held a special place among nations, because it was a country of immigrants and the first modern democracy.
 a. Adam Smith
 b. Economic impact of immigration
 c. International-Communist-Judaeo-Masonic Conspiracy
 d. American exceptionalism

3. _____ is a term used in accounting relating to the increase in value of an asset. In this sense it is the reverse of depreciation, which measures the fall in value of assets over their normal life-time.

_____ is a rise of a currency in a floating exchange rate.

 a. ACCRA Cost of Living Index
 b. ACEA agreement
 c. AD-IA Model
 d. Appreciation

4. In finance, the _____s between two currencies specifies how much one currency is worth in terms of the other. It is the value of a foreign natione;s currency in terms of the home natione;s currency. For example an _____ of 102 Japanese yen to the United States dollar means that JPY 102 is worth the same as USD 1.
 a. Exchange rate
 b. ACEA agreement
 c. Interbank market
 d. ACCRA Cost of Living Index

5. In economics, _____ is the total demand for final goods and services in the economy (Y) at a given time and price level. It is the amount of goods and services in the economy that will be purchased at all possible price levels. This is the demand for the gross domestic product of a country when inventory levels are static.
 a. Aggregate demand
 b. Aggregate expenditure
 c. Aggregate supply
 d. Aggregation problem

6. _____ is money accepted for exchange of goods in an economy. The prevalence of one money over another arises, usually, when a government designates through decrees that the government shall accept only particular notes and coins in payment for taxes. Typically, money of _____ consists of stamped coins and minted paper bills.
 a. Currency
 b. Local currency
 c. Security thread
 d. Totnes pound

Chapter 35. THE INTERNATIONAL MONETARY SYSTEM: ORDER OR DISORDER? 305

7. Economics:

    - _____, the desire to own something and the ability to pay for it
    - _____ curve, a graphic representation of a _____ schedule
    - _____ deposit, the money in checking accounts
    - _____ pull theory, the theory that inflation occurs when _____ for goods and services exceeds existing supplies
    - _____ schedule, a table that lists the quantity of a good a person will buy it each different price
    - _____ side economics, the school of economics at believes government spending and tax cuts open economy by raising _____

    a. McKesson ' Robbins scandal
    b. Variability
    c. Production
    d. Demand

8. _____ is the a method of technical and economic research of the systems for purpose to optimize a parity between system's consumer functions or properties and expenses to achieve those functions or properties.

This methodology for continuous perfection of production, industrial technologies, organizational structures was developed by Juryj Sobolev in 1948 at the 'Perm telephone factory'

- 1948 Juryj Sobolev - the first success in application of a method analysis at the 'Perm telephone factory' .
- 1949 - the first application for the invention as result of use of the new method.

Today in economically developed countries practically each enterprise or the company use methodology of the kind of functional-cost analysis as a practice of the quality management, most full satisfying to principles of standards of series ISO 9000.

- Interest of consumer not in products itself, but the advantage which it will receive from its usage.
- The consumer aspires to reduce his expenses
- Functions needed by consumer can be executed in the various ways, and, hence, with various efficiency and expenses. Among possible alternatives of realization of functions exist such in which the parity of quality and the price is the optimal for the consumer.

The goal of _____ is achievement of the highest consumer satisfaction of production at simultaneous decrease in all kinds of industrial expenses Classical _____ has three English synonyms - Value Engineering, Value Management, Value Analysis.

a. Staple financing
b. Willingness to pay
c. Function cost analysis
d. Monopoly wage

9. In economics, the _____ can be defined as the graph depicting the relationship between the price of a certain commodity, and the amount of it that consumers are willing and able to purchase at that given price. It is a graphic representation of a demand schedule. The _____ for all consumers together follows from the _____ of every individual consumer: the individual demands at each price are added together.

a. Wage curve
c. Kuznets curve
b. Cost curve
d. Demand curve

10. _____ is a reduction in the value of a currency with respect to other monetary units. In common modern usage, it specifically implies an official lowering of the value of a country's currency within a fixed exchange rate system, by which the monetary authority formally sets a new fixed rate with respect to a foreign reference currency. In contrast, (currency) depreciation is used for the unofficial decrease in the exchange rate in a floating exchange rate system.
   a. Reserve currency
   b. Petrodollar recycling
   c. Devaluation
   d. Texas redbacks

11. The _____ is an economic and political union of 27 member states, located primarily in Europe. It was established by the Treaty of Maastricht on 1 November 1993, upon the foundations of the pre-existing European Economic Community. With a population of almost 500 million, the _____ generates an estimated 30% share (US$18.4 trillion in 2008) of the nominal gross world product.
   a. European Court of Justice
   b. ACEA agreement
   c. ACCRA Cost of Living Index
   d. European Union

12. A _____ or a flexible exchange rate is a type of exchange rate regime wherein a currency's value is allowed to fluctuate according to the foreign exchange market. A currency that uses a _____ is known as a floating currency. The opposite of a _____ is a fixed exchange rate.
   a. Floating currency
   b. Trade Weighted US dollar Index
   c. Foreign exchange market
   d. Floating exchange rate

13. A _____ is a theoretical term that economists use to describe a market which is free from government intervention (i.e. no regulation, no subsidization, no single monetary system and no governmental monopolies.) In a _____, property rights are voluntarily exchanged at a price arranged solely by the mutual consent of sellers and buyers. By definition, buyers and sellers do not coerce each other, in the sense that they obtain each other's property without the use of physical force, threat of physical force, or fraud, nor is the coerced by a third party (such as by government via transfer payments) and they engage in trade simply because they both consent and believe that it is a good enough choice.
   a. Leninism
   b. Third camp
   c. Delegation
   d. Free market

14. _____ is a type of trade policy that allows traders to act and transact without interference from government. Thus, the policy permits trading partners mutual gains from trade, with goods and services produced according to the theory of comparative advantage.

Under a _____ policy, prices are a reflection of true supply and demand, and are the sole determinant of resource allocation.

   a. 130-30 fund
   b. Free trade
   c. 100-year flood
   d. 1921 recession

15. A _____ is any systematic process enabling many market players to bid and ask: helping bidders and sellers interact and make deals. It is not just the price mechanism but the entire system of regulation, qualification, credentials, reputations and clearing that surrounds that mechanism and makes it operate in a social context.

Chapter 35. THE INTERNATIONAL MONETARY SYSTEM:ORDER OR DISORDER?

Because a _____ relies on the assumption that players are constantly involved and unequally enabled, a _____ is distinguished specifically from a voting system where candidates seek the support of voters on a less regular basis.

   a. Competitive equilibrium
   c. Price mechanism
   b. Contestable market
   d. Market system

16. _____ in economics and business is the result of an exchange and from that trade we assign a numerical monetary value to a good, service or asset. If Alice trades Bob 4 apples for an orange, the _____ of an orange is 4 apples. Inversely, the _____ of an apple is 1/4 oranges.

   a. Price
   c. Price book
   b. Price war
   d. Premium pricing

17. In economics, a _____ is any economic system that effects its distribution of goods and services with prices and employing any form of money or debt tokens. Except for possible remote and primitive communities, all modern societies use _____s to allocate resources. However, _____s are not used for all resource allocation decisions today.

   a. Hanseatic League
   c. Price system
   b. Neomercantilism
   d. Family economy

18. _____ means a rise of a price of goods or products. This term is specially used as _____ of a currency, where it means a rise of currency to the relation with a foreign currency in a fixed exchange rate. In floating exchange rate correct term would be appreciation.

   a. Death spiral financing
   c. Legal monopoly
   b. Deglobalization
   d. Revaluation

19. A _____, reserve bank, or monetary authority is the entity responsible for the monetary policy of a country or of a group of member states. It is a bank that can lend money to other banks in times of need. Its primary responsibility is to maintain the stability of the national currency and money supply, but more active duties include controlling subsidized-loan interest rates, and acting as a lender of last resort to the banking sector during times of financial crisis (private banks often being integral to the national financial system.)

   a. Central bank
   c. 100-year flood
   b. 130-30 fund
   d. 1921 recession

20. In economics, a _____ is a table that lists the quantity of a good a person will buy it each different price See Demand curve.

   a. Free contract
   c. Federal Reserve districts
   b. Rational irrationality
   d. Demand schedule

21. _____ is an economic model based on price, utility and quantity in a market. It predicts that in a competitive market, price will function to equalize the quantity demanded by consumers, and the quantity supplied by producers, resulting in an economic equilibrium of price and quantity. The model incorporates other factors changing equilibrium as a shift of demand and/or supply.

   a. Rational addiction
   c. Joint demand
   b. Deferred gratification
   d. Supply and demand

Chapter 35. THE INTERNATIONAL MONETARY SYSTEM: ORDER OR DISORDER?

22. _____ is a phrase that may take on different meanings in different contexts.

In the language of crime, _____ refers to stolen currency that can easily be traced back to the crime, such as marked bills or new currency with consecutive serial numbers. It is also known as bait money.

   a. Hot money
   b. Comparative advantage
   c. Small open economy
   d. Gravity model of trade

23. _____ is a fee paid on borrowed assets. It is the price paid for the use of borrowed money, or, money earned by deposited funds. Assets that are sometimes lent with _____ include money, shares, consumer goods through hire purchase, major assets such as aircraft, and even entire factories in finance lease arrangements.
   a. Internal debt
   b. Interest
   c. Asset protection
   d. Insolvency

24. An _____ is the price a borrower pays for the use of money they do not own, for instance a small company might borrow from a bank to kick start their business, and the return a lender receives for deferring the use of funds, by lending it to the borrower. _____s are normally expressed as a percentage rate over the period of one year.

_____s targets are also a vital tool of monetary policy and are used to control variables like investment, inflation, and unemployment.

   a. Arrow-Debreu model
   b. ACCRA Cost of Living Index
   c. Enterprise value
   d. Interest rate

25. _____ refers to a business or organization attempting to acquire goods or services to accomplish the goals of the enterprise. Though there are several organizations that attempt to set standards in the _____ process, processes can vary greatly between organizations. Typically the word '_____' is not used interchangeably with the word 'procurement', since procurement typically includes Expediting, Supplier Quality, and Traffic and Logistics (T'L) in addition to _____.
   a. 130-30 fund
   b. Free port
   c. 100-year flood
   d. Purchasing

26. _____ is the number of goods/services that can be purchased with a unit of currency. For example, if you had taken one dollar to a store in the 1950s, you would have been able to buy a greater number of items than you would today, indicating that you would have had a greater _____ in the 1950s. Currency can be either a commodity money, like gold or silver, or fiat currency like US dollars.
   a. Purchasing power
   b. Compliance cost
   c. Human Poverty Index
   d. Genuine progress indicator

27. The _____ theory uses the long-term equilibrium exchange rate of two currencies to equalize their purchasing power. Developed by Gustav Cassel in 1920, it is based on the law of one price: the theory states that, in ideally efficient markets, identical goods should have only one price.

This purchasing power SEM rate equalizes the purchasing power of different currencies in their home countries for a given basket of goods.

Chapter 35. THE INTERNATIONAL MONETARY SYSTEM: ORDER OR DISORDER?

a. Purchasing power parity
c. Gross national product
b. Measures of national income and output
d. Bureau of Labor Statistics

28. _____s is the social science that studies the production, distribution, and consumption of goods and services. The term _____s comes from the Ancient Greek oá¼°κονομῖα from oá¼¶κος (oikos, 'house') + vÏŒμος (nomos, 'custom' or 'law'), hence 'rules of the house(hold)'. Current _____ models developed out of the broader field of political economy in the late 19th century, owing to a desire to use an empirical approach more akin to the physical sciences.
    a. Inflation
    c. Energy economics
    b. Economic
    d. Opportunity cost

29. _____ is a broad label that refers to any individuals or households that use goods and services generated within the economy. The concept of a _____ is used in different contexts, so that the usage and significance of the term may vary.

Typically when business people and economists talk of _____s they are talking about person as _____, an aggregated commodity item with little individuality other than that expressed in the buy/not-buy decision.

    a. 100-year flood
    c. 1921 recession
    b. 130-30 fund
    d. Consumer

30. A _____ is a measure of the average price of consumer goods and services purchased by households. A _____ measures a price change for a constant market basket of goods and services from one period to the next within the same area (city, region, or nation.) It is a price index determined by measuring the price of a standard group of goods meant to represent the typical market basket of a typical urban consumer.
    a. Consumer Price Index
    c. CPI
    b. Cost-of-living index
    d. Lipstick index

31. A _____ is a normalized average (typically a weighted average) of prices for a given class of goods or services in a given region, during a given interval of time. It is a statistic designed to help to compare how these prices, taken as a whole, differ between time periods or geographical locations.

Price indices have several potential uses.

    a. Product sabotage
    c. Transactional Net Margin Method
    b. Two-part tariff
    d. Price Index

32. In economics, _____ is a rise in the general level of prices of goods and services in an economy over a period of time. When the general price level rises, each unit of currency buys fewer goods and services; consequently, _____ is also a decline in the real value of money--a loss of purchasing power in the medium of exchange which is also the monetary unit of account in the economy. A chief measure of general price-level _____ is the general _____ rate, which is the percentage change in a general price index (normally the Consumer Price Index) over time.
    a. Opportunity cost
    c. Inflation
    b. Economic
    d. Energy economics

33. In economics, the _____ measures the payments that flow between any individual country and all other countries. It is used to summarize all international economic transactions for that country during a specific time period, usually a year. The _____ is determined by the country's exports and imports of goods, services, and financial capital, as well as financial transfers.

   a. Skyscraper Index
   b. Gross world product
   c. Gross domestic product per barrel
   d. Balance of payments

34. A _____, sometimes called a pegged exchange rate, is a type of exchange rate regime wherein a currency's value is matched to the value of another single currency or to a basket of other currencies such as gold.

A _____ is usually used to stabilize the value of a currency, vis-a-vis the currency it is pegged to. This facilitates trade and investments between the two countries, and is especially useful for small economies where external trade forms a large part of their GDP.

   a. Law of supply
   b. Monetary economics
   c. Leading indicators
   d. Fixed exchange rate

35. A _____ is a legal document that is often passed by the legislature, and approved by the chief executive-or president. For example, only certain types of revenue may be imposed and collected. Property tax is frequently the basis for municipal and county revenues, while sales tax and/or income tax are the basis for state revenues, and income tax and corporate tax are the basis for national revenues.

   a. Lump-sum tax
   b. Right-financing
   c. Structural deficit
   d. Government budget

36. A _____ is the transfer of wealth from one party (such as a person or company) to another. A _____ is usually made in exchange for the provision of goods, services or both, or to fulfill a legal obligation.

The simplest and oldest form of _____ is barter, the exchange of one good or service for another.

   a. Soft count
   b. Payment
   c. Going concern
   d. Social gravity

37. The _____ of monetary management established the rules for commercial and financial relations among the world's major industrial states in the mid 20th Century. The _____ was the first example of a fully negotiated monetary order intended to govern monetary relations among independent nation-states.

Preparing to rebuild the international economic system as World War II was still raging, 730 delegates from all 44 Allied nations gathered at the Mount Washington Hotel in Bretton Woods, New Hampshire, United States, for the United Nations Monetary and Financial Conference.

   a. 100-year flood
   b. 1921 recession
   c. 130-30 fund
   d. Bretton Woods system

38. In financial accounting, the _____ is one of the accounts in shareholders' equity. Sole proprietorships have a single _____ in the owner's equity. Partnerships maintain a _____ for each of the partners.

Chapter 35. THE INTERNATIONAL MONETARY SYSTEM:ORDER OR DISORDER?

a. Net national product
b. Compensation of employees
c. Capital account
d. Current account

39. The _____ is a monetary system in which a region's common medium of exchange are paper notes that are normally freely convertible into pre-set, fixed quantities of gold. The _____ is not currently used by any government, having been replaced completely by fiat currency. Gold certificates were used as paper currency in the United States from 1882 to 1933, these certificates were freely convertable into gold coins.

In the 1790s Britain suffered a massive shortage of silver coinage and ceased to mint larger silver coins.

a. 1921 recession
b. 100-year flood
c. Gold standard
d. 130-30 fund

40. _____, often referred to by his initials _____, was the 32nd President of the United States. He was a central figure of the 20th century during a time of worldwide economic crisis and world war. Elected to four terms in office, he served from 1933 to 1945 and is the only U.S. president to have served more than two terms.
a. Adolph Fischer
b. Adolf Hitler
c. Adam Smith
d. Franklin Delano Roosevelt

41. The _____ is an international organization that oversees the global financial system by following the macroeconomic policies of its member countries, in particular those with an impact on exchange rates and the balance of payments. It is an organization formed to stabilize international exchange rates and facilitate development. It also offers financial and technical assistance to its members, making it an international lender of last resort.
a. ACCRA Cost of Living Index
b. International Monetary Fund
c. ACEA agreement
d. Office of Thrift Supervision

42. In cases of extreme appreciation or depreciation, a central bank will normally intervene to stabilize the currency. Thus, the exchange rate regimes of floating currencies may more technically be known as a _____. A central bank might, for instance, allow a currency price to float freely between an upper and lower bound, a price 'ceiling' and 'floor'.
a. Triangular arbitrage
b. Continuous linked settlement
c. Foreign exchange reserves
d. Managed float

43. The _____ is the largest national economy in the world. Its gross domestic product (GDP) was estimated as $14.2 trillion in 2008. The U.S. economy maintains a high level of output per person (GDP per capita, $46,800 in 2008, ranked at around number ten in the world.)
a. ACEA agreement
b. AD-IA Model
c. ACCRA Cost of Living Index
d. Economy of the United States

44. The _____ is the official currency of 16 of the 27 member states of the European Union (EU.) The states, known collectively as the Eurozone, are Austria, Belgium, Cyprus, Finland, France, Germany, Greece, Ireland, Italy, Luxembourg, Malta, the Netherlands, Portugal, Slovakia, Slovenia, and Spain. The currency is also used in a further five European countries, with and without formal agreements and is consequently used daily by some 327 million Europeans.
a. Import and Export Price Indices
b. Euro
c. Equity capital market
d. IRS Code 3401

45. An economic and _____ is a single market with a common currency. It is to be distinguished from a mere currency union, which does not involve a single market. This is the fifth stage of economic integration.
   a. Commercial invoice
   b. Free trade zone
   c. Monetary union
   d. Customs union

46. In economics, the _____ is one of the two primary components of the balance of payments, the other being the capital account. It is the sum of the balance of trade (exports minus imports of goods and services), net factor income (such as interest and dividends) and net transfer payments (such as foreign aid.)

$$\text{Current account} = \text{Balance of trade} \\ + \text{Net factor income from abroad} \\ + \text{Net unilateral transfers from abroad}$$

The _____ balance is one of two major metrics of the nature of a country's foreign trade (the other being the net capital outflow.)

   a. Compensation of employees
   b. Gross private domestic investment
   c. National Income and Product Accounts
   d. Current account

Chapter 36. EXCHANGE BATES AND THE MACROECONOMY

1. An _____ is an economy in which people, including businesses, can trade in goods and services with other people and businesses in the international community at large. This contrasts with a closed economy in which international trade cannot take place.

The act of selling goods or services to a foreign country is called exporting.

 a. Indicative planning
 b. Attention work
 c. Information economy
 d. Open economy

2. In economics, _____ is the total demand for final goods and services in the economy (Y) at a given time and price level. It is the amount of goods and services in the economy that will be purchased at all possible price levels. This is the demand for the gross domestic product of a country when inventory levels are static.

 a. Aggregate demand
 b. Aggregate supply
 c. Aggregation problem
 d. Aggregate expenditure

3. The term _____ refers to economy-wide fluctuations in production or economic activity over several months or years. These fluctuations occur around a long-term growth trend, and typically involve shifts over time between periods of relatively rapid economic growth (expansion or boom), and periods of relative stagnation or decline (contraction or recession.)

These fluctuations are often measured using the growth rate of real gross domestic product.

 a. Consumer theory
 b. Nominal value
 c. Tobit model
 d. Business cycle

4. The _____ is the central banking system of the United States. Created in 1913 by the enactment of the Federal Reserve Act (signed by Woodrow Wilson), it is a quasi-public and quasi-private (government entity with private components) banking system that comprises (1) the presidentially appointed Board of Governors of the _____ in Washington, D.C.; (2) the Federal Open Market Committee; (3) twelve regional Federal Reserve Banks located in major cities throughout the nation acting as fiscal agents for the U.S. Treasury, each with its own nine-member board of directors; (4) numerous other private U.S. member banks, which subscribe to required amounts of non-transferable stock in their regional Federal Reserve Banks; and (5) various advisory councils. Since February 2006, Ben Bernanke has served as the Chairman of the Board of Governors of the _____.

 a. Federal Reserve System
 b. Federal Reserve System Open Market Account
 c. Term auction facility
 d. Monetary Policy Report to the Congress

5. In economics, an _____ is any good (e.g. a commodity) or service brought into one country from another country in a legitimate fashion, typically for use in trade. It is a good that is brought in from another country for sale. _____ goods or services are provided to domestic consumers by foreign producers. An _____ in the receiving country is an export to the sending country.

 a. Economic integration
 b. Import
 c. Import quota
 d. Incoterms

6. _____ is exchange of capital, goods, and services across international borders or territories. In most countries, it represents a significant share of gross domestic product (GDP.) While _____ has been present throughout much of history, its economic, social, and political importance has been on the rise in recent centuries.

a. Import license
c. Incoterms
b. Intra-industry trade
d. International trade

7. Economics:

- _____, the desire to own something and the ability to pay for it
- _____ curve, a graphic representation of a _____ schedule
- _____ deposit, the money in checking accounts
- _____ pull theory, the theory that inflation occurs when _____ for goods and services exceeds existing supplies
- _____ schedule, a table that lists the quantity of a good a person will buy it each different price
- _____ side economics, the school of economics at believes government spending and tax cuts open economy by raising _____

a. Production
c. McKesson ' Robbins scandal
b. Variability
d. Demand

8. In economics, the _____ can be defined as the graph depicting the relationship between the price of a certain commodity, and the amount of it that consumers are willing and able to purchase at that given price. It is a graphic representation of a demand schedule. The _____ for all consumers together follows from the _____ of every individual consumer: the individual demands at each price are added together.
   a. Wage curve
   c. Cost curve
   b. Demand curve
   d. Kuznets curve

9. In finance, the _____s between two currencies specifies how much one currency is worth in terms of the other. It is the value of a foreign natione;s currency in terms of the home natione;s currency. For example an _____ of 102 Japanese yen to the United States dollar means that JPY 102 is worth the same as USD 1.
   a. Interbank market
   c. ACEA agreement
   b. ACCRA Cost of Living Index
   d. Exchange rate

10. In economics, an _____ is any good or commodity, transported from one country to another country in a legitimate fashion, typically for use in trade. _____ goods or services are provided to foreign consumers by domestic producers. _____ is an important part of international trade.
    a. ACCRA Cost of Living Index
    c. AD-IA Model
    b. ACEA agreement
    d. Export

11. In economics, a _____ is a general slowdown in economic activity over a sustained period of time, or a business cycle contraction. During _____s, many macroeconomic indicators vary in a similar way. Production as measured by Gross Domestic Product (GDP), employment, investment spending, capacity utilization, household incomes and business profits all fall during _____s.
    a. Recession
    c. Monetary economics
    b. Treasury View
    d. Leading indicators

12. _____ is the a method of technical and economic research of the systems for purpose to optimize a parity between system's consumer functions or properties and expenses to achieve those functions or properties.

Chapter 36. EXCHANGE BATES AND THE MACROECONOMY 315

This methodology for continuous perfection of production, industrial technologies, organizational structures was developed by Juryj Sobolev in 1948 at the 'Perm telephone factory'

- 1948 Juryj Sobolev - the first success in application of a method analysis at the 'Perm telephone factory' .
- 1949 - the first application for the invention as result of use of the new method.

Today in economically developed countries practically each enterprise or the company use methodology of the kind of functional-cost analysis as a practice of the quality management, most full satisfying to principles of standards of series ISO 9000.

- Interest of consumer not in products itself, but the advantage which it will receive from its usage.
- The consumer aspires to reduce his expenses
- Functions needed by consumer can be executed in the various ways, and, hence, with various efficiency and expenses. Among possible alternatives of realization of functions exist such in which the parity of quality and the price is the optimal for the consumer.

The goal of _____ is achievement of the highest consumer satisfaction of production at simultaneous decrease in all kinds of industrial expenses Classical _____ has three English synonyms - Value Engineering, Value Management, Value Analysis.

a. Staple financing
c. Willingness to pay
b. Function cost analysis
d. Monopoly wage

13. The _____ or gross domestic income (GDI), a basic measure of an economy's economic performance, is the market value of all final goods and services produced within the borders of a nation in a year. _____ can be defined in three ways, all of which are conceptually identical. First, it is equal to the total expenditures for all final goods and services produced within the country in a stipulated period of time (usually a 365-day year.)

a. Gross domestic product
c. Market structure
b. Countercyclical
d. Monopolistic competition

14. _____ in economics and business is the result of an exchange and from that trade we assign a numerical monetary value to a good, service or asset. If Alice trades Bob 4 apples for an orange, the _____ of an orange is 4 apples. Inversely, the _____ of an apple is 1/4 oranges.

a. Price book
c. Premium pricing
b. Price war
d. Price

15. An _____, in economics, is the amount by which the real Gross domestic product exceeds potential GDP. The real GDP is also known as GDP 'adjusted for inflation', 'constant prices' GDP or 'constant dollar' GDP, because it measures the aggregate output in a country's income accounts in a given year, expressed in base-year prices. On the other hand, the potential GDP is the quantity of real GDP when a country's economy is at full-employment.

a. ACCRA Cost of Living Index
c. Inflationary gap
b. ACEA agreement
d. AD-IA Model

Chapter 36. EXCHANGE BATES AND THE MACROECONOMY

16. _____ is the price of a commodity such as a good or service in terms of another; ie, the ratio of two prices. A _____ may be expressed in terms of a ratio between any two prices or the ratio between the price of one particular good and a weighted average of all other goods available in the market. A _____ is an opportunity cost.
    - a. Relative price
    - b. False economy
    - c. Food cooperative
    - d. False shortage

17. In economics, _____ is the total supply of goods and services produced by a national economy during a specific time period. It is the total amount of goods and services in the economy available at all possible price levels.
    - a. Aggregate supply
    - b. Aggregate expenditure
    - c. Aggregation problem
    - d. Aggregate demand

18. In finance, a _____ is a debt security, in which the authorized issuer owes the holders a debt and, depending on the terms of the _____, is obliged to pay interest (the coupon) and/or to repay the principal at a later date, termed maturity. A _____ is a formal contract to repay borrowed money with interest at fixed intervals.

    Thus a _____ is like a loan: the issuer is the borrower (debtor), the holder is the lender (creditor), and the coupon is the interest.

    - a. Prize Bond
    - b. Callable
    - c. Zero-coupon
    - d. Bond

19. A consumer price index (_____) is a measure of the average price of consumer goods and services purchased by households. A consumer price index measures a price change for a constant market basket of goods and services from one period to the next within the same area (city, region, or nation.) It is a price index determined by measuring the price of a standard group of goods meant to represent the typical market basket of a typical urban consumer.
    - a. Cost-of-living index
    - b. Lipstick index
    - c. Hedonic price index
    - d. CPI

20. _____ is a broad label that refers to any individuals or households that use goods and services generated within the economy. The concept of a _____ is used in different contexts, so that the usage and significance of the term may vary.

    Typically when business people and economists talk of _____s they are talking about person as _____, an aggregated commodity item with little individuality other than that expressed in the buy/not-buy decision.

    - a. 1921 recession
    - b. 130-30 fund
    - c. 100-year flood
    - d. Consumer

21. A _____ is a measure of the average price of consumer goods and services purchased by households. A _____ measures a price change for a constant market basket of goods and services from one period to the next within the same area (city, region, or nation.) It is a price index determined by measuring the price of a standard group of goods meant to represent the typical market basket of a typical urban consumer.
    - a. Lipstick index
    - b. CPI
    - c. Consumer Price Index
    - d. Cost-of-living index

Chapter 36. EXCHANGE BATES AND THE MACROECONOMY

22. _____ and Keynesian Theory) is a macroeconomic theory based on the ideas of 20th-century British economist John Maynard Keynes. _____ argues that private sector decisions sometimes lead to inefficient macroeconomic outcomes and therefore advocates active policy responses by the public sector, including monetary policy actions by the central bank and fiscal policy actions by the government to stabilize output over the business cycle.

The theories forming the basis of _____ were first presented in The General Theory of Employment, Interest and Money, published in 1936.

   a. Market failure
   b. Deflation
   c. Rational choice theory
   d. Keynesian economics

23. A _____ is a normalized average (typically a weighted average) of prices for a given class of goods or services in a given region, during a given interval of time. It is a statistic designed to help to compare how these prices, taken as a whole, differ between time periods or geographical locations.

Price indices have several potential uses.

   a. Price Index
   b. Product sabotage
   c. Transactional Net Margin Method
   d. Two-part tariff

24. The balance of trade (or net exports, sometimes symbolized as NX) is the difference between the monetary value of exports and imports in an economy over a certain period of time. It is the relationship between a nation's imports and exports. A favorable balance of trade is known as a trade surplus and consists of exporting more than is imported; an unfavorable balance of trade is known as a _____ or, informally, a trade gap.

   a. Trade deficit
   b. Complementary asset
   c. Demographics of India
   d. Computational economic

25. A _____, reserve bank, or monetary authority is the entity responsible for the monetary policy of a country or of a group of member states. It is a bank that can lend money to other banks in times of need. Its primary responsibility is to maintain the stability of the national currency and money supply, but more active duties include controlling subsidized-loan interest rates, and acting as a lender of last resort to the banking sector during times of financial crisis (private banks often being integral to the national financial system.)

   a. 1921 recession
   b. 100-year flood
   c. 130-30 fund
   d. Central bank

26. An autarky is an economy that is self-sufficient and does not take part in international trade, or severely limits trade with the outside world. Likewise the term refers to an ecosystem not affected by influences from the outside, which relies entirely on its own resources. In the economic meaning, it is also referred to as a _____.

   a. Closed economy
   b. Network Economy
   c. Digital economy
   d. Transition economy

27. The _____ is the largest national economy in the world. Its gross domestic product (GDP) was estimated as $14.2 trillion in 2008. The U.S. economy maintains a high level of output per person (GDP per capita, $46,800 in 2008, ranked at around number ten in the world.)

a. ACCRA Cost of Living Index
b. ACEA agreement
c. AD-IA Model
d. Economy of the United States

28. The term _____ refers to government debt, expenditures and revenues, or to finance (particularly financial revenue) in general.

- _____ deficit is the budget deficit of federal or local government
- _____ policy is the discretionary spending of governments. Contrasts with monetary policy.
- _____ year and _____ quarter are reporting periods for firms and other agencies.

a. Bucket shop
b. Procter ' Gamble
c. Drawdown
d. Fiscal

29. _____ is the process by which the government, central bank (ii) availability of money, and (iii) cost of money or rate of interest, in order to attain a set of objectives oriented towards the growth and stability of the economy. Monetary theory provides insight into how to craft optimal _____.

_____ is referred to as either being an expansionary policy where an expansionary policy increases the total supply of money in the economy, and a contractionary policy decreases the total money supply.

a. Monetary policy
b. 1921 recession
c. 100-year flood
d. 130-30 fund

30. In financial accounting, the _____ is one of the accounts in shareholders' equity. Sole proprietorships have a single _____ in the owner's equity. Partnerships maintain a _____ for each of the partners.
a. Current account
b. Compensation of employees
c. Net national product
d. Capital account

31. In economics, the _____ is one of the two primary components of the balance of payments, the other being the capital account. It is the sum of the balance of trade (exports minus imports of goods and services), net factor income (such as interest and dividends) and net transfer payments (such as foreign aid.)

$$\text{Current account} = \text{Balance of trade} \\ + \text{Net factor income from abroad} \\ + \text{Net unilateral transfers from abroad}$$

The _____ balance is one of two major metrics of the nature of a country's foreign trade (the other being the net capital outflow.)

a. Current account
b. Gross private domestic investment
c. National Income and Product Accounts
d. Compensation of employees

Chapter 36. EXCHANGE BATES AND THE MACROECONOMY

32. The _____ is an economic and political union of 27 member states, located primarily in Europe. It was established by the Treaty of Maastricht on 1 November 1993, upon the foundations of the pre-existing European Economic Community. With a population of almost 500 million, the _____ generates an estimated 30% share (US$18.4 trillion in 2008) of the nominal gross world product.
   a. European Court of Justice
   b. ACCRA Cost of Living Index
   c. ACEA agreement
   d. European Union

33. A _____ occurs when an entity spends more money than it takes in. The opposite of a _____ is a budget surplus. Debt is essentially an accumulated flow of deficits.
   a. Budget deficit
   b. Funding body
   c. Public Financial Management
   d. Lump-sum tax

34. To _____ is to impose a financial charge or other levy upon a taxpayer by a state or the functional equivalent of a state.

   _____es are also imposed by many subnational entities. _____es consist of direct _____ or indirect _____, and may be paid in money or as its labour equivalent (often but not always unpaid.)

   a. 1921 recession
   b. 130-30 fund
   c. 100-year flood
   d. Tax

35. To tax is to impose a financial charge or other levy upon a taxpayer by a state or the functional equivalent of a state.

   _____ are also imposed by many subnational entities. _____ consist of direct tax or indirect tax, and may be paid in money or as its labour equivalent (often but not always unpaid.)

   a. Taxes
   b. 1921 recession
   c. 100-year flood
   d. 130-30 fund

Chapter 1
1. a	2. d	3. c	4. a	5. d	6. d	7. d	8. c	9. d	10. a
11. b	12. d	13. a	14. b	15. d	16. c	17. d	18. d	19. d	20. c
21. d	22. b	23. d	24. d	25. a	26. d	27. a	28. c	29. c	30. d
31. b	32. d								

Chapter 2
1. d	2. b	3. d	4. d	5. d	6. d	7. a	8. d	9. d	10. d
11. c	12. b	13. c	14. b	15. d	16. d	17. c	18. d	19. c	20. d
21. d	22. d	23. d	24. b	25. d	26. a	27. c	28. d	29. a	30. a
31. d	32. d	33. c	34. d	35. d	36. b	37. d	38. d	39. a	40. b
41. b	42. b	43. b	44. a	45. b	46. d	47. a	48. a	49. c	50. d
51. d	52. b	53. d	54. b	55. d	56. a	57. d	58. d	59. c	60. a
61. c	62. d	63. d	64. d	65. d					

Chapter 3
1. b	2. d	3. c	4. d	5. d	6. b	7. d	8. d	9. b	10. d
11. b	12. d	13. d	14. d	15. d	16. c	17. b	18. d	19. d	20. b
21. b	22. d	23. c	24. d	25. d	26. b	27. c	28. d	29. d	30. d
31. d	32. c	33. a	34. d	35. c	36. d				

Chapter 4
1. d	2. d	3. c	4. b	5. a	6. a	7. d	8. d	9. b	10. c
11. a	12. c	13. b	14. d	15. d	16. b	17. d	18. c	19. b	20. d
21. d	22. b	23. d	24. a	25. d	26. c	27. d	28. d	29. a	30. a
31. a									

Chapter 5
1. d	2. c	3. c	4. b	5. a	6. c	7. d	8. c	9. d	10. c
11. d	12. d	13. d	14. b	15. a	16. c	17. a	18. b	19. b	20. a
21. d	22. b	23. d	24. d						

Chapter 6
1. a	2. b	3. c	4. d	5. a	6. d	7. d	8. d	9. d	10. d
11. c	12. a	13. c	14. d	15. d	16. d	17. a	18. c	19. b	20. d
21. b	22. d	23. d	24. d	25. d	26. d	27. b	28. c		

Chapter 7
1. a	2. b	3. a	4. c	5. d	6. d	7. b	8. d	9. d	10. d
11. d	12. a	13. d	14. a	15. b	16. c	17. d	18. d	19. d	20. b
21. a	22. b	23. c	24. a	25. a	26. a	27. d	28. d	29. d	30. c
31. d	32. c	33. c	34. c	35. d	36. c	37. d	38. d		

ANSWER KEY

Chapter 8
1. a	2. d	3. d	4. d	5. a	6. c	7. b	8. a	9. d	10. d
11. b	12. d	13. d	14. d	15. d	16. d	17. c	18. d	19. d	20. d
21. c	22. d	23. d	24. b	25. d	26. d	27. d	28. d	29. c	30. d
31. a									

Chapter 9
1. d	2. d	3. a	4. d	5. a	6. d	7. d	8. d	9. a	10. c
11. d	12. a	13. b	14. d	15. b	16. c	17. b	18. d	19. c	20. d
21. a	22. d	23. d	24. d	25. d	26. b	27. a	28. d	29. d	30. c
31. d	32. b	33. d	34. c	35. a	36. a	37. c	38. d	39. d	40. d
41. d	42. d	43. d	44. b						

Chapter 10
1. d	2. d	3. d	4. b	5. a	6. b	7. d	8. d	9. a	10. d
11. d	12. b	13. b	14. c	15. d	16. d	17. b	18. a	19. b	20. d
21. d	22. a	23. d	24. b	25. b	26. d	27. d	28. d	29. b	30. c
31. d	32. c	33. d	34. a	35. c	36. d	37. b	38. d	39. a	40. a

Chapter 11
1. c	2. b	3. b	4. d	5. d	6. d	7. c	8. d	9. d	10. d
11. d	12. a	13. b	14. a	15. d	16. c	17. d	18. d	19. b	20. d
21. d	22. d	23. d	24. c	25. a	26. d	27. d	28. a	29. c	30. d
31. d	32. a	33. d	34. c	35. b					

Chapter 12
1. a	2. a	3. c	4. c	5. d	6. d	7. c	8. d	9. a	10. b
11. d	12. d	13. b	14. d	15. d	16. c	17. d	18. a	19. d	20. a
21. d	22. b	23. c	24. a	25. b	26. d	27. b	28. a	29. d	30. a
31. d	32. d	33. b	34. a	35. a	36. d	37. d	38. d	39. d	40. c
41. d	42. d	43. d							

Chapter 13
1. a	2. a	3. d	4. b	5. d	6. d	7. d	8. b	9. c	10. d
11. d	12. b	13. a	14. b	15. d	16. d	17. d	18. a	19. d	20. d
21. a	22. d	23. a	24. d	25. d	26. c	27. c	28. d	29. a	30. c
31. d	32. d	33. c	34. d	35. d	36. c	37. d	38. d	39. d	40. b
41. c	42. c	43. b	44. d	45. d	46. d	47. a			

Chapter 14
1. d	2. d	3. c	4. d	5. c	6. d	7. a	8. a	9. c	10. a
11. d	12. d	13. d	14. b	15. d	16. b	17. c	18. d	19. d	20. b
21. b	22. c	23. b	24. c	25. b	26. c	27. d	28. a	29. a	30. d
31. a	32. c	33. d	34. a						

Chapter 15

1. b	2. d	3. d	4. a	5. d	6. d	7. c	8. d	9. b	10. d
11. d	12. d	13. c	14. d	15. a	16. d	17. d	18. d	19. c	20. d
21. d	22. a	23. b	24. a	25. d	26. c	27. d	28. d	29. d	30. b
31. d	32. d	33. d	34. d	35. d	36. d	37. c	38. d	39. b	40. a
41. a	42. d	43. b	44. d	45. d	46. d	47. d	48. d	49. d	50. d
51. c	52. a	53. b							

Chapter 16

1. b	2. d	3. d	4. d	5. d	6. d	7. d	8. a	9. b	10. d
11. c	12. d	13. b	14. a	15. d	16. d	17. d	18. c	19. c	20. d
21. b	22. d	23. d	24. c	25. d	26. d	27. d	28. d	29. b	30. c
31. c	32. d	33. c	34. c	35. d	36. d	37. b	38. d	39. d	40. b
41. c	42. d	43. a	44. d	45. c	46. b	47. d			

Chapter 17

1. a	2. d	3. c	4. d	5. d	6. a	7. d	8. d	9. d	10. b
11. d	12. d	13. a	14. d	15. d	16. b	17. a	18. c	19. d	20. d
21. c	22. d	23. d	24. d	25. b	26. c	27. a	28. c	29. d	

Chapter 18

1. d	2. a	3. d	4. d	5. d	6. a	7. b	8. b	9. d	10. b
11. d	12. d	13. b	14. a	15. d	16. a	17. b	18. c	19. c	20. d
21. d	22. b	23. d	24. d	25. d	26. d	27. d	28. d	29. b	30. b
31. c	32. b	33. b	34. b	35. c	36. a	37. d	38. a		

Chapter 19

1. d	2. d	3. c	4. a	5. d	6. b	7. c	8. a	9. d	10. d
11. c	12. d	13. d	14. c	15. c	16. b	17. d	18. d	19. c	20. d
21. d	22. c	23. d	24. a	25. a	26. d	27. c	28. d	29. d	30. c
31. a	32. c	33. d	34. b	35. d	36. d	37. d	38. c	39. d	40. c
41. b									

Chapter 20

1. d	2. d	3. d	4. d	5. c	6. d	7. c	8. d	9. d	10. b
11. b	12. d	13. a	14. d	15. c	16. b	17. d	18. d	19. d	20. a
21. b	22. c	23. d	24. d	25. c	26. a	27. d	28. d	29. d	30. d
31. b	32. d	33. d	34. a	35. b	36. a	37. d	38. b	39. a	40. b
41. d	42. d	43. d	44. d	45. a	46. c	47. d	48. d	49. d	50. b
51. d	52. a	53. c	54. b	55. d	56. d	57. d	58. d		

ANSWER KEY

Chapter 21

1. c	2. a	3. d	4. d	5. d	6. a	7. a	8. d	9. b	10. d
11. c	12. b	13. d	14. d	15. b	16. b	17. a	18. b	19. d	20. d
21. a	22. c	23. c	24. d	25. b	26. b	27. d	28. d	29. c	30. b
31. d	32. d	33. d	34. d	35. c	36. a	37. d	38. c	39. d	40. c
41. d	42. a	43. d							

Chapter 22

1. d	2. d	3. c	4. c	5. d	6. c	7. d	8. c	9. d	10. c
11. d	12. b	13. c	14. d	15. d	16. d	17. b	18. d	19. d	20. d
21. c	22. c	23. c	24. a	25. d	26. a	27. c	28. b	29. d	30. a
31. c	32. a	33. d	34. b	35. d	36. b	37. b	38. c	39. b	40. d
41. d	42. d	43. b	44. c	45. d	46. d	47. d	48. d	49. d	50. b
51. d	52. d	53. c	54. a	55. d	56. d	57. d	58. c		

Chapter 23

1. d	2. d	3. d	4. d	5. a	6. d	7. d	8. d	9. a	10. d
11. c	12. d	13. d	14. d	15. d	16. d	17. d	18. a	19. a	20. d
21. a	22. d	23. b	24. c	25. a	26. d	27. d	28. a	29. a	30. a
31. d	32. c	33. a	34. a	35. b	36. a	37. d	38. d	39. d	40. c
41. d	42. c	43. d	44. d	45. a	46. d	47. d	48. d	49. d	50. d
51. b	52. b	53. b	54. d	55. b	56. c	57. a			

Chapter 24

1. d	2. d	3. b	4. d	5. a	6. b	7. b	8. b	9. d	10. c
11. d	12. d	13. b	14. a	15. c	16. b	17. c	18. a	19. a	20. b
21. c	22. d	23. d	24. c	25. d	26. d	27. a	28. d	29. d	30. b
31. d	32. c	33. a	34. d	35. d	36. b	37. d	38. d	39. d	40. b
41. d	42. b	43. a	44. a	45. d	46. c	47. d	48. a	49. d	50. b
51. a	52. d	53. d	54. d						

Chapter 25

1. d	2. d	3. d	4. a	5. a	6. a	7. c	8. a	9. d	10. d
11. b	12. d	13. d	14. d	15. d	16. b	17. b	18. c	19. a	20. d
21. c	22. a	23. a	24. d	25. b	26. d	27. d	28. d	29. c	30. d
31. d	32. d	33. d	34. d	35. d	36. a	37. c	38. d	39. d	40. c
41. d	42. d	43. d	44. d	45. d	46. d	47. d	48. d	49. b	50. b
51. a	52. d	53. a	54. c	55. d	56. d	57. a	58. a		

Chapter 26

1. d	2. d	3. b	4. c	5. a	6. d	7. b	8. b	9. b	10. d
11. d	12. c	13. a	14. d	15. d	16. d	17. d	18. d	19. d	20. d
21. a	22. a	23. d	24. c	25. a	26. c	27. b	28. d	29. d	30. d
31. c	32. d	33. d	34. a	35. d					

Chapter 27

1. d	2. c	3. d	4. d	5. a	6. c	7. c	8. b	9. d	10. d
11. d	12. a	13. d	14. b	15. c	16. d	17. d	18. d	19. d	20. d
21. d	22. a	23. d	24. a	25. b	26. c	27. d	28. b	29. d	30. a
31. a	32. d	33. d	34. b	35. c	36. d	37. d	38. b		

Chapter 28

1. d	2. a	3. b	4. a	5. a	6. c	7. a	8. d	9. d	10. d
11. a	12. a	13. d	14. d	15. b	16. d	17. d	18. b	19. d	20. c
21. b	22. b	23. a	24. d	25. c	26. d	27. d	28. d	29. d	30. a
31. a	32. a	33. d	34. d	35. d	36. d	37. c	38. d	39. c	40. d

Chapter 29

1. d	2. b	3. a	4. d	5. b	6. d	7. d	8. c	9. b	10. d
11. d	12. d	13. a	14. c	15. d	16. b	17. d	18. c	19. c	20. d
21. c	22. d	23. c	24. c	25. d	26. b	27. a	28. d	29. a	30. d
31. c	32. a	33. a	34. d	35. d	36. d	37. d	38. d	39. b	40. c

Chapter 30

1. b	2. b	3. b	4. d	5. c	6. d	7. d	8. c	9. c	10. b
11. d	12. d	13. c	14. b	15. d	16. a	17. d	18. d	19. a	20. d
21. b	22. d	23. d	24. d	25. c	26. d	27. d	28. d	29. d	30. a
31. c	32. d	33. d	34. b	35. b	36. d	37. c	38. d	39. d	40. b
41. d									

Chapter 31

1. d	2. d	3. c	4. a	5. d	6. a	7. b	8. d	9. d	10. d
11. b	12. d	13. d	14. d	15. d	16. b	17. d	18. c	19. d	20. a
21. a	22. a	23. c	24. d	25. d	26. c	27. d	28. d	29. c	30. d
31. d	32. d	33. d	34. a	35. d	36. b	37. a	38. b	39. b	40. b
41. d	42. d	43. d	44. d	45. a	46. d	47. d			

Chapter 32

1. d	2. d	3. d	4. d	5. d	6. a	7. c	8. a	9. c	10. d
11. c	12. b	13. d	14. a	15. b	16. d	17. a	18. d	19. b	20. b
21. d	22. d	23. d	24. b	25. b	26. d	27. b	28. d	29. b	30. a
31. d	32. a	33. a	34. d	35. a	36. d	37. d	38. b	39. b	40. a

Chapter 33

1. d	2. d	3. d	4. d	5. d	6. a	7. a	8. a	9. d	10. d
11. d	12. d	13. d	14. d	15. d	16. b	17. d	18. c	19. c	20. b
21. d	22. d	23. b	24. a	25. b	26. d	27. d	28. d	29. a	30. a
31. d	32. d	33. d	34. b	35. d	36. c	37. a	38. c	39. c	40. a
41. d	42. c								

ANSWER KEY

Chapter 34
1. d	2. c	3. d	4. d	5. d	6. c	7. b	8. a	9. d	10. c
11. d	12. b	13. d	14. c	15. a	16. c	17. a	18. c	19. d	20. d
21. c	22. b	23. d	24. d	25. a	26. c	27. b	28. b	29. a	30. d
31. c	32. d	33. d	34. b	35. d	36. a	37. a	38. d	39. d	40. d
41. a	42. d	43. b							

Chapter 35
1. b	2. d	3. d	4. a	5. a	6. a	7. d	8. c	9. d	10. c
11. d	12. d	13. d	14. b	15. d	16. a	17. c	18. d	19. a	20. d
21. d	22. a	23. b	24. d	25. d	26. a	27. a	28. b	29. d	30. a
31. d	32. c	33. d	34. d	35. d	36. b	37. d	38. c	39. c	40. d
41. b	42. d	43. d	44. b	45. c	46. d				

Chapter 36
1. d	2. a	3. d	4. a	5. b	6. d	7. d	8. b	9. d	10. d
11. a	12. b	13. a	14. d	15. c	16. a	17. a	18. d	19. d	20. d
21. c	22. d	23. a	24. a	25. d	26. a	27. d	28. d	29. a	30. d
31. a	32. d	33. a	34. d	35. a					

www.ingramcontent.com/pod-product-compliance
Lightning Source LLC
Chambersburg PA
CBHW082144230426
43672CB00015B/2844